CHRISTIANITY .

What impact has Christianity had on the law from its beginnings to the present day? This introduction explores the main legal teachings of Western Christianity, set out in the texts and traditions of Scripture and theology, philosophy and jurisprudence. It takes up the weightier matters of the law that Christianity has profoundly shaped – justice and mercy, rule and equity, discipline and love – as well as more technical topics of canon law, natural law, and state law. Some of these legal creations were wholly original to Christianity. Others were converted from Jewish and classical traditions. Still others were reformed by Renaissance humanists and Enlightenment philosophers. But whether original or reformed, these Christian teachings on law, politics and society have made and can continue to make fundamental contributions to modern law in the West and beyond.

JOHN WITTE, JR. is Jonas Robitscher Professor of Law and Director of the Center for the Study of Law and Religion at Emory University. His many publications include *The Reformation of Rights: Law, Religion and Human Rights in Early Modern Calvinism* (2007) and *Law and Protestantism: The Legal Teachings of the Lutheran Reformation* (2002).

FRANK S. ALEXANDER is Professor of Law and Founding Director of the Center of the Study of Law and Religion at Emory University. He is co-editor with John Witte Jr. of *The Teachings of Modern Christianity on Law, Politics and Human Nature* (2006).

CHRISTIANITY AND LAW: AN INTRODUCTION

Edited by

JOHN WITTE, JR.
FRANK S. ALEXANDER
Center for the Study of Law and Religion
Emory University

CAMBRIDGE
UNIVERSITY PRESS

CAMBRIDGE UNIVERSITY PRESS
Cambridge, New York, Melbourne, Madrid, Cape Town,
Singapore, São Paulo, Delhi, Tokyo, Mexico City

Cambridge University Press
The Edinburgh Building, Cambridge CB2 8RU, UK

Published in the United States of America by Cambridge University Press, New York

www.cambridge.org
Information on this title: www.cambridge.org/9780521697491

First published 2008

A catalogue record for this publication is available from the British Library

ISBN 978-0-521-87462-5 Hardback
ISBN 978-0-521-69749-1 Paperback

To Milner S. Ball
Inspiring leader, courageous scholar

Contents

List of illustrations   *Page*   ix
List of contributors   xii
Preface   xiv

Introduction   1
John Witte, Jr., Emory University

1. Law and religion in Judaism   33
David Novak, University of Toronto

2. Law in early Christianity   53
Luke Timothy Johnson, Emory University

3. Western canon law   71
R.H. Helmholz, University of Chicago

4. Natural law and natural rights   89
Brian Tierney, Cornell University

5. Conscientious objection, civil disobedience, and resistance   105
Kent Greenawalt, Columbia University

6. The Christian sources of general contract law   125
Harold J. Berman, Emory University

7. Proof, procedure, and evidence   143
Mathias Schmoeckel, University of Bonn

8. Family law and Christian jurisprudence   163
Don S. Browning, University of Chicago

9. Poverty, charity, and social welfare   185
Brian S. Pullan, University of Manchester

10. Property and Christian theology   205
    Frank S. Alexander, Emory University

11. Christian love and criminal punishment   219
    Jeffrie G. Murphy, Arizona State University

12. Christianity and human rights   237
    Michael J. Perry, Emory University

13. Religious liberty   249
    David Little, Harvard University

14. Modern church law   271
    Norman Doe, Cardiff University

15. Religious organizations and the state: the laws of ecclesiastical
    polity and the civil courts   293
    William W. Bassett, University of San Francisco

16. Christianity and the large-scale corporation   311
    David A. Skeel, Jr., University of Pennsylvania

Index to biblical texts   329
General index   333

Illustrations

Cover frontispiece
"The King Administering Justice," from *Justiniani in Fortiatum* (vellum), folio 3r, French School (fourteenth century). Used by permission of the Bridgeman Art Library.

1   "The Newly Discovered Book of the Law Read to King Josiah," from Nicolas Fontaine, *The History of the Old and New Testament: Extracted out of Sacred Scripture and Writings of the Fathers* (Exeter, 1780), s.v. 2 Kings 22. Used by permission of the Pitts Theological Library, Emory University.   2

2   "Moses and the People Make a Sacrifice to God Confirming the Covenant,"from Christoph Weigel, *Biblia ectypa: Bildnussen auss heiliger Schrifft Alt und Neuen Testaments* (Augsburg, 1695), s.v. Exodus 24. Used by permission of the Pitts Theological Library, Emory University.   34

3   "Paul Arrives in Rome," from Julius Schnorr von Carolsfeld, *Die Bibel in Bildern* (Leipzig, 1853), s.v. Acts 28. Used by permission of the Pitts Theological Library, Emory University.   54

4   "Table Showing the Forbidden Degrees of Affinity," (vellum) (Italian, fourteenth century). Used by permission of the Fitzwilliam Museum, University of Cambridge and Bridgeman Art Library.   70

5   "Historiated Title Page Border Depicting Thomas Aquinas with Several Classical and Medieval Authorities," cover page from Thomas Aquinas, *Summa Contra Gentiles* [1523], repr. edn (Turin, 1933). Used by permission of the Pitts Theological Library, Emory University.   88

6   "Martin Luther King, Jr. Waits to Address the Combined
     Session of the Massachusetts State Legislature at the
     Massachusetts State House in Boston on April 23, 1965."
     Used by permission of Bettmann/CORBIS.   104

7   "Boaz Purchases all the Property of Ruth's Dead
     Husband by Removing his Sandal," from Christoph Weigel,
     *Biblia ectypa: Bildnussen auss heiliger Schrifft Alt und Neuen
     Testaments* (Augsburg, 1695), s.v, Ruth 4. Used by permission
     of the Pitts Theological Library, Emory University.   124

8   "The Judicial Duel," (litho), from Paul Lacroix, *Le Moyen Age
     et la Renaissance* (Paris, 1847). Used by permission of the
     Bridgeman Art Library.   144

9   "A Proposal," by Otto Erdmann (1834–1905): German
     private collection (nineteenth century). Used by permission
     of the Bridgeman Art Library.   164

10   "The Good Samaritan," from Christoph Weigel, *Biblia ectypa:
     Bildnussen auss heiliger Schrifft Alt und Neuen Testaments*
     (Augsburg, 1695), s.v. Luke 10. Used by permission of the
     Pitts Theological Library, Emory University.   184

11   "Lazarus Begging for Scraps from the Rich Man's Table,"
     from Julius Schnorr von Carolsfeld, *Die Bibel in Bildern*
     (Leipzig, 1853), s.v. Luke 16. Used by permission of the
     Pitts Theological Library, Emory University.   204

12   "Jesus Forgiving the Adulteress," from Julius Schnorr von
     Carolsfeld, *Die Bibel in Bildern* (Leipzig, 1853), s.v. Luke 7.
     Used by permission of the Pitts Theological Library, Emory
     University.   218

13   Eleanor Roosevelt holding a poster of the Universal
     Declaration of Human Rights, November 1949. In the public
     domain and reproduced from: http//www.nps.gov/archive/elro/
     teach-er-vk/lesson-plans/er-and-udhr.htm.   236

14   "Decree Instituting the Freedom of Worship, November
     1799" (colored engraving) French School (eighteenth century).
     Used by permission of the Bridgeman Art Library.   250

15   "Christ Giving the Keys to St. Peter," from a Psalter of Don
      Appiano from the Church of the Badia Fiorentina, Florence,
      1514–1515. Used by permission of the Bridgeman Art Library.   272

16   "United States Supreme Court Building," Washington, DC.
      Used by permission of Dennis Degnan/CORBIS.   292

17   "Erie Railway, Bradford Division, Bridge 27.66." In the
      public domain and reproduced from:
      http://commons.wikimedia.org/w/index.
      php?title=Image:Kinzuabridgeold3.jpg&oldid=3214582   312

Contributors

FRANK S. ALEXANDER is Professor of Law and Founding Director of the Center for the Study of Law and Religion at Emory University.

WILLIAM W. BASSETT is Professor of Law at the University of San Francisco.

HAROLD J. BERMAN is Robert W. Woodruff Professor of Law and Senior Fellow at the Center for the Study of Law and Religion at Emory University and James Barr Ames Professor of Law Emeritus at Harvard University.

DON S. BROWNING is Alexander Campbell Professor of Religious Ethics and the Social Sciences Emeritus at the University of Chicago Divinity School and Senior Fellow in the Center for the Study of Law and Religion at Emory University.

NORMAN DOE is Professor of Law at Cardiff University and Director for the Centre for Law and Religion, Cardiff Law School.

KENT GREENAWALT is University Professor at Columbia University.

R. H. HELMHOLZ is Ruth Wyatt Rosenson Distinguished Service Professor of Law at the University of Chicago.

LUKE TIMOTHY JOHNSON is Robert W. Woodruff Professor of New Testament and Christian Origins in the Candler School of Theology and Senior Fellow in the Center for the Study of Law and Religion at Emory University.

DAVID LITTLE is Professor in the Practice of Religion, Ethnicity, and Global Conflict at Harvard University.

JEFFRIE G. MURPHY is Regents' Professor of Law, Philosophy, and Religious Studies at Arizona State University.

DAVID NOVAK is J. Richard and Dorothy Shiff Chair of Jewish Studies, Professor of the Study of Religion, and Professor of Philosophy at the University of Toronto.

MICHAEL J. PERRY is Robert W. Woodruff Professor of Law and Senior Fellow of the Center for the Study of Law and Religion at Emory University.

BRIAN S. PULLAN is Professor of History Emeritus at the University of Manchester, UK.

MATHIAS SCHMOECKEL is Professor of Private Law and German Legal History at the University of Bonn.

DAVID A. SKEEL, JR. is S. Samuel Arsht Professor of Corporate Law at University of Pennsylvania Law School.

BRIAN TIERNEY is Bryce and Edith M. Bowmar Professor of Humanistic Studies Emeritus at Cornell University.

JOHN WITTE, JR. is Jonas Robitscher Professor of Law and Director of the Center for the Study of Law and Religion at Emory University.

Preface

This volume provides an authoritative but accessible introduction to some of the main legal teachings of the Western Christian tradition – as set out in the texts and traditions of Scripture and theology, philosophy and jurisprudence. The sixteen chapters that follow address "the weightier matters of the law" (Matthew 25:23) – justice and mercy, rule and equity, discipline and love. They also address the more technical topics of canon law and natural law, conscience and commandment, contract and promise, evidence and proof, marriage and family, crime and punishment, property and poverty, liberty and dignity, church and state, business and commerce. These topics and others were perennial staples of both jurisprudence and theology in the West, and Christianity gave rise to many of the legal ideas and institutions that still dominate the West today. Some of these legal creations were wholly original to Christianity, born of keen new biblical insight and theological ingenuity. Others were converted and recast from Hebrew and classical prototypes. Still others were reworked and reformed by Renaissance humanists and Enlightenment *philosophes* and their ample modern progeny. But whether original or reformed, canonical or casuistical, Western Christian teachings on law, politics, and society have made enduring contributions to the development of law as we know it today. And these teachings still hold essential insights for legal reform and renewal in the new millennium.

This volume focuses on the Western Christian tradition – the Patristic, Catholic, and Protestant worlds of Western Europe and eventually North America – and leaves the legal analysis of non-Western and non-Christian religious traditions to other volumes. The interaction of law and Christianity in Europe and North America is a huge topic, and it has proved hard enough to wrestle the most essential material into a manageably sized volume. This volume of necessity only introduces part of the story of law and Christianity. Particularly the riches of the historical and contemporary Eastern Orthodox Churches as well as the numerous forms of Asian, African, and Latin American Christianity deserve their own treatment. Many of these forms of Christianity now rival Western Christianity in sheer numbers if not world influence, and many of them have made and are making their own unique contributions to law, politics, and society. We hope that the publication of this volume will catalyze the production of parallel volumes on law and religion in these other quarters of Christianity – as well as in Judaism, Islam, Hinduism, Buddhism, and Confucianism.

This volume is part and product of an ongoing project on Christian Legal Studies, undertaken by our Center for the Study of Law and Religion at Emory University. This project, which has involved more than 200 scholars over the past twenty years, explores the historical and contemporary influence of Christian ideas, institutions, and individuals on Western law, politics, and society. In its earlier phases, the project analyzed some of the Christian foundations and fundamentals of Western constitutionalism, democracy, religious liberty, and human rights, yielding a score of volumes that have appeared in a score of languages. In its current phase, the project has commissioned thirty new volumes on the past and potential contributions of Catholic, Protestant, and Orthodox Christianity to the cardinal legal and political questions that are now challenging and dividing church, state, and society.

This volume provides a brief introduction to some of these questions and some of the answers that the Western Christian tradition has offered. A general introduction puts the main themes of the volume in historical context. Each chapter fills in more detail and nuance about discrete figures and themes, charts the challenges that remain open in each area of law under discussion, and concludes with recommended readings to enhance the value of this text as a teaching resource and research guide. Further research guidance is available through the other volumes and projects described on our Law and Religion Center website (www.law.emory. edu/clsr).

This volume – and the broader project of Christian legal studies of which it is a part – was made possible by generous grants to our Center for the Study of Law and Religion by the Alonzo L. McDonald Family Foundation and the Lilly Endowment, Inc. We express our profound gratitude to Alonzo, Peter, and Suzie McDonald, and Robert Pool of the McDonald Foundation and to Craig Dykstra and his Lilly colleagues for their generous and genial support. We express our warm thanks to our Center colleagues – April Bogle, Eliza Ellison, Linda King, Anita Mann, and Amy Wheeler – for their effective and efficient administrative work on this and related projects, as well as to our students, Amos Davis and Judd Treeman, for their careful editorial work. Finally, we wish to thank Kate Brett, Gillian

Dadd, and their colleagues at Cambridge University Press for taking on this volume and bringing it to print with their usual excellence and professionalism.

This volume is dedicated to our dear friend and brother, Milner S. Ball, who has long been a great leader of the field of law and religion and has long blessed us with his wit, wisdom, and *Wissenschaft*. May it long continue!

John Witte, Jr. and Frank S. Alexander

Introduction

John Witte, Jr.

Over the past two generations, a new interdisciplinary movement has emerged dedicated to the study of the religious dimensions of law, the legal dimensions of religion, and the interaction of legal and religious ideas and institutions, norms and practices. This study is predicated on the assumptions that religion gives law its spirit and inspires its adherence to ritual and justice. Law gives religion its structure and encourages its devotion to order and organization. Law and religion share such ideas as fault, obligation, and covenant and such methods as ethics, rhetoric, and textual interpretation. Law and religion also balance each other by counterpoising justice and mercy, rule and equity, discipline and love. This dialectical interaction gives these two disciplines and dimensions of life their vitality and their strength.

To be sure, the spheres and sciences of law and religion have, on occasion, both converged and contradicted each other. Every major religious tradition has known both theonomism and antinomianism – the excessive legalization and the excessive spiritualization of religion. Every major legal tradition has known both theocracy and totalitarianism – the excessive sacralization and the excessive secularization of law. But the dominant reality in most eras and most cultures, many scholars now argue, is that law and religion relate dialectically. Every major religious tradition strives to come to terms with law by striking a balance between the rational and the mystical, the prophetic and the priestly, the structural and the spiritual. Every major legal tradition struggles to link its formal structures and processes with the beliefs and ideals of its people. Law and religion are distinct spheres and sciences of human life, but they exist in dialectical interaction, constantly crossing-over and cross-fertilizing each other.[1]

---

[1] See especially the early anchor text in this field by Harold J. Berman, *The Interaction of Law and Religion* (Nashville, TN: Abingdon Press, 1974), updated in Harold J. Berman, *Faith and Order: The Reconciliation of Law and Religion* (Grand Rapids, MI: Wm. B. Eerdmans Publishing, 1993). See further Howard O. Hunter, ed., *The Integrative Jurisprudence of Harold J. Berman* (Boulder, CO: Westview Press, 1996).

I "The Newly Discovered Book of the Law Read to King Josiah," from Nicolas Fontaine,
*The History of the Old and New Testament: Extracted out of Sacred Scripture and Writings of
the Fathers* (Exeter, 1780), s.v. 2 Kings 22.

It is these points of cross-over and cross-fertilization that are the special province of the scholarly field of law and religion. How do legal and religious ideas and institutions, methods and mechanisms, beliefs and believers influence each other – for better and for worse, in the past, present, and future? These are the cardinal questions that the burgeoning field of law and religion study has set out to answer. Over the past two generations, scholars of various confessions and professions throughout the world have addressed these questions with growing alacrity.[2]

This volume surveys and maps one part of the broad field of law and religion – law and Christianity in the Western tradition. Using the "binocular of law and religion," the chapters that follow view afresh many familiar ideas and institutions that traditionally were studied through the "monocular of law" or the "monocular of religion" alone.[3] In the opening chapters herein, David Novak and Luke Johnson mine the Ur texts of Western law and religion, the Hebrew Bible and the New Testament, both viewed in classical and cultural context, and both the subjects of enormous bodies of juridical learning in the Jewish and Christian traditions respectively. R. H. Helmholz analyzes the Christian church's own internal laws that were built on these biblical and classical foundations – the two millennium-old canon law of the Catholic tradition, and the more recent Protestant church orders and ordinances. Brian Tierney analyzes the Western tradition's perennial attachment to concepts of natural law, and its development of a distinctive understanding of natural rights and liberties. Kent Greenawalt takes up one important form of natural law, the law of conscience, and how it has informed Western understandings of conscientious objection, civil disobedience, and resistance. The natural law in various biblical and rational forms, Harold Berman and Mathias Schmoeckel show, has also been critical to guide and to govern the words of testimony and evidence used in judicial proceedings and the words of promise and contract used in social and economic life. Among the most important such words, Don Browning shows, are those that form the marriage contract, an institution of such critical importance in the Western tradition that the church has elevated it to

---

[2] See, e.g., F. C. DeCoste and Lillian MacPhearson, *Law, Religion, Theology: A Selective Annotated Bibliography* (West Cornwall, CT: Locust Press, 1997); "Reviews on New Books in Law and Religion," *Journal of Law and Religion* 16 (2001): 249–1035 and 17 (2002): 97–459, and ongoing scholarship reflected and reviewed in such specialty journals as the *Ecclesiastical Law Journal, Studia Canonica, Bulletin of the Medieval Canon Law Society, Zeitschrift der Savigny-Stiftung (Kanonisches Abteilung), Ius Commune, Journal of Law and Religion, Journal of Church and State*, and others.

[3] The phrase is from Jaroslav Pelikan, "Foreword," to John Witte, Jr. and Frank S. Alexander, eds., *The Weightier Matters of the Law: Essays on Law and Religion in Tribute to Harold J. Berman* (Atlanta, GA: Scholars Press, 1988), xi–xii.

a covenant or sacrament as well. Another vital institution, embraced from the start, is that of property. Frank Alexander shows how property shapes our identity, power, and relationships in modern society, and carries with it the primeval commandments of dominion and stewardship – "to dress and keep the Garden" (Genesis 2:15). One critical use of property for Christians, Brian Pullan reminds us, is to relieve the plight of the poor and needy, and Christians over the centuries have elaborated structures and programs to discharge their obligations of charity and love to the "least" in society (Matthew 25:40). Christian love extends beyond the poor and needy, Michael Perry reminds us. The Bible commands us to love all others as ourselves, and this universal love command is a critical foundation of our modern understanding of human dignity and human rights. Christians are called to love even their enemies, and Jeffrie Murphy shows how this startling ethic must work to transform our understanding of punishment of one such enemy, the criminal.

The concluding chapters of the volume shift to issues of religious liberty, and to the relations of churches and other associations to the state. David Little maps the Christian foundations and modern institutions of religious liberty for individuals and for groups, showing how these norms have both captured and challenged national and international law today. Norman Doe and William Bassett describe the complex internal legal structures of modern churches, and show how these institutions interact with, and sometimes conflict with, the modern state. The institutional church, of course, is only one of many associations recognized at law. The law recognizes countless associations for other things – not only families, charities, schools, and the like, as we have seen, but also corporations, partnerships, unions, and other groups focused on commerce and business. For many centuries, David Skeel shows, the church chartered and Christians ran many of the business associations of the West, and defined a good bit of the law of associations that governed these institutions. Today, business corporations are governed by complex state laws, which modern Christians have largely accepted, albeit with some critique of corporate excesses and exploitation.

The balance of this Introduction seeks to contextualize these chapters a bit more. I set "the binocular of law and religion" at its most panoramic setting to survey the grand civilizational pictures of law and Christianity in Western history. My argument is that there is a distinctive Western legal tradition – rooted in the ancient civilizations of Israel, Greece, and Rome. This Western legal tradition was nourished for nearly two millennia by Christianity and for more than two centuries by the Enlightenment. It has developed enduring postulates about justice and mercy, rule and equity, nature and custom, canon and commandment. It has featured evolving ideas about authority and power, rights and liberties, individuals and associations, public and private. It has developed distinctive methods of legislation and adjudication, of negotiation and litigation, of legal rhetoric and textual interpretation, of legal science and legal philosophy. The precise shape and balance of the Western legal tradition at any period has been determined, in part, by the Western religious tradition. And when the prevailing ideas, officials, symbols, and methods of the Western religious tradition have changed, the shape and balance of the Western legal tradition have changed as well.

Four major shifts in the Western religious tradition have triggered the most massive transformations of the Western legal tradition: (1) the Christian conversion of the Roman Empire in the fourth through sixth centuries; (2) the Papal Revolution of the late eleventh to thirteenth centuries; (3) the Protestant Reformation of the sixteenth century; and (4) the Enlightenment movements of the eighteenth and nineteenth centuries. The Western legal tradition was hardly static between these four watershed periods. Regional and national movements – from the ninth century Carolingian Renaissance to the Russian Revolution of 1917 – had ample ripple effects on the tradition. But these were the four watershed periods, the civilizational moments and movements that permanently redirected the Western legal tradition. What follows is a quick sketch of the interactions of law and Christianity in these four watershed eras, which sets up the more refined and colorful portraits of individual topics offered in the succeeding chapters.[4]

LAW AND CHRISTIANITY IN THE ROMAN EMPIRE

The first watershed period came with the Christian conversion of the Roman emperor and Empire in the fourth through sixth centuries CE. Prior to that time, Roman law reigned supreme throughout much of the West. Roman law defined the status of persons and associations and the legal actions and procedures available to them. It proscribed delicts (torts) and crimes. It governed marriage and divorce, households and children, property and inheritance, contracts and commerce, slavery and labor. It protected the public property and welfare of the Roman state, and created the

---

[4] The following section is distilled in part from my *God's Joust, God's Justice: Law and Religion in the Western Tradition* (Grand Rapids, MI: Wm. B. Eerdmans Publishing, 2006).

vast hierarchies of government that allowed Rome to rule its far-flung Empire for centuries.[5]

A refined legal theory began to emerge in Rome at the dawn of the new millennium, built in part on Greek prototypes. The Roman Stoics, Cicero (106–43 BCE) and Seneca (d. 65 CE), among other Roman philosophers, cast in legal terms the topical methods of reasoning, rhetoric, and interpretation inherited from the Greek philosopher, Aristotle (384–322 BCE). They also greatly expanded the concepts of natural, distributive, and commutative justice developed by Aristotle and Plato (CA. 426–387 BCE). The Roman jurists, Gaius (d. *c.* 180 CE), Ulpian (*c.* 160–228 CE), and others drew what would become classic Western distinctions among: (1) civil law (*ius civile*), the statutes and procedures of a particular community to be applied strictly or with equity; (2) the law of nations (*ius gentium*), the principles and customs common to several communities and often the basis for treaties; and (3) natural law (*ius naturale*), the immutable principles of right reason, which are supreme in authority and divinity and must prevail in cases of conflict with civil or common laws. The Roman jurists also began to develop the rudiments of a concept of subjective rights (*iura*), freedoms (*libertates*), and capacities (*facultates*) in private and public law.

Roman law also established the imperial cult. Rome was to be revered as the eternal city, ordained by the gods and celebrated in its altars, forum, and basilicas. The Roman emperor was to be worshiped as a god and king in the rituals of the imperial court and in the festivals of the public square. The Roman law itself was sometimes viewed as the embodiment of an immutable divine law, appropriated and applied through the sacred legal science of imperial pontiffs and jurists. The Roman imperial cult claimed no monopoly; each of the conquered peoples in the Empire could maintain their own religious faith and practices, so long as they remained peaceable and so long as they accepted the basic requirements of the imperial cult that were prescribed by Roman law.

The early Christian church stood largely opposed to this Roman law and culture – as had the Jewish communities in which the church was born.[6] Early Christians certainly adopted a number of Roman legal institutions and practices – putting "a complex spin or twist on them," in Don Browning's apt phrase, in light of Gospel narratives and imperatives.[7] But

---

[5] See the chapter by Luke Timothy Johnson herein.
[6] On Judaism, see the chapter by David Novak herein.
[7] See the chapter by Don Browning herein, with further examples of early adaptation in the chapters by Luke Johnson, Brian Tierney, R. H. Helmholz, Mathias Schmoeckel, and David Skeel herein.

early Christians could not easily accept the Roman imperial cult nor readily partake of the pagan rituals required for participation in commerce, litigation, military life, and other public forums and activities. Emulating the sophisticated legal communities of Judaism, the early churches thus organized themselves into separate communities, largely withdrawn from official Roman society, and increasingly dissociated from Jewish communities as well. Early church constitutions, such as the *Didache* (*c.* 90–120), set forth internal rules for church organization, clerical life, ecclesiastical discipline, charity, education, family, and property relations, and these laws were amply augmented by legislation and decrees by bishops and church councils from the later second century onward.[8] Early Christian leaders – building on biblical injunctions to "render to Caesar the things that are Caesar's" (Matthew 22:21) and to "honor the authorities" (Romans 13:1; 1 Peter 2:13–17) – taught the faithful to pay their taxes, to register their properties, and to obey the Roman rulers up to the limits of Christian conscience and commandment.[9] But these early Christian leaders also urged their Roman rulers to reform the law in accordance with their new teachings – to respect liberty of conscience and worship, to outlaw concubinage and infanticide, to limit easy divorce, to expand charity and education, to curb military violence, to mitigate criminal punishments, to emancipate slaves, and more. Such legal independence and reformist agitation eventually brought forth firm imperial edicts which condemned Christianity as an "illicit religion" and exposed Christians to intermittent waves of brutal persecution.

The Christian conversion of Emperor Constantine in 312 and the formal establishment by law of Trinitarian Christianity as the official religion of the Roman Empire in 380 ultimately fused these Roman and Christian laws and beliefs. The Roman Empire was now understood as the universal body of Christ on earth, embracing all persons and all things. The Roman emperor was viewed as both pope and king, who reigned supreme in spiritual and temporal matters. The Roman law was viewed as the pristine instrument of natural law and Christian morality. This new convergence of Roman and Christian beliefs allowed the Christian church to imbue the Roman law with a number of its basic teachings, and to have those enforced throughout much of the Empire – notably and brutally against such heretics as Arians, Apollonarians, and Manicheans. Particularly in the great synthetic texts of Roman law that have survived – the *Codex Theodosianus* (438) and the *Corpus*

---

[8] See the chapters by Luke Johnson and R. H. Helmholz herein.
[9] See the chapter by Kent Greenawalt herein.

Iuris Civilis (529–534) – Christian teachings on the Trinity, the sacraments, liturgy, holy days, the Sabbath Day, sexual ethics, charity, education, and much else were copiously defined and regulated at law. The Roman law also provided special immunities, exemptions, and subsidies for Christian ministers, missionaries, and monastics, who thrived under this new patronage and eventually extended the church's reach to the farthest corners of the Roman Empire. The legal establishment of Trinitarian Christianity contributed enormously both to its precocious expansion throughout the West and to its canonical preservation for later centuries.

This new syncretism of Roman and Christian beliefs, however, also subordinated the church to imperial rule. Christianity was now, in effect, the new imperial cult of Rome, presided over by the Roman emperor. The Christian clergy were, in effect, the new pontiffs of the Christian imperial cult, hierarchically organized and ultimately subordinate to imperial authority. The church's property was, in effect, the new public property of the empire, subject both to its protection and to its control. Thus the Roman emperors and their delegates convoked many of the church councils and major synods; appointed, disciplined, and removed the high clergy; administered many of the church's parishes, monasteries, and charities; and legally controlled the acquisition, maintenance, and disposition of much church property.

This "caesaropapist" pattern of substantive influence but procedural subordination of the church to the state, and of the Christian religion to secular law, met with some resistance by strong clerics, such as Bishop Ambrose of Milan (339–397), Pope Gelasius (d. 496), and Pope Gregory the Great (*c.* 540–604). In several bold pronouncements, they insisted on the maintenance of two powers, if not "two swords" (Luke 22:38), to govern the affairs of Western Christendom – one held by the spiritual authorities, the other by the temporal authorities. But the more enduring political formulation came from St. Augustine (354–430), who saw in this new imperial arrangement a means to balance the spiritual and temporal dimensions and powers of the earthly life. In his famous political tract, *City of God,* Augustine contrasted the city of God with the city of man that coexist on this earth. The city of God consists of all those who are predestined to salvation, bound by the love of God, and devoted to a life of Christian piety, morality, and worship led by the clergy. The city of man consists of all the things of this sinful world, and the legal, political, and social institutions that God has created to maintain a modicum of order and peace on the earth. Augustine sometimes depicted this dualism as two walled cities separated from each other – particularly when he was describing the sequestered life and discipline of monasticism, or the earlier plight of the Christian churches under pagan Roman persecution. But Augustine's more dominant teaching was that, in the Christianized Roman Empire, these two cities overlapped in responsibility and membership. Christians would remain dual citizens until these two cities were fully and finally separated on the Return of Christ and at the Last Judgment of God. A Christian remained bound by the sinful habits of the world, even if he aspired to greater purity of the Gospel. A Christian remained subject to the power of both cities, even if she aspired to be a citizen of the city of God alone. If the rulers of the city of man favored Christians instead of persecuting them, so much the better.[10]

This Roman imperial understanding of law and Christianity largely continued in the West after the fall of Rome to various Germanic tribes in the fifth century. Before their conversion, many of the pagan Germanic rulers were considered to be divine and were the cult leaders as well as the military leaders of their people. Upon their conversion to Christianity, they lost their divinity, yet continued as sacral rulers of the Christian churches within their territories. They found in Christianity an important source of authority in their efforts to extend their rule over the diverse peoples that made up their regimes. The clergy not only supported the Germanic Christian kings in the suppression of pagan tribal religions, but many of them also looked upon such leaders as the Frankish Emperor Charlemagne (r. 768–814) and the Anglo-Saxon King Alfred (r. 871–899) as their spiritual leaders. Those Germanic rulers who converted to Christianity, in turn, supported the clergy in their struggle against heresies and gave them military protection, political patronage, and material support, as the Christian Roman emperors before them had done. Feudal lords within these Germanic domains further patronized the church, by donating lands and other properties for pious causes in return for the power to appoint and control the priests, abbots, and abbesses who occupied and used these new church properties.

LAW AND MEDIEVAL CATHOLICISM

The second watershed period of the Western legal tradition came with the Papal Revolution or Gregorian Reform of the late eleventh through thirteenth centuries. Building on the conflict over lay investiture of clergy, Pope

---

[10] On Augustine, see further the chapters by Brian Tierney, Kent Greenawalt, Jeffrie Murphy, and David Little herein.

Gregory VII (1015–1085) and his successors eventually threw off their civil
rulers and established the Roman Catholic Church as an autonomous legal
and political corporation within Western Christendom. This event was
part and product of an enormous transformation of Western society in the
late eleventh to thirteenth centuries. The West was renewed through the
rediscovery and study of the ancient texts of Roman law, Greek philosophy,
and Patristic theology. The first modern Western universities were established in Bologna, Rome, and Paris with their core faculties of theology,
law, and medicine. A number of small towns were transformed into burgeoning city-states. Trade and commerce boomed. A new dialogue was
opened between Christianity and the sophisticated cultures of Judaism and
Islam. Great advances were made in the natural sciences, in mechanics, in
literature, in art, music, and architecture. And Western law, particularly the
law of the church, was transformed.[11]

From the twelfth to fifteenth centuries, the Catholic Church claimed a
vast new jurisdiction – literally the power "to speak the law" (*jus dicere*).
The church claimed personal jurisdiction over clerics, pilgrims, students,
the poor, heretics, Jews, and Muslims. It claimed subject matter jurisdiction over doctrine and liturgy; ecclesiastical property, polity, and patronage; sex, marriage and family life; education, charity, and inheritance; oral
promises, oaths, and various contracts; and all manner of moral, ideological, and sexual crimes. The church also claimed temporal jurisdiction over
subjects and persons that also fell within the concurrent jurisdiction of one
or more civil authorities.

Medieval writers pressed four main arguments in support of these jurisdictional claims. First, this new jurisdiction was seen as a simple extension
of the church's traditional authority to govern the seven sacraments –
baptism, confirmation, penance, eucharist, marriage, ordination, and
extreme unction. By the fifteenth century, the sacraments supported whole
bodies of sophisticated church law, called "canon law." The sacrament of
marriage supported the canon law of sex, marriage, and family life.[12] The
sacrament of penance supported the canon law of crimes and torts (delicts)
and, indirectly, the canon law of contracts, oaths, charity, and inheritance.[13] The sacrament of penance and extreme unction also supported a
sophisticated canon law of charity and poor relief, and a vast network of
church-based guilds, foundations, hospitals, and other institutions
that served the *personae miserabiles* of Western society.[14] The sacrament of

---

[11] See the chapter by Harold J. Berman herein.   [12] See the chapter by Don Browning herein.
[13] See the chapter by Harold J. Berman herein.   [14] See the chapter by Brian Pullan herein.

ordination became the foundation for a refined canon law of corporate rights and duties of the clergy and monastics, and an intricate network of corporations and associations that they formed. The sacraments of baptism and confirmation supported a new constitutional law of natural rights and duties of Christian believers.

Second, church leaders predicated their jurisdictional claims on Christ's famous delegation to the Apostle Peter: "I will give you the keys of the kingdom of heaven, and whatever you bind on earth shall be bound in heaven, and whatever you loose on earth shall be loosed in heaven" (Matthew 16:19). According to conventional medieval lore, Christ had conferred on St. Peter two keys – a key of knowledge to discern God's word and will, and a key of power to implement and enforce that word and will throughout the church. St. Peter had used these keys to help define the doctrine and discipline of the apostolic church. Through apostolic succession, the pope and his clergy had inherited these keys to define the doctrine and discipline of the contemporary church. This inheritance, the canonists believed, conferred on the pope and his clergy a legal power, a power to make and enforce canon laws. This argument of the keys readily supported the church's claims to subject matter jurisdiction over core spiritual matters of doctrine and liturgy – the purpose and timing of the mass, baptism, eucharist, confession, and the like. The key of knowledge, after all, gave the pope and his clergy access to the mysteries of divine revelation, which, by use of the key of power, they communicated to all believers through the canon law. The argument of the keys, however, could be easily extended. Even the most mundane of human affairs ultimately have spiritual and moral dimensions. Resolution of a boundary line dispute between neighbors implicates the commandment to love one's neighbor. Unaccountable failure to pay one's civil taxes or feudal dues is a breach of the spiritual duty to honor those in authority. Printing or reading a censored book is a sin. Strong clergy, therefore, readily used the argument of the keys to extend the subject matter jurisdiction of the church to matters with more attenuated spiritual and moral dimensions, particularly in jurisdictions where they had no strong civil rivals.

Third, medieval writers argued that the church's canon law was the true source of Christian equity – "the mother of exceptions," "the epitome of the law of love," and "the mother of justice," as they variously called it. As the mother of exceptions, canon law was flexible, reasonable, and fair, capable either of bending the rigor of a rule in an individual case through dispensations and injunctions, or punctiliously insisting on the letter of an agreement through orders of specific performance or reformation of documents. As the epitome of love, canon law afforded special care for the disadvantaged – widows, orphans, the poor, the handicapped, abused wives, neglected children, maltreated servants, and the like. It provided them with standing to press claims in church courts, competence to testify against their superiors without their permission, methods to gain succor and shelter from abuse and want, opportunities to pursue pious and protected careers in the cloister. As the mother of justice, canon law provided a method whereby the individual believer could be reconciled to God, neighbor, and self at once. Church courts treated both the legality and the morality of the conflicts before them. Their remedies enabled litigants to become righteous and just not only in their relationships with opposing parties and the rest of the community, but also in their relationship to God. This was one reason for the enormous popularity and success of the church courts in much of medieval Christendom. Church courts treated both the legality and the morality of the conflicts before them.[15]

Fourth, some writers reworked the traditional "two swords" theory to support claims that the church's jurisdiction was superior to that of secular authorities. In its high medieval form, the two swords theory taught that the pope was the vicar of Christ on earth, in whom Christ vested the plenitude of his authority. This authority was symbolized in the "two swords" discussed in the Bible (Luke 22:38), a spiritual sword and a temporal sword. Christ had metaphorically handed these two swords to the highest being in the human world – the pope, the vicar of Christ. The pope and lower clergy wielded the spiritual sword, in part by establishing canon law rules for the governance of all Christendom. The clergy, however, were too holy to wield the temporal sword. They thus delegated this temporal sword to those authorities below the spiritual realm – emperors, kings, dukes, and their civil retinues, who held their swords "of" and "for" the church. These civil magistrates were to promulgate and enforce civil laws in a manner consistent with canon law. Under this two swords theory, civil law was by its nature inferior to canon law. Civil jurisdiction was subordinate to ecclesiastical jurisdiction. The state answered to the church.

While each of these four arguments had its detractors, together they provided the Catholic Church with a formidable claim to a sweeping jurisdiction. By the later twelfth century, church officials emerged as both the new legislators and new judges of Western Christendom. Church authorities issued a steady stream of new canon laws through papal decretals and bulls, conciliar and synodical decrees and edicts, and more discrete orders by local

---

[15] See the chapter by Mathias Schmoeckel herein.

bishops and abbots. Church courts adjudicated cases in accordance with the substantive and procedural rules of the canon law. Periodically, the pope or a strong bishop would deploy itinerant ecclesiastical judges, called *inquisitores*, with original jurisdiction over discrete questions that would normally lie within the competence of the church courts. The pope also sent out his legates who could exercise a variety of judicial and administrative powers in the name of the pope. Cases could be appealed up the hierarchy of church courts, ultimately to the papal rota. Cases raising novel questions could be referred to distinguished canonists or law faculties called assessors, whose learned opinions *(consilia)* on the questions were often taken by the church court as edifying if not binding.[16]

Alongside these legislative and judicial functions, the church developed a vast network of ecclesiastical officials, who presided over the church's executive and administrative functions. The medieval church registered its citizens through baptism. It taxed them through tithes. It conscripted them through crusades. It educated them through schools. It nurtured them through cloisters, monasteries, chantries, foundations, and guilds. The medieval church was, in F. W. Maitland's famous phrase, "the first true state in the West." Its medieval canon law was the first international law of the West since the eclipse of the classical Roman law half a millennium before.

From the twelfth century onward, the jurists of the canon law, called "canonists," began to systematize this vast new body of law, using the popular dialectical methods of the day. Thousands of legal and ethical teachings drawn from the apostolic constitutions, patristic writings, and Christianized Roman law of the first millennium were collated and harmonized in the famous *Decretum Gratiani* (c. 1140), the anchor text of medieval canon law. The *Decretum* was then heavily supplemented by collections of papal and conciliar legislation and juridical glosses and commentaries. All these texts were later integrated in the five-volume *Corpus Iuris Canonici* published in the 1580s, and in hundreds of important canon law texts on discrete legal topics that emerged with alacrity after the invention of the printing press in the early fifteenth century.[17]

This complex new legal system of the church also attracted sophisticated new legal and political theories. The most original formulations came from such medieval jurists as John of Salisbury (d. 1180), Hostiensis (1200–1271) and Baldus de Ubaldis (c. 1327–1400) and such medieval theologians and philosophers as Hugh of St. Victor (c. 1096–1141), Thomas Aquinas (1225–1274), John of Paris (c. 1240–1306) and William of Ockham

---

[16] See the chapter by Mathias Schmoeckel herein.   [17] See the chapter by R. H. Helmholz herein.

(*c.* 1280–*c.* 1349). These scholars reclassified the sources and forms of law, ultimately distinguishing: (1) the eternal law of the creation order; (2) the natural laws of the Bible, reason, and conscience; (3) the positive canon laws of the church; (4) the positive civil laws of the imperial, royal, princely, ducal, manorial and other authorities that comprised the medieval state; (5) the common laws of all nations and peoples; and (6) the customary laws of local communities.[18] These scholars also developed enduring rules for the resolution of conflicts among these types of laws, and contests of jurisdiction among their authors and authorities. They developed refined concepts of legislation, adjudication, and executive administration, and core constitutional concepts of sovereignty, election, and representation. They developed a good deal of the Western theory and law of chartered corporations, private associations, foundations, and trusts, built in part on early Roman law and later civil law prototypes.[19]

In these juridical writings, the language and concept of rights (*iura,* the plural of *ius)* became increasingly common. Medieval writers differentiated all manner of rights (*iura*) and liberties (*libertates*), and associated them variously with a power (*facultas*) inhering in rational human nature and with the property (*dominium*) of a person or the power (*potestas*) of an office of authority (*officium*). Particularly, the canonists worked out a whole complex latticework of what we now call rights, freedoms, powers, immunities, protections, and capacities for different groups and persons.[20] Most important were the rights that protected the "freedom of the church" (*libertas ecclesiae*) from the intrusions and control of secular authorities. Medieval writers specified in great detail the rights of the church and its clergy to make its own laws, to maintain its own courts, to define its own doctrines and liturgies, to elect and remove its own clergy. They also stipulated the exemptions of church property from civil taxation and takings, and the right of the clergy to control and use church property without interference or encumbrance from secular authorities. They also guaranteed the immunity of the clergy from civil prosecution, military service, and compulsory testimony, and the rights of church entities like parishes, monasteries, charities, and guilds to form and dissolve, to accept and reject members, and to establish order and discipline. In later twelfth- and thirteenth-century decrees, the canon law defined the rights of church councils and synods to participate in the election and discipline of bishops, abbots, and other clergy. It defined the rights

[18] See the chapter by Brian Tierney herein.
[19] See the chapters by Brian Pullan and David Skeel herein.
[20] See the chapter by Brian Tierney herein.

of the lower clergy vis-à-vis their superiors. It defined the rights of the laity to worship, evangelize, maintain religious symbols, participate in the sacraments, travel on religious pilgrimages, and educate their children. It defined the rights of the poor, widows, and needy to seek solace, succor, and sanctuary within the church. It defined the rights of husbands and wives, parents and children, masters and servants within the household. The canon law even defined the (truncated) rights that Orthodox Christians, Jews, Muslims, and heretics had in Western Christendom.

These medieval canon law formulations of rights and liberties had parallels in later medieval common law and civil law. Particularly notable sources were the thousands of medieval treaties, concordats, charters, and other constitutional texts that were issued by religious and secular authorities. These were often detailed, and sometimes very flowery, statements of the rights and liberties to be enjoyed by various groups of clergy, nobles, barons, knights, urban councils, citizens, universities, monasteries, and others. These were often highly localized instruments, but occasionally they applied to whole territories and nations. A familiar example of the latter type of instrument was the Magna Carta (1215), the great charter issued by the English crown at the behest of the church and barons of England. The Magna Carta guaranteed that "the Church of England shall be free (*libera*) and shall have all her whole rights (*iura*) and liberties (*libertates*) inviolable" and that all "free-men" (*liberis hominibus*) were to enjoy their various "liberties" (*libertates*).[21] These liberties included sundry rights to property, marriage, and inheritance, to freedom from undue military service, and to freedom to pay one's debts and taxes from the property of one's own choosing. The Magna Carta also set out various rights and powers of towns and of local justices and their tribunals, various rights and prerogatives of the king and of the royal courts, and various procedural rights in these courts (including the right to jury trial). These charters of rights, which were common throughout the medieval West, became important prototypes on which early modern Catholic, Protestant, and Enlightenment-based revolutionaries would later call to justify their revolts against tyrannical authorities.

LAW AND PROTESTANTISM

The third watershed period in the Western legal tradition came with the transformation of canon law and civil law, and of church and state, in the

---

[21] *The Statutes at Large of England and of Great Britain from the Magna Carta to the Union of the Kingdoms of Great Britain and Ireland*, 20 vols. (London: G. Eyre and J. Strahan, 1811), 1:1.

Protestant Reformation. The Protestant Reformation was inaugurated by Martin Luther (1483–1546) of Wittenberg in his famous posting of the Ninety-Five Theses in 1517 and his burning of the canon law and confessional books in 1520. It ultimately erupted in various quarters of Western Europe in the early sixteenth century, settling into Lutheran, Anglican, Calvinist, and Free Church (or Anabaptist) branches.

The early Protestant reformers – Luther, John Calvin (1509–1564), Menno Simons (1496–1561), Thomas Cranmer (1489–1556), and others – all taught that salvation comes through faith in the Gospel, not by works of law. Each individual stands directly before God, seeks God's gracious forgiveness of sin, and conducts life in accordance with the Bible and Christian conscience. To the Protestant reformers, the medieval Catholic canon law obstructed the individual's relationship with God and obscured simple biblical norms for right living. The early Protestant reformers further taught that the church is at heart a community of saints, not a corporation of politics. Its cardinal signs and callings are to preach the Word, to administer the sacraments, to catechize the young, to care for the needy. To the reformers, the Catholic clergy's legal rule in Christendom obstructed the church's divine mission and usurped the state's role as God's vice-regent. To be sure, the church must have internal rules of order to govern its own polity, teaching, and discipline. The church must critique legal injustice and combat political illegitimacy. But, according to classic Protestant lore, law is primarily the province of the state not of the church, of the magistrate not of the minister.

These new Protestant teachings helped to transform Western law in the sixteenth and seventeenth centuries. The Protestant Reformation permanently broke the international rule of the Catholic Church and the canon law, splintering Western Christendom into competing nations and territories. Each of these polities had its own (often conjoined) religious and political rulers, many of whom fought violently with each other in a century of bloody religious warfare that finally ended with the Peace of Westphalia (1648). The Protestant Reformation also triggered a massive shift of power, property, and prerogative from the church to the state. Political rulers now assumed jurisdiction over numerous subjects previously governed principally by the Catholic Church and its canon law – marriage and family life, property and testamentary matters, charity and education, contracts and oaths, moral and ideological crimes. Particularly in Lutheran and Anglican polities, political authorities also came to exercise considerable control over the clergy, polity, and property of the church – in self-conscious emulation of the laws and practices of Christianized Rome, and in implementation of the budding new Christian theories of absolute monarchy developed by Niccolò Machiavelli (1469–1527), Jean Bodin (1530–1596), Robert Filmer (d. 1653), and others.

These massive shifts in legal power and property from cleric to magistrate and from church to state did not separate Western law from its Christian foundations. Catholic canon law remained part of a good deal of early modern Western common law and civil law – predictably so in Catholic lands, but also surprisingly so in many Protestant lands. Despite the loud condemnation of the canon law by several early reformers, Protestant magistrates and jurists readily plucked many legal provisions and procedures from the medieval canon law that they regarded as consonant with their new teachings. Moreover, in the Catholic regions of Eastern Europe and the Holy Roman Empire, as well as in France, Spain, Portugal, Italy and their many Latin and North American colonies, Catholic clerics and canonists continued to have a strong influence on the content and character of early modern state law. This influence was strengthened by the resurgence of refined legal learning in Spain and Portugal, led by such scholars as Thomas Vitoria (*c.* 1486–1546), Fernando Vázquez (b. 1512), Francisco Suarez (1548–1617), and Thomas Sanchez (1550–1610). This influence was further strengthened by the sweeping legal and theological reforms of the Council of Trent (1545–1563) and by the wave of early modern concordats and constitutions that ensured the Catholic Church of a privileged, if not legally established, status in many Catholic nations and their colonies.

In the Protestant nations of early modern Europe and their later transatlantic colonies, many new Protestant theological views came to direct and dramatic expression at state law. For example, Protestant theologians replaced the traditional sacramental understanding of marriage with a new idea of the marital household as a "social estate" or "covenantal association" of the earthly kingdom. On that basis, Protestant magistrates developed a new state law of marriage, featuring requirements of parental consent, state registration, church consecration, and peer presence for valid marital formation, a severely truncated law of impediments and annulment, and the introduction of absolute divorce on grounds of adultery, desertion, and other faults, with subsequent rights to remarry at least for the innocent party.[22] Protestant theologians replaced the traditional understanding of education as a teaching office of the church with a new understanding of the public school as a "civic seminary" for all persons to prepare for their

---

[22] See the chapter by Don Browning herein.

peculiar vocations. On that basis, Protestant magistrates replaced clerics as
the chief rulers of education, state law replaced church law as the principal
law of education, and the general callings of all Christians replaced the
special calling of the clergy as the *raison d'être* of education.

Lutheranism

Beyond these common changes in Reformation Europe, each of the four
original branches of Protestantism made its own distinctive contributions to
Western law, politics, and society. The Lutheran Reformation of Germany
and Scandinavia territorialized the Christian faith, and gave ample new
political power to the local Christian magistrate. Luther replaced medieval
teachings with a new two-kingdoms theory. The "invisible" church of the
heavenly kingdom, he argued, was a perfect community of saints, where all
stood equal in dignity before God, all enjoyed perfect Christian liberty, and
all governed their affairs in accordance with the Gospel. The "visible" church
of this earthly kingdom, however, embraced saints and sinners alike. Its
members still stood directly before God and still enjoyed liberty of conscience, including the liberty to leave the visible church itself. But, unlike the
invisible church, the visible church needed both the Gospel and human
law to govern its members' relationships with God and with fellow believers.
The clergy must administer the Gospel. The magistrate must administer
the law.

Luther and his followers regarded the local magistrate as God's vice-
regent called to elaborate natural law and to reflect divine justice in his local
domain. The best source and summary of natural law was the Ten
Commandments and its elaboration in the moral principles of the Bible.
The magistrate was to cast these general principles of natural law into
specific precepts of human law, designed to fit local conditions. Luther and
his followers also regarded the local magistrate as the "father of the community" (*Landesvater, paterpoliticus*). He was to care for his political subjects as if they were his children, and his political subjects were to "honor"
him as if he were their parent. Like a loving father, the magistrate was to
keep the peace and to protect his subjects in their persons, properties, and
reputations. He was to deter his subjects from abusing themselves through
drunkenness, sumptuousness, gambling, prostitution, and other vices. He
was to nurture his subjects through the community chest, the public
almshouse, the state-run hospice. He was to educate them through
the public school, the public library, the public lectern. He was to see to
their spiritual needs by supporting the ministry of the local church, and

encouraging attendance and participation through civil laws of religious worship and tithing.

These twin metaphors of the Christian magistrate – as the lofty vice-regent of God and as the loving father of the local community – described the basics of Lutheran legal and political theory for the next three centuries. Political authority was divine in origin, but earthly in operation. It expressed God's harsh judgment against sin but also his tender mercy for sinners. It communicated the Law of God but also the lore of the local community. It depended upon the church for prophetic direction but it took over from the church all jurisdiction. Either metaphor of the Christian magistrate standing alone could be a recipe for abusive tyranny or officious paternalism. But both metaphors together provided Luther and his followers with the core ingredients of a robust Christian republicanism and budding Christian welfare state. These ideas were central to German and Scandinavian law and politics until modern times.

Anglicanism

Anglicanism pressed to more extreme national forms the Lutheran model of a unitary local Christian commonwealth under the final authority of the Christian magistrate. Building in part on Lutheran and Roman law precedents, King Henry VIII severed all legal and political ties between the church in England and the pope. The Supremacy Act (1534) declared the monarch to be "Supreme Head" of the Church and Commonwealth of England as well as the Defender of the Faith. The English monarchs, through their parliaments, established a uniform doctrine and liturgy and issued the Book of Common Prayer (1559), Thirty-Nine Articles (1576), and eventually the Authorized (King James) Version of the Bible (1611). They also assumed jurisdiction over poor relief, education, and other activities that had previously been carried on under Catholic auspices, and dissolved the many monasteries, foundations, and guilds through which the church had administered its social ministry and welfare. Communicant status in the Church of England was rendered a condition for citizenship status in the Commonwealth of England. Contraventions of royal religious policy were punishable both as heresy and as treason.

The Stuart monarchs moved slowly, through hard experience, toward greater toleration of religious pluralism and greater autonomy of local Protestant churches. From 1603 to 1640, King James I (1566–1625) and Charles I (1600–1649) persecuted Protestant non-conformists with a growing vengeance, driving tens of thousands of them to the Continent and often from there to North America. In 1640, the Protestants who remained led a revolution against King Charles, and ultimately deposed and executed him in 1649. They also passed laws that declared England a free Christian commonwealth, free from Anglican establishment and aristocratic privilege. This commonwealth experiment was short-lived. Royal rule and traditional Anglicanism were vigorously reestablished in 1660, and repression of Protestant and Catholic dissenters renewed. But when the dissenters again rose up in revolt, Parliament passed the Bill of Rights and Toleration Act in 1689 that guaranteed a measure of freedom of association, worship, self-government, and basic civil rights to all peaceable Protestant churches. Many of the remaining legal restrictions on Protestants fell into desuetude in the following century, though Catholicism and Judaism remained formally proscribed in England until the Emancipation Acts of 1829 and 1833.

Despite these intermittent waves of revolt, restoration, and constitutional reform, much English law remained rather strikingly traditional in the early modern period. Unlike other Protestant lands, England did not pass comprehensive new legal reformations that reflected and implemented its new Protestant faith. Armed with the conservative legal syntheses of Richard Hooker (1553–1600) and others, England chose to maintain a good deal of its traditional medieval common law and canon law, which was only gradually reformed over the centuries by piecemeal parliamentary statutes and judicial precedents. Moreover, after divesting the church of its lands and jurisdiction during the early Reformation era, Queen Elizabeth I (1533–1603) and her successors turned anew to established Anglican church institutions to help administer the English laws of charity, education, domestic relations, and more.

Anabaptism

Contrary to Lutherans and Anglicans, early Anabaptists advocated the separation of the redeemed realm of religion and the church from the fallen realm of politics and the state. In their definitive Schleitheim Confession (1527), the Anabaptists called for a return to the communitarian ideals of the New Testament and the ascetic principles of the apostolic church. The Anabaptists eventually splintered into various groups of Amish, Brethren, Hutterites, Mennonites, and others. Some of these early splinter groups were politically radical or utopian, particularly those following Thomas Müntzer (1489–1525) of Germany. But most Anabaptist communities by the later sixteenth century had become quiet Christian separatists.

Anabaptist communities ascetically withdrew from civic life into small, self-sufficient, intensely democratic communities. When such communities grew too large or too divided, they deliberately colonized themselves, eventually spreading Anabaptists from Russia to Ireland to the furthest frontiers of North America. These communities were governed internally by biblical principles of discipleship, simplicity, charity, and non-resistance. They set their own internal standards of worship, liturgy, diet, discipline, dress, and education. They handled their own internal affairs of property, contracts, commerce, marriage, and inheritance – so far as possible by appeal to biblical laws and practices, not those of the state.

The state and its law, most Anabaptists believed, was part of the fallen world, which was to be avoided in accordance with biblical injunctions that Christians should "be in the world, but not of the world" or "conformed" to it (John 15:18–19, 17:14–16; Romans 12:2; 1 John 2:15–17). Once the perfect creation of God, the world was now a sinful regime that lay beyond "the perfection of Christ" and beyond the daily concern of the Christian believer. God had allowed the world to survive through his appointment of magistrates and laws who were empowered to use coercion and violence to maintain a modicum of order and peace. Christians should thus obey the laws of political authorities, so far as Scripture enjoined, such as in paying their taxes or registering their properties. But Christians should avoid active participation in and unnecessary interaction with the world and the state. Most early modern Anabaptists were pacifists, preferring derision, exile, or martyrdom to active participation in war. Most Anabaptists also refused to swear oaths, or to participate in political elections, civil litigation, or civic feasts and functions.[23] This aversion to political and civic activities often earned Anabaptists severe reprisal and repression by Catholics and Protestants alike – violent martyrdom in many instances.

While unpopular in its genesis, Anabaptist theological separatism ultimately proved to be a vital source of later Western legal arguments for the separation of church and state and for the protection of the civil and religious liberties of minorities. Equally important for later legal reforms was the new Anabaptist doctrine of adult baptism. This doctrine gave new emphasis to religious voluntarism as opposed to traditional theories of birthright or predestined faith. In Anabaptist theology, each adult was called to make a conscious and conscientious choice to accept the faith – metaphorically, to scale the wall of separation between the fallen world and

---

[23] See the chapter by Kent Greenawalt herein.

the realm of religion to come within the perfection of Christ. In the later eighteenth century, Free Church followers, both in Europe and North America, converted this cardinal image into a powerful platform of liberty of conscience and free exercise of religion not only for Christians but eventually for all peaceable believers.[24]

A number of these early Anabaptist ideas from Europe entered into the hearts and minds of American Evangelicals. Especially after the eighteenth- and early nineteenth-century Great Awakenings, American Evangelicals emphasized the act of Christian conversion, the necessary spiritual rebirth of each sinful individual. On that basis, they strongly advocated the liberty of conscience of each individual and the free speech and free press rights of missionaries to evangelize, both on the American frontier and abroad. Evangelicals had a high view of the Christian Bible as the infallible text- book for human living. On that basis, they celebrated the use of the Bible in public and private life, and they castigated Jews, Catholics, Mormons, and others for using what they considered to be partial, apocryphal, or sur- rogate scriptures. Evangelicals emphasized sanctification, the process of each individual becoming holier before God, neighbor, and self. On that basis, they underscored a robust ethic of spiritual and moral progress, edu- cation, and improvement of all.

Departing from their Anabaptist forebearers, many early American Evangelicals coupled this emphasis on personal conversion and sanctifica- tion with a concern for legal reform and moral improvement of the nation. Great numbers of Evangelicals joined mainline Protestants, Catholics, Jews, Quakers, and others in the national campaign to end slavery – though this issue sharply divided their northern and southern constituents, espe- cially during the Civil War (1861–1865). Nineteenth-century Evangelicals were more united in their support for successive campaigns concerning the laws of dueling, freemasonry, lotteries, drunkenness, Sunday mails, Sabbath-breaking, industrial exploitation, corporate corruption, and more. In the later nineteenth century, many Evangelicals also joined the struggle for the rights and plights of emancipated blacks, poor workers, women suffragists, and labor union organizers – none more forcefully than Walter Rauschenbusch (1861–1918), the leader of the Social Gospel Movement. Though they engaged these big national issues, however, most American Evangelicals were generally suspicious of big government, especially federal government. Most prized federalism and the fostering of voluntary associ- ations – families, schools, clubs, charities, businesses, unions, corporations,

---

[24] See the chapter by David Little herein.

learned societies, and more – as essential forces and forums of law and order.[25]

Calvinism

Calvinists charted a course between the Erastianism of Lutherans (and Anglicans) that subordinated the church to the state, and the asceticism of early Anabaptists that withdrew the church from the state and society. Like Lutherans, Calvinists insisted that each local polity be an overtly Christian commonwealth that adhered to the general principles of natural law and that translated them into detailed new positive laws of religious worship, Sabbath observance, public morality, marriage and family, crime and tort, contract and business, charity and education. Like Anabaptists, Calvinists insisted on the basic separation of the offices and operations of church and state, leaving the church to govern its own doctrine and liturgy, polity and property, without interference from the state. But, unlike these other Protestants, Calvinists stressed that both church and state officials were to play complementary roles in the creation of the local Christian common-wealth and in the cultivation of the Christian citizen.

Calvinists emphasized more fully than other Protestants the educational use of the natural and positive law. Lutherans stressed the "civil" and "the-ological" uses of the natural law – the need for law to deter sinners from their sinful excesses and to drive them to repentance. Calvinists emphasized the educational use of the natural law as well – the need to teach persons both the letter and the spirit of the law, both the civil morality of common human duty and the spiritual morality of special Christian aspiration. While Lutheran followers of Philip Melanchthon (1497–1560) had included this educational use of the natural law in their theology, Calvinists made it an integral part of their politics as well. They further insisted that not only the natural law of God but also the positive law of the state could achieve these three civil, theological, and educational uses.

Calvinists also emphasized more fully than other Protestants the legal role of the church in a Christian commonwealth. Lutherans, after the first two generations, left law largely to the Christian magistrate. Anabaptists gave the church a strong legal role, but only for voluntary members of the ascetically withdrawn Christian community. By contrast, Calvinists, from the start, drew local church officials directly into the enforcement of law for the entire Christian commonwealth and for all citizens, regardless of their

---

[25] See the chapter by David Skeel herein.

church affiliation. In Calvin's Geneva, this political responsibility of the church fell largely to the consistory, an elected body of civil and religious officials, with original jurisdiction over cases of marriage and family life, charity and social welfare, worship and public morality. Among most later Calvinists – French Huguenots, Dutch Pietists, Scottish Presbyterians, German and Hungarian Reformed, and English and American Puritans and Congregationalists – the Genevan-style consistory was transformed into the body of pastors, elders, deacons, and teachers that governed each local church congregation, and played a less structured political and legal role in the broader Christian commonwealth. But local clergy still had a strong role in advising magistrates on the positive law of the local community. Local churches and their consistories also generally enjoyed autonomy in administering their own doctrine, liturgy, charity, polity, and property and in administering ecclesiastical discipline over their members.

Later Calvinists also laid some of the foundations for Western theories of democracy and human rights.[26] One technique, developed by Calvinist writers like Christopher Goodman (c. 1530–1603), Theodore Beza (1519–1605), and Johannes Althusius (1557–1638), was to ground rights in the duties of the Decalogue and other biblical moral teachings. The First Table of the Decalogue prescribes duties of love that each person owes to God – to honor God and God's name, to observe the Sabbath day and to worship, to avoid false gods and false swearing. The Second Table prescribes duties of love that each person owes to neighbors – to honor one's parents and other authorities, not to kill, not to commit adultery, not to steal, not to bear false witness, not to covet. The reformers cast the person's duties toward God as a set of rights that others could not obstruct – the right to religious exercise: the right to honor God and God's name, the right to rest and worship on one's Sabbath, the right to be free from false gods and false oaths. They cast a person's duties toward a neighbor, in turn, as the neighbor's right to have that duty discharged. One person's duties not to kill, to commit adultery, to steal, or to bear false witness thus gives rise to another person's rights to life, property, fidelity, and reputation.

Another technique, developed especially by English and New England Puritans, was to draw out the legal and political implications of the signature Reformation teaching, coined by Luther, that a person is at once sinner and saint (*simul justus et peccator*). On the one hand, they argued, every person is created in the image of God and justified by faith in God. Every person is called to a distinct vocation, which stands equal in dignity and sanctity to

---

[26] See the chapter by David Little herein.

all others. Every person is a prophet, priest, and king, and responsible to exhort, to minister, and to rule in the community. Every person thus stands equal before God and before his or her neighbor. Every person is vested with a natural liberty to live, to believe, to love and serve God and neighbor. Every person is entitled to the vernacular Scripture, to education, to work in a vocation.

On the other hand, Protestants argued, every person is sinful and prone to evil and egoism. Every person needs the restraint of the law to deter him from evil, and to drive him to repentance. Every person needs the association of others to exhort, minister, and rule her with law and with love. Every person, therefore, is inherently a communal creature. Every person belongs to a family, a church, a political community.

These social institutions of family, church, and state, later Protestants argued, are divine in origin and human in organization. They are created by God and governed by godly ordinances. They stand equal before God and are called to discharge distinctive godly functions in the community. The family is called to rear and nurture children, to educate and discipline them, to exemplify love and cooperation. The church is called to preach the Word, administer the sacraments, educate the young, aid the needy. The state is called to protect order, punish crime, promote community. Though divine in origin, these institutions are formed through human covenants.[27] Such covenants confirm the divine functions, the created offices, of these institutions. Such covenants also organize these offices so that they are protected from the sinful excesses of officials who occupy them. Family, church, and state are thus organized as public institutions, accessible and accountable to each other and to their members. Calvinists especially stressed that the church is to be organized as a democratic congregational polity, with a separation of ecclesiastical powers among pastors, elders, and deacons, election of officers to limited tenures of office, and ready participation of the congregation in the life and leadership of the church.

By the turn of the seventeenth century, Calvinists began to recast these theological doctrines into democratic norms and forms. Protestant doctrines of the person and society were cast into democratic social forms. Since all persons stand equal before God, they must stand equal before God's political agents in the state. Since God has vested all persons with natural liberties of life and belief, the state must ensure them of similar civil liberties. Since God has called all persons to be prophets, priests, and kings,

---

[27] See the chapters by David Novak and Harold J. Berman herein.

the state must protect their constitutional freedoms to speak, to preach, and to rule in the community. Since God has created persons as social creatures, the state must promote and protect a plurality of social institutions, particularly the church and the family.

Protestant doctrines of sin, in turn, were cast into democratic political forms. The political office must be protected against the sinfulness of the political official. Political power, like ecclesiastical power, must be distributed among self-checking executive, legislative, and judicial branches. Officials must be elected to limited terms of office. Laws must be clearly codified, and discretion closely guarded. If officials abuse their office, they must be disobeyed. If they persist in their abuse, they must be removed, even if by revolutionary force and regicide. These Protestant teachings were among the driving ideological forces behind the revolts of the French Huguenots, Dutch Pietists, and Scottish Presbyterians against their monarchical oppressors in the later sixteenth and seventeenth centuries. They were critical weapons in the arsenal of the revolutionaries in England and America, and important sources of inspiration and instruction during the great age of democratic construction in later eighteenth- and nineteenth-century North America and Western Europe.

LAW AND CHRISTIANITY IN THE MODERN AGE

The fourth watershed period in the Western legal tradition came with the Enlightenment of the eighteenth and nineteenth centuries. The Enlightenment was no single, unified movement, but a series of diverse ideological movements in various academic disciplines and social circles of Western Europe and North America. Enlightenment philosophers such as David Hume (1711–1776), Jean Jacques Rousseau (1712–1778), Thomas Jefferson (1743–1826), and others offered a new theology of individualism, rationalism, and nationalism to supplement, if not supplant, traditional Christian teachings. To Enlightenment exponents, the individual was no longer viewed primarily as a sinner seeking salvation in the life hereafter. Every individual was created equal in virtue and dignity, vested with inherent rights of life and liberty and capable of choosing his or her own means and measures of happiness. Reason was no longer the handmaiden of revelation, rational disputation no longer subordinate to homiletic declaration. The rational process, conducted privately by each person, and collectively in the open marketplace of ideas, was considered a sufficient source of private morality and public law. The nation-state was no longer identified with a national church or a divinely blessed covenant people. The nation-state was to be glorified in its own right. Its constitutions and laws were sacred texts reflecting the morals and mores of the collective national culture. Its officials were secular priests, representing the sovereignty and will of the people.

Such teachings transformed many modern Western legal systems. They helped shape new constitutional provisions for limited government and ample liberty, new injunctions to separate church and state, new criminal procedures and methods of criminal punishment, new commercial, con-tractual, and other laws of the private marketplace, new laws of private property and inheritance, shifts toward a fault-based law of delicts and torts, the ultimate expulsion of slavery in England and America, and the gradual removal of discrimination based on race, religion, culture, and gender.[28] Many Western nations also developed elaborate new codes of public law and private law, transformed the curricula of their faculties of law, and radically reconfigured their legal professions.

The new theology of the Enlightenment penetrated Western legal phil-osophy. Spurred on by Hugo Grotius's (1583–1645) impious hypothesis that natural law could exist "even if there is no God," jurists offered a range of new legal philosophies – often abstracted from or appended to earlier Christian and classical teachings. Many Enlightenment writers postulated a mythical state of nature that antedated and integrated human laws and natural rights. Nationalist myths were grafted onto this paradigm to unify and sanctify national legal traditions: Italian jurists appealed to their utopic Roman heritage; English jurists to their ancient constitution and Anglo-Saxon roots; French jurists to their Salic law; German jurists to their ancient constitutional liberties.

A triumvirate of new increasingly secular legal philosophies came to prominence in the later eighteenth and nineteenth centuries. Legal posi-tivists such as John Austin (1790–1859) and Christopher Columbus Langdell (1826–1906) contended that the ultimate source of law lies in the will of the legislature and its ultimate sanction in political force. Natural law theorists as diverse as Immanuel Kant (1724–1804) and Adam Smith (1723–1790) sought the ultimate source of law in pure reason and its ulti-mate sanction in moral sentiment. Historical jurists such as Friedrich Karl von Savigny (1814–1875) and Otto von Gierke (1841–1921) contended that the ultimate source of law is the custom and character of the *Volk*, and its ultimate sanction is communal condemnation. These juxtaposed positivist, naturalist, and historical legal philosophies have lived on in sundry forms

---

[28] See the chapters by David Little and Michael Perry herein.

in the modern Western legal academy, now heavily supplemented by an
array of realist, socialist, feminist, and various critical schools of legal
thought and with a growing number of interdisciplinary approaches that
study law in interaction with the methods and texts of economics, science,
literature, psychology, sociology, and anthropology.

Though these recent reforms have removed most traditional norms
and forms of Christian legal influence, contemporary Western law still
retains important connections with Christian and other religious ideas and
institutions. Even today, law and religion continue to cross-over and cross-
fertilize each other. Law and religion remain conceptually related. They
both draw upon prevailing concepts of the nature of being and order, the
person and community, knowledge and truth. They both embrace closely
analogous doctrines of sin and crime, covenant and contract, righteousness
and justice that invariably bleed together in the mind of the legislator, judge,
and juror.[29] Law and religion are methodologically related. They share overlapping hermeneutical methods of interpreting authoritative texts, casuistic
methods of converting principles to precepts, systematic methods of
organizing their subject matters, pedagogical methods of transmitting the
science and substance of their craft to students. Law and religion are insti-
tutionally related, through the multiple relationships between political and
religious officials and the multiple institutions in which these officials
serve.[30]

Even today, the laws of the secular state retain strong moral and religious
dimensions. These dimensions are reflected not only in the many substantive doctrines of public, private, and criminal law that were derived from
earlier Christian theology and canon law. They are also reflected in the
characteristic forms of contemporary legal systems in the West. Every legitimate legal system has what Lon L. Fuller called an "inner morality," a set
of attributes that bespeak its justice and fairness. Like divine laws, human
laws are generally applicable, publicly proclaimed and known, uniform,
stable, understandable, non-retroactive, and consistently enforced. Every
legitimate legal system also has what Harold J. Berman calls an "inner sanctity," a set of attributes that command the obedience, respect, and fear of
both political authorities and their subjects. Like religion, law has authority – written or spoken sources, texts or oracles, which are considered to be
decisive or obligatory in themselves. Like religion, law has tradition – a
continuity of language, practice, and institutions, a theory of precedent and

---

[29] See the chapters by Jeffrie Murphy and Frank S. Alexander herein.
[30] See the chapters by David Little, Norman Doe, and William Bassett herein.

preservation. Like religion, law has liturgy and ritual – the ceremonial procedures, decorum, and words of the legislature, the courtroom, and the legal document aimed to reflect and dramatize deep social feelings about the value and validity of the law.

Even today, Christianity and other forms of religion maintain a legal dimension, an inner structure of legality, which gives religious lives and religious communities their coherence, order, and social form. Legal "habits of the heart" structure the inner spiritual life and discipline of religious believers, from the reclusive hermit to the aggressive zealot. Legal ideas of justice, order, dignity, atonement, restitution, responsibility, obligation, and others pervade the theological doctrines of countless religious traditions, not least Christianity.[31] Legal structures and processes, including Catholic and Orthodox canon law and Protestant forms of ecclesiastical discipline, continue to organize and govern religious communities and their distinctive beliefs and rituals, mores and morals.[32] All these religious beliefs, values, and practices the modern Western state still protects, respects, and reflects in its law.

Moreover, in the twentieth and early twenty-first centuries, Western Christians have remained forceful and effective legal advocates – albeit as minority voices in much of Europe and Canada today. Catholic legal and political advocacy has grown in depth and power over the past century. Beginning with Pope Leo XIII (1810–1903) and his successors, the Catholic Church has revived and reconstructed for modern use much of the religious, political, and legal thought of the thirteenth-century sage, Thomas Aquinas. This neo-Thomist movement, along with other revival movements within Catholicism, helped launch the early political experiments of the Christian Democratic Party in Europe, the rise of sophisticated subsidiarity theories of society and politics on both continents, and the powerful new natural law and natural rights theories of Jacques Maritain (1882–1973), John Courtney Murray (1904–1967), and their many students. It also helped pave the way for the Church's great Second Vatican Council (1962–1965) with its transforming vision of religious liberty, human dignity, and democracy and with its ambitious agenda to modernize the Catholic Church's legal, political, and social teachings on numerous subjects. A good deal of the energy and ingenuity of these earlier Catholic reform movements are now captured in legally sophisticated Catholic "social teachings" movements and in various schools of

---

[31] See the chapters by Frank Alexander, Jeffrie Murphy, and Michael Perry herein.
[32] See the chapters by Norman Doe and William Bassett herein.

Catholic natural law theory. It has also helped to drive a whole cottage industry of legal and political activism: Catholic non-governmental associations, news media, litigation and lobbying groups have become deeply embroiled in contested national and international legal issues of religious liberty, capital punishment, marriage, abortion, social welfare, education, and more.

Protestant teachings on law, politics, and society have also been influential, albeit less comprehensive and more focused in the United States. In the first half of the twentieth century, great Protestant figures like Abraham Kuyper (1827–1920), Karl Barth (1886–1968), Dietrich Bonhoeffer (1906–1945), and Reinhold Niebuhr (1892–1971) charted provocative new legal and political pathways for Protestantism, building on neo-Reformation models. But their successors have not developed a comprehensive legal and political program on the order of Roman Catholicism after the Second Vatican Council – despite important advances made by the World Council of Churches and various world Evangelical gatherings. After World War II, most European Protestants tended to fade from legal influence, and many North American Protestants tended to focus on hot button political issues, like abortion or prayer in schools, without developing a broader legal theory or political program. There have been notable advances and achievements in recent times. One was the civil rights movement of the 1950s–1960s, led by the Baptist preacher Martin Luther King, Jr. and others, that helped to bring greater political and civil equality to African-Americans through a series of landmark statutes and cases. Another was the rise of the Christian right in America in the 1970s to 1990s – a broad conservative political and cultural campaign designed to revitalize public religion, restore families, reform schools, reclaim unsafe neighborhoods, and support faith-based charities through new statutes and law suits. Another has been the recent energetic involvement of Protestant and other Christian intellectuals in campaigns of family law reform, human rights, environmental protection, and social welfare. Also promising has been the rise of articulate public intellectuals like Wolfgang Huber, Jürgen Habermas, and John Stott in Europe, and Robert Bellah, Jean Elshtain, Carl Henry, and Martin Marty in North America, who from various perspectives have called fellow Protestants to take up anew the great legal, political, and social questions of our day. Whether these recent movements are signposts for the development of a comprehensive new Protestant jurisprudence and political theology remains to be seen.

RECOMMENDED READING

Ball, Milner S. *Called By Stories: Biblical Sagas and Their Challenge for Law.* Durham, NC: Duke University Press, 2000.

The Word and the Law. Chicago: University of Chicago Press, 1993.

Berman, Harold J. *Faith and Order: The Reconciliation of Law and Religion.* Grand Rapids, MI: Wm. B. Eerdmans Publishing, 1993.

Law and Revolution: The Formation of the Western Legal Tradition. Cambridge, MA: Harvard University Press, 1983.

Law and Revolution II: The Impact of the Protestant Reformations on the Western Legal Tradition. Cambridge, MA: Harvard University Press, 2003.

Brundage, James A. *Law, Sex, and Christian Society in Medieval Europe.* Chicago: University of Chicago Press, 1987.

Medieval Canon Law. London: Longman, 1995.

Daube, David. *Collected Works*, ed. Calum Carmichael. Berkeley, CA: Robbins Collection, 1992– .

Ehler, Sidney Z. and John B. Morrall. *Church and State Through the Centuries: A Collection of Historic Documents with Commentaries.* Newman, MD: Burnes & Oates, 1954.

Field, Lester L. *Liberty, Dominion and the Two Swords: On the Origins of Western Political Theology.* Notre Dame, IN: University of Notre Dame Press, 1998.

Fuller, Lon L. *The Morality of Law*, rev. edn. New Haven, CT: Yale University Press, 1969.

Helmholz, R. H. *Canon Law in Protestant Lands.* Berlin: Dunker and Humbolt, 1992.

The Spirit of the Classical Canon Law. Athens, GA: University of Georgia Press, 1996.

Roman Canon Law in Reformation England. Cambridge: Cambridge University Press, 1990.

Huber, Wolfgang. *Gerechtigkeit und Recht: Grundlinien christlicher Rechtsethik.* Gütersloh: Chr. Kaiser, 1996.

Klaassen, Walter A. *Anabaptism in Outline: Selected Primary Sources.* Scottdale, PA: Herald Press, 1981.

Marty, Martin E. *Religion and Republic: The American Circumstance.* Boston: Beacon Press, 1987.

The One and the Many: America's Struggle for the Common Good. Cambridge, MA: Harvard University Press, 1997.

McConnell, Michael W., Robert F. Cochran, Jr. and Angela C. Carmella, eds. *Christian Perspectives on Legal Thought.* New Haven, CT: Yale University Press, 2001.

Noll, Mark A. *America's God: From Jonathan Edwards to Abraham Lincoln.* New York and Oxford: Oxford University Press, 2002.

O'Donovan, Oliver and Joan Lockwood O'Donovan, eds. *From Irenaeus to Grotius: A Sourcebook in Christian Political Thought 100–1625.* Grand Rapids, MI: Wm. B. Eerdmans Publishing, 1999.

Perry, Michael. *Toward a Theory of Human Rights: Religion, Law, Courts.*
    Cambridge: Cambridge University Press, 2007.
    Under God? Religious Faith and Liberal Democracy. Cambridge and New York:
    Cambridge University Press, 2003.
Tellenbach, Gerd. *Church, State, and Christian Society at the Time of the Investiture
    Conflict.* 1940; reprinted Toronto: University of Toronto Press, 1991.
Tierney, Brian. *The Crisis of Church and State, 1050–1300.* Englewood Cliffs, NJ:
    Prentice Hall, 1964.
    *The Idea of Natural Rights: Studies on Natural Rights, Natural Law, and Church
    Law, 1150–1625.* Grand Rapids, MI: Wm. B. Eerdmans Publishing, 1997.
    Religion, Law, and the Growth of Constitutional Thought, 1150–1625. Cambridge:
    Cambridge University Press, 1982.
Vallauri, Luigi, and Gerhard Dilcher, eds. *Christentum, Säkularisation und
    Modernes Recht,* 2 vols. Baden-Baden: Nomos Gesellschaft, 1981.
Witte, John, Jr. *Law and Protestantism: The Legal Teachings of the Lutheran
    Reformation.* Cambridge: Cambridge University Press, 2002.
    *The Reformation of Rights: Law, Religion, and Human Rights in Early Modern
    Calvinism.* Cambridge: Cambridge University Press, 2007.
Witte, John, Jr. and Frank S. Alexander, eds. *The Teachings of Modern Christianity
    on Law, Politics, and Human Nature,* 2 vols.; 3 vols. pbk. New York: Columbia
    University Press, 2006–2007.

CHAPTER ONE

Law and religion in Judaism

David Novak

LAW AND RELIGION

While today many regard law and religion as separate spheres and sciences of life, Judaism has long regarded these phenomena as overlapping, if not virtually identical. Indeed, by the early Middle Ages, Jewish writers used the same Hebrew word *dat* to denote the concepts both of "law" and "religion."[1] By that time, there was no legitimate law, whether Jewish or non-Jewish, that was not regarded as religious. All law was assumed to be derived from the will of God, whether immediately experienced in revelation, or transmitted via continuous tradition, or discerned by public discursive reasoning. And religion, being the human relationship with God, was assumed to consist of accepting, understanding, applying, and obeying God's commandments. These commandments comprise the body of the law governing any religiously legitimate community which, for medieval Jews, would be a community characterized by its monotheistic religion. Thus the fourteenth-century rabbinical scholar, Menahem ha-Meiri, judged both Christianity and Islam to be worthy of the respect of Jews because "they are bound by the ways of religion/law," namely by "religious law" or by "lawful religion."[2] Christians and Muslims were now like the Jews, but unlike the ancient idolaters who either had no law or whose law was not willed by the one true God, the creator of the universe and of humankind within it, the God who continues to govern his universe according to his law. Jewish thinkers regarded Jewish law to be theologically superior even to the revealed law of Christians and Muslims, but that superiority was assumed to be one of degree

---

[1] The word *dat* is not originally Hebrew but, rather, a Hebraicized form of the Persian words *dâta*, meaning statutory law. See F. D. Brown, S. R. Driver, C. A. Briggs, *A Hebrew and English Lexicon of the Old Testament*, corrected edn (Oxford: Clarendon Press, 1966), 206.

[2] See David Novak, *Jewish–Christian Dialogue* (New York: Oxford University Press, 1989), 42–56. For the basis of assuming Gentile normativity, see *Tosefta*: Sanhedrin 13.2 re. Ps. 9:18.

2 "Moses and the People Make a Sacrifice to God Confirming the Covenant." from
Christoph Weigel, *Biblia ectypa: Bildnussen auss heiliger Schrifft Alt und Neuen Testaments*
(Augsburg, 1695), s.v. Exodus 24.

rather than one of kind. Jews were not the only people to have authentic *dat*.

This identification of law with religion was not always the case in the history of Judaism. In early antiquity, religion was regarded as more than law, and law was regarded as only one institution in the overall theological–political reality of the people of Israel. It was not until the second century CE that the law gained its total hegemony in Jewish religious life, and it has remained so for traditional Jews to this day.

This chapter recounts briefly the stages of interaction between law and religion in the history of Judaism. This story is significant not just for Jews, but also for Christians interested in the religious foundations and dimensions of Western law. Although Jews and Christians have had a tempestuous, and sometimes tragic, relationship during the first two millennia of the common era, Christians have sometimes drawn on the Jewish texts and traditions recounted herein in developing their own internal religious legal systems, as well as in shaping the secular laws of the various political regimes that governed them.

BIBLICAL LAW

When looking at the relation of law and religion in Judaism, we need to begin by carefully looking at that relation in the Hebrew Bible (what Christians have called the "Old Testament"): first, because that is where Judaism begins; second, because that relation of law and religion is the one that had the most profound influence on Christian (and subsequent Western) thought on the issue of law and religion, especially in discussions of what we now call "church–state relations."

In biblical Hebrew, "religion" as the relationship between God and humans is best denoted by the word *berit*, usually translated into English as "covenant." That translation of *berit* is helpful as long as "covenant" is not confused with "contract," as is often the case in modern parlance.[3] Covenants are either made by God with humans, or they are made by humans before God as their guarantor. The correlation of covenant and law (*torah*) in ancient Israel needs to be understood first.

The covenant made at Sinai between God and Israel is considered to be *the* covenant par excellence. Indeed, creation itself, with its reconstitution in the Noahide covenant, is for the sake of *the* covenant of Sinai.[4] "Were

---

[3] See David Novak, *The Jewish Social Contract* (Princeton: Princeton University Press, 2005), 30–64.
[4] See Exodus 34:28–35.

My covenant not by day and not by night, I would not have established the laws of heaven and earth" (Jeremiah 33:25). And the law that emerges from this covenant of all covenants is the Torah, specifically the commandments (*mitzvoth*) that were revealed to the people of Israel through Moses, and are recorded by Moses in the biblical books of Exodus, Leviticus, Numbers, and Deuteronomy. According to late rabbinic tradition, there are 613 commandments in the Mosaic Torah, which are considered to be binding on all Israel until at least the time of the coming of the Messiah, and perhaps even thereafter. Also, according to many of the ancient Rabbis, these perpetual commandments are not found in the Pentateuch until the first Passover precepts are given in the twelfth chapter of Exodus. Hence commandments that seem to be assumed in Genesis are almost always taken to be precepts for both Jews and Gentiles.

Except for the Ten Commandments presented in Exodus 20 and again in Deuteronomy 5, the various commandments in the Pentateuch seem to be given randomly in no particular order. Thus it is difficult to call any of the groupings of the commandments a "code." Some modern biblical scholars have noted that there are two kinds of law given in the Pentateuch: apodictic and casuistic. An example of an apodictic law would be: "You shall not kill" (Exodus 20:13). An example of a casuistic law would be: "When you draw near to a city to fight against it, offer terms of peace to it" (Deuteronomy 20:10). The first type of law is what philosophers call a "categorical imperative." There are no exceptions and no preconditions. The second type of law is what philosophers call a "hypothetical imperative." Here there could be exceptions, such as when the war is a defensive war against an enemy who would not accept peace terms. As for preconditions, it seems left to the leadership of the people to decide if and when the people might or might not engage in an offensive war.

Modern biblical scholars, beginning most famously with Baruch Spinoza, have gone to great lengths to argue that the various groupings of commandments in the Pentateuch were written by different authors writing at different times. The traditional Jewish view is that all the commandments – however they are presented in the Pentateuch and in whatever style they are presented – are God's revelation to Moses for the people of Israel, and some of them are even God's revelation to the people directly. Whatever its historical merits, the traditional view is the one that shaped the way subsequent generations of Jewish teachers interpreted the Pentateuch or "Written Torah." For rabbinic tradition, the whole Pentateuch is taken to be a seamless garment. As such, anything in one part of the "Five Books of Moses" could be a complement to anything in another part. All contradictions are assumed to be apparent rather than real. Thus it became the task of post-biblical scholars both to explicate what seems obscure in the Written Torah and to resolve seeming contradictions by recontextualizing the opposing passages so that they are now seen to be talking about different matters. In that sense, the rabbinic tradition made a systematic code out of what seems to be several random collections of laws in the Pentateuch. And, despite all their differences with the Rabbis over the ultimate value of the law, early Christian exegetes had no disagreement with the Rabbis in their reading of the Pentateuch and its commandments as a unified, totally coherent, whole.

There are two other covenants in the Bible that have legal significance: one preceding the covenant at Sinai, the other still to come in the future.

The future messianic covenant, promising ultimate redemption of Israel and humankind along with them, is considered to have been fulfilled when the Gentiles come to Zion. "For out of Zion shall go forth the law . . . [God] shall judge between nations, and shall decide for many peoples" (Isaiah 2:3–4). The first covenant, that made between God and Noah and his descendants, did not bring its own law; instead, it was instituted as a sign that God will enforce the law for humans that is coequal with their very creation, the law whose violation had led to the near destruction of all humankind.[5] Moreover, even certain private agreements between individuals and between nations were not to contradict what was already considered to be divine law. Indeed, the covenantal oaths that solemnized such agreements were to be made in the name of the divine lawgiver. Such was also the case with any new law that had to be made by Jewish authorities: optimally, this new law was to enhance the old law; minimally, it was not to contradict the old law.

In the days before the destruction of the First Temple in Jerusalem (586 BCE), the law (*torah*) was only one part of the covenant between God and Israel. In fact, three institutions were at work in the overall covenantal reality of pre-exilic Israel: (1) the Temple and its priesthood (*kehunah*); (2) the monarchy (*melukhah*); and (3) the prophecy of the prophets (*nevu'ah*). Whereas the Temple seemed to have operated according to usually undisputed cultic practices, and the monarchy seemed to have had the prerogative to override divine laws in the public interest, the authority of the law itself as the means for governing human affairs seemed to require prophetic endorsement, even at times prophetic initiation.[6] Without

---

[5] See Genesis 6:11; 9:1–17.   [6] See I Samuel 8:4–22. Cf. Deuteronomy 17:14–20.

prophetic endorsement or initiation, the law lacked authority, inasmuch as the prophet was considered the one who brought either divine approval or divine disapproval of any human action or plan of action. Without that approval, any human proposal was considered to be presumptively illegal – contrary to God's justice (*mishpat*). This is what is meant by Moses' admonition to Israel, just before his death and their departure from the Wilderness for the Promised Land, to hearken to the prophet, whom "the Lord your God will raise up for you a prophet, who is like me" (Deuteronomy 18:15). If not the actual lawgivers, the prophets were certainly the only legitimate conduits of the law for the authors of the Bible.

In the biblical period before the destruction of the First Temple in 586 BCE, the very authenticity of the law itself depended on the endorsement of a prophet.[7] Thus, in the last days of the First Temple, when a Torah scroll was found in the Temple, which seemed to contain normative data theretofore unknown, King Josiah commanded the high priest and some of his other officials to take the Torah scroll to the prophet Huldah for official sanction of its authenticity. Since the people were being held accountable for their violation of the law written in this scroll, Huldah seemed to be holding them responsible for having forgotten the law of Moses, the very model for her prophetic authority.[8] Accordingly, the Torah, as law, depended on a prophet for its authority, and it depended on a prophet for the renewed authentication of its text.

With the return of the Jews (the remnant of the larger people of Israel) to the Land of Israel from Babylonian exile under the political leadership of Nehemiah and the religious leadership of Ezra around 538 BCE, the religio-legal situation changed considerably. When the returning people gathered in Jerusalem to be politically reconstituted, they sent for Ezra the Scribe (*ha-sofer*) to "bring the book (*sefer*) of the law (*torah*) of Moses that which the Lord had given to Israel" (Nehemiah 8:1). The important point to note here is that although Ezra was a priest (*kohen*), he was acting neither in a priestly capacity nor in a prophetic capacity (even though some saw him as being identical with the prophet Malachi).[9] Unlike the earlier prophets who had to authenticate the divine law, Ezra's authority became that of the interpreter of the divine law, whose text by then seemed to be undisputed. So, rather than requiring a prophet to bring a new law or even a new endorsement of the old law, Ezra re-presented *the text of* the old law of Moses as being sufficient to govern the entire life of the Jewish people.

---

[7] Cf. *Babylonian Talmud*: Yevamot 90b re Deut. 18:15.
[8] See 2 Kings 22:8–23:3; 2 Chronicles 34:14–33.
[9] See *Babylonian Talmud*: Megillah 15a re Mal. 2:11.

That text now only needed current interpretation, but the people needed no new further revelation.[10]

The prophets had already completed their task of saving the Torah from utter oblivion at the hands of antinomian factions in Israel. In the days of the Second Temple (538 BCE–70 CE), the synagogue became the primary locus of the Written Torah – understood as the first five books of Moses, called the Pentateuch, plus selections from the Prophets and the Hagiographa. The regular reading of the Torah became the central feature of the synagogue service, when most of the members of any Jewish community were regularly assembled for both worship and instruction in God's law. The synagogue was called the "House of the Book" (*bet ha-sefer*) because of the centrality of "the book (*sefer*) of the Torah" that was there. The synagogue was also the primary place of primary education for the masses.[11] The ark holding the Torah scrolls became the focal point of every synagogue. And, although the synagogue did not replace the Temple, the fact that the reading of the Torah became a regular feature of the synagogue service, rather than only a special event in the Temple, as it had been, meant that the interpretation of the law was considered to be much more within the purview of the scribes than that of the priests. Since the scribes, unlike the priests, were not a hereditary caste, the connection of law and religion also became more pervasive among the whole people, since the synagogues, unlike the Temple, were open to all. That is how the synagogue also came to be known as the "House of Assembly" (*bet ha-keneset*).

RABBINIC LAW

By around 538 BCE, the Jewish people saw the simultaneous reassertion of the total hegemony of the written Torah of Moses over all of Jewish life, plus the first manifestation of the tradition of interpretation and supplementation of the official Torah text known as the "Oral Torah." This second Torah was entered into the public discourse being conducted within the synagogue service. The discourse focused on the meaning, especially the practical meaning, of the portions of the Torah and the Prophets regularly read there.[12] Nevertheless, the oral rather than the written character of this public discourse seemed to insure that it would never surpass, let alone

---

[10] See D. W. Halivni, *Revelation Restored* (Boulder, CO: Westview Press, 1997), 11–45.
[11] See *Palestinian Talmud*: Maasrot 3.7/50d.
[12] See Josephus, *Contra Apionem*, 2.175; *Antiquities*, 16.43.

supplant, the Written Torah upon which its scribal interpreters continually sought to base it by a process called *midrash* (literally, "enquiry").

The oral character of this secondary, supplementary Torah, in effect, created a class of interpreters to be the recipients and developers of the oral tradition, who came to be known as "Pharisees," and later as "Rabbis." Whereas the synagogue became the public locale of the Written Torah because all the people were there to hear it read aloud regularly, the rabbinic academy or "House of Interpretation" (*bet midrash*) became the locale of more specialized study of the sacred text and the traditions built upon it.[13] Only a portion of what was developed there by the Rabbis was brought into the synagogue for direct public acceptance and application. This was especially so with the law (*halakhah*) that emerged from the discussions of the rabbinic academy, law that seemed to have been formulated as generalizations of rulings the Rabbis originally made as jurists when they were presented with important cases. In fact, it was out of the specialized discussions of the rabbinic academy that the Talmud emerged.

While initially subordinate and supplemental, rabbinic law came to dominate Jewish religious life after the destruction of the Second Temple in Jerusalem in 70 CE. That was mainly due to the fact that the rabbinic academy was the only one of the three religio-political institutions of early Israel to survive this catastrophe. Not only was the Temple destroyed, but the monarchy as an independent Jewish political institution had, for all intents and purposes, already ended with the destruction of the First Temple six centuries before, and now even its vestigial form was stamped out with the destruction of Jerusalem. The centuries after the diaspora saw the full flowering of what we now call "rabbinic Judaism," out of which all subsequent versions of Judaism until the present day have emerged in one way or another. Here we find the most complete amalgam of law and religion in Judaism. As the Talmud put it: "After the destruction of the Temple, God only has the four cubits of the law left in his world."[14] When the Temple still stood, God had more than the Law. God had the place where his presence (*shekhinah*) dwelled. With the demise of the Temple and its establishment, the prophetic–pharisaic–rabbinic institution of law/religion was left without a rival institution to challenge the full merger of law and religion in Jewish life (as many of their Sadducee opponents were priests).

Even though some traditional norms (*halakhot*) were considered to have been given to Moses along with the Written Torah, in fact, this Mosaic attribution was only specifically invoked when dealing with normative

---

[13] See *Babylonian Talmud*: Berakhot 28a.   [14] *Ibid.*, 8a re. Ps. 87:2.

Jewish practices whose origins were obscure enough that they were attributed to the earliest time possible: the beginning of Jewish tradition at the time of the revelation of the Written Torah to Moses.[15] And, even though there are rabbinic statements that seem to attribute the whole Oral Torah to the time of revelation of the Written Torah at Sinai, that only meant that nothing in the Oral Torah contradicted or overturned the Written Torah. In effect, the Written Torah was viewed as holding the potential that the Oral Torah would later develop.[16] So, when one examines most discussions in the Talmud, whether legal (*halakhic*) or theologically reflective (*aggadic*), it becomes quite evident that these discussions are being represented as the reasoned conclusions and even innovations of the Rabbis who uttered them.

Most of the early rabbinic interpretations of biblical norms are *midrashic*, that is, they are attempts to show that certain normative Jewish practices are really grounded in the words of Scripture, once the deeper meaning of these scriptural words are uncovered by proper exegesis. Though there were attempts to derive new law exegetically, the process of *halakhic midrash* was most often a retrospective enterprise; its goal was to show that what the people had long been doing is what Scripture had always intended. Thus *halakhic midrash* was more heuristic and more conservative than legally innovative.

But while conservative, this rabbinic interpretation was not without innovation. Because the legal norms recorded in the Bible were frequently quite random, the Rabbis constructed a more conceptual ordering of the commandments (both biblical and traditional). This process of conceptual ordering of the law culminated in what might well be seen as the first humanly constructed code of Jewish law: the Mishnah, edited by Judah the Prince in the late second century CE. Drawing upon earlier rabbinic rulings (and even some earlier orderings of the law), "Rabbi" (as Judah alone was called), organized and edited the material into six major divisions.

The six major divisions of the Mishnah are as follows: (1) *Zeraim*, which deals with agricultural laws pertaining to the land of Israel. The first tractate, *Berakhot*, deals with worship and liturgy, thus making it more useful than the other tractates for subsequent generations. (2) *Moed*, which deals with the Sabbath and festivals. (3) *Nashim*, which deals with marital and family matters. (4) *Neziqin*, which deals with civil and criminal matters. (5) *Qodashim*, which deals with the Temple cult. The tractate, *Hullin*,

---

[15] See *Babylonian Talmud*: Menahot 28a; also, Niddah 72b.
[16] See *Palestinian Talmud*: Peah 2.4/17a re Eccl. 1:10.

which deals with the dietary laws, has become the most useful tractate to subsequent generations. (6) *Tohorot*, which deals with matters of ritual purity, mostly having significance only when the Temple is in operation. The tractate, *Niddah*, which deals with menstruation and its effects on marital relations, an issue independent of the Temple, has become *the* tractate in this division of the Mishnah, generating the most discussion in subsequent generations.

The rabbinic discussions that followed in the *Tosefta* (200 CE), the *Babylonian Talmud* (500 CE), and the *Palestinian Talmud* (400 CE) were all organized according to Rabbi Judah's sixfold division and its subdivisions. His achievement was so important and his religious and political authority so revered, that he was able to override the old rabbinic prohibition of publishing the Oral Torah. Rabbi Judah justified this great innovation as an emergency measure. That is, due to the dispersion of the Jews in 70 CE, after the failed Bar Kokhba revolution and the harsh Roman reprisals and destruction of Jerusalem and its Temple, the continuity of rabbinic transmission of oral traditions had been gravely disrupted. Without a written document that could be consulted (with or without a living recipient of authentic tradition), the Oral Torah would be lost. So Rabbi Judah persuaded his rabbinic colleagues to accept his codification in the Mishnah.[17]

The Mishnah was a compendium of a huge amount of traditional and mostly legal material. Rabbi Judah, however, was a selective editor. He deliberately left a number of old traditions and rabbinic opinions out of the Mishnah. While Rabbi Judah evidently intended the Mishnah to be the exclusive code of law, which would govern all of Jewish normative practice (including Jewish religion), his rabbinic successors after the second century CE seemed to have other ideas about the role of the Mishnah in their legal deliberations and decisions. For them, the Mishnah did not function as a code having prima facie, let alone preeminent, authority. Instead, it functioned more as a compendium or legal encyclopedia, *from which* subsequent discussions could draw, but *to which* they were not bound.[18]

Rabbinic law grew not only by the interpretation and elaboration of biblical norms. Most post-Talmudic commentators regarded these rabbinic interpretations and elaborations, especially those derived through specific hermeneutical principles, to have the status of scriptural law (*d'oraita*). Hence the legal innovations of the Rabbis themselves (*de-rabbanan*), even if they could not be attributed to biblical exegesis, were justified as deriving

---

[17] See D. Zlotnick, *The Iron Pillar – Mishnah* (Jerusalem: Bialik Institute, 1988), 11–23, 160–217.
[18] See *Babylonian Talmud*: Baba Metsia 33a–b.

from the *general* power that Scripture granted the Rabbis not only to interpret the law, but to supplement it as well. In this process of legislation, the Rabbis considered themselves to be the successors of the *Sanhedrin*, the institution that was remembered as having functioned in the days of the Second Temple as the supreme court and parliament of the Jewish people. The Sanhedrin, however, gradually ceased to have its old authority in the century following the destruction of the Second Temple in 70 CE.

This supplementary rabbinical legislation was of two kinds. First, the Rabbis made laws called "decrees" (*gezerot*) for the sake of protecting a specific law of the Torah from eventual violation. So, for example, the Torah prohibited intermarriage between Jews and Gentiles.[19] In order to protect this prohibition from eventual violation, the Rabbis decreed that Jews should not drink the wine of Gentiles. Now the original reason for this prohibition was that the wine of Gentiles might have been dedicated to a pagan god. But, the Rabbis reasoned, even when that was no longer a concern, drinking the wine of Gentiles – usually in the company of Gentiles – might still lead to romantic involvements of Jews with Gentiles, considering the loosening of inhibitions that social wine drinking often entails. And, of course, such romantic involvements often lead to intermarriage, which was prohibited.[20]

Second, the Rabbis made laws called "enactments" (*taqqanot*) for the sake of promoting what they considered to be the overall ends or purposes of the Torah. Sometimes, such rabbinic enactments simply codified customary practices. So, for example, the Rabbis enacted a *halakhic* structure for the festival of *Hanukkah*.[21] Clearly, *Hanukkah* was not invented by the Rabbis. It had been observed by the people since the Maccabean victories in the second century BCE – centuries before the Rabbis formally and officially structured it. The initial reason for the observance of *Hanukkah* had been to celebrate the *human* victory over both Jewish and Gentile Hellenizers by the Hasmonean kings. The Rabbis, however, declared that *Hanukkah* was a feast to celebrate the *divine* miracle that the oil burned for eight days rather than for one day during the rededication of the Temple as the place where the Jewish people most closely engaged the presence of God (*shekhinah*).[22] In other words, the Rabbis regarded a theological

---

[19] Deuteronomy 7:3–4. See *Babylonian Talmud*: Kiddushin 68b.

[20] See *Babylonian Talmud*: Avodah Zarah 36b; also, Shabbat 17b.

[21] In fact, this became the paradigm for all specifically rabbinic legislation, which is generally mandated by the Written Torah. See *Babylonian Talmud*: Shabbat 23a re. Deut. 17:11. For requirements that there had to be good reasons for such legislation to be accepted and that there had to be popular acceptance of such legislation, see *Palestinian Talmud*: Horayot 45d re. Deut. 17:11; *Babylonian Talmud*: Avodah Zarah 35a; also, Maimonides, *Mishneh Torah*: Rebels, 2.5–7.

[22] See *Babylonian Talmud*: Shabbat 21b.

justification for *Hanukkah* more appropriate than a merely political reason. The Rabbis' invocation of such theological considerations in this case is one of many examples that could be adduced to dispel the too common caricature that rabbinical Judaism was merely "legalistic" – preoccupied with mechanical behavior rather than with the inward intent and the transcendent ends that intelligent observance of the law should always be seeking to know and instantiate.

Sometimes, the Rabbis radically reinterpreted specific biblical norms, particularly when the perceived purpose of a law would be disserved were the specifics of the law retained. The best known example is the institution of *prosbul*, enacted by Hillel the Elder early in the first century CE. This enactment, which enabled a rabbinic court to collect a debt during the sabbatical year when debts were normally cancelled, involved both a reiteration of the purpose of the law of release of debts (*shemittah*) and an innovative (and *fictio juris*) reinterpretation of the specifics of that biblical law.[23]

The purpose of the biblical law on point was clear enough: the release of debts in the sabbatical year was to benefit poor people who could not pay their debts. Most loans and other debts at the time were much shorter term; persons who could not pay their debts by the seventh (or sabbatical) year were to be given immunity from payment. But, what if the poor person was dishonest and conspired to delay his or her debt payment until the seventh year in order to evade moral and legal responsibility? And, what if richer people capable of lending their money to the poor suspected that the poor would deliberately avoid payment of their debts by using the law of sabbatical year release as a legal loophole? If the rich stopped lending money to the poor, out of fear of such fraud, then the practical effect of the literal interpretation of the specifics of the law of release would be to disadvantage the poor, who now were foreclosed even from loans. This defeated the very purpose of the law of release in the Torah, namely to help the poor gain access to loans but not be crushed by them if their poverty persisted. By radically reinterpreting this law, and allowing for the collection of debts in certain cases even in the sabbatical year, Hillel the Elder enabled the actual purpose of the law to be fulfilled in fact. And he did this by interpreting the requirement that a debt not be collected during the sabbatical year to apply only to a debt owed to an individual creditor. The court, as a communal rather than as an individual creditor, collected the debt, and then turned over the proceeds to the original creditor.[24]

---

[23] See *ibid.*: Gittin 36a–b re. Deut. 15:1–3; also, David Novak, *Jewish Social Ethics* (New York: Oxford University Press, 1992), 206–24.   [24] See *Mishnah*: Sheviit 10.4–5.

Because the Rabbis were reluctant to exercise the right of repeal of earlier laws, earlier rabbinic decrees and enactments were often allowed to remain in force even when the social circumstances for which some of them were originally legislated were no longer extant. However, such old decrees or enactments would lead to real hardship under the changed social circumstances. In some such cases, the Rabbis used the type of judicial recontextualization that we have already seen at work. In other cases, they simply allowed these older laws to fall into long disuse and ignored them. The Rabbis assumed that the people would not listen to their ordering the reinstatement of these long forgotten practices, and thus did not want to turn involuntary ignorance into voluntary defiance of the law.[25]

POST-TALMUDIC LAW

The principal legal authority (*hora'ah*) of the Rabbis ended with the deaths of their last major figures, Rav Ashi and Ravina in the fifth century CE. Thereafter, the *Babylonian Talmud* (codified around 500 CE) gradually became *the* authoritative literary source of Jewish law.[26] The apodictic rulings of these bona fide Talmudic figures represented in the Talmud now came to be quoted from the Talmud, without any justification other than their connection to either biblical norms or rabbinic norms formulated earlier. But, for most of the rulings of the authorities presented in the Talmud, the editors of the *Babylonian Talmud*, now sometimes called the *stammaim* (literally, "anonymous ones"), did make reasoned arguments.

Unlike the codification of the Mishnah, which almost immediately thereafter occasioned legal interpreters to cite parallel texts as being equally authoritative (even when these texts contradicted the Mishnah), the *Babylonian Talmud* came to be unchallenged by parallels in texts outside the Talmud. The only debates allowed among interpreters were about the correct wording and meaning of texts from the *Babylonian Talmud*; its authoritative truth, however, was uncontested. The *Babylonian Talmud* had a canonical status greater than that of the *Mishnah*; in fact, its canonical authority became second only to that of the Bible itself.[27] And its practical authority, as the most immediately applicable body of law in many areas of life, actually became greater than that of the Bible. The preeminent source of law and religion was now the explicit teaching of the *Babylonian*

---

[25] See *Babylonian Talmud*: Baba Batra 60b.   [26] See *ibid.*: Baba Metsia 86a re. Ps. 73:18.
[27] See Alfasi, *Eruvin/* end; *Babylonian Talmud*: Sanhedrin 24a and *Tosafot*, s.v. "belulot" *ad locum*.

Talmud; other rabbinic sources like the *Tosefta* or the *Palestinian Talmud* or various *midrashim*, were regarded as extra-canonical sources and could have validity only as sources when supplementing rather than contradicting the *Babylonian Talmud*.

The canonical primacy of the *Babylonian Talmud* – now often just "the Talmud" – became the basis for two modes of legal discourse and writing in Judaism. The first was the rabbinic responsum.[28] Even in the Talmud itself, there are examples of responsa (*teshuvot*), which are answers to questions submitted by someone having communal authority to someone having greater communal authority.[29] However, as a specifically recognizable literary form, responsa writing became developed during the post-Talmudic period when questions of law (and occasionally questions of biblical exegesis and of theology) were addressed to and answered by the heads of the Babylonian academies. These questions, which were looking for authoritative answers, came not only from the Babylonian Jewish community but also from the newer Jewish communities in places as far away as North Africa and Spain.

As the method of responsa writing developed, especially when later practiced by Rabbis having less political authority than the Babylonian *geonim*, these responsa became less and less like authoritative rulings and much more like professional consultations. Moreover, by becoming more akin to consultations, rabbinic responsa themselves functioned less and less like authoritative precedents (as that term functions in common law tradition today). This did not mean that earlier responsa were never cited. They sometimes were cited, but only because the later respondent (*poseq*) had been persuaded by a reasoned interpretation of the earlier respondent of the Talmudic source that the later respondent wanted to apply to the legal question he had to address then and there. This form of legal interpretation and application is still employed within traditional law-abiding Jewish communities today.

The second mode of post-Talmudic legal discourse and writing was that of codification.[30] Because the Talmud was often the edited record of what seem to be inconclusive normative discussions, post-Talmudic jurists attempted to conclude the authoritative ruling implicit in the Talmudic discussion of a question of normative import. They used two criteria for coming to their own conclusions: first, because somewhere else in the

---

[28] See S. B. Freehof, *The Responsa Literature* (New York: KTAV Publishing House, 1973).
[29] See e.g., *Babylonian Talmud*: Gittin 81a.
[30] See Louis Ginzberg, "The Codification of Jewish Law," in *On Jewish Law and Lore* (Philadelphia: Jewish Publication Society of America, 1955), 153–84.

Talmud some later authority accepted one opinion over another on a question of normative import, or, second, because a codifier of the Talmud decided to prefer the opinion of Rabbi X over Rabbi Y in any case where the two were disputing a question of law.[31] And sometimes, based on his own explicit or implicit jurisprudential criteria, a codifier simply decided that one legal position was more appropriate in general than another, irrespective of who originally uttered it. Furthermore, with the notable exception of the code of Maimonides, all other codes of Jewish law only dealt with normative issues that were of practical concern in their own day. Hence, they could always invoke actual precedents for the application of the law they were representing.

Although there were some earlier attempts at codification, the first major code of Jewish law was that of Isaac Alfasi in the eleventh century CE. It is significant that this code was published in and for a Jewish community in North Africa, which no longer looked to the Babylonian *geonim* for authoritative rulings. Thus a code became a substitution for a body of lawmakers who still considered themselves the rightful extensions of Talmudic prima facie legal authority. The code of Moses Maimonides (d. 1204 CE), called *Mishneh Torah*, was very much beholden to Alfasi, yet it constructed a much more conceptually structured code. Due to its codification of all of Jewish law, especially Jewish law that pertained to statecraft, some scholars have concluded that Maimonides hoped his code would be the constitution of a reestablished Jewish state in the land of Israel. Nevertheless, because of what seemed to be overweening, imprudent, political ambition, plus its rather abstract approach to legal institutions and often obscure connection to Talmudic sources (the work has no references, and only biblical texts are quoted verbatim), *Mishneh Torah* did not in the long run become *the* code of Jewish law. Instead, it functioned more as an encyclopedia of Jewish law and as the best conceptualization of Jewish law ever. But that conceptualization was more suited to theoretical reflection *about* the law than it was to the practical application *of* the law.

Closer, however, to verbatim Talmudic interpretations and rulings was the *Arbaah Turim* (called the *Tur* for short) of Jacob ben Asher in the fourteenth century CE. This code gained centrality in Jewish legal discourse primarily due to the massive commentary thereon by Joseph Karo (d. 1575 CE), called *Bet Yosef*, which brought Talmudic and other post-Talmudic sources to supplement the terse wording of the *Tur*. And, finally, there is the digest of *Bet Yosef*, which follows the format of the *Tur*'s four main divisions,

---

[31] See *Babylonian Talmud*: Eruvin 46b.

written by Karo himself, called *Shulhan Arukh* (literally, "the set table").
This digest has become *the* code of Jewish law, whose rulings still have
prima facie authority for traditional Jewish communities today. The
popularity of the *Shulhan Arukh* was greatly enhanced by the glosses of
Moses Isserles (d. 1572 CE), a leading Polish scholar and rabbinical leader.
Isserles' achievement for the *Shulhan Arukh* was to connect the jurisprudence of Central European Jewry (*Ashkenazim*) with that of Spanish and
North African Jewry (*Sephardim*), of which Karo was the leading exposi-
tor. The legal power of the *Shulhan Arukh* is evidenced by the fact that
when a contemporary legal respondent wants to get around a ruling of the
Shulhan Arukh, he has to employ casuistry to show that his own ruling does
not really contradict the *Shulhan Arukh*, arguing that he is actually dealing
with a different situation than the one dealt with by the *Shulhan Arukh*.
Such recontextualization has been greatly aided by employing some of the
critical-historical scholarship developed by rabbinic scholars in the last two
hundred years or so.

Besides these emerging codes, individual Jewish communities occasionally legislated local ordinances (*taqqanot ha-qehilot*) for their own membership, and some of these originally local ordinances gained acceptance in
other communities. The most famous of these ordinances was the tenth-
century ban on polygamy (something not prohibited in the Bible or the
Talmud), promulgated by Gershom of Mainz for his community in the
Rhineland, a rule which eventually took hold in all of European Jewry.

The interpretation and application of Jewish law by Jewish communities
and their leaders (both rabbinic and lay) differed in some important ways
in Jewish communities living under Muslim rule and in Jewish communities living under Christian rule. In both realms, Jewish communities did not
have national sovereignty, but only relative internal independence within a
larger polity that had ultimate political control over them. The political
security of the Jewish communities varied between Islam and Christendom:
at times things were better under Muslim rule; at times things were better
under Christian rule. Nevertheless, there was a fundamental difference of
legal status of the Jews in Christendom and in Islam. In Islamic law, the Jews
had a definite status. Because they (and Christians, too) were monotheists,
having what Muslim authorities considered to be at least a partial revelation
from God, Jews were not to be forcibly converted to Islam. Instead, they
were to have a second-class or *dhimmi* status. This gave a certain legal stability to the Jewish communities within Muslim polities of which individual Jews were members. By contrast, in Christendom, the legal status of the
Jews was dependent upon a contract with the ruler of the Christian polity

in which the particular Jewish community happened to be living. Since rulers come and go, and are subject to all kinds of unexpected political pressures, the legal status of Jews in Christendom was always precarious. Political and economic persecution – even wholesale expulsions (the most famous being the expulsions from Spain in 1492 CE and from Portugal in 1497 CE) – was often the case for Jews in Christendom, even though in a number of lands the Jews enjoyed a relatively stable and sometimes even prosperous condition.

The rabbinic responsa written in places of Christian dominance at times differ from the responsa written in places of Muslim dominance. For example, even though both Christians and Muslims were anxious to convert Jews to either Christianity or Islam, there were, on the whole, greater pressures on Jews to convert to Christianity than to Islam. As such, the question of apostasy or the denial of Judaism and the simultaneous affirmation of Christianity entailed some considerable legal (and even theological) problems for Jewish jurists. Thus, there were questions about the status of the Jewish wife of a man who had converted to Christianity, or questions about the status of converted Jews who, subsequently, wanted to return to the Jewish community. Then there were questions of Jewish use of the wine of Christians, since wine played such an important role in Christian worship. Even today, when *Christendom* is no longer a political issue for Jews (or for anyone) and when Jews have more political problems with Muslims than with Christians, Jewish law still retains several elements that clearly come from the time when Christianity, at least *de jure*, was more of a problem for Jews than was Islam.

LAW AND RELIGION IN MODERN JUDAISM

Even though traditional Jewish communities have been governed by the law as codified in the *Shulhan Arukh* since the French Revolution (or what modern Jews call the "Emancipation"), even the most traditional Jewish communities have been governed by that law in a radically changed political context.[32] After the French Revolution, the semi-autonomous Jewish communities that existed throughout the Middle Ages lost their quasi-sovereignty. That is, Jewish communal courts no longer had police power to enforce the decisions of Jewish courts for the Jews living under their jurisdiction, a jurisdiction that extended into areas of familial and civil matters. First in Western Europe, then in North America, and thereafter in

---

[32] See Jacob Katz, *Tradition and Crisis* (New York: Schocken Books, 1971).

Eastern Europe, Jews as autonomous individuals became full citizens of secular nation-states. As such, Jewish communities, like the communities of other minority religions became, in effect, corporations, membership in which and resignation from which were now strictly voluntary. This meant that Jewish courts lost their old civil jurisdiction (though they did not have much criminal jurisdiction even in the Middle Ages). Even in marital matters, individual Jews were now required to register their marriages and divorces with the non-Jewish civil authorities before freely subjecting themselves to Jewish legal procedures in these areas. This created problems when the free compliance of both parties to the decisions of a religious court was required, but only one complied.[33] Unlike its predecessors, the modern religious court had little leverage to force compliance with its divorce and other decrees, as it could do in pre-Emancipation times.

One can see, in fact, this radically new religio-legal situation of the Jews as a consequence of the growing privatization of religion in modern secular nation-states. Religion, including religious law, in all Western democracies came to be viewed increasingly as a matter of private preference, something with which the state did not interfere unless it saw its own moral hegemony challenged by religious laws and authorities. Thus, a system of religious law like *halakhah* (traditional Jewish law) has come to lose most of its public character in modernity. Jewish law has become "religious" according to the modern Western notion of religion; it is a private matter among consenting individuals who have already ceded (explicitly or tacitly) public legal and even much moral authority to the secular society and its nation-state. As such, *halakhah* no longer functions as a form of public law because the religious community, governed according to its norms, is nothing more than a private corporation. So, even if the old correlation of law and religion still operates in and for traditional Jewish communities, which have become religious *denominations* rather than local *communities* in the old sense, that correlation is no longer co-extensive with all of life even there.

In addition to the contraction of the domain of law and religion in modern Judaism, two other developments have even challenged the old correlation itself between law and religion: first, Reform Judaism, and, second, Zionism. By the middle of the nineteenth century, Reform Judaism, first in Western Europe and then (even more radically) in the United States, attempted to sever Jewish religion from Jewish law. For Reform Judaism, Jewish law was only a source of guidance rather than

[33] See David Novak, "Jewish Marriage and Civil Law: A Two-Way Street?" *George Washington Law Review* 68 (2000): 1059–78.

governance, even in areas thickly structured by *halakhah,* such as synagogue worship and marriage and divorce. Even the Jewish "community," whose normative domain was by now limited to "religious" or ritual matters, was redefined as an association of those of like-minded *belief* rather than a community of common practice, governed by its own public law. This has led to serious problems with more traditionally oriented Jews, since many of the latter do not recognize such things as conversions to Judaism and marriages conducted according to Reform rites. The question raised to Reform Jews (and which some of them are taking with increasing seriousness) by more traditional Jews is how long it will be before what is perceived to be their antinomianism will make them a community apart from the rest of Jewry, unable to distinguish themselves from the surrounding non-Jewish world and its cultures, and with whom traditional Jews will be unable to engage in such community-building activities as marriage.

Zionism, as the Jewish movement for the reestablishment of a Jewish state in the homeland of Israel, has taken three different approaches to the correlation of law and religion in Judaism.[34] First, most conservatively, what is called "Religious Zionism" has advocated that the now reestablished Jewish State of Israel be governed according to Jewish law, including governance in civil and criminal matters. (As of now in the State of Israel, Jewish law only governs some areas of public ritual and marriage and divorce among Jews.) The political likelihood of this happening in the foreseeable future is remote. Second, at the other end of the philosophical spectrum, secularist Zionists would like to sever Israeli law and government from Jewish law altogether, regarding it as an incorrigibly religious hold from the Jewish past on the secular Jewish present (and future). Most of the leading Israeli jurists today fall into this secularist camp. Third, there is a movement called "Hebrew Jurisprudence" (*mishpat ivri*) that attempts to argue for Jewish law, in civil and criminal matters, to be included more and more in the secular system of Israeli law. That, of course, means that the adherents of this school of thought think that Jewish civil and criminal law can function coherently outside the traditional, theologically grounded and structured, system of *halakhah.* Critics of this approach have come from both the right and the left. Critics on the right (religiously speaking) argue that Jewish law severed from its theological roots and interpretation will quickly lose its uniquely Jewish identity. Critics on the left (who are

---

[34] For the background of this whole complex issue, see Menachem Elon, *Jewish Law,* 4 vols., trans. B. Auerback and M. J. Sykes (Philadelphia/Jerusalem: Jewish Publication Society of America, 1994), IV:1620–52 and throughout.

often either atheists or at least public agnostics) have argued that the incorporation of religious law into the Israeli legal system, no matter how secularized that process is, will inevitably turn Israel into a theocracy in fact, governed by the rabbinical interpreters of traditional Jewish law *in toto*.

The most interesting and important developments regarding the correlation of law and religion in Judaism will, it seems, take place in the State of Israel, where both Jewish law and Jewish religion are matters of public significance unlike their greater privatization in the diaspora.

RECOMMENDED READING

Broyde, Michael J. *The Pursuit of Justice and Jewish Law*. New York: Yeshiva University Press, 1996, rev. edn 2007.

Cohn, Haim H. *Human Rights in Jewish Law*. New York: KTAV Publishing House, 1984.

Dorff, Elliot N. and L. E. Newman, eds. *Contemporary Jewish Ethics and Morality*. New York: Oxford University Press, 1995.

Elon, Menachem. *Jewish Law*. 4 vols. Translated by B. Auerbach and M. J. Sykes. Philadelphia/Jerusalem: Jewish Publication Society of America, 1994.

Falk, Ze'ev W. *Law and Religion*. Jerusalem: Mesharim Publishers, 1981.

Religious Law and Ethics. Jerusalem: Mesharim Publishers, 1991.

Freehof, S. B. *The Responsa Literature*. New York: KTAV Publishing House, 1973.

Katz, Jacob. *Tradition and Crisis*. New York: Schocken Books, 1971.

Novak, David. "Halkhah", *Encyclopedia of Religion* (1987), 6: 164–173.

Jewish Social Ethics. New York: Oxford University Press, 1992.

Natural Law in Judaism. Cambridge: Cambridge University Press, 1998.

Silberg, Moshe. *Talmudic Law and the Modern State*. Translated by B. Z. Bokser. New York: United Synagogue of America, 1973.

CHAPTER TWO

Law in early Christianity

Luke Timothy Johnson

Christianity began as a Jewish sect in the first third of the first century CE and in the course of less than a century became a distinct religion whose Gentile members far outnumbered Jews. From the start, this religious movement associated with Jesus of Nazareth fell athwart the two great law systems of the Mediterranean world, the Roman and the Jewish, and it took some time before Christianity fully established its position with respect to either system and articulated its own version of law. This chapter examines the period before the fourth century, when Christianity became the imperial religion and things fundamentally changed. It identifies some of the tensions the first Christians experienced with respect to law and the ways they resolved those tensions in some of Christianity's earliest litera-ture – the canonical writings of the New Testament (written between 50 and 100 CE) – and in some pertinent compositions from the second and third centuries.

THE ROMAN AND JEWISH CONTEXT

The history of Roman law can be traced in a thousand-year arc from the Law of the Twelve Tables (*Lex Duodecim Tabularum*) in 449 BCE to the great compilation of law (*Corpus Iuris Civilis*) issued between 529 and 534 CE by the Emperor Justinian. The composition of the New Testament roughly coincided with the period considered to be the most creative in the devel-opment of Roman jurisprudence, as the demands of world-empire forced both expansion and creativity with respect to earlier, simpler, and more formal rules and procedures. Roman administration included a variety of ordinary magistrates (Consuls, Praetors, Quaestors, Promagistrates, Aediles, Tribunes, Censors, Governors, Prefects, and Procurators) and extraordinary (Consular Tribune and Dictator), whose decisions set precedents for further decisions. In the Principate (27 BCE–313 CE), to be sure, the decrees of the Roman Emperor served as the principal source of empire-wide legislation.

3 "Paul Arrives in Rome" from Julius Schnorr von Carolsfeld, *Die Bibel in Bildern* (Leipzig, 1853), s.v. Acts 28.

And while the Roman law was certainly concerned with the settlement of disputes over property and of the punishment of criminals, the most compelling concern for all involved in imperial administration was the security and prosperity of the Empire itself.[1] This meant that in threatened or unsettled territories (such as the province of Syria-Palestine tended chronically to be), considerable latitude was accorded local prefects such as Pontius Pilate (Prefect of Palestine under whom Jesus of Nazareth was executed) to act *extra ordinem* in the interests of peace and security.[2]

The Jewish system of law, traditionally ascribed to Moses but developed over a long period of ancient Israel's history, was also in a period of creative expansion. Laws first established to regulate the commerce and cult of a nation became otiose in dramatically altered circumstances, such as the occupation of the land by a foreign power (Rome) and the loss of the Temple (in the year 70 CE). The twin pressures placed upon the Mediterranean world's only monotheistic and separatist population by a hegemonic Greek culture and an imperial Roman order, generated a variety of responses from Jews, all of which, in some fashion or other, involved the reaffirmation of the covenant between God and Israel by a renegotiation of the *mitzvoth* (commandments) that spelled out the demands of the covenant in concrete terms.[3]

All Jews recognized the requirement to observe God's laws, but their specific circumstances generated distinct ways of interpreting those commandments. Thus, Philo of Alexandria regarded the *politeia* of Mosaic legislation as superior to that found in Greek culture, but he felt free to employ the same allegorical modes of interpretation as those used by Stoic contemporaries in the search for the deeper philosophical meaning of the literal commands.[4] Among the sectarians at Qumran, who considered only themselves to be authentic Jews, a rigorous interpretation of Torah was carried out in accord with the dualistic ideology and purity practices of the community.[5] The Pharisees, in turn, employed the textual expertise of the scribes to adapt ancient legislation to changing circumstances through

---

[1] See the essays in *Aufstieg und Niedergang der römischen Welt*, ed. H. Temporini and W. Haase (Berlin: Walter de Gruyter, 1980) II Principat, vols. XIII–XV (Recht).

[2] A. N. Sherwin-White, *Roman Society and Roman Law in the New Testament* (Oxford: Clarendon Press, 1963), 1–23.

[3] E. P. Sanders, *Judaism: Practice and Belief, 63 BCE–66 CE* (London: SCM Press, 1992); *Jewish Law from Jesus to the Mishna: Five Studies* (London: SCM Press, 1990). See further chapter 1 by David Novak herein.

[4] E. R. Goodenough, *An Introduction to Philo Judaeus*, 2nd edn (New York: Barnes and Noble, 1963).

[5] F. M. Cross, *The Ancient Library at Qumran and Modern Biblical Studies* 3rd edn (Minneapolis: Fortress Press, 1995).

midrash, developing an understanding of a "second *Torah*" consisting in oral interpretation of the written text.[6]

After the destruction of the Jerusalem temple at the climax of the Jewish war against Rome in 70 CE, the Pharisees emerged as the dominant form of Judaism. Their convictions and practices of interpretation formed the basis of classical or Talmudic Judaism, the norm for Jewish existence in the diaspora for two millennia. The first codification of oral interpretation was the *Mishnah*, carried out by Judah ha Nasi (*c.* 200 CE).[7] Continuing legal conversation led to the massive collections of law and lore known as the *Babylonian Talmud* and the *Talmud of the Land of Israel* (between the fifth and seventh centuries CE).[8]

Christianity would eventually form its own system of law, but in the first stages of its development, it had deep ambivalence toward both the Roman and Jewish legal systems, and it took time for law to claim an honored place within Christian thought and practice. In contrast both to Judaism and Islam, whose embrace of law was immediate and thorough, and whose understanding of obedience of God was completely consonant with the ordering of society, the nature of the early Christian experience made its stance toward law problematic. Throughout the history of Christianity, indeed, some continued to regard a positive perception of law as a corruption of the primitive Christian spirit.

JESUS AND LAW

Statements concerning the historical Jesus are necessarily tentative because our primary sources – the canonical Gospels – are documents of faith composed in light of convictions concerning Jesus as the resurrected Son of God, and this faith perspective pervades their narratives.[9] In addition, the Gospels work with traditions that were passed on orally for some forty years before the first Gospel narrative was composed, and the experiences of the early believers are in some instances read back into the story of Jesus.[10] There is insufficient evidence to support any notion that Jesus, in

---

[6] J. Neusner, "The Formation of Rabbinic Judaism: Yavneh (Jamnia) from 70 to 100," in *Aufsieg und Niedergang der römischen Welt*, ed. H. Temporini and W. Haase (Berlin: Walter de Gruyter, 1979), II. 19.2, pp. 3–42. [7] See further discussion in chapter 1 herein by David Novak.

[8] J. Neusner, *The Formation of the Babylonian Talmud: Studies in the Achievements of Late Nineteenth and Twentieth Century Historical and Literary-Critical Research*, Studia Post-Biblica 17 (Leiden: E. J. Brill, 1970).

[9] L. T. Johnson, *The Writings of the New Testament: An Interpretation*, 2nd rev. edn with Todd Penner (Minneapolis: Fortress Press, 1999), 107–257, 525–57.

[10] R. Bultmann, *The History of the Synoptic Tradition*, rev. edn, trans. J. Marsh (New York: Harper and Row, 1963).

the manner of a Moses or a Muhammad, deliberately sought to legislate for a later community; even the passages like Matthew 5–7, 10, 16, 18 that might seem to point in this direction fall far short of a *Shari'a.*

Some historical judgments concerning Jesus and the legal systems that dominated first-century Palestine are possible. We can confidently assert that Jesus did not directly engage or challenge the Roman order. The strong thesis that Jesus was a Zealot who led resistance against Rome is far-fetched,[11] and the weaker thesis that his teaching program was motivated by an anti-imperial agenda has little support beyond the ambiguous saying: "Give to Caesar the things that are Caesar's, and to God the things that are God's" (Mark 12:13–17 and parallels).[12]

On the other side, it is difficult to dispute that some aspect of Jesus' behavior led to his being crucified by command of the Roman Prefect Pontius Pilate under the *titulus,* "King of the Jews" (Mark 15:15–25 and parallels).[13] The tension between the Gospels' representation of Jesus' ministry as one of religious reform and their unflinching portrayal of his death as public and political remains a historical puzzle. Perhaps the most reasonable explanation is that the threat of political instability caused by an insurrection in the city (see Luke 23:19) led Pilate to exercise the *ius gladii* decisively *extra ordinem* in order to preserve order.[14]

The canonical Gospels also portray Jesus as a teacher of Torah – albeit without formal training (Mark 6:1–6) – whose interpretation of a righteousness that "exceeds that of the Scribes and Pharisees" (Matthew 5:20) came into direct conflict with those experts in Jewish legal interpretation. Precisely how much Jesus himself interpreted Torah in such fashion as to generate controversy, and how much this role was projected back on him by early Christians struggling to define their own understanding of Torah over against the synagogue is another historical puzzle. What seems historically clearer is that aspects of Jesus' behavior with respect to Torah observance caused offense: his breaking of the Sabbath, his neglect of purity regulations, his non-payment of the temple-tax, his association with notorious flouters of Jewish piety, the "sinners and tax-collectors," his claim to a special relationship with God, and his prophetic gesture in the precincts of the Jerusalem Temple.[15]

---

[11] S. G. F. Brandon, *Jesus and the Zealots: A Study of the Political Factor in Primitive Christianity* (New York: Scribner, 1967).

[12] J. D. Crossan, *The Historical Jesus: The Life of a Mediterranean Jewish Peasant* (San Francisco: HarperSanFrancisco, 1992).

[13] M. Hengel, *Crucifixion in the Ancient World and the Folly of the Cross* (Philadelphia: Fortress Press, 1977).   [14] Sherwin-White, *Roman Society and Roman Law,* 24–47.

[15] J. P. Meier, *A Marginal Jew: Rethinking the Historical Jesus,* 3 vols. (New York: Doubleday, 1991–2001).

Cumulatively, these charges could seriously compromise any claim made for or by him of being a messiah, and could even be construed as the signs of a "false messiah," one who "led the people astray" (see, for example, Luke 23:5). Faced with the growing popularity of such a charlatan, it is not inconceivable that members of the Jewish Sanhedrin could have met in rump session to condemn Jesus and stage-manage his appearance before the Roman prefect. The role even of Jewish leadership in the death of Jesus is understandably a sensitive subject, after centuries of Christian anti-Semitism and the horrors of the Holocaust, but a sober historical assessment allows for the combination of religious and political, Jewish and Roman legal systems in the execution of Jesus.[16] What is certain is that for strict adherents of Torah, Jesus' death was one cursed by God (see Deuteronomy 21:23; Galatians 3:13), the decisive "sign" that he was not God's anointed.

CHRISTIAN BEGINNINGS AND LAW

The first Christians' claims concerning the resurrection of Jesus and their distinctive manner of life in associations (*ekklesiai*), analogous to but separate from recognized forms of association in the Empire and in Judaism, ensured that Jesus' followers would continue to experience some of the same tensions vis-à-vis Roman and Jewish legal systems.

The conviction that a man executed as a "robber" (*lestes*; see Mark 15:27) should not only "rise from the dead" but be exalted to a share in God's power and be designated as "Lord" (*kyrios*) and "King" (*basileus*; see Revelation 17:14) could not but have been perceived by imperial authorities – when the movement broke the surface of obscurity – as inherently subversive of an *oikoumene* in which only Caesar could legitimately be designated Lord and King. The same confession that "Jesus is Lord" inevitably brought nascent Christianity into conflict with formative Judaism, whose monotheism was strict. Claiming that Jesus inherited the very name of Israel's God (*kyrios* translates *YHWH* in the Greek translation of Torah used by all the New Testament writers) meant, in the eyes of loyal Jews, that Jesus' followers had made "two powers in heaven," and were, in fact, not Jews at all but polytheists.[17] The fact that the movement won far fewer adherents among

---

[16] On the historicity of the trial of Jesus, see P. Winter, *On the Trial of Jesus* (Berlin: Walter de Gruyter, 1961); E. Bammel, ed., *The Trial of Jesus* (Naperville, IL: Allenson, 1970); more recent and less sober, J. D. Crossan. *Who Killed Jesus? Exposing the Roots of Anti-Semitism in the Gospel Story of the Death of Jesus* (San Francisco: HarperSanFrancisco, 1995).

[17] A. F. Segal, *Two Powers in Heaven: Early Rabbinic Reports about Christianity and Gnosticism*, Studies in Judaism in Late Antiquity (Leiden: E. J. Brill, 1977).

Jews than among Gentiles only sharpened the perception that Christianity was not a form of Judaism but a variety of Gentile idolatry.

The tension between the Jews who confessed Jesus as Messiah and those who regarded such confession as a form of blasphemy forced a separation of Jesus' followers from the synagogue sometime between the destruction of the temple (70 CE) and the end of the first century. The Jewish "Benediction against Heretics" (*birkat ha minim*) formalized a rift that had begun decades earlier.[18] A result of Christianity's clear separation from the synagogue was that it was more clearly exposed as a novel cult with possibly subversive tendencies, no longer to be confused with the ancient *religio licita* of Judaism, whose distinctive customs and independent laws were recognized (as were other ancient national traditions) by the Empire and protected them from persecution.[19] A now thoroughly Gentile Christianity could no longer claim or enjoy the privilege of passing as a form of Judaism.

The writings of the New Testament provide glimpses of these tensions in the period of Christianity's first great expansion across the Mediterranean world, especially in connection with the figure of Paul. Before encountering the risen Jesus and becoming an apostle, Paul (then Saul) was a Pharisee who, by his own admission, "persecuted the church" because of his great zeal for Torah, in all likelihood because of his conviction that a crucified Messiah was a contradiction in terms (Deuteronomy 21:23; Galatians 3:13). The Acts of the Apostles shows Paul, now converted to the messianic movement, seeking to persuade his fellow Jews in the context of synagogue worship, but, being rebuffed by them, then turning to the Gentiles (Acts 13:46–47; 18:6; 28:25–28). Acts probably simplifies a genuine historical process that is suggested also by Paul's letters and the Gospels (Romans 1:16; 9:1–11:36; Matthew 28:18).[20]

For the most part, the harassment of Christians in the first generations came from the side of Jews rather than Gentiles (see Acts 4:1–22; 5:17–40; 6:12–8:1; 9:1–2; 13:50; 21:27–31; 1 Thessalonians 2:14–16; 2 Corinthians 11:23–29; Galatians 6:11–12). The Acts of the Apostles does suggest the vulnerability of a cult movement within the Empire, when it narrates how Paul was imprisoned by the magistrate of the Roman colony of Philippi on the charge of subversion: "These men are Jews and they are disturbing

---

[18] R. Kimelman, "*Birkat Ha-Minim* and the Lack of Evidence for an Anti-Christian Jewish Prayer in Late Antiquity," in *Jewish and Christian Self-Definition*, 3 vols., vol. II: *Aspects of Judaism in the Greco-Roman World*, ed. E. P. Sanders, A. I. Baumgarten, and A. Mendelson (Philadelphia: Fortress Press, 1981), 226–44.

[19] E. M. Smallwood, *The Jews Under Roman Rule from Pompey to Diocletian* (Leiden: E. J. Brill, 1976).

[20] A. F. Segal, *Paul the Convert: The Apostolate and Apostasy of Saul the Pharisee* (New Haven, CT: Yale University Press, 1990).

our city. They advocate customs which it is not lawful for us Romans to accept or practice" (Acts 16:20–21). Nevertheless, Acts shows Paul using his citizenship in the city of Rome – a possible though unusual claim for a provincial Jew of the first century[21] – to avoid local Jewish opposition and local Roman magistrates likely to be swayed by Jewish pressure. He appeals to Caesar, confident that the system of Roman law will protect him (Acts 25:11). Acts shows that it does: he arrives safely in Rome, and, under house-arrest, continues his ministry unimpeded (Acts 28:16, 30–31).

The relatively positive experience of the imperial order had by many early Christians – not all, for the Book of Revelation shows intense hostility to the "whore of Babylon" that sits on the seven hills and enslaves humans (see Revelation 17:1–18) – is indicated by the stunningly optimistic appreciation for imperial governance expressed by Paul's letter to the Roman church (Romans 13:1–7) and Peter's first letter, addressed to Christians scattered throughout the imperial provinces of Pontus, Bithynia, Cappadocia, and Asia (1 Peter 2:13–17). These passages see the imperial authority as benign, punishing the wicked and rewarding the virtuous, even serving as ministers of God. Such human authority, declares Paul, is from God, is indeed instituted by God (Romans 13:1–2). These pronouncements would have a long after-life in imperial and medieval Christianity as support for both royal and ecclesiastical rule.[22] It is noteworthy as well that Paul exhorts Christians in Ephesus to pray "for all men, for kings and all who are in high positions" (1 Timothy 2:1–2), adopting the strategy of diaspora Jews, who also offered such prayer for rulers (see Philo, *Legation to Gaius* 157, 317; *Against Flaccus* 49), thus neatly avoiding the (for them, idolatrous) recognition of the Emperor as *kyrios* ("Lord") while simultaneously extending good will to the government itself.

Persecution from the side of Roman rule was at first local and sporadic. Nero blamed Christians for the fire in Rome and may have executed Peter and Paul, but this was an isolated incident (Suetonius, *Life of Nero* VI, 16, 2). A letter from the Governor of Bythinia, Pliny the Younger, to the Emperor Trajan (*c.* 112 CE) suggests that Christians were in danger if they persisted in their "stubborn superstition," but were not treated as criminals simply for being Christian (*Letter* X, 96). From the middle of the second century to the time of Constantine in the early fourth century, however, the profession of Christianity became more dangerous, and the persecution of it

---

[21] Sherwin-White, *Roman Society and Roman Law*, 144–85.
[22] See E. Käsemann, "Principles of the Interpretation of Romans 13," in *New Testament Questions of Today* (Philadelphia: Fortress Press, 1969), 196–216.

became more direct and general, reaching a climax in the great persecution of Diocletian (303 CE), which continued until Constantine's Edict of Milan (313 CE).

The greater intensity of persecution was due to the greater exposure of Christians caused by their greater Gentile membership and their decisive split from Judaism, the historical eclipse of Jewish power signaled by Rome's crushing defeat of the Jews' final rebellion (135 CE), and by the impressive Christian growth in numbers, not only among society's marginal but increasingly among the powerful. In this light, Constantine's conversion (of himself and eventually of the Empire) to Christianity was as much a matter of shrewd politics as religious conviction.[23]

CHRISTIAN ENGAGEMENT WITH JEWISH LAW

In Christianity's early years, the nature of the movement, its social location, and its preoccupation with working out its distinct identity, made contacts with Roman law few and largely accidental (as in Paul's trial; see Acts 25:1–12; Philippians 1:12; 2 Timothy 4:16). Roman law as such played no important or positive role in shaping Christian ethos. The exact opposite is the case with Jewish law, and for the same reasons. When Christians in the first century used the term *nomos* or *lex*, they would almost invariably be speaking of Jewish law, for it was in the immediate context of Judaism that Christians had to work out their identity, and Judaism was all about law.

Coming to grips with the law was both necessary and difficult. The first believers in Jesus, we remember, were Jews. For them, the term "Torah," usually translated into Greek as *nomos*, meant far more than the commandments; it included teaching, prophecy, wisdom, and the stories of the Israelite people, of its heroes and villains, of its triumphs and failures. Law in this sense formed the symbolic world within which Jews lived and by which they perceived the world. This Torah, moreover, was widely thought by Jews to be inspired by God, and authoritative for Jewish life in every word, syllable, and letter. Unlike the laws of the Greeks and Romans that owed their existence to mere human wisdom, Torah revealed God's own mind concerning how the world should run.[24]

In order to speak of Jesus as Messiah at all, therefore, believers had to engage Torah, simply because the very term "Christ" (*Christos*) or "Anointed

---

[23] J. Pelikan, *The Excellent Empire: The Fall of Rome and the Triumph of the Church* (San Francisco: Harper and Row, 1987).

[24] See J. L. Kugel, *The Bible as it Was* (Cambridge, MA: Harvard University Press, 1997).

One" meant nothing in Greco-Roman culture outside the symbolic world of Torah. The difficulty of engaging Torah is that Jesus was not the sort of Messiah that other Jewish readers of these texts would recognize. Indeed, a strict reading of Deuteronomy 21:23, "Cursed be everyone who hangs upon a tree" could be, and apparently was, used as a text disproving messianic claims made for Jesus.

The impetus for Christian engagement with Jewish law, then, was the need to resolve the cognitive dissonance created by two opposing convictions: on one side, Torah reveals God's will and declares a crucified messiah to be cursed by God; on the other side, the conviction that the crucified Jesus has been raised as Lord and is the source of God's Holy Spirit. We see the struggle most vividly displayed in the letters of Paul, for he represents in himself and in extreme form, both sides of the dissonance: he was a Pharisee totally dedicated to the law who persecuted Christians as blasphemers, and he directly experienced the power of the resurrected Christ: "Have I not seen our Lord" (1 Corinthians 9:1).

Paul's conviction that the good news extended to all humans led him to convert Gentiles. In his letter to the Galatians, Paul defended their freedom from the observance of Jewish law against those who, like the earlier Paul, insisted that righteousness could be adequately measured only by Torah. Torah required that Gentile believers should be circumcised and observe the law. He argued that instead of trying to fit Jesus into the frame of Torah, Jesus must be taken as the starting point for a complete rereading of Torah. It is Paul's impassioned insistence that in Christ there is a "new creation" (2 Corinthians 5:17; Galatians 6:15), and the basis for a "new humanity" (see Romans 5; Colossians 3) based in the experience of the risen Jesus as "life-giving spirit" (1 Corinthians 15:45) and "Lord" (1 Corinthians 12:3; Romans 10:9; Philippians 2:11), with the consequence that "the written code kills, but the Spirit gives life" (2 Corinthians 3:6). A reexamination of these texts began an enduring bias, which found particular expression in the sixteenth-century Protestant reformer Martin Luther against the adequacy of any law to express the authentic Christian reality.

Paul was not alone in struggling to find a way to affirm both the heritage of Jewish law, thought to be God's word, and the new experience of God in Jesus. Other New Testament writers, above all the author of the Letter to the Hebrews, also engaged the symbolic world of Torah, and from their joint efforts emerged the first and most significant resolution of the tension between faith and law. Insofar as Torah was considered as narrative, wisdom, or prophecy, it was universally affirmed as the necessary background for understanding the identity of Jesus as Messiah, Lord, and God's

Son. But the ancient texts are background: they point to and find their fulfillment in the story of Jesus. As Paul stated succinctly, "Christ is the end (*telos*) of the law" (Romans 10:4). Thus, the New Testament compositions are studded with texts from Torah that show Jesus to be the goal of the story, the embodiment of wisdom, and the fulfillment of prophecy. Matthew's Gospel, in particular, is fond of showing how events in Jesus' ministry "fulfilled the saying of the prophets" (see, e.g., Matthew 1:23; 2:17).

The normative character of law in the proper sense – God's commandments to the people – required delicate negotiation. The most broadly accepted position among the New Testament writings is that the ritual commandments that made Jews a distinctive people (Sabbath, purity, circumcision, diet, worship) were no longer binding, but that the moral commandments (as in the Ten Commandments) retained their force. Among the moral commands, furthermore, the law of love of neighbor stated in Leviticus 19:18 becomes the most widely pervasive summation of the Jewish law's intent. In the Gospels, Jesus responds to the Jewish legal experts by identifying the love of God and the love of neighbor as the commandments on which all others depend (Mark 12:29–31; Matthew 22:37–39; Luke 10:25–27).

In the letters of Paul and James, Leviticus 19:18 is singled out as the law binding on Christians (James 2:7–13; Romans 13:8–10; Galatians 5:14). The commandment of love of neighbor finds specific expression in the example of Jesus' self-giving service to others. Paul speaks of living by "the mind of Christ," (1 Corinthians 2:16; Philippians 2:5) and even of "fulfilling the law of Christ" or, perhaps better, "the law that is Christ" (*nomos christou*). How is this done? Paul says it is by "bear[ing] one another's burdens" (Galatians 6:2). For many Christians, "the law of love" is the perfect expression of Christian ethics and the ground for any notion of Christian law.[25] The ritual commandments of Torah, in turn, found continuing significance only through their ability to prefigure Christian mysteries (of Christ's life, of the sacraments), the meaning of which were unlocked by the employment of allegorical interpretation.[26]

STEPS TOWARD CHRISTIAN LAW

The commandment to love one's neighbor as oneself, however powerful an expression of the *telos* of the Holy Spirit's activity among believers, was too

---

[25] E.g. B. Haring, *The Law of Christ: Moral Theology for Priests and Laity*, 3 vols., trans. E. G. Kaiser (Westminster, MD: Newman Press, 1961–1966).

[26] See J. Danielou, *From Shadows to Reality: Studies in the Biblical Typology of the Fathers*, trans. W. Hibberd (Westminster, MD: Newman Press, 1960).

broad to provide practical guidance for many of the issues faced by the earliest Christians, even when it was given specific content by the example of Jesus – an example everywhere implicit in the New Testament's letters and explicit in the Gospel narratives. It was inevitable that other resources for community guidance and governance should be sought, and it is in these first attempts to secure specific principles and rules for conduct within the assembly (*ekklesia*) that we find the first intimations of Christian law.

The occasional, sporadic, and non-systematic character of these efforts should be noted. They arose spontaneously, either through the need to address a practical problem or as the application of the memory of Jesus to their common life, and in no manner represent a legal system in the proper sense. These first steps were all addressed, moreover, to the internal life of the community. Christians were not in a position to legislate for the larger world, and, still largely unknown to Roman authorities, would not experience their ad hoc arrangements as constituting a challenge to the legal systems that ran the *oikoumene*.

Perhaps the earliest expression of norms directly linked to the eschatological convictions of the first Christians (that with the resurrection of Jesus they were living in the "end-times") are designated "statements of holy law" that promise divine retribution for certain acts. Examples are found in 1 Corinthians 3:17, "If any one destroys God's temple, God will destroy him," and 1 Corinthians 14:38, "If anyone does not recognize this, he is not recognized." Such statements could well have been stated by those regarded as prophets within the community who "spoke in the name of the Lord" (see 1 Corinthians 14:1–33), but are also found placed in the mouth of the human Jesus: "For whoever is ashamed of me and of my words in this adulterous and sinful generation, of him will the Son of man also be ashamed, when he comes in the glory of his Father with the holy angels" (Mark 8:38).[27]

Some authoritative statements of Jesus are found in Paul's letters as well as in the Gospels. Thus, Paul declares that "the Lord commanded that those who proclaim the Gospel should get their living by the Gospel" (1 Corinthians 9:14) and says "the laborer deserves to be paid" (1 Timothy 5:17), statements that are supported by the saying of Jesus in Luke 10:7, "the laborer deserves his wages." Similarly, in his discussion of marriage and virginity, Paul refers to a "command of the Lord" in support of the prohibition of divorce (see 1 Corinthians 7:10). The Gospels, in turn, show Jesus expressing that precise prohibition during his ministry. In the earliest

---

[27] E. Käsemann, "Sentences of Holy Law," in *New Testament Questions of Today*, 66–81.

Gospel, Jesus' declaration occurs in a debate with the Pharisees (Mark 10:2–11). They cite the legal precedent provided by Deuteronomy 24:1–4, in which Moses allows divorce. Jesus responds by quoting another part of Torah, the account of creation in Genesis, pronouncing the "way it was in the beginning" when "the two become one flesh" as normative rather than the decree of Moses, which was attributed to "your hardness of heart." The passage concludes with a statement that in form resembles a legal *sententia*: "Whoever divorces his wife and marries another commits adultery against her, and if she divorces her husband and marries another, she commits adultery" (Mark 10:11–12). Although placed in the context of a Jewish dispute over *halakhah*, Jesus' statement actually reflects Greco-Roman rather than Jewish practice, since either party can initiate the divorce.

In Luke's Gospel, Jesus' statement is removed from the context of a controversy story and stands with a number of other *sententiae*: "Every one who divorces his wife and marries another commits adultery, and he who marries a woman divorced from her husband commits adultery" (Luke 16:18). The command is absolute, and as in Mark, appears to allow for the possibility of mutual divorce. The Gospel of Matthew has two versions of Jesus' statement concerning divorce. The first occurs in the Sermon on the Mount as one of the antithetical statements by which Matthew shows Jesus to be revealing a "righteousness exceed[ing] that of Scribes and Pharisees" (Matthew 5:20): "It was also said, 'whoever divorces his wife, let him give her a certificate of divorce.' But I say to you that anyone who divorces his wife, except on the grounds of unchastity, makes her an adulteress, and whoever marries a divorced woman commits adultery." Notable here is the thoroughly Jewish character of the statement, with its explicit rebuttal of the law in Deuteronomy 24:1–4, and its assumption that divorce is initiated only by males. The exceptive clause, "except for unchastity (*porneia*)," although open to a variety of interpretations, represents a legal amendment of the absolute prohibition found in Paul, Mark, and Luke.

The same features are present in Matthew's second version of Jesus' statement, found in his redaction of Mark's account of a controversy with Pharisees (Matthew 19:3–9). This account concludes, however, with a startling declaration by Jesus concerning the superiority of being a "eunuch for the sake of the kingdom of heaven" to the condition of being married (Matthew 19:10–12). Jesus' absolute prohibition of divorce was clearly taken with utter seriousness by early Christians, so seriously that they were required to interpret it in ways that fit the less than ideal circumstances. Such is the start of legal/*halachic* thinking within the messianic community, with Jesus' teachings as the precedents to be construed. Through the centuries, Christians continued to parse Jesus' statements concerning adultery and lust, murder and anger, non-retribution, the taking of oaths (Matthew 5–7), the sharing of possessions, the demands of discipleship (Luke 12–14), mutual correction and excommunication (Matthew 18), not simply because Jesus said them, but because they addressed essential elements of their life within the community. Other statements of Jesus within the Gospels, such as the *logion* concerning taxes, "[r]ender to Caesar the things that are Caesar's, and to God the things that are God's" (Mark 12:13–17), took on additional significance – and extended application – when Christians began to engage the imperial order more directly and eventually governed a Christian empire.[28]

Still other statements of Jesus were made to support political agendas that would certainly have surprised and puzzled him. Such is the case with the use of "you are Peter, and on this rock I will build my church" (Matthew 16:18–19) to support papal authority over a world-wide church,[29] and the employment of Jesus' cryptic comment at the last supper in response to his disciples' statement, namely, "Look, Lord, here are two swords . . . It is enough" (Luke 22:38), as support for the political arrangements between the medieval church and state.[30] These developments, however, belong to a time considerably later than the period that is the concern of the present chapter.

In addition to the eschatological "sentences of Holy Law" and the sayings of Jesus, Paul's letters reveal other small steps in the direction of a distinctively Christian law. I have noted already how Paul drew from Graeco-Roman and Jewish precedents to state an attitude toward the Empire and its rulers. We find in his letters other elements drawn from moral philosophers (both Gentile and Jewish) that provide guidance to early Christian communities, such as lists of vices and virtues, the use of language associated with moral discernment (*phronesis*), and tables of household ethics that address appropriate domestic arrangements and attitudes. A fascinating display of such elements as well as prescriptions concerning behavior at public worship, the moral qualifications of leaders, the settling of disputes concerning leaders, and the administration of the community support of widows is found in two of Paul's letters to his delegates (1 Timothy and Titus). They take the literary form of letters that had been

---

[28] R. J. Cassidy, *Christians and Roman Rule in the New Testament* (New York: Crossroad Publishing, 2001).
[29] J. E. Bigane, *Faith, Christ, or Peter: Matthew 16:18 in Sixteenth Century Roman Catholic Exegesis* (Washington, DC: University Press of America, 1981).
[30] L. L. Field, *Liberty, Dominion, and the Two Swords: On the Origins of Western Political Theology (180–398)* (Notre Dame, IN: University of Notre Dame Press, 1998).

written by kings and governors to their delegates since the start of the Hellenistic period (called *mandata principis* letters), combining elements of personal advice to the delegate with specific prescriptions for the community the delegate is sent to administer.[31]

At the beginning of the second century, such elements continued to be deployed through letters written by leaders to communities – *1 Clement* (*c.* 95 CE) and *Letter of Polycarp* (*c.* 130 CE) – but increasingly as well in compositions that come to be called "Church Orders." The earliest of these were the *Didache* (the *Teaching of the Lord through the Twelve Apostles*), which comes from Syria (*c.* 100 CE). Other examples include the *Apostolic Church Order* (Egypt, *c.* 300 CE), the *Didascalia Apostolorum* (third-century Syria), and *The Apostolic Tradition* of Hippolytus (third-century Rome). The fullest version is the fourth-century compilation of ecclesiastical law from Syria called the *Apostolic Constitutions*, whose eight books build on and expand earlier collections. By this point, it is possible to speak of a genuine "Christian law," the precedent for medieval canon law.[32]

DISTINCTIVE LEGAL CONTRIBUTIONS OF EARLY CHRISTIANITY

The most important contributions of early Christianity to later law – both religious and secular – did not derive from its own struggles to establish procedure within the community or to find a place within the context of Jewish and Greco-Roman societies. They come rather from certain basic elements of the early Christian experience that, given expression in the New Testament, continued to exercise influence wherever and whenever the New Testament was taken seriously as a norm for Christian life.

Perhaps the most powerful was the simple notion of "the church" as a society that was defined by religious choice, rather than by kinship or national identity. Not only did Christianity draw its adherents from Jew and Gentile and Scythian and Barbarian, it made those former allegiances less important than the commitment to a "commonwealth [that] is in heaven" (Philippians 3:20), a *politeuma* defined not in terms of worldly standards but by the paradoxical experience of a crucified and raised Messiah whose Holy Spirit was considered to be the life-force by which the community lived. The eschatological character of Christianity – its insistence on obedience to God rather than to any human institution – has never completely been lost, even when the church itself seemed most

---

[31] L. T. Johnson, *The First and Second Letters to Timothy*, Anchor Bible 35A (New York: Doubleday, 2001). [32] See further discussion in chapter 3 herein by R. H. Helmholz.

compromised by worldly standards, and this religious tradition has shown itself repeatedly capable of astonishing internal renewal. Such movements of renewal within Christianity have usually led to a less comfortable place for Christians within the larger society. At its best, Christianity has offered an alternative to totalitarian systems that demand complete allegiance to human rule, since Christians could claim to belong to a "City of God" that was incommensurate with any human politics.

The Pauline image of the church as "the Body of Christ" also offered a vision of a society whose members are mutually bound together through reciprocity of gifts and whose joint care is for the health of the body as a whole rather than the success or power of individuals, whose obedience is owed to the Head who is the risen Christ, rather than to secular or ecclesiastical leaders, and within which the forms of status that in every secular society are used to separate humans through degrees of status (race, gender, social position, wealth) are relativized. Forms of status served now as opportunities to gift others rather than to establish precedence over them.

A further contribution of Christianity to future systems of law again came from Paul, who insisted on the integrity of the individual conscience as the ultimate determinant of moral action, to the point that even doing the "right thing" against one's inner sense of right and wrong is equivalent to doing "the wrong thing." This insistence on the primacy of the individual human conscience would have a significant impact on the development of later legal systems, and formed the basis for the development of the notion of religious liberty as a fundamental human right.[33]

Christianity did not begin as a system of law but as a set of experiences and convictions centered in the ministry, death, and resurrection of Jesus. Each of these aspects of Jesus presented challenges to the dominant systems of Roman and Jewish law. In seeking to define its distinctive new identity, Christians were necessarily engaged with various aspects of Roman and (especially) Jewish law, but in the development of its own law, it depended less on precedents provided by those systems than on the experiences and convictions associated with Jesus. At the core of this religion, and its most fundamental contribution to later law, is a vision of humanity that values the conscience of each individual yet uses human diversity to build a body of Christ that is organically interconnected and whose every activity responds to an authority that is divine rather than human.

---

[33] L. T. Johnson, "Religious Rights and Christian Texts," in *Religious Human Rights in Global Perspective: Religious Perspectives,* ed. J. Witte, Jr. and J. D. van der Vyver (The Hague: Martinus Nijhoff Publishers, 1996), 65–96.

RECOMMENDED READING

Bammel, E., ed. *The Trial of Jesus.* Naperville, IL: Allenson, 1970.

Cassidy, R. J. *Christians and Roman Rule in the New Testament.* New York: Crossroad Publishing, 2001.

Danielou, J. *From Shadows to Reality: Studies in the Biblical Typology of the Fathers.* Translated by W. Hibberd. Westminster, MD: Newman Press, 1960.

Haring, B. *The Law of Christ: Moral Theology for Priests and Laity,* 3 vols. Translated by E. G. Kaiser. Westminster, MD: Newman Press, 1961–1963.

Johnson, L. T. *The Writings of the New Testament: An Interpretation.* 2nd rev. edn with Todd Penner. Minneapolis: Fortress Press, 1999.

Kugel, J. L. *The Bible as it Was.* Cambridge, MA: Harvard University Press, 1997.

Meier, J. P. *A Marginal Jew: Rethinking the Historical Jesus,* 3 vols. New York: Doubleday, 1991–2001.

Pelikan, J. *The Excellent Empire: The Fall of Rome and the Triumph of the Church.* San Francisco: Harper and Row, 1987.

Sanders, E. P. *Jewish Law from Jesus to the Mishnah: Five Studies.* London: SCM Press, 1990.

Segal, A. F. *Paul the Convert: The Apostolate and Apostasy of Saul the Pharisee.* New Haven, CT: Yale University Press, 1990.

Sherwin-White, A. N. *Roman Society and Roman Law in the New Testament.* Oxford: Clarendon Press, 1963.

Smallwood, E. M. *The Jews under Roman Rule from Pompey to Diocletian.* Leiden: E. J. Brill, 1976.

4 "Table Showing the Forbidden Degrees of Affinity," (vellum) (Italian, fourteenth century).

CHAPTER THREE

Western canon law

R. H. Helmholz

The law of the church is called the canon law. The term itself comes from a Greek word that means a measuring rod, taken figuratively in the West to be a measure of right conduct. In the broadest sense, canons are intended to lead men and women to act justly in the world so that they may ultimately stand before God unashamed. The *salus animarum* (soul's health) has always been their most vital guiding principle, even though some of the rules embraced over the course of the canon law's history now seem very remote from spiritual principles as we understand them. The canon law's greatest sanction has always been a spiritual one, the sentence of excommunication – the separation of an individual from the body of Christians. Physical or monetary penalties have sometimes been used in practice, but they have been compromises with stubborn human nature. The canon law has thus always been connected with the "internal forum" of conscience. It is also separate, however, because it is designed to govern the conduct of Christian people in the world, doing so by a combination of prohibition, command, and moral guidance.

Canon law is not all spirit. Inevitably, a large part of it has provided detailed rules for the governance of the church – regulations of conduct by the clergy, instructions for the performance of the sacraments, and directions for decision-making within the church. By design, the canons create conditions that promote harmony within the church and freedom from interference from without. But this has never been their sole aim. The canon law has also aimed higher, assuming to provide salutary rules for the lives of ordinary Christians and to exert an influence on the content of temporal law. In some matters, the canon law has also claimed to stand outside and even above the rules applied in the secular law courts. The justification for its claimed authority has been that its aim is higher and more important – nothing less than leading men and women toward God and establishing a Christian social order.

That aspiration has sometimes become a source of dispute. Can law really promote sanctity of life? Should not things of the spirit be kept out of the law courts? Many spiritually minded Christians have minimized the place that law should play in the life of a church whose founder's statements about law, or at least lawyers, were equivocal at best (e.g., Luke 11:45). They have regarded rigid rules of law as a barrier to the workings of the Holy Spirit. Selected words from St. Paul have encouraged critical attitudes toward law (e.g., Galatians 3:10), and they have sometimes been taken to antinomian conclusions. However, the leaders of the church have been all but unanimous over the centuries in concluding that some form of law is necessary to enable the church to carry out its mission in the world. Formally at least, they have prevailed. Today, virtually all Christian churches have adopted codes of canon law or ecclesiastical discipline. Some have maintained elaborate court systems, entrusting them with the power to determine questions involving marriage and divorce, misconduct by the clergy, and the disposition of ecclesiastical property.

THE *IUS ANTIQUUM*

The early manifestations of canon law, like so much else in the history of Christianity, came out of the East. The oldest surviving example, dating from about 100 CE, is said to be the collection of precepts and rules for the running of the church called the *Didache* or *Doctrine of the Twelve Apostles*.[1] Its brevity and simplicity may disqualify it as a candidate for the foundation stone for the later history of the church's law, but it was assuredly a sign of future direction. After the establishment of Christianity within the Roman Empire in the fourth century, a way that would eventually lead to the creation of a separate law for the church was more clearly staked out. Councils of the church met and enacted canons. The great ecumenical councils, like those of Nicaea (325) or Chalcedon (451), are best known for their decrees on religious doctrine, but they also enacted numerous regulations for governance of the church.[2] The Nicaean Fathers, for example, enacted canons to regulate the choice of bishops, to set requirements for ordination to lesser offices, and to forbid clerical participation in usury. The bishops at Chalcedon adopted canons against simony, required that diocesan synods be held twice a year, and forbade the marriage of diaconesses. As these examples suggest, most such canons regulated the church and clergy, including monks and nuns. However, some also touched the laity, as for example, those defining heresy and anathematizing those who held

---

[1] See chapter herein by Luke Timothy Johnson on law in the early church.
[2] See Norman P. Tanner, ed., *Decrees of the Ecumenical Councils*, 2 vols. (Washington, DC: Georgetown and Sheed & Ward, 1990), 1: 1–19, 77–103.

heretical opinions. A few even touched social life, such as encouraging charity or forbidding the forcible abduction of women. This general pattern was to endure. Many such councils were held. One of them, held at Sardica *c.* 343, included an early provision for appeals to the Bishop of Rome in its disciplinary canons dealing with bishops accused of offenses against church order.

Knowing the rules laid down by the canons enacted by the various councils long presented problems. No single code or other source provided authoritative answers. The councils were sporadic and their canons quite miscellaneous. Enterprising men, therefore, began to bring the existing canons together in canonical collections. To them they added extracts from the writing of the Church Fathers, parts of the Bible, letters of the popes, and other miscellaneous sources in attempts to state the law by which the church should be governed in a more complete fashion. Some (but not all of them) were arranged by subject matter for ease in consultation, and they are called systematic for that reason. The seventh-century *Collectio Hispana*, for example, was reworked several times; some versions put the canons and papal decretals into chronological order, while others (presumably later versions) provided users with a more convenient systematic arrangement of the texts.

Many such collections were made during the early Middle Ages. An example is the *Libri duo de synodalibus causis*, collected by Abbot Regino of Prüm. Dating from *c.* 906, Regino's work included, among others, canons from seventh-century Spanish collections and from the Pseudo-Isidorian Decretals, an influential and large compendium of genuine conciliar canons and papal letters interspersed with forged canons put together in the diocese of Reims in the ninth century. Regino lamented the "perilous times" in which he lived, "when many kinds of disgraceful things were being perpetrated," hoping that his collection would restore a measure of discipline to the church. His preface stated that he had preferred to include canons from Gaul and German lands, where he lived, so that it might be seen that Christians might differ among themselves "in kind, customs, language, and laws" even though they were "joined in the unity of faith."[3]

Despite Regino's apparent faith that his texts would be employed in governing the life of the clergy and the laity, it is not easy to say what actual use was made of the collections of canons like his in early medieval practice. They were incomplete in coverage, and most of them were local in

---

[3] A Latin edition was published by F. G. A. Wasserschleben in 1840; for an English introduction, see Robert Somerville and Bruce C. Brasington, *Prefaces to Canon Law Books in Latin Christianity: Selected Translations, 500–1245* (New Haven, CT: Yale University Press, 1998), 69–70, 92–94.

orientation. None was regarded as authoritative throughout the West, and they often contained more theology than hard law. Little evidence exists to show how they were actually employed to settle legal questions, if indeed they were so used. The church of the early Middle Ages had no regular court system in which canons could be enforced and disputes determined. Diocesan synods, which were to be held yearly, provided the principal forum for litigation and public discipline. The institution of the *audiencia episcopalis* of the late Empire, under which bishops acted to settle legal disputes where the parties were willing, also provided a model and justification for a wider jurisdiction. However, as an institution, that step was to take place only in the second millennium of the church's existence.

The pace of compiling canonical collections quickened with the stirrings of the reform movement within the church during the eleventh century. Indeed, the compilers were themselves instrumental in the promotion of reform, and the names of the greatest of them, Burchard of Worms and Ivo of Chartres, for example, are still known and admired by historians of the canon law. Their work advanced the reformers' attack upon the evil of simony, the trading in spiritual things that hindered the church's independence, and also their efforts to undermine acceptance of the marriage of the clergy, a long-standing compromise regarded as standing in the way of an independent and purified clerical order. These collections asserted the primacy of the church both in things of the spirit and in matters of governance. The major steps were taken under the leadership of the papacy. At least to judge by the number of surviving manuscripts, these new efforts in collecting achieved a greater acceptance in the West than had any one of the earlier collections. As a practical matter, however, they were swept away by the appearance in the twelfth century of the compilation which came to be known simply as the *Decretum* of Gratian. It laid the foundation for a canon law worthy of the name.[4]

THE *IUS NOVUM*

Decretum was shorthand for the collection's official title, *Concordia discordantium canonum*, or the *Harmonization of Discordant Canons*. Its compiler is known only by the name of Gratian; traditionally he was thought to be a monk who taught in Bologna, the site of the revival of legal learning during the twelfth century and home to Europe's first university. In fact, little is known about the man himself, or indeed of the way in which the

---

[4] See chapter herein by Brian Tierney on the legal theory of the *Decretum*.

Decretum was compiled. Scholars debate, for instance, about whether he himself incorporated texts from the Roman law into the *Decretum* or whether this was done only later by his followers.[5] The final form of the text was at length established, and although not approved by the papacy or any other official body, it soon was accepted throughout the West as the first law book of the church.

A hurried glance at the *Decretum* will not explain its appeal. Although some of it consisted of canons stating the accepted law of the church, the larger part consisted of long strings of apparently contradictory canons that Gratian reconciled using the scholastic methods of the classroom. He began with a statement of the questions raised by a proposed set of facts. Like Abelard's famous *Sic et Non*, Gratian's treatment produced canons that bore upon the questions raised, but gave opposite answers. Unlike Abelard, however, Gratian proposed answers to the contradictions his texts raised; they were the "harmonization" in his title. For example, in *Causa* II, Gratian supposed that one cleric had sued another cleric over rights in an estate; the defendant had objected to the forum, claiming his right to be heard in a court of the church, but the plaintiff continued nonetheless, causing the defendant to be dispossessed. In consequence, the bishop of the clerics suspended the plaintiff from his clerical office. The *Decretum* asked, first, whether a cleric could be sued before a secular judge, and produced twenty-six authorities against this proposition. Clergy were only accountable to their bishops was the upshot of these texts. Then came four authorities, including extracts from the Bible itself, that seemed to point in the opposite direction. Secular causes should not come before spiritual tribunals, effectively precluding this dispute from being brought before any but a secular court. Gratian thus reconciled the authorities by distinguishing between criminal and civil disputes, treating the first group of authorities as having involved criminal disputes, even though not all of them seem to have fitted neatly into this scheme. He went on, however, to refine his distinctions, and in the process further limited the situations in which secular jurisdiction was permissible under the canons. The question of the reach of secular jurisdiction was important in medieval Europe and was much disputed at the time. The *Decretum* gave an answer of sorts, but more importantly for the history of the canon law, it did so by using the dialectic method of reconciling seemingly opposing authorities. This method marked out the future of the canon law. It was a source of strength, but also

---

[5] Anders Winroth, *The Making of Gratian's Decretum* (Cambridge: Cambridge University Press, 2000).

of weakness, for it opened the canon law to charges of over-subtlety and hair-splitting. It also left a great many matters open to dispute.

Despite its shortcomings, Gratian's text was an immediate and lasting success. It was expanded by adding canons, and it was glossed within a decade of its appearance. We do not yet know the details of this process of expansion, but we do know that in short order, glossators began working to understand and comment upon the canons in the *Decretum* and in Gratian's own dicta. Chief among these workers was Johannes Teutonicus (d. 1245), whose *glossa ordinaria* became the standard guide to the contents and meaning of the texts. Without this gloss, it is unlikely that Gratian's work would have had the long-term influence it did. Later commentators would take note that "What the gloss does not recognize, the courts do not recognize" – a tribute to the difficulty of using Gratian's work without the working guide provided by the ordinary gloss and also to the great influence of the academic jurists on the course of the church's law.

Gratian's *Decretum*, based as it was on ancient authorities, turned out not to state the evolving law of the church on some questions of moment. The canon law was subject to change and to newer legislation. For example, the canon law regulating the formation of marriage took a different direction than that found in the *Decretum*. Whereas Gratian had taken the position that an indissoluble marriage did not come into existence until the exchange of consent between man and woman had been followed by sexual intercourse, the evolving law of the twelfth century chose to follow the example of the marriage between Joseph and the Virgin Mary. It held that the exchange of words of present consent, without more, constituted a true and indissoluble marriage. This was a view that was to cause many practical problems in the future; it required no public ceremony or event, but it did require fine distinctions between words of future consent and words of present consent. For instance, whether the words "I will have you as my wife (husband)" were the one or the other was disputed for centuries. However, the test of present words of consent was recognized by Pope Alexander III (1159–1181) and became the law of the church. It lasted a long time – until the new rules of the Council of Trent (1545–1563) adopted in most of Catholic Europe and in England until the passage of Lord Hardwicke's Marriage Act in 1753.

The way in which this decision about the church's law occurred is worthy of note. It happened through a papal determination, giving express sanction to one position taken in the contemporary schools. That decision was contained in decretal letters issued by the papal chancery in Rome. Rarely was it the product of legislation properly speaking. Most of the papal decretals in fact were answers to questions put to the popes by bishops or other judges throughout the Western church. Faced with a hard case, they asked for instructions on how to deal with it. Some cases also came to Rome by the process of appeal. Only a few decretals were immediate products of papal initiative. Whatever their specific origin, during the twelfth century they became the normal means by which the church's law was stated, clarified, and amended.

Of course, church councils did also meet and enact canons. The great Fourth Lateran Council of 1215, for example, reduced the scope of the prohibited degrees of consanguinity and affinity that prevented men and women from marrying those to whom they were related by blood or marriage. It enacted other rules of fundamental importance, giving approval for example to the system of inquisitorial procedure in order to sharpen the church's ability to deal with criminal offenses. Local synods and ecclesiastical assemblies also continued to enact canons to meet the problems of their own regions and to give specific force to the more general law of the church. This regional legislation was not to be in direct conflict with the law of the Western church, but was meant to supplement and strengthen it.

However, it was the papal decretal that took center stage in the evolution of the canon law. Decretals came thick and fast from the papal court; they were much in demand. Canonists, teaching in the nascent universities and also acting as judges and administrators, turned their efforts away from the ancient canons and toward the law stated in current papal decretals. Indeed, the collection of contemporary decretals was an urgent task. They contained the latest formulations of the church's law, and with the heightened attention to law that was a feature of intellectual life in the thirteenth century, they were the natural objects of study. In short order, five of these decretal collections – known as the *Quinque compilationes antiquae* – emerged as the most reliable. However, even these five "victors" were rendered obsolete by the work of a single editor commissioned by Pope Gregory IX to bring the law of the decretals together into a single work: that of Raymond of Peñaforte, a Spanish canonist. He was given a free hand in selecting and editing the existing decretals, and he made good use of it. He eliminated superfluous information from the existing decretals, suppressed contradictions in them, altered words and phrases for the sake of accuracy, and divided their contents into separate titles and chapters according to the subject matter they contained. The result was not a legal code in the sense later centuries would use the term to mean a complete statement of the law of church. It left too many gaps and left too much to local custom for that. However, it was (and is) an impressive and orderly statement of the canon law as it stood in the thirteenth century. Raymond completed his work in 1234 and his collection was made "official" in that same year, when Gregory IX sent it to the University at Bologna to be incorporated into the teaching of the canon law.

This collection, *The Decretals*, as it came to be commonly known, was divided into five books. The first dealt with the constitution and basic law of the church, the second with jurisdictional and procedural rules to be used in practice, the third with the clerical order and the sacraments, the fourth with matrimonial law, and the fifth with the church's penal law. Just as happened with Gratian's *Decretum*, the Gregorian *Decretals* were glossed almost immediately in the Schools. By the 1260s, the *glossa ordinaria* was put together by Bernard of Parma, using existing comments on the texts. The *Decretals* stood as the basic law of the Catholic Church until 1917 and (in spite of their papal sponsorship) they determined many of the legal principles adopted by the Protestant churches in the sixteenth century and beyond.

Of course, the medieval canon law did not stand still. It could not. New problems arose. Improvements in procedural rules were desired. New challenges appeared. In consequence, papal decretals were issued, and church councils met to deal with changed circumstances. The new texts from both were placed into collections in their turn, and recognized officially by Pope Boniface VIII in 1298 by issuance of the so-called *Liber sextus*. Its name came from the notion that it was the sixth book of the *Decretals*, though in fact it was divided into five books that followed the pattern of the earlier collection. Its contents mirror contemporary concerns. On the one hand, the *Liber sextus* has almost nothing new in its fourth book about marriage – only five decretals in all. Here the law stated in the Gregorian *Decretals* must have seemed sufficient to contemporaries, however unworkable it now seems to us.[6] On the other hand, the penal law of the church exploded. The title devoted to prosecution of heresy in the *Liber sextus* contained twenty separate decretals. That related to the sanction of excommunication contained twenty-four. Extensive and extraordinary powers were given to inquisitorial tribunals – a tribute to the panicky reaction of the medieval church to the perceived dangers of religious dissent and the conviction that a popular neglect of the moral law had arisen.[7]

Similar, though smaller, compilations of the canon law were later made and incorporated into the *Corpus iuris canonici*. Notable were the *Clementines*, planned by Pope Clement V to incorporate decrees from

---

[6] See chapter herein by Don Browning on marriage.
[7] See chapter by Mathias Schmoeckel herein on criminal procedure and evidence.

the Council of Vienne (1311–1312) and actually published in 1316, early in the reign of his successor, Pope John XXII. Also notable were the *Extravagantes*, published a few years later and finally incorporated in the canon law in two separate editions. They were brought together finally in the standard *Corpus iuris canonici* in the 1580s.

THE MATURE CANON LAW

The juristic literature based on the *Corpus iuris canonici* was an essential part of the law of the church. It quickly took on a life of its own. At the start, much of it, like the *glossa ordinaria* itself, was directly related to scholastic instruction. The *Lectura* or *Commentaria* on the Gregorian *Decretals*, for instance, followed the teacher on an orderly march through the texts. Many such commentaries were compiled. Henricus de Susa, called Hostiensis (d. 1271), described this method. First, he put the case and its subject; second, he read the text and explained it; third, he took note of related texts found elsewhere in the *Decretals*; fourth, he brought forward apparently contrary authorities and reconciled them; fifth, he discussed questions raised by the text and answered them where possible; and sixth, he spoke of other notable matters relating to the chapter under discussion. With few variations, other lecturers did the same, though the points they covered might differ among themselves.

From these relatively modest beginnings eventually sprang a literature of great size and complexity. Some were also linked to the Schools, as the *Quaestiones* and *Repetitiones* that raised difficult points in the academic law. Others were tied to practice, like the *Ordines iudiciarii* that provided forms and advice for use in litigation. Still others dealt with a single aspect of the learned laws, such as the *Speculum iudiciale* by William Durantis (d. 1296) on the law of procedure, the treatise on canonical elections compiled by William of Mandagoto (d. 1321), or the inquisitors' manual written by Nicholaus Eymericus (d. 1399). The great age of specialized treatise writing did not arrive till the Middle Ages had passed, but the direction was apparent already by 1400. Some of the great treatises, such as those of Nicholas de Tudeschis, known as Panormitanus (d. 1445 or 1453), are still regarded with respect by students of the canon law.

Among the treatises composed during the late medieval period were several that dealt with the relationship between the Roman civil law and the canon law. *De differentiis legum et canonum* was a common title.[8] They

---

[8] That written by Prosdocimus de Comitibus (d. 1438) won a place in the *Tractatus universi iuris*.

point to an important point about the law of the church; it was linked with
the law of the Roman Empire. The link had existed from the earliest days.
The church and its clergy were said to "live by the Roman law." The mature
canon law was both different and more restricted in its substantive coverage than the law found in the *Corpus iuris civilis* that had been compiled
under the Emperor Justinian in the 530s. However, the link was maintained. Whether it was Gratian himself or one of his followers who inserted
extracts from the Roman law into the *Decretum*, the fact remained that the
ancient law filled many of the gaps in the canon law. Both were taught in
the European universities, although normally in separate faculties, and
lawyers who served the church were normally trained in both laws. When
reading through a commentary on the canon law from the thirteenth or
fourteenth centuries, one is immediately struck by the presence of citations
to Roman law; they were used to augment, explain, and interpret the texts
of the canon law itself.

At first, the Roman law was the senior partner in this alliance. The
jurists of the civil law, called civilians, felt entitled to despise the rude
efforts of the canonists. But the balance gradually swung toward greater
equality between the two laws, and from the combination of canon and
Roman law there emerged an amalgam now called the *ius commune*, the
common law of Europe. It was something like a blend of both laws,
making room also for adaptation to new and local conditions. Each preserved its own identity and maintained many of its own legal rules. For
example, the Roman law of marriage was quite different from the law of
the church. Each took quite different views on the legality of usury. The
overlap in coverage, too, was not complete. For example, the canon law of
testamentary succession was modest in scope, whereas the civil law was
quite extensive and sophisticated. The canon law of the sacraments (e.g.,
baptism), by contrast, was not matched by anything found in the Roman
law. However, overall the two laws were brought into tolerable harmony,
and in some areas, the law of procedure for instance, a more unitary set of
rules developed. What differences existed could be explained by the
difference in aim of the two laws, and in many areas the differences were
many fewer than the similarities. The two could scarcely have existed
without the aid of the other.

This connection was cemented by the emergence of a system of courts
and of a legal profession to serve in them. On the church's side, this happened during the second half of the thirteenth century. In this respect, the
canon law was a century or so behind the secular law. There must have been
a resistance to the creation of a permanent system of spiritual courts

and lawyers to administer the law of the church. It all but admitted the normality of discord among Christians. But the step was taken, and on the Continent, the same men who served in the secular courts could also serve in the courts of the church. Their training in the schools would have been little different. It was easy and natural that they should have applied the same tools in their practice.

In England, this did not happen. The ecclesiastical courts and a legal profession to act in them did come into being during the thirteenth century, but it was a different group of men and a different procedural setting than had come into being in the royal courts. On the secular side, the customary English common law and the institution of the jury prevailed. From the start, the English ecclesiastical courts made use of written pleadings and procedures; they entrusted the duty of fact finding to a judge learned in the law rather than to a jury of laymen.

There were, of course, also differences between the secular courts and the courts of the church throughout Europe, but the contrast was particularly marked in lands where the English common law prevailed. When the New World came under the dominance of Europeans, it is worthy of note that no ecclesiastical courts were created in North America at the time the English colonies were being organized. The courts inherited from the common law had to deal as best they could with legal problems and controversies that, in England, had been and remained the preserve of tribunals of the church and the canon law.

The thirteenth century witnessed the high water mark of the canon law's influence in European history. But diminution of that influence was not abrupt. The Western church long possessed a relatively well-ordered system of courts. Archbishops, bishops, archdeacons, and many lesser ecclesiastical dignitaries held jurisdiction over the clergy and laymen within the lands subject to them. Appeals from their sentences lay to higher courts, ultimately to the papal court, where an institution known as the *Rota Romana* dealt with them in the name of the popes. During the later medieval period, it appears that the greater part of the litigation there dealt with ecclesiastical benefices, that is, the rights of the clergy to hold offices in the church and to enjoy the revenues that went with them. We know this from the *Decisiones* of the *Rota*, which began to be collected during the first half of the fourteenth century; they exist in virtually unbroken sequence to the present day.

In the present state of knowledge, it is not so easy to describe the inner workings of the tribunals held on the local level during the later Middle Ages. Historians have not yet explored anything like all the records that do exist, and in some places, Scandinavia for instance, no contemporary records seem to have survived. Moreover, the scope of jurisdiction these courts exercised in fact was dependent as much on local custom and the acquiescence of temporal rulers as it was on the formal canon law. In some places, the Netherlands for example, litigants apparently made their own choice. The weaknesses of the secular tribunals caused the majority of civil cases to be brought in the ecclesiastical forum.[9] In some other places, by seeming contrast, the temporal courts effectively restricted the ability of the courts of the church to deal with cases involving the laity.

It does appear that the law of marriage provided a substantial part of ecclesiastical litigation in many places, at least before the very end of the Middle Ages. French, English, Belgian, and Italian archives contain much evidence on the subject.[10] In some places, England for example, the courts went further; they attempted to police the sexual mores of the laity, routinely prosecuting men and women for adultery and fornication. In other places, Spain for example, these matters appear to have been left either to the penitential forum of the confessional or to the temporal courts. Jurisdictional variation was more often the rule than the exception, despite the uniformity of the canonical sources. In France, the clerical privilege of being sued in civil matters only before an ecclesiastical tribunal, called the *privilegium fori*, was respected for the most part during the later Middle Ages. In England, by contrast, it was a dead letter almost from the start. By the same token, in some parts of Europe special inquisitorial tribunals were established, famously under the leadership of the Dominican friars, to root out and punish heresy. In other parts no such tribunals were established; heresy and blasphemy were left to the ordinary courts or to tribunals set up ad hoc to deal with specific cases. We know such things in part and in outline only. It will be many years before historians have worked through the records and understood the details.

We do know enough already to see that the canon law continued to be a force to be reckoned with during the later Middle Ages. Viewed from close up, its most obvious accomplishment was to keep the institutional church running. Tithes were collected to support the clergy; refusal to pay one's tithes or other customary dues to a parish church could be met by

---

[9] John Witte, Jr., "The Plight of Canon Law in the Early Dutch Republic," in *Canon Law in Protestant Lands*, ed. R. H. Helmholz (Berlin: Duncker & Humblot, 1992), 135–64; 137.

[10] See Anne Lefebvre-Teillard, *Les officialités à la veille du Concile de Trente* (Paris: Librairie général de droit, 1973); R. H. Helmholz, *Marriage Litigation in Medieval England* (Cambridge: Cambridge University Press, 1974); *Liber sentenciarum van de Officialiteit van Brussel 1448–1459*, ed. Cyril Vleeschouwers and Monique van Malkebeek (Brussels: Ministry of Justice, 1982); Silvana Seidel Menchi and Diego Quaglioni, *Matrimonio in dubbio* (Bologna: Il Mulino, 2001).

a suit for collection in the bishop's court. Attempts to take away or "secularize" property belonging to the church might equally be met with hostile legal action, some of it rather grandly styled "for the protection of ecclesiastical liberty." Assaults upon the clergy, including monks and nuns, were punished in the courts with sanctions that threatened offenders with having to make a trip to distant Rome to be absolved.

The canon law's contemporary influence extended far beyond the church's walls. In commercial life, for example, the doctrines worked out by the canonists counted. The just price, the prohibition of usury, and the institution of annuities touched the lives of ordinary people.[11] In political life, representative institutions came into being under the influence of provisions taken from the canon law.[12] In social life, the creation and regulation of poor relief was accomplished, in part at least, with resources found in the canon law.[13] We cannot say that all canonical rules were obeyed. What law can claim that? Nor can we assert that the courts of the church were never resented or satirized. Chaucer's summoner was taken from life. But it is too cynical a conclusion to say that the canon law's most fundamental goals – promotion of the *salus animarum* and creation of a more perfect society – were not in some measure accomplished. We can be certain that the law's purposes were not achieved in full, but we cannot know that they were not achieved at all.

THE PROTESTANT REFORMATION TO THE PRESENT

The religious Reformation of the sixteenth century brought many changes to the legal life of the church in the West, including life in Catholic lands, but it did not usher in an age of lawlessness. A few of the Protestant reformers, Martin Luther in particular, had hard things to say about the law; indeed he consigned the *Decretals* to the flames. Almost all the reformers criticized features of the existing canonical structure, such as the system of dispensations that licensed evasions of the law and filled the coffers of the Roman pontiff. However, no divorce between law and the Protestant churches took place. Books of church order and discipline were compiled, and a different court system was established in some places. Jurisdiction over some aspects of human life was transferred from ecclesiastical to civil

[11] John Gilchrist, *The Church and Economic Activity in the Middle Ages* (London/New York: Macmillan, 1969).
[12] See Gaines Post, "Plena Potestas and Consent in Medieval Assemblies," in *Studies in Medieval Legal Thought* (Princeton, NJ: Princeton University Press, 1964), 60–162.
[13] Brian Tierney, *Medieval Poor Law: A Sketch of Canonical Theory and its Application in England* (Berkeley/Los Angeles: University of California Press, 1959).

tribunals to accord with Protestant understanding of the Christian polity, but actual substantive changes in the law were not inevitable. *Faute de mieux*, much of the canon law remained in place. Even in those parts of Germany where Luther's influence prevailed, jurists continued to teach the *ius commune* and courts continued to seek its enforcement.[14] The procedural law of the church, with some necessary variations, remained the touchstone of much of Protestant law. The innate strength of the *ius commune* was a bulwark against dramatic change.

Protestant England preserved its links with the past in an even stronger sense than did the Continental churches. Replacement of the inherited canon law was envisioned, but the statute which authorized the process specified that, with the exception of papal powers held to be contrary to English custom and royal rights, the old law should remain in effect, pending revision. In the end, the revision failed, and the old law kept its hold on practice. The traditional courts met as they had before the Reformation, and their jurisdiction remained pretty much as it had been. Over the centuries that followed, legislation was passed and inroads were made in the church's sphere of legal competence in England, as indeed happened throughout Europe. But in fact the English ecclesiastical courts exercised a wide competence over the life of the laity, wider than was true in Catholic lands, until the major part of their jurisdiction was withdrawn by statute in the mid nineteenth century.[15]

Today, the links with the classical canon law are difficult to discern in most Protestant churches, even in the Church of England. However, this has not meant the displacement of law altogether. There must be rules to facilitate the life of a church, and they are contained in a miscellaneous, and apparently unconnected, series of church constitutions.[16] In the United States, where links with the past seem at their weakest, churches nonetheless live by rules of law. For example, a work called *The Constitution and Bylaws of the United Church of Christ* (2001) serves that function for a body of Christians. The Methodists have a *Book of Discipline*, and so on.[17] Typically, these collections are not called books of canon law, but they are not different in function. They define the government and offices of the

---

[14] Johannes Heckel, "Das Decretum Gratiani und das deutsche evangelische Kirchenrecht," *Studia Gratiana* 3 (1955): 483–537; John Witte, Jr., *Law and Protestantism: The Legal Teachings of the Lutheran Reformation* (Cambridge: Cambridge University Press, 2002).

[15] See R. B. Outhwaite, *The Rise and Fall of the English Ecclesiastical Courts, 1500–1860* (Cambridge: Cambridge University Press, 2006).

[16] See the chapter by Norman Doe herein on modern Protestant, Catholic, and Orthodox church laws.

[17] See *The Book of Discipline of the United Methodist Church* (Nashville: United Methodist Publishing House, 1989).

church, outline the process of calling and disciplining ministers, and state the sanctions at the disposal of ecclesiastical bodies. The Presbyterians in the USA have spelled out a quite elaborate set of rules for the conduct of trials.[18]

Parallels with these developments took place in the Catholic Church. The Council of Trent (1545–1563) was the most dramatic manifestation of changing times. It reaffirmed in the strongest terms some of the traditional canonical prohibitions, citing "the calamities of our times and the cunning of advancing heresies."[19] It reformed other parts of the canon law. For instance, it reduced the scope of the prohibited degrees in the law of marriage and most famously, in the decree *Tametsi* (1563) required the presence of the parish priest for the validity of a marriage. Where fully implemented, this decree worked to solve the great predicament of clandestine marriages – valid in law but hard to prove in fact – that had troubled the ecclesiastical courts and created real dilemmas of conscience since the twelfth century.

The process was one of addition and careful amendment. No major changes in court structure took place, although the hands of the Inquisition were strengthened and special "Congregations" were created in Rome and entrusted to cardinals appointed by the popes; they were given the duty of dealing with special areas of religious life. The Congregation of the Council, for example, was given the responsibility of interpreting and executing the Tridentine decrees. Other Congregations established by Pope Sixtus V at the end of the sixteenth century supervised the Catholic Church's *Index of Prohibited Books*, the administration of sacraments, the process of canonization, and even the Vatican printing press. Multiplication and changes have occurred in the jurisdiction assigned to each Congregation from that day to this, but the same pattern has been followed, leading to a level of bureaucratization likely to bewilder and repel those who arrive from outside.

The basic canon law in the Catholic Church also remained the *Corpus iuris canonici*. New canons and provisions were added, after Trent most of them being issued directly from the papacy, but education of future canonists in the universities continued to be tied to the traditional sources and taught by the traditional methods. In canon law scholarship, there was both stability and development. Commentaries on the *Decretals* did not cease; for instance, Prospero Fagnani (d. 1678), secretary of the Congregation of

---

[18] See *The Constitutions of the Presbyterian Church in the United States of America* (Philadelphia: Presbyterian Board of Publications, 1942), 385–436.
[19] Sess. 25; De Ref. c. 2, in *Decrees of the Ecumenical Councils*, II:785.

the Council, produced a *Commentaria in libros Decretalium* in 1661. Shorter works attempting to state the law in a more methodical fashion, like the famous *Institutiones iuris canonici* of 1563 by Paulo Lancelloti, also appeared. At the same time, works on individual subjects, some of them lengthy and impressive in the ways of traditional scholarship, were more often undertaken by scholars. The huge treatise by the Spanish Jesuit, Thomas Sanchez (d. 1610), called *De sancto matrimonii sacramento*, is one good example. The *Praxis beneficiorum* by a French jurist, Petrus Rebuffus (d. 1557) is another. They stated the old law, added recent changes to it, and discussed at length the issues about the subjects of marriage and ecclesiastical benefices that arose in practice and in the Schools.

It was only in 1917 that a more definitive step away from the old law was taken. In that year, acting in response to a long-stated desire among the bishops for an up-to-date statement of the church's law and following the codification movement in nineteenth-century secular law, a new *Codex iuris canonici* was promulgated at last by the Apostolic See. It remained the law of the Catholic Church until 1983, when a revised code of canon law was adopted.

RECOMMENDED READING

Bellomo, Manlio. *The Common Legal Past of Europe 1000–1800*. Washington, DC: Catholic University of America Press, 1995.
Berman, Harold J. *Law and Revolution: The Formation of the Western Legal Tradition*. Cambridge, MA: Harvard University Press, 1983.
Brundage, James A. *Medieval Canon Law*. London/New York: Longman, 1995.
Doe, Norman. *The Legal Framework of the Church of England*. Oxford: Oxford University Press, 1996.
Gallagher, Clarence. *Church Law and Church Order in Rome and Byzantium: A Comparative Study*. Aldershot: Ashgate Publishing, 2002.
Helmholz, R. H. *The Spirit of the Classical Canon Law*. Athens, GA: University of Georgia Press, 1996.
Helmholz, R. H. ed., *Canon Law in Protestant Lands*. Berlin: Duncker & Humblot, 1996.
Kemp, Eric Waldron, *An Introduction to Canon Law in the Church of England*. London: Hodder & Stoughton, 1957.
Kéry, Lotte, *Canonical Collections of the Early Middle Ages (ca. 400–1140)*. Washington, DC: Catholic University of America Press, 1999.
Kuttner, Stephan, *Harmony from Dissonance*. Latrobe, PA: Archabbey Press, 1960.
Pennington, Kenneth. *Pope and Bishops: The Papal Monarchy in the Twelfth and Thirteenth Centuries*. Philadelphia: University of Pennsylvania Press, 1984.

Ullmann, Walter. *Law and Politics in the Middle Ages.* Ithaca, NY: Cornell University Press, 1975.

Witte, John, Jr. *Law and Protestantism: The Legal Teachings of the Lutheran Reformation.* Cambridge: Cambridge University Press, 2002.

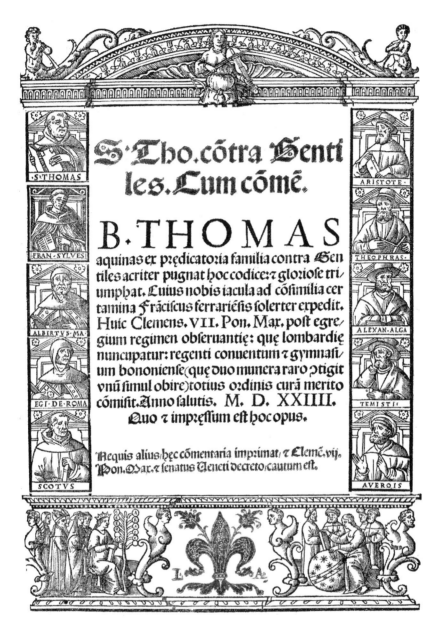

5 "Historiated Title Page Border Depicting Thomas Aquinas with Several Classical and Medieval Authorities," cover page from Thomas Aquinas, *Summa Contra Gentiles* [1523], repr. edn (Turin, 1933).

CHAPTER FOUR

Natural law and natural rights

Brian Tierney

The idea of natural law exercised a persistent influence on Christian thought and Western jurisprudence from ancient times down to the eighteenth century, and the concept has undergone a significant revival in modern times. This tradition of thought, rooted in classical Greek and early Christian sources, affirms that standards of justice and right order exist that are not derived from positive enacted laws but that are inherent in the nature of humankind.

STOICS AND CHRISTIANS

Among the ancient Greeks, Aristotle distinguished between "natural justice" and "legal justice." Natural justice was the same everywhere, but legal justice varied from place to place according to the opinions of different peoples. Aristotle, however, was thinking of justice only within the Greek polis; he regarded the masses of "barbarian" peoples outside the Hellenic world as natural slaves, incapable of forming just societies.

During the following centuries, Stoic thinkers created a more cosmopolitan theory of natural law. In the Stoic vision, the whole cosmos was pervaded by a divine intelligence that directed all its activities in accordance with a universal natural law. Human reason was a part of the divine reason that pervaded the universe, and, by virtue of their possessing reason, all humans were by nature free and equal. Stoic thought, however, did not leave much room for the exercise of human free will. The philosophy was basically deterministic. Humans could at best freely choose to accept the chain of cause and effect that shaped their lives; but by so choosing, by living in harmony with nature, a Stoic sage could achieve a state of serenity, undisturbed by the passing vicissitudes of life, sickness or health, riches or poverty.

Stoic doctrines were passed on to later ages principally in the writings of Cicero and in fragments of Roman law. In his *De republica*, Cicero gave an eloquent defense of natural law: "True law," he wrote, "is right reason in agreement with nature; it is universal, unchanging and everlasting . . . neither Senate nor people can loose us from this law." Cicero's fullest treatment of this theme was presented in his *De legibus*. There he wrote that justice had its origin in law and that law was supreme reason implanted in nature and in human minds, commanding what should be done and forbidding the opposite. All humans shared the same reason and a common sense of justice, and so they were all members of one great commonwealth. The gift of reason even gave them a likeness to God and so distinguished them from all other creatures.[1]

Traces of Cicero's influence and of earlier Stoic doctrines can be found in the writings of the Roman jurists of the next three centuries. A text of Marcianus, attributed to the Stoic philosopher Chrysipus, described natural law as "sovereign over divine and human affairs . . . a standard of justice and injustice." The Roman jurist Ulpian gave an influential tripartite division of law in which natural law was defined as "what nature has taught all animals"; this law included such things as procreation and the rearing of offspring. Other texts, however, treated natural law as pertaining only to humans. Some of them identified natural law with the law of nations (*ius gentium*). Others treated the *ius gentium* as a body of human conventions that had in part replaced a primordial natural law. They maintained, for instance, that by natural law all humans were free and that servitude had been introduced by the law of nations.[2] The Roman jurists seem to have treated the natural law as only an abstract philosophical concept; they did not argue that the law of nature could prevail over enacted law if the two conflicted. Nevertheless, their sometimes conflicting texts attracted a great body of juristic commentary in later centuries.

The Christian view of the universe was different from that of the Stoics. Stoics were pantheists and materialists; Christians believed that the universe was created *ex nihilo* by an omnipotent God whose will was revealed to man in the teachings of sacred scripture. But Christians also believed that the whole universe was ruled by a divine providence, and there were many points of resemblance between Stoic ethics and Christian moral teachings. The version of natural law presented by Cicero proved attractive to some of the early Christian writers and their works helped to transmit his teachings

---

[1] Cicero, *De republica. De legibus*, with an English translation by C. W. Keyes, Loeb Classical Library, repr. edn (London: William Heinneman Ltd., 1970), 210, 317, 320–22.
[2] *Digesta* in T. Mommsen and P. Krueger, eds., *Corpus Juris Civilis*, 2 vols. (Berlin: Weidmann, 1868), I: 1.3.2, 1.1.1.3, 1.1.4.

to later thinkers. For instance, we know Cicero's famous definition of natural law in the *De republica* only because it was copied into a surviving work of the Christian author, Lactantius.

St. Paul provided a key text for Christian authors. In his Epistle to the Romans, he wrote that "when Gentiles who have not the law do by nature what the law requires," they "show that what the law requires is written on their hearts" (Romans 2:14–15). This law "written on the hearts" of men was commonly identified with the moral teachings of the Ten Commandments. Among the early Christians, Irenaeus, followed by other Church Fathers, wrote that God had implanted the natural precepts of the law in our hearts from the beginning and had then set them down on tablets of stone in the Decalogue given to Moses.

Augustine emphasized especially God's eternal law as the source of the natural law in man. For Augustine, eternal law was "the divine reason or will of God, commanding that the natural order be preserved." Augustine also wrote of divine providence as a natural law transcribed in the rational soul. The natural order of the universe, ruled by divine reason, was paralleled by a natural order in the human soul where reason could and should rule over the passions. But humans, unlike brute animals, also possessed free will. Reason showed them the law they should observe, but free will gave them the ability to sin against it.[3] Augustine especially emphasized human sinfulness as distorting a natural order of freedom and innocence established by God; servitude and coercive government, he held, existed only because of the human proclivity to sin.

Certain tensions in the understanding of natural law were inherent in the dual origins of the concept in Greek philosophy and Christian theology, and some important problems were left unresolved. Is there some essential rightness or "oughtness" in the whole structure of the universe, or is it only in rational human beings? Is natural law grounded primarily on the command of God or on reason? Does it guide the whole conduct of human life or only a limited range of moral choices?

MEDIEVAL CANONISTS

The culture of the twelfth century was characterized by a great upsurge of jurisprudence. First came the rediscovery of the whole corpus of Roman law, then an immensely influential codification of the canon law of the church in Gratian's *Concordance of Discordant Canons*, soon known simply

---

[3] Augustine, *Contra Faustum*, ed. J. Zycha (Vienna: F. Tempsky, 1881), 621–23. See further discussion of Augustine's views of law and politics in the chapter by Kent Greenawalt herein.

as the *Decretum* (*c.* 1140).[4] The very first words of Gratian's work gave a definition of natural law as the Golden Rule of Scripture. "Natural law is what is contained in the Law and the Gospel, by which each one is commanded to do to another what he wants done to himself and is forbidden to do to another what he does not want done to himself."[5] This seems a fine beginning for a work of Christian jurisprudence. But problems soon arose. For instance, Gratian went on to state that by natural law all things were common and that private property had been introduced by custom and civil law; but then he added that any custom or law contrary to natural law was null and void.[6] And yet the existence of private property as licit and just was taken for granted in other parts of the *Decretum*.

A text taken from the seventh-century writer, Isidore of Seville, raised further problems. According to Isidore, natural law was held everywhere by instinct of nature; it included such things as the union of men and women, the rearing of children, the common possession of all things, the common liberty of all, the acquisition of anything taken by land, sea, or air, the return of a thing deposited, the repelling of force with force. All these things "and anything similar," Isidore wrote, were just and equitable.[7] But this is a very mixed group of definitions, held together, if at all, by some kind of metonymic association with an underlying idea of natural rightness or natural justice. Moreover, the array of examples seems to include without distinction natural laws and what we should call natural rights. To return a deposit is a precept of natural law, but to act in self-defense ("the repelling of force with force") seems more like a natural right.

Commenting on this text, a later canonist, Huguccio noted in *c.* 1190 that "Not all the examples of natural law given here refer to the same meaning of natural law," and he added: "But lest the mind of some idiot be confused, we will diligently explain each one."[8] This was typical of the canonists' approach. They were not philosophers, and they did not seek to construct a unified philosophy of natural law; they saw their task rather as one of clarifying the meaning of their texts by investigating all the different senses in which the term *ius naturale* was employed in them.

Odo of Dover wrote in *c.* 1170 that natural law could be defined in three ways. In the most general sense, it was the law that God had implanted in the whole of creation, the law that kept the stars in their courses. In another

---

[4] See chapter herein by R. H. Helmholz on medieval canon law.
[5] *Decretum Magistri Gratiani*, ed. E. Friedberg (Leipzig: Tauchnitz, 1879), *dictum ante* Dist.1 c.1.
[6] *Ibid.*, *dictum ante* Dist. 8 c.1, *dictum post* Dist. 8 c.1.   [7] *Ibid.*, Dist. 1 c.7.
[8] Quoted in Brian Tierney, *The Idea of Natural Rights. Studies on Natural Rights, Natural Law and Church Law, 1150–1625* (Grand Rapids, MI: Wm. B. Eerdmans Publishing, 1997), 61 n. 63.

sense, natural law applied to all animate creation, and here Odo quoted the text of Ulpian: "Natural law is what nature has taught all animals." And, finally, in a still more limited sense, natural law could mean a law peculiar to humans that led them to just and honorable conduct.[9] Other canonists succeeded in finding up to ten meanings of *ius naturale*.

Among all the canonists' treatments of natural law, there were two that would greatly influence the future development of the idea of natural rights. The first was the idea of *ius naturale* as a kind of permissive law. Some modern scholars have held that the idea of natural rights that came to be emphasized in later centuries was incompatible with traditional ideas of natural law because, they argued, natural law restrains our actions with its precepts and prohibitions while natural rights define an area where we are free to act as we choose. But the argument overlooks the fact that, ever since the twelfth century, the natural law itself had been understood in one sense as defining an area of human free choice. This way of thinking provided a ready solution to some of the apparent contradictions in Gratian's texts. For instance, the natural law pertaining to common property was often explained as only a permissive law that did not impose any binding obligations, and so left the way open for the institution of private property.

Several canonists of the late twelfth century built this doctrine of *ius naturale* as permissive law around some words of St. Paul at 1 Corinthians 6:12. One of them wrote:

In another way *ius naturale* means what is permitted and approved, not commanded or prohibited by the Lord or any statute . . . as, for instance, to claim one's own or not to claim it, to put away an unbelieving wife or not to put her away, to eat or not to eat something. Whence upon the words of the Apostle, "All things are permitted to me," Ambrose wrote. "By the law of nature (*lege naturae*)."[10]

Another canonist referred to things permitted by the power of free will and by natural law. From this time onward, down to the eighteenth century, permissive law, considered as an intrinsic part of natural law, was treated as a ground of natural rights. Toward the end of the period, the German philosopher Christian Wolff wrote simply that natural law is called permissive when it gives us right to act.

The other canonistic discussions that were important in the growth of later natural rights theories were those that defined *ius naturale* in a subjective sense as an inherent attribute of human persons. Cicero had written that natural law was something that an innate force implanted in us. The canonists often wrote that *ius naturale* (natural law, natural right) was itself a force

---

[9] *Ibid.*, 63.   [10] *Ibid.*, 67.

residing in humans – a force associated with reason and free will. Then, varying Cicero's terminology, they sometimes wrote of *ius naturale* as a power or faculty or ability inherent in humankind.[11] Such language was not at first intended to define a modern idea of a natural right; it meant primarily a power or faculty to distinguish between right and wrong. But once a subjective definition of *ius naturale* came to be widely accepted – and associated with ideas of reason and free will – the language could readily be used to define the natural rights that humans could exercise in acting freely or claiming something due. The first such natural right that the canonists recognized around 1200 was a right of the needy poor to be supported from the wealth of the rich. In subsequent centuries a long line of thinkers – including William of Ockham, Jean Gerson, Francisco Vitoria, Francisco Suarez, and Hugo Grotius – used the terms "power" or "faculty" or "ability" in their definitions of *ius* as a subjective right. The medieval canonists themselves did not develop a coherent theory of natural rights, but they created a language in which such theories could later be expressed.

AQUINAS AND OCKHAM

After a century of canonistic analysis, thirteenth-century teachings on natural law were often embedded in major works of theological synthesis. The most important and enduring contribution came from the thirteenth-century Dominican friar, Thomas Aquinas, who presented a far-ranging argument in which natural law was placed within a whole hierarchy of laws and related to each of them.

In his *Summa theologiae*, Aquinas first defined law in general as "an ordinance of reason for the common good promulgated by one who has charge of the community."[12] Then he considered, in turn, eternal law, natural law, human law, and divine law. For Aquinas, as for Augustine, eternal law was the divine plan of the universe existing in the mind of God, "the rule of divine wisdom moving all things to their due ends." All other law, insofar as it was in accord with right reason, was derived from this eternal law.[13]

Turning next to natural law, Aquinas noted that, since all things were regulated by eternal law, they all derived from this law their tendencies to their own proper ends. Irrational creatures acted through blind determinism, but humans could discern and obey the principles of eternal law that

---

[11] *Ibid.*, 62–65.

[12] Thomas Aquinas, *Summa theologiae*, vol. XXVIII, *Law and Political Theory*, ed. T. Gilby and T. C. O'Brien (New York: McGraw Hill Publishing, 1964–), 1.2ae.90.4, p. 16.

[13] *Ibid.*, 1.2ae.93.1, p. 52; 1.2ae.93.3, p. 58.

guided their conduct through the exercise of reason and will. Aquinas therefore concluded that "Natural law is nothing other than the participation of the eternal law in the rational creature." He was familiar with Ulpian's teaching about a natural law in all animals but wrote that the term could be used in this way only by way of analogy.[14]

When Aquinas considered the content of natural law, he first stated as an axiomatic first principle that "Good is to be done and sought after, and evil avoided." All other precepts of the law were dependent on this maxim, Aquinas held; but the maxim would seem to be an empty one unless we can know the further precepts that show us the particular things to be done or avoided. Aquinas held that such knowledge could be derived from reflection on the natural inclinations implanted in us, and he went on to discuss several such inclinations or tendencies. There was first a natural inclination to self-preservation that humans shared with all other substances, then a natural inclination to procreate and rear offspring that humans shared with other animals and, finally, natural inclinations that were proper to humans alone. These were inclinations to know the truth about God and to live in society with other humans. Some natural laws followed immediately from these last inclinations – for instance, to shun ignorance and not to injure others with whom we must live together.[15]

Aquinas went on next to consider human positive laws. He understood, of course, that humans have bad inclinations as well as good ones, and he held that reason could distinguish between them. But Aquinas also noted that reason could be distorted by lust or some other passion or by corrupt habits. Coercive human laws were therefore needed to enforce those basic rules of natural law that were essential if humans were to live peacefully together – for instance, laws against murder and theft. Human laws were also needed because natural law provided only general principles without specifying how they should be applied in different circumstances. For instance, natural law indicated that crime should be punished, but it did not lay down an appropriate punishment for each offense, and this could vary from people to people.[16] Aquinas concluded that all rules of human law must conform to natural law in one of two ways – either as conclusions derived from premises of natural law or as supplements intended to provide a common rule where natural law left some issue undetermined. The latter category corresponded roughly to the canonists' idea of a realm of permissive natural law.

[14] *Ibid.*, 1.2ae.91.2, p. 22.   [15] *Ibid.*, 1.2ae.94.2, p. 80
[16] *Ibid.*, 1.2ae.94.6, p. 96; 1.2ae.95.1, p. 100.

When Aquinas turned finally to the divine law of Scripture, he explained that the natural law accessible to human reason could guide men to their proximate end of felicity in their life here on earth, but it could not lead them to the final end of beatitude, the vision of God in heaven. Natural law could not teach all the necessary truths of the Christian faith. Moreover, although the moral teachings of natural law were in principle knowable by human reason, not all persons would in fact come to a knowledge of them, and for them, the law laid down in Scripture provided another way of knowledge. Divine law therefore both supplemented the natural law and confirmed its moral teachings.[17]

Aquinas was criticized in his own day on the ground that his emphasis on divine reason implied some kind of restraint on God's exercise of his omnipotent will. In the next generation, the Franciscan philosopher John Duns Scotus argued, in response, that will was not necessarily determined by reason. Then, fellow Franciscan William of Ockham propounded a more radically voluntarist philosophy. He maintained that the whole universe, including the world of moral values, existed as it did simply because God willed it so; God could have created some other universe if he had so willed in which it would be virtuous to steal and lie and commit adultery. However, the significance of this doctrine for Ockham's teaching on natural law and natural rights has sometimes been misunderstood. Although Ockham believed that God could have created some other, different kind of universe, he did not doubt that, in this existing world that God had actually chosen to make, human reason could provide a guide to human moral conduct.

When Ockham wrote on natural law, he gave three definitions of the term, all related to human reason. Natural law, he wrote, could mean immutable moral precepts "in conformity with natural reason," such as the commandments of the Decalogue. Natural law could also mean the law that had existed in the state of innocence and that would still exist if humans always lived in accordance with reason. In a third sense, natural law could be derived by natural reason from human experience; this was a "suppositious law" that supposed the actual existing state of humanity, not an ideal condition. There is nothing revolutionary in these doctrines and, in fact, Ockham found texts in Gratian's *Decretum* to support each one of them.[18]

Ockham's most significant contribution to natural law theory is found in an innovative doctrine of natural rights that Ockham presented in the

---

[17] *Ibid.*, 1.2ae.95.2, p. 104, 1.2ae.91.4, p. 28.
[18] H. S. Offler, "The Three Modes of Natural Law in Ockham. A Revision of the Text," *Franciscan Studies* 23 (1977): 207–18.

course of a bitter dispute between Pope John XXII and the leaders of Ockham's Franciscan order. In a series of polemical works directed against the pope, Ockham developed a new theory of rights based on both reason and Scripture. He defined a right as a power conformed to reason, but he also appealed to the texts of the New Testament that referred to Christian law as a law of liberty. Christian freedom, Ockham argued, required that a pope's power be limited by the natural rights of his subjects. The argument was presented most clearly in Ockham's *Breviloquium*, a treatise against tyranny. There Ockham began with a declaration that papal tyranny was "opposed to the rights and liberties granted by God and nature," and he added that "to neglect common rights is a vice." In his defense of natural rights, Ockham was mainly concerned to argue that the powers of temporal rulers and the rights of property owners were derived from natural law and not from the pope, but he also recognized a sphere of moral autonomy where individuals must be free to shape their own lives. Such things as taking a vow of virginity or entering the priesthood were good in themselves, but they could not be commanded by the pope. Such choices, Ockham wrote, were "liberties granted to mortals by God and nature."[19]

French philosopher, Jean Gerson, writing around 1400, developed Ockham's argument in a new way. Like Ockham he defined a right as a power in accordance with right reason. But then Gerson went on to argue that, since all creatures were directed by the reason of God, they could all be said to have a right to their own way of being. "The sun has a right to shine," he wrote, ". . . the swallow has a right to build its nest."[20] The argument was often discussed in the neo-scholastic writings of the sixteenth century, but it was seldom approved by later theologians.

MEDIEVAL TO MODERN

The philosophy of natural law developed by the Spanish neo-scholastics of the sixteenth century was Janus-faced. The authors wove together threads of thought from the past in new syntheses, but they also emphasized themes that would be important for the future, especially ideas concerning natural rights and the sources and limits of political power.

In the early part of the century, Spanish philosopher Francisco Vitoria vigorously defended the natural rights of the Native Americans in the

---

[19] William of Ockham, *A Short Discourse on Tyrannical Government*, ed. A. S. McGrade, trans. J. Killcullen (Cambridge: Cambridge University Press, 1992), 39, 44, 57, 90–91.
[20] Jean Gerson, *Oeuvres completes, vol. 3, De vita spirituali anime*, ed. P. Glorieux (Paris: Desclée, 1965), 142.

lands conquered by Spain, but in the course of his argument he rather impatiently brushed aside Gerson's view that rights could inhere also in irrational creatures. We do not injure any right, Vitoria wrote, when we deprive a wolf of its prey or close a shutter against the sun.[21] When considering the source of political authority Vitoria maintained that government must be based on consent, because at first everyone had an equal right to self-defense and there was no intrinsic reason why one should rule over others. But Vitoria also held that once a ruler was instituted, he held his power directly from God, not as a grant from the community.[22]

Writing two generations later, around 1600, Francisco Suarez rejected any idea of a divine right of kings. He held that political power came from God only as a remote cause, in the sense that God had implanted in humans from the beginning a capacity to form political communities which then possessed the power to institute governments "by the force of natural law alone."[23] Suarez's own teaching on natural law was based principally on the work of Aquinas, supplemented by ideas of later theologians, and by frequent references to juristic sources. When, for instance, Suarez considered the origin of property, he turned back to the old canonistic argument about a permissive natural law.

In the field of legal philosophy, Suarez made a notable contribution by his solution of a problem that had become a matter of urgent concern in late medieval thought. Are the precepts of natural law binding on humans because they are commands of God? Or do they derive obligatory force from the power of human reason itself to distinguish between good and evil? Suarez presented a compromise solution, arguing that reason both distinguished between good and evil and commanded the one and forbade the other. But this was because the reason implanted in man was itself a sufficient sign of the divine will for humans.[24]

A little later in the seventeenth century, the ideas of Suarez and his medieval predecessors were taken up and developed further by the Dutch scholar Hugo Grotius, later renowned as a major founder of modern international law. Grotius was a Protestant and a noted humanist who wrote in an ornate Latin style, decked out with innumerable references to classical authors. Other Protestant humanists, who deplored the "barbarous" Latin

---

[21] Francisco Vitoria, *De Indis recenter inventis*, in *Obras de Francisco de Vitoria*, ed. T. Urdanoz (Madrid: Biblioteca de Autores Cristianos, 1960), 661.   [22] Vitoria, *De potestate civili*, in *Obras*, 159, 164.

[23] Francisco Suarez, *De legibus ac Deo legislatore*, in *Selections from Three Works of Francisco Suarez S. J.*, vol. I, ed. James Brown Scott (Oxford: Clarendon Press, 1944), 3.2.4, p. 202.

[24] *Ibid.*, 2.6.24, p. 128.

of the neo-scholastics, as well as their Catholic religious teachings, could more readily accept some of their teachings on natural law when they came filtered through the works of Grotius.

In his own work on natural law Grotius held, like Suarez, that the moral judgments of human reason were a sufficient indication of the will of God; but he also wrote that the rules of natural law could be derived from the fact of human sociability. He added, in a famous phrase, that such rules would be valid "even if we were to grant, what cannot be granted without the greatest wickedness, that there is no God . . ."[25] Grotius himself was no skeptic, but his "impious hypothesis" could encourage the growth of more secular doctrines of natural law. The major thinkers of the next century were indeed seldom atheists. Most of them were Protestant Christians (of varying degrees of fervor), but there was a change of emphasis in their writings. Aquinas and Suarez had both started out from the eternal law of God, and then moved on to consider the reflection of eternal law in the natural law known to man. The writers of the early modern period usually retained the idea of a divinely ordained natural law, but they argued, as it were, "from the bottom up". They began from an undifferentiated human nature existing in a "state of nature", and then explained how institutions of law and government emerged from this original condition by freely made contracts among individuals. One might say that their first rule of natural law was not "Good must be done," but "Contracts must be kept."

Inevitably perhaps, the various authors projected on their hypothetical states of nature the characteristics that would readily lead on to the form of government they preferred. Thomas Hobbes, living amidst the turmoil of the English Civil War, favored the institution of an absolute monarchy. Accordingly, he presented an ugly picture of life in a state of nature as a war of every man against every man, a condition that reasonable people would want to escape from at any cost. In this state of nature, Hobbes wrote, every man had a right to protect his own life and this was an absolute right, a right "even to another's body." Hobbes's law of nature was developed as a way of implementing this right. Security of life could best be attained by the establishment of peace, so the first law of nature was that peace should be sought. Hobbes went on to spell out a series of rules of behavior conducive to this end. But at a later point he wrote that real laws must be commands of a superior, so that the rules of natural law he had enumerated were mere "theorems" unless indeed we consider them also as commands

---

[25] Hugo Grotius, *De iure belli et pacis*, vol. I, *Prolegomena*, trans. Francis Kelsey (Oxford: Clarendon Press, 1925), sec. 11.

of God.[26] Whether Hobbes believed in such a God is, however, far from certain.

Hobbes's solution to the anarchy of a state of nature was not to trust in divine law but to institute an absolute sovereign, a "mortal god," here on earth. In Hobbes's theory, every man made a covenant with all the others to submit his will to a sovereign chosen by a majority of them. Such a sovereign was necessarily absolute because the subjects, in submitting to him, had authorized all his acts in advance. And in Hobbes's theory, there was no covenant establishing mutual obligations between ruler and community, but only a transfer of power to the ruler.[27]

John Locke set out with a different purpose from that of Hobbes; he wanted to justify resistance to tyranny, specifically to the supposed tyranny of King James II of England in the 1680s. Locke therefore presented a more traditional account of natural law – a law ordained by God but knowable through human reason – and described a more benign state of nature. In Locke's state of nature everyone was free and equal. This was not a state of license, however, because humans had a natural law to guide them. They were free to act "within the permission of the law of nature," and this law required them to preserve their own lives and not to injure others. For Locke, the fundamental law of nature was "the preservation of mankind."[28]

Although Locke's state of nature was kindlier than that of Hobbes, it had one major defect. There was no impartial authority to enforce the law; instead, each individual had the power to execute the law of nature by punishing offenders. But this could lead to a state of chaos. The remedy was for the people to institute a government whose purpose was "the mutual preservation of their lives, liberties, and estates." To establish such a government, a group of individuals first "incorporated." Each individual agreed with all the others to give up his own executive power to the community that they formed; then a government was created by a second agreement between the community and the rulers. The government could take several forms, but one type of regime was excluded in Locke's argument – an absolute arbitrary sovereignty with power of life and death over the subjects. Humans did not have an arbitrary power over their own lives, so they could not transfer such power to a ruler.[29]

Locke repeatedly referred to government power as a "trust" held from the people, a trust that conveyed an authority to act for the good of all and to

---

[26] Thomas Hobbes, *Leviathan*, ed. M. Oakeshott (Oxford: Basil Blackwell Publishing, 1944), I. 13–15, pp. 80–85, 105.   [27] *Ibid.*, II. 17, pp. 112–13.
[28] John Locke, *Two Treatises of Government*, ed. P. Laslett, 2d edn (Cambridge: Cambridge University Press, 1970), II. 2,9, pp. 287–90, 370.   [29] *Ibid.*, II. 8–9,15, pp. 348–51, 368–69, 400–01.

rule according to standing laws. If a ruler betrayed his trust by ruling as a tyrant, the people had a right to revoke the trust, to rebel and depose him. They would not then fall into a state of anarchy but would revert to the political community they had originally formed, which could then institute a new government.[30]

Samuel Pufendorf, another major thinker of the seventeenth century, presented a voluntarist theory of a natural law grounded on divine command. But he, too, held that reason could ascertain God's will for humans. Writing before Locke, Pufendorf also held that two stages were necessary in the institution of a government – first a compact that established a civil society, then a second compact between ruler and people in which the ruler promised to maintain peace and security. But Pufendorf's state was more absolutist than Locke's. Where Locke inveighed against tyranny Pufendorf complained about "turbulent and querulous subjects." He did, however, distinguish between an absolute power to rule for the public good and a power to "murder a man for mere pleasure,", and he conceded an ultimate right of resistance against such arbitrary abuse of power.[31]

During the eighteenth century, Pufendorf's ideas were used to defend enlightened absolutism in Germany. Locke's work helped to shape the thought of the founding fathers of the American republic. In France, the ideas of universal liberty and equality that had always been inherent in the natural law tradition took on an explosive force with the outbreak of the French Revolution of 1789.

MODERN TRENDS

After the excesses of the French Revolution, theories of natural law fell out of favor with jurists and philosophers. Already in the eighteenth century, Scottish philosopher David Hume had attacked all such theories by arguing that we cannot infer moral values from factual observations of nature, including human nature. Then, in the following century, anthropological relativism began to undermine belief in a moral law common to all peoples. At the same time, new movements of political thought grew up that rejected the old tradition – utilitarianism for liberals and Marxism for socialists. To many thinkers, natural law seemed only an outmoded relic of the past.

[30] *Ibid.*, II. 19, pp. 430–32, 445–46.
[31] Samuel von Pufendorf, *De iure naturae et gentium*, 8 vols. (Oxford: Clarendon Press, 1934), I: 7.8.3, 7.8.7, pp. 756, 761.

A major change came in the second half of the twentieth century, inspired mainly by moral revulsion against the atrocities of the Nazis in World War II. One reaction was defined by Isaiah Berlin as a return to the ancient notion of natural law. But the aspect of the natural law tradition that was most prominently revived was the idea of natural rights, now renamed human rights. The United Nations *Universal Declaration of Human Rights* of 1948 was followed by many covenants and treaties designed to give effect to its principles and extend them. The language of rights became so prevalent in moral discourse that some enthusiasts applied it indiscriminately to humans and animals and even trees, and this, in turn, evoked criticisms of abuses of "rights talk."[32]

Modern rights are not grounded on any one philosophical system; there are now Kantian and Aristotelian and utilitarian theories of rights in vogue. But we need not deplore the diversity. The fact that a doctrine can be defended within several different systems of thought suggests that it has an intrinsic vitality or even indispensability. Religiously grounded theories of rights continue to flourish alongside secular ones. Martin Luther King, Jr. quoted Augustine and Aquinas in his famous "Letter From a Birmingham Jail"; Archbishop Tutu's struggle against apartheid in South Africa was inspired by his Christian faith; Pope John XXIII led the Catholic Church to a new commitment to human rights in the decrees of the Second Vatican Council (1962–1965).[33]

The body of modern writing on natural law is not so great as the voluminous literature on human rights, and often natural law concepts are implied rather than overtly articulated in modern criticisms of legal positivism or consequentialist ethics. Among the more influential contributors to the discussion, Ronald Dworkin based a theory of justice on the doctrine that all persons are entitled to equal concern and respect; in earlier discourse this would have been called a principle of natural law. Lon Fuller argued that the procedures through which the law is actually shaped depend on underlying, taken-for-granted ideas of natural justice. Leo Strauss defended "classical natural right" against relativist criticisms. Probably the most fully worked out modern theory of natural law is the one presented by John Finnis. Arguing against Hume and in the spirit of Aquinas (though without Aquinas's metaphysics), Finnis maintains that "practical reasonableness" can discern some goods essential to human flourishing – such things as life itself, health, knowledge, friendship, aesthetic joy – and can guide our moral choices in instantiating them.

---

[32] See further the chapter by Michael Perry herein.
[33] See further the chapter by Kent Greenawalt herein.

Whether or not a tradition of natural law persists in jurisprudence and moral philosophy, it seems certain at least that humans will continue to grapple with the concerns that inspired the tradition, concerns about the relationship between religion, morality, and law, and about the possibility of discerning universal moral values amid all the variety of human experience.

RECOMMENDED READING

Crowe, M. B. *The Changing Profile of the Natural Law.* The Hague: Martinus Nijhoff Publishers, 1977.

D'Entrèves, A. P. *Natural Law: An Historical Survey.* New York: Harper and Row, 1965.

Finnis, John. *Natural Law and Natural Rights.* Oxford: Clarendon Press, 1979.

Gierke, Otto von. *Natural Law and the Theory of Society, 1500–1800.* Translated by Ernst Barker. Cambridge: Cambridge University Press, 1958.

Mäkinen, V. and Korkman, P., eds. *Transformations in Medieval and Early Modern Rights Discourse.* Dordrecht: Springer, 2006.

Maritain, Jacques. *The Rights of Man and Natural Law.* Translated by D. C. Anson. New York: Gordian Press, 1971.

Strauss, Leo. *Natural Right and History.* Chicago: University of Chicago Press, 1965.

Tierney, Brian. *The Idea of Natural Rights. Studies on Natural Rights, Natural Law and Church Law, 1150–1625.* Grand Rapids, MI: Wm. B. Eerdmans Publishing, 1997.

Tuck, Richard. *Natural Rights Theories: Their Origin and Development,* Cambridge: Cambridge University Press, 1979.

6 "Martin Luther King, Jr. Waits to Address the Combined Session of the Massachusetts State Legislature at the Massachusetts State House in Boston on April 23, 1965."

CHAPTER FIVE

Conscientious objection, civil disobedience, and resistance

Kent Greenawalt

When are people justified in disobeying the law? This has been a central question for Christians who have reflected on the relation between their religion and the demands of the governments under which they live. An essay on the subject could comfortably be organized exclusively along historical lines, tracing attitudes in the early church up to the present. My treatment of this question indicates historical developments, including social circumstances that have helped to produce various theories, but it also tries to show how fundamental differences in Christian understandings about human nature and about how to discern the truth can influence attitudes toward compliance with law. One of my aspirations is to help people who read this chapter – whether Christians or not – to sort out their own sense of when an individual is morally justified in breaking legal rules. A brief historical survey of past understandings may assist their contemporary appraisal of relevant considerations.

DEFINING KEY TERMS

I begin by clarifying our modern understanding of the three crucial concepts in the chapter. A person who has a "conscientious objection" to performing an act believes she should not perform the act, even though the immediate upshot is a harshly negative consequence for herself or for people she cares about.[1] In modern life, the paradigm of conscientious objection is conscientious objection to military service. A person who has a conscientious objection to killing in war thinks he should suffer death rather than kill. He may not have the moral courage actually to suffer death but he believes he should. Perhaps we would concede that someone has a conscientious objection to performing jury duty even if she believes she

---

[1] See further Kent Greenawalt, *Conflicts of Law and Morality* (Oxford: Clarendon Press, 1987), 311–47; Kent Greenawalt, *Religion and the Constitution, Vol. I, Free Exercise and Fairness* (Princeton, NJ: Princeton University Press, 2006).

should serve rather than die, but she would need to believe she should suffer other harsh penalties the state might mete out, rather than serve. Not every moral complaint about the law's compulsion amounts to a conscientious objection. A citizen whose work is aiding desperately ill persons and their families might conclude that being required to sit around all day to see if lawyers will pick her for a jury is such a ludicrous waste of her time it amounts to an outrage, but she would rather show up for jury service than spend a month in jail. She has a moral complaint against serving but not a conscientious objection.

The basis for conscientious objection tends to be deontological and absolute, not consequentialist. The objector thinks that certain actions are wrong without finely evaluating likely earthly consequences – good or bad – and that in no (or almost no) circumstances should he perform those actions. That is not to deny that conscientious objectors often have strong opinions about consequences and that some are drawn to their positions by the prospect of horrible consequences. Thus, many pacifists who object to military service assert that only a pacifist approach can bring peace among nations, and the terrors of modern warfare lead some to their pacifist outlook. Religious conscientious objectors often have a rather different view about consequences. Whatever one making an ordinary secular evaluation of probable consequences might conclude, they trust that God will make sure – in this realm or the next – that living by God's word will not ultimately do harm to one's self or others. With such a faith, a person might suppose that refusing to try to stop a Hitler by force will in some final analysis yield good rather than unmitigated disaster.

By "resistance," I mean forcible opposition or resistance to the government in power, like the American Revolutionary War and the Communist Revolution in Russia, as well as violent acts, such as assassinations of high government officials, aimed at dislodging those exercising political power. Justifications of resistance rely on particular circumstances and consequences in ways not typical for conscientious objection. Apart from violent anarchists who believe that all government should be overthrown, a supporter of resistance needs to explain why particular governments are bad enough to warrant being overthrown. Violent resistance costs human lives and is deeply unsettling; a government must be failing in very important ways before such measures are warranted. And violent resistance is definitely not desirable unless it promises some likelihood of success. Here we can distinguish a "right to resist" from "justified resistance" and a "duty to resist." A truly atrocious tyranny may itself create a right of citizens to resist, but they would engage in justified resistance only if they had a chance to succeed and if the consequences they would produce would probably not overwhelm any good they might accomplish. We might speak of a "duty to resist" only if the reasons to overthrow a government were especially compelling and the likely gain much greater than any probable harm.

In the evaluation of likely success and the standard of proportionality of good to harm, these aspects of claims about justified resistance connect to theories of just war (a subject that receives brief mention but not close examination in later parts of this chapter). Questions about resistance and just war both bear on a vital concern in the modern international order: when may international or regional organizations or powerful individual countries justifiably intervene to replace a government or to stop it from harming its own citizens? When the ground for intervention is one country's threat to other countries, outside intervention *might* be justified even though the citizens within the threatening country would lack a right to overthrow their government. But when the basis for justified outside intervention is what a government does to its own citizens – one part of the rationale offered for the war the United States, with allies, waged against Iraq early in the twenty-first century – it follows that the citizens themselves had a right to resist (although internal resistance might have been unjustified because it was doomed to futility).

With resistance and just war, questions arise as to what measures are morally legitimate if the effort itself is justifiable. If a group of revolutionaries is attempting to overthrow an evil government, may it intentionally kill innocent citizens to disrupt the regime? This chapter does not explore these questions of justifiable and unjustifiable means of resistance, though that is the subject of a substantial literature, historical and current, on just war.

"Civil disobedience" falls somewhere between conscientious objection and resistance. Identifying the requisites for civil disobedience is itself a complex topic, but I shall use a "minimalist" definition that I believe is appropriate.[2] Acts of disobedience to law must be non-violent. They must be open (violators act in the open for all to see, or they quickly reveal themselves). Violators must aim to alter the behavior of officials or private individuals or organizations. And violators must be willing to submit to punishment. These conditions are put abstractly, so a word may help about exactly what they require. The disobedience must be non-violent, but that does not mean it has to be non-coercive. Demonstrators who block traffic

---

[2] See further Greenawalt, *Conflicts of Law and Morality*, 226–43. Perhaps the best known proposal of a more restrictive definition is in John Rawls, *A Theory of Justice* (Cambridge, MA: Harvard University Press, 1971), 363–68.

in order to get a traffic light installed may hope that the inconvenience they generate will cause officials to provide the light. That is a kind of weak coercion. Most civil disobedience takes place in open view, but my sense of openness embraces persons who secretly break into a government office and pour blood on draft files, so long as they quickly announce what they have done. Civil disobedience is typically aimed at government policies, such as war and racial segregation, but I include similar disobedience, such as a trespass on a private power company's nuclear facility, aimed at getting a private company to alter its behavior. Finally, those who commit civil disobedience must make themselves available for punishment. They can neither hide nor use coercive tactics, such as shutting down facilities, to extract a promise from authorities not to punish them. They do not have to submit to punishment in the sense of agreeing that they *should* be punished; they can be engaged in civil disobedience even if they think the government's response should not include punishment.

Given disagreements over exactly what *constitutes* civil disobedience and over what conditions are requisites for *justified* civil disobedience, we must avoid getting too tangled in the various definitions and remember that the crucial concern is when disobeying the law might be morally justified. It is worth noting that many acts called civil disobedience during the civil rights movement were believed by the demonstrators to be constitutionally protected, and on many occasions their understandings were vindicated by courts. Acts that people believe are legally protected do not count as civil disobedience in the sense I am using the term here.

The fundamental idea behind civil disobedience is that some instances of it may be justified even though violent or secret acts, or acts committed by people determined to avoid punishment, would not be justified. Of course, civil disobedience *might* be a desirable tactic when outright resistance would also be justified. If peaceful means may work as well as violent ones, better to try them. The interesting question is what makes civil disobedience distinctively different from other illegal actions, so that it may be justified although violent or secret acts would not be.

It bears noting that some other illegal acts directed against government injustice might be defensible in conditions that would not warrant outright resistance.[3] To take a stark example from American history, a citizen of New York in 1840 might have been justified in using force to prevent the capture of a fugitive slave, even though his state government was sufficiently legitimate to make resistance wrongful.

---

[3] See Greenawalt, *Conflicts of Law and Morality*, 244–68.

BASIC STRANDS OF CHRISTIAN UNDERSTANDING

A Christian's attitude toward conscientious objection, resistance, and civil disobedience is likely to be closely related to his or her overall religious understanding. In this section, I point out some basic divisions, leaving for subsequent sections the working out of particular attitudes toward law violation.[4]

Natural reasoning versus the authority of Scripture or tradition

Some Christian writers adopt positions that they believe can be defended on the basis of a natural reason shared by non-Christians; others rely heavily on distinctly religious sources. The greater one's reliance on specific Christian sources, the greater the likelihood her approach to disobedience will not fit the views of people whose approach is secular.

Commandment, model, or inspiration

What one takes as the nature of religious guidance can also be tremendously important. To oversimplify greatly, we might find in the Bible or church teachings commandments or rules about how to live, a model in the lives of Jesus and others, or a more diffuse source of inspiration about what matters in a human life.

Perfectionist or consequentialist

A Christian who discerns in the Gospels a perfectionist ethic that should guide our behavior will adopt a very different attitude from one who believes that any perfectionist ethic one finds there is meant to illuminate the degree of human imperfection, not to guide behavior in this world. A central illustration is Jesus' encouragement to turn the other cheek (Matthew 5:39–40). Does that mean we should never return military force with counterforce? Christian pacifists and non-pacifists disagree.

The political realm as important or not

Some Christians believe the political realm is fundamentally unimportant, that Christians should concentrate on their spiritual lives. Others assume

---

[4] See elaboration in Kent Greenawalt, "Reflections on Christian Jurisprudence and Political Philosophy," in *The Teachings of Modern Christianity on Law, Politics, and Human Nature*, 2 vol., ed. John Witte, Jr. and Frank S. Alexander (New York: Columbia University Press, 2006), I: 715–51.

that the political realm is a significant domain for people leading fulfilling lives and for achieving a degree of justice, both of which matter from a Christian perspective.

Human beings as good or fallen

Over time, Christians have embraced radically different perspectives on human nature. Putting aside modern views about the social construction of human characteristics, the basic division has been between a relatively benign view of human rationality and moral capacity, represented by scholars like Thomas Aquinas (who drew from Aristotle), and a sense that people are mired in sin, unable by their own devices to come close to lives that are rational and moral, an outlook shared by Augustine and Martin Luther. Among those who hold the latter view, a critical division exists between those who believe that lives on this earth can be radically transformed for the good by Christian conversion and commitment, and those who think that our inclinations to immoderate and irrational pursuit of self-interest are affected only modestly by becoming Christian.

Governments promoting good lives or maintaining minimal order

Closely connected to divergent views about human nature and the importance of the political realm are contesting conceptions of the role of government. Can it help in a substantial way to promote good lives among its citizens, or is its function to preserve a modicum of order among essentially sinful people? Thomas Aquinas took the former position, Augustine the latter.

Whom to trust?

Christians over the centuries have differed greatly over whom to trust. We may cast the basic division as whether, in matters of religion, ethics, and government, to trust ordinary people or those in authority; but matters are much more complicated than that. First, we need to distinguish between religious authorities and political authorities. A modern Roman Catholic believer in traditional hierarchical religion might nonetheless distrust secular political authorities in comparison with ordinary citizens; a Protestant who accepts "the priesthood of all believers" in matters of religion might place greater trust for political subjects in officials than in average citizens. Second, one might believe that people in general are deeply untrustworthy, but that true Christians (however defined) can be trusted in the political as well as religious realm. Third, some Christian writers have distinguished lower political authorities from the highest authorities and from ordinary citizens, trusting those subsidiary authorities to keep the higher authorities in line. Fourth, the basis for trust might or might not depend upon religious sources, and "trust" may be less trust in the ordinary sense than a kind of resignation. Christian sources going back to Paul have spoken of political authority as ordained by God (see Romans 13:1–7). This idea could underlie a belief that, for the most part, those exercising the power of government will act for the common welfare, but sometimes it has been taken to mean that regardless of whether rulers are good or bad, competent or incompetent, Christians should accept them and what they do.

Fear of tyranny or fear of anarchy

Someone who fears anarchy as by far the worst political condition may accept even bad government as preferable to the risk of ineffective government. If, on the other hand, one's primary fear is of tyranny, believing it can be worse than anarchy or that overthrowing tyrants will not lead to anarchy, one may support actions to deprive bad governments of power.

Emphasis on right or duty

Christianity, like religions generally, has emphasized moral duties over rights. People are called to live in a certain way; what they may or may not claim against others is of secondary importance. Yet, claims of moral and political rights are common to Christian leaders in the modern era. John Locke, perhaps the most influential political theorist for American revolutionaries, relied significantly on Christian premises in developing his theory of natural rights.[5] His fundamental ideas, repeated in many American pulpits in the late eighteenth century, continue to affect political thought across religious lines. Along with rights go correlative duties, and duties can usually (though not always) be translated into rights; but the relative emphasis matters. A rights theory fits more comfortably with notions that government needs to justify itself and that if it fails miserably, it can be overthrown.

---

[5] See Jeremy Waldron, *God, Locke and Equality* (Cambridge: Cambridge University Press, 2002) and the chapters by Brian Tierney and Michael J. Perry herein.

Standards for the select or for everyone?

Adherents to a religion may believe that the standards for their behavior should or should not also govern how outsiders act. Within Judaism, many guides to behavior are meant only for Jews, and Jews do not proselytize outsiders to become Jewish. Christianity is universalist in aspiration; traditionally Christians have believed that the truth they accept should also be accepted by others. In this sense, they rarely assume that standards of behavior are ultimately only for those who happen to be Christian. But many groups of Christians, especially those who embrace a perfectionist understanding of the Gospel, have conceived of themselves as a small distinct remnant in a broader society, most of whose members will never accept Christianity in its pure form. Members of these groups may follow strict standards of behavior, neither expecting those in the mainstream culture to do likewise, nor making efforts to persuade them to do so. In modern American society, one can compare the Amish with the Jehovah's Witnesses in this respect. The Amish do not reach out to persuade outsiders to accept Amish beliefs and practices; the Jehovah's Witnesses devote substantial efforts to convert others to their perspectives.

SUBMISSION TO POLITICAL AUTHORITY AND CONSCIENTIOUS OBJECTION

One important strand in Christian thought and practice has been submission to political authority, except on certain matters which a good Christian does not and cannot obey. According to this understanding, the primary motivation for refusing to obey is not to change the government's demands, but rather because the Christian cannot in good conscience perform those demands. This was the approach of the early Christian church,[6] influenced by some combination of passages in what became the New Testament, by the absence of any overtly political aspect in the teachings of Jesus, by the belief that the fast approaching end of days rendered mundane political life insignificant, and perhaps by the overwhelming power of Roman government.

Among the crucial biblical passages was Christ's injunction to "[r]ender therefore to Caesar the things that are Caesar's, and to God the things that are God's" (Matthew 22:21) and his comment that his kingdom was "not

---

[6] See Herbert A. Deane, *The Political and Social Ideas of St. Augustine* (New York: Columbia University Press, 1963), 5–10.

of this world" (John 8:23). Christ's refusal of earthly power when tempted by the devil in the wilderness (Matthew 4:8–10) was also taken as suggesting that Christians should not concern themselves much with processes of government. Paul's Letter to the Romans was more explicit: "Let every person be subject to the governing authorities. For there is no authority except from God, and those that exist have been instituted by God. Therefore he who resists the authorities resists what God has appointed, and those who resist will incur judgment" (Romans 13:1–2). Paul went on to say that those whose behavior is good need not fear magistrates who are there to serve God for their benefit, but those who break the law should be afraid of authorities who carry out God's revenge by inflicting punishment. People should obey political authority not only to avoid punishment but also for conscience's sake (Romans 13:3–6; see also 1 Peter 2:13–17).

This passage from Paul has been a major point of reference for theorists reflecting on what Christians owe to government.[7] Because Paul did not assume that the political authorities would themselves be Christian, he was asserting that non-Christian governments are established by God. Paul did not directly address perversions of government power when officials fail to act for the good of those they govern. What if they reward evil and punish good? Does that change the responsibility to comply, or should people nevertheless submit on the assumption that the exercise of political power remains within God's purposes, however incomprehensible at the moment? Paul does not tell us, but he gives no indication that subjects are to measure the legitimacy of their governments.

In one crucial respect early Christians did not submit to governmental authority, and many suffered death as a consequence. They believed they should not deny their religious faith or swear allegiance to pagan gods.[8] That most people within the Empire may have regarded the Roman religion as more civic than transcendent did not matter. Adherence to the true God was rendering to God what was God's. One can easily imagine a consequentialist argument that it is better temporarily to deny one's faith publicly than to suffer a terrible fate, but one does not find such arguments in Christian writings down through the centuries. However most modern Christians might respond to such dire circumstances, the prevailing assumption has been that one should not deny one's Christian faith, even if the law requires it.

In the history of Christianity, what we would now classify as conscientious

---

[7] See further the chapters by Luke Johnson and Mathias Schmoeckel herein.
[8] Deane, *The Political and Social Ideas of St. Augustine*, 8–9.

objection has usually, though not always, been accompanied by an attitude of general submission to political authority. For many early Christians, this attitude was qualified by a belief that they should not participate in the army or other government service.

Some radical Protestants have found various injunctions in the Bible not to behave in certain ways. Notably, in Matthew, Jesus says that one should not seek "an eye for an eye" or "a tooth for a tooth;" rather "Do not resist one who is evil. But if anyone strikes you on the right cheek, turn to him the other also" (Matthew 5:38–39). Among groups trying to live by this New Testament ethic, these passages are taken to support pacifism and non-violence more generally. Responding to the passage where Jesus, having remarked on the traditional saying that people should keep their oaths to the Lord, tells his audience "Do not swear at all" (Matthew 5:33–37), some Christians have believed they should never take oaths, even if required by law to do so. Jehovah's Witnesses believe that other biblical passages (e.g., Leviticus 24:10–14; Acts 15:20, 28–29) indicate that people should never consume blood; these underlie their refusal to accept blood transfusions, even in cases of medical emergency.

Some radical Protestants, like many early Christians, feel called upon to withdraw from participation in the state more broadly. Although they may not resist the law, and although they may believe political governance is required for those who are not saved, they nonetheless feel they cannot join actively in the institutions of government – refusing to serve on juries, never voting, and perhaps refusing to pay some forms of taxes. For groups that rely on the Bible to conclude that particular acts of participation in government are forbidden, conscientious objection to performing legal duties bears little or no connection to acts of resistance or civil disobedience.

That is not true for Christians whose conscientious objection has more of a basis in likely consequences on this earth. One thinks, for example, of many modern Quakers whose pacifism is informed both by Christian values *and* estimates that non-violence is far more likely to lead to peace and stability than military responses. Such beliefs fit well with a sense that civil, non-violent, disobedience of law can be a constructive tactic toward a more just society.

Questions about conscientious objection concern not only individual attitudes about obeying laws but also how the state should respond to objectors. A government can punish those who refuse to comply. Or it can decline to require behavior it might otherwise require. Or it can make a specific exception for conscientious objectors. The second approach is taken by Article VI of the US federal constitution with respect to oaths; people can "affirm" rather than swear an oath. With few exceptions, no relief is given to those who object in conscience to paying taxes. They must pay their taxes or live so they do not incur the relevant tax liabilities. Throughout American history, military conscription has been accompanied by an exemption for pacifists. Historically, objectors would often have to send a horse and provisions in their stead; in modern times, objectors have been required to perform alternative civilian service.

One might address the issue of an appropriate government response from the standpoint of non-religious political philosophy or from one's own religious outlook. Without going into detail, I shall simply assert that in a country like the United States whose population is dominantly Christian, in at least some sense, a tradition that has long had perfectionist and pacifist threads, government should accommodate strong claims of conscience, so long as it can do so without serious fraud, injury, or unfairness to others. I believe this conclusion holds whether one examines the issue from (most) religious premises or from a perspective that refrains from any judgment about religious truth. (This may well be the right approach for *any* modern society.)

RESISTANCE

Since the time of the early church, Christian theorists have asked what Christians should do in response to tyrannical government. We may break down varying attitudes into three rough categories. The first is that resistance is never justified, that one should submit to the government, however tyrannical. The second is that resistance is warranted when a government suppresses the true faith. Early Christians did not resist Roman government even when they were victims of harsh persecution, but many Christians of later eras have believed that governments that suppress true religion may be overthrown. The third attitude is that other great injustices may warrant resistance. Although various Christians in colonial America objected to the treatment of their specific religions, it was other injustices in how the mother country treated her colonies that were thought to warrant military rebellion. Among Christians who have defended resistance to tyranny, some have discerned a right and responsibility in ordinary citizens, others have looked to subsidiary political authorities.

The duty to submit to political authorities was developed in its most uncompromising form in the writings of Augustine, who lived during the political and cultural disintegration of Rome's classical Empire in the late fourth and fifth centuries.[9] Augustine believed that the nature of most people is deeply sinful; members of a "worldly city," they are moved by greed, lust for domination, and pride. In contrast to this worldly city is a small City of God, whose citizens live by faith and serve one another in charity. Rejecting the Donatist notion of a "pure" church, Augustine was careful not to identify the City of God with the much larger visible church.

Persons who receive God's grace are incapable of living perfect lives in this world; they continue to be drawn to sin. A government's role is to suppress sin by fear of punishment and by earthly rewards, achieving a kind of negative peace that guards against overt conflict. An institution created by God in response to the fall into sin, government is not a means by which human beings attain genuine virtue or happiness. Nevertheless in this life, members of the City of God, as well as those of the worldly city, require the coercion of government and law to create a minimal order.

Although Augustine had a decidedly limited view of what government could do, he nevertheless urged that political authorities were divinely ordained and even the most evil rulers must be obeyed as a matter of conscience. Their deeds will chastise the wicked and test the fortitude of good people. Bad government is far preferable to anarchy and chaos. The only kind of laws Christians need not obey are those contrary to God's ordinances, and even then people have no right to resist or rebel. Augustine claimed that pagan religion had much to do with the fall of the Roman Empire, but his views about submission to authority applied to pagan as well as Christian governments.

Augustine differed from many of the early Church Fathers, as he rejected pacifism and approved of participation by Christians in government. Good men who have the talent to rule have an obligation to do so. Rulers may fight just wars to punish other rulers whose acts are contrary to norms of worldly justice. They may defend against aggressors and even fight an offensive war if another ruler has failed to repair certain wrongs. The decision whether a war is just is exclusively the ruler's; the soldier's duty is to obey.

During the medieval period, in which the church exercised powerful political authority, Augustine's pessimistic appraisal of human nature, his sense of government's limited role, and his belief in an absolute duty to obey played a less significant part, but similar understandings reemerged with Martin Luther and John Calvin. Little interested in politics, Luther wrote: "It is in no wise proper for anyone who would be a Christian to set

---

[9] My account draws heavily on *ibid.*

himself up against his government, whether it acts justly or unjustly. There are no better works than to obey and serve all those who are set over us as superiors."[10]

Calvin had a somewhat more positive view than Luther of what government could do, but, with limited equivocations, he also asserted a duty of passive obedience. God may punish evil rulers, but that is not the responsibility of subjects. "We are not only subject to the authority of princes who perform their office towards us uprightly and faithfully as they ought, but also to the authority of all who, by whatever means, have got control of affairs, even though they perform not a whit of the princes' office."[11] Calvin did note constitutional schemes in which "inferior magistrates" have a duty to resist tyranny (a theory greatly expanded by his successors), but this was far from a general right of citizens to resist.

At least within Western Christendom, one of the main competitors to the Augustinian understanding of human nature and law has been the natural law approach strongly identified with Thomas Aquinas, still the prevailing philosophy within the Roman Catholic Church today. Human beings are essentially social, said Aquinas; with rational and moral capacities, they can identify the good and are inclined toward it. All people are subject to the natural law. Christian revelation may be a surer avenue to truth than natural reason, but revelation confirms and complements (rather than departs from) what natural reason indicates. Apart from the church, the state, serving the common good, is the highest form of community. It can promote the full flourishing of its citizens, helping them to lead virtuous and happy lives. On this view, the state is more than a device made necessary by fallen man; it is a healthy, positive aspect of human life.

For Aquinas, human law was derived from natural law. A positive human law that violates natural law is, in some sense, not really law. Although he indicated that people may need to comply to avoid "scandal or disturbance," such laws do not have the same claim to obedience as laws that conform with natural law. Human laws can violate natural law if they are not directed to the common good, or if they impose liabilities and benefits in unjust proportion. These violations expand well beyond Augustine's notion of laws that violate God's ordinances.[12]

---

[10] Quoted in George H. Sabine, *A History of Political Theory*, 2nd edn (New York: Henry Holt & Co., Inc., 1950), 361.

[11] Quoted in Quentin Skinner, *The Age of Reformation*, in *The Foundations of Political Thought*, 2 vols. (Cambridge: Cambridge University Press, 1978), II: 194.

[12] See Greenawalt, *Conflicts of Law and Morality*, 187–89. See further the chapter by Brian Tierney herein.

The ruler has a responsibility to act for the common good; he exercises a trust bestowed upon him by the community. The consent of the people is necessary to establish legitimate political authority, but when they establish a lawful ruler, people alienate, rather than delegate, their original authority. Drawing in this respect more from earlier classical authors and from medieval theorists than from Aristotle, Aquinas distinguished tyranny from "lawful" government, and justified resistance to tyranny by the people, subject to the condition that their actions will injure the common good less than the abuses they aim to eliminate.

As the Protestant Reformation developed in the last half of the sixteenth century, more robust Protestant theories of resistance emerged. The seeds of these theories were found in defenses of the independence of Italian city-states, in pre-Protestant arguments against the political authority of the Catholic Church, and in medieval Catholic scholastic writings about the conditions for legitimate political authority.[13] When Emperor Charles V after 1530 threatened military force to suppress the Lutheran heresy, Lutheran leaders, including Luther himself in later life, began to accept the lawfulness of resistance. They relied on a "constitutionalist" theory that the emperor had obligations to the various princes, who were also rulers, albeit subordinate ones; the inferior magistrates might meet force with force to defend their rights. More particularly, they should not submit if the highest ruler is suppressing the true religion. Lutheran leaders also advanced a "private-law" theory: just as people can defend themselves from unlawful force, rulers who proceed outside their jurisdiction and do serious harm may also be resisted.[14]

Calvinists from the Continent and the British Isles drew from and developed these two theories to justify resistance. During the reign of Roman Catholic queens, Mary Tudor in England and Mary Guise in Scotland, John Knox urged Scottish nobles as inferior magistrates that they had a religious obligation to revolt. In response to St. Paul's comment that political power is ordained by God, the most radical Calvinists of the mid sixteenth century onward argued that rulers who fail to discharge their duties are not ordained by God. These Calvinists adopted a somewhat broader idea of *who* might resist than the inferior magistrates emphasized by Lutherans.

During the sixteenth century, Catholic theorists of the Counter-Reformation made significant contributions toward a modern theory of the state that included a right to resist. Francisco Suarez explained how people

---

[13] See Skinner, *The Age of Reformation* and *The Renaissance*, in *The Foundations of Modern Political Thought* (Cambridge: Cambridge University Press, 1978), I.

[14] Skinner, *The Foundations of Modern Political Thought*, II:191–205.

living in a natural and pre-political community might submit themselves by consent to a rule of positive law. If a ruler threatens the life of a community, the community has a right to resist, but that right may be exercised only after a representative assembly deliberates.[15]

The exact role of various theoretical influences is debatable, but Quentin Skinner's conclusion is that, despite common reference to a "Calvinist theory of revolution," virtually no elements are specifically Calvinist. The first Calvinists drew heavily from Lutherans who themselves drew from civil and canon law, and the new arguments of Calvinists after 1570 were largely scholastic. Thus, "we may say with very little exaggeration that the main foundations of the Calvinist theory of revolution were in fact constructed entirely by their Catholic adversaries."[16]

The writings of French Protestant Huguenots developed the theory of rightful resistance in important respects.[17] Arguing that the basic condition of people is one of natural liberty, they claimed that free consent must ground legitimate government. Appealing to France's "ancient constitution," they urged that the French parlements had a right to check kings who became tyrants. Reaching out to members of the Catholic majority, they no longer emphasized a *duty* to resist that depended on a ruler's failure to protect the true faith, but rather a *right* to resist that grew out of natural rights and the people's sovereignty.

In his study of the English Puritans, Michael Walzer suggests that they went beyond ideas of resistance to urge that the faithful should reconstruct government and society to fulfill God's purposes, relying not on those with hereditary positions but on the work of those with understanding and talent.[18]

The Calvinist expansion of a theory of resistance was taken somewhat further in the influential theory of John Locke in the later seventeenth century.[19] According to Locke, persons in authority who exceed their power cease to be magistrates and may be resisted not only by inferior magistrates but by the citizens themselves. Resistance is a political and moral right to hold rulers to their legitimate functions. Although Locke's theory rested significantly on religious ideas, his emphasis on natural rights and social contract could be understood without reference to Christian premises. Rulers might violate their obligations to citizens by forms of overreaching

---

[15] *Ibid.*, II:160–63, 177–78.   [16] *Ibid.*, II:321.   [17] *Ibid.*, II:239–348.

[18] Michael Walzer, *The Revolution of the Saints* (Cambridge, MA: Harvard University Press, 1965).

[19] See John Locke, *Two Treatises of Government*, 2nd edn with an Introduction by Peter Laslett (Cambridge: Cambridge University Press, 1967). Skinner calls this work of Locke's "the classical text of radical Calvinist politics." Skinner, *The Foundations of Modern Political Thought*, II:239. See further the chapter by David Little herein.

that were not necessarily forms of religious oppression. In contrast to the Puritans, Locke did not think the government has a fundamental responsibility to promote the true religion; its proper role is to tolerate divergent religious views.

After Locke, much political theorizing within Christian countries was no longer distinctly Christian. Theorists writing from a Christian perspective have, down to the present, made contributions to ideas about resistance to tyranny, but perhaps we can say that they have adopted some variant of one of the four conceptions we have identified. (1) Government is divinely ordained to deal with human sin, and active resistance to political authority is never justified. (2) Government fulfills a natural human need and contributes to virtuous lives; resistance is warranted only when a government deviates seriously from the requisites of natural law. (3) Resistance is justified if government suppresses, or fails to promote, the true religion. (4) Government rests on the consent of the governed or to serve the common good, or both. It must protect the rights of citizens, including the right to worship according to conscience. When a government substantially violates these rights, resistance is warranted.

In the modern era, it is only some small perfectionist groups that reject violent resistance in all circumstances. Thinkers like Reinhold Niebuhr, who have accepted an Augustinian view of human nature, have not followed him in assuming that even the worst governments are ordained by God.[20] Few Christians now believe the government should promote true religion by suppressing false religion. Most think, along with citizens who think about these questions without direct reliance on religious perspectives, that the way in which governments violate rights in respect to religion is in not allowing the free exercise of religion. Most modern Christians join non-Christians in believing that if a government is *oppressive enough*, forcible resistance is warranted; Hitler's Nazi Germany is the most cited example. Extreme oppression may concern religion itself or other matters. Ethnic genocide and stark racial injustice, as in the apartheid of the Union of South Africa, are two illustrations. Christians, like others, disagree about the gravity of various injustices and about what degree of injustice is so great that people have a right to mount violent resistance.

In this era of globalization and the development of theories of universal human rights, what injustices warrant intervention by outsiders – international organizations and other countries? There is no distinctly Christian

---

[20] Reinhold Niebuhr, *The Nature and Destiny of Man: A Christian Interpretation* (New York: Charles Scribner's Sons, 1947).

outlook on that topic, but any individual's view will be affected by what she thinks citizens of one country owe to those of other countries, by her sense of whether we can divide governments into basically good and basically evil or should acknowledge that the mixture of good and evil is usually much more nuanced, and by the prospect of likely success as compared with the prospect of making bad situations worse. Insofar as the war in Iraq that started in 2003 was motivated by genuine concern with the plight of its citizens, and insofar as we can take such political rhetoric seriously, the Bush Administration did believe that the government of Saddam Hussein was strikingly evil and that the prospects of generating a much better, effective government were very promising. As of early 2007, this latter prognosis is far from confirmed.

CIVIL DISOBEDIENCE

Civil disobedience is a much more modern idea than passive conscientious objection and active resistance, and it lies between those two ideas of when one should disobey the law. It is more disruptive than passive non-submission but less disruptive than violence; unlike passive refusal, it aims at change but typically not at overthrow of government. Although the modern idea of civil disobedience owes much to Mahatma Gandhi's campaign against the English in India, the approach of the civil rights movement in the United States rested on both democratic theory and Christian ethics. (That does not mean, of course, that all Christians accepted civil disobedience against legitimate governments. Many thought that Christians should not blatantly disobey the laws of such governments.)

Viewed from the standpoint of democratic theory, civil disobedience, unlike violent action, shows a respect for fellow citizens and for ordinary political processes. This is true even if, in contrast to many of the ostensibly illegal acts during the civil rights movement in the United States, those engaging in the acts recognize that they are in genuine violation of the law, including any possible constitutional standards. The actors do not injure other people (though they may inconvenience them). Furthermore, their willingness to submit to punishment both demonstrates a degree of acceptance of the rules governing illegal behavior and counters the reality (or perception) that actors are seeking to take unfair advantage of their fellows. American political philosopher John Rawls suggested that a condition of civil disobedience is that one appeal to a sense of justice shared by fellow citizens. I believe that is too strict a requirement for what *counts* as civil disobedience, ruling out, as it probably would, peaceful demonstrations in favor of animal rights. But it may well be that when disobedience does appeal to shared sentiments of justice, it can be more easily defended as only a limited breach of processes of liberal democratic rule.

The distinctly Christian elements of civil disobedience, along with its democratic elements, were emphasized by American Baptist preacher, Martin Luther King, Jr.[21] The non-violent element of civil disobedience fits the Christian traditions of non-violence and of love for one's enemies. As hostile as many whites, including many in political authority, were to efforts to desegregate aspects of American society, King emphasized the transforming power of love. If civil rights demonstrators refused to return violence with violence, this could help change their opponents. Although a realist about the injustice of many political conditions, King rested on an optimism about what loving non-violence could accomplish that is not to be found in Augustine and other "realists."

When one thinks about civil disobedience from a modern Christian perspective, one needs to take account of the threads of democratic theory and of the extent to which Christians aiming to achieve change are called to act non-violently. This includes the question of how consistent non-violence by those seeking change can affect their opponents over time. Whatever the Christian religion may tell us about acts that one should not perform because they are wrong from some transcendental perspective (a typical basis for instances of conscientious objection), it is an open question whether, when facing questions about resistance and civil disobedience in modern life, one should conceive of a peculiarly Christian outlook. My own perspective on this is skeptical. Although I do not believe we should try to divorce threads of understanding we have gleaned from our religion traditions, I do not perceive a Christian approach to these topics that is sharply distinct from an approach grounded in "detached" political philosophy. Nonetheless, I find some value in perceiving the strikingly different approaches various Christian thinkers have adopted over two millennia.

RECOMMENDED READING

Burns, J. H., ed. *The Cambridge History of Political Thought 1450–1700*. Cambridge: Cambridge University Press, 1991.

Deane, Herbert A. *The Political and Social Ideas of St. Augustine*. New York: Columbia University Press, 1963.

---

[21] Martin Luther King, Jr., "Letter from Birmingham City Jail" (1963), reprinted in Hugo Adam Bedau, ed., *Civil Disobedience: Theory and Practice* (New York: Pegasus Books, 1969), 72–89.

Gooch, G. P. *English Democratic Theory in the Seventeenth Century.* Cambridge: Cambridge University Press, 1932.

Greenawalt, Kent. *Conflicts of Law and Morality.* Oxford: Clarendon Press, 1987.
  Religion and the Constitution, Vol. 1, Free Exercise and Fairness. Princeton, NJ: Princeton University Press, 2006.

Klaasen, Walter, ed. *Anabaptism in Outline.* Scottdale, PA: Herald Press, 1981.

Niebuhr, Reinhold. *The Nature and Destiny of Man: A Christian Interpretation.* New York: Charles Scribner's Sons, 1947.

Rawls, John. *A Theory of Justice.* Cambridge, MA: Harvard University Press, 1971.

Skinner, Quentin. *The Foundations of Modern Political Thought,* 2 vols. Cambridge: Cambridge University Press, 1978.

Waldron, Jeremy. *God, Locke, and Equality.* Cambridge: Cambridge University Press, 2002.

Walzer, Michael. *The Revolution of the Saints.* Cambridge, MA: Harvard University Press, 1968.

Witte, John, Jr. and Frank S. Alexander, eds. *The Teachings of Modern Christianity on Law, Politics, and Human Nature,* 2 vols. New York: Columbia University Press, 2006.

RUTH c. IV.
Propinquus Ruth suo juri cedit.

Ruth. IV. 8.
Der Bluts freünd und Erbe Ruth, be,
gibt sich seines Rechtes, in dem er, nach
landes gebrauch, seine Schurch ausziehet.

7 "Boaz Purchases all the Property of Ruth's Dead Husband by Removing his Sandal,"
from Christoph Weigel, *Biblia ectypa: Bildnussen auss heiliger Schrifft Alt und Neuen
Testaments* (Augsburgh, 1695), s.v, Ruth 4

CHAPTER SIX

The Christian sources of general contract law

Harold J. Berman

In his dramatic, if not mystical, account of the birth, growth, senescence, and death of American contract law, and of its ultimate dissolution into the law of tort, Grant Gilmore certainly did not intend to join forces with those who would later seize on his story as evidence that both contract and tort, and, indeed, law all together, are merely artificial devices to support a hierarchical and hegemonic political structure and to facilitate economic exploitation of the weak by the strong.[1] Yet Gilmore's exposé of the logical circularities and fallacies of contract doctrine (especially as it is taught in first-year courses in American law schools) does add fuel to the already raging fires of skepticism – skepticism not only about the coherence of individual branches of the legal tree (contracts, torts, property, etc.) but also about the validity of doctrinal legal analysis, and ultimately of law itself.

Arthur Corbin – Gilmore's mentor and the hero of his book – did not share that skepticism, although he strongly opposed the rigidities of the then prevailing contract doctrine, especially as represented in the teachings of his friend and rival, Samuel Williston. Unlike Williston, Corbin was pre-pared to give a contractual remedy for losses caused by reliance on a promise, and thus to bring contract and tort into a common focus. He was also more willing than Williston to expand concepts of fairness at the expense of strict liability for breach. Nevertheless, Corbin did not doubt, and surely did not seek to undermine, the coherence of contract law.

Although Gilmore went farther than Corbin in his critique of traditional doctrine, he, too, was concerned to restructure contract law, not to destroy it. Above all, Gilmore retained a commercial lawyer's respect for contracts – in the plural. His attack was rather on the notion of *contract* – in the singular – as an abstract entity, a thing-in-itself, reflecting in its very essence the coherent body of concepts, principles, and rules that had come to

---

[1] Grant Gilmore, *The Death of Contract* (Columbus, OH: Ohio State University Press, 1974).

surround it: offer and acceptance, consideration, formal requirements, defenses of fraud and duress and mistake, excuse based on impossibility or frustration, and the rest. This entire body of learning was now thought to be based on a questionable theory of the priority of intent, or will, which in turn was based on a questionable theory of the priority of party autonomy. It was the logical symmetry of the doctrines and their basis in the will-theory and the autonomy-theory of contract law that came under attack in Gilmore's *Death of Contract*, as it had been under attack for the preceding fifty years.

Looking back at what happened to contract law in action during the twentieth century, and especially to accepted contract practices, one is struck by the fact that the priorities of contractual intent and party autonomy, which still form the basis of contract law in theory, no longer correspond to reality in most situations. Contracts of adhesion, regulated contracts, contracts entered into under economic compulsion, and other types of prefabricated contractual arrangements, are now typical rather than exceptional. Doctrines of frustration and of substantial performance have been greatly expanded. The defense of unconscionability has become a reality in consumer sales and is a potential obstacle to contractual autonomy in other types of transactions as well. Duties of cooperation and of mitigation of losses have begun to change the nature of many types of contractual relationships. Promissory estoppel has spawned non-promissory estoppel, notably in the form of implied warranties which, though contractual in theory, nevertheless "run with the chattel."

The breakdown of traditional contract law in practice has given some support to those legal theorists who contend that all law must be judged not in terms of doctrinal consistency but in terms of social consequences. To understand the significance of the attack that has been launched against general contract law in the past two or three generations, however, one must go back much farther in time than Gilmore went. One must also go much farther in space. Gilmore imagined that American jurists, Christopher Columbus Langdell and Oliver Wendell Holmes, Jr., had invented the modern system of contract doctrine, which Williston later refined. In fact, Langdell in 1870 carried over into American legal thought ideas that had been propounded in France, Germany, England, and elsewhere for a hundred years. The Enlightenment of the late eighteenth century stimulated the desire to rationalize and systematize the law in new ways. In England, Jeremy Bentham called for the "codification" – a word of his own creation – of the various branches of law. In the wake of the

French Revolution, France adopted separate codes for civil law, civil procedure, criminal law, criminal procedure, administrative law, and commercial law. The idea was taken up everywhere in the West that the entire body of civil law, and, within it, its component parts, should be rationalized and systematized anew, whether in a code (as in France), or in scholarly treatises (as in Germany), or in court decisions collected by law teachers (as in England and the United States). Indeed, in the United States, a generation before Langdell, William Story wrote *A Treatise on the Law of Contracts Not Under Seal* (1844) and Theophilus Parsons wrote *The Law of Contracts* (1853). And so, Langdell and others did for American contract law what others had done for English and other legal systems. They attempted to reduce it to a set of concepts, principles, and rules which would be applicable to all contracts.

It is, however, a great mistake to suppose that this was the first time that any such attempt at systematizing contract law had been made, and an even greater mistake to suppose that the nineteenth-century systematizers simply invented the concepts, principles, and rules upon which they founded their new system. The "general law of contract" was, in fact, invented much earlier, and the nineteenth-century jurists drew upon the older learning in establishing their new version of it.

Yet the nineteenth-century jurists differed from their predecessors in several crucial respects. Perhaps the most important of these was their concern to cut the general law of contract loose from its moorings in a religious – more specifically, a Christian – belief system. They sought to replace those moorings with their own belief system, based on rationalism and individualism. It was that secular faith which found expression, in nineteenth-century contract law, in the overriding principles of freedom of will and of party autonomy. Those principles were applied, however, to an already existing system of contract law, many of whose basic features were preserved.

THE ORIGINS OF MODERN CONTRACT LAW IN CANON LAW

Modern contract law originated in Europe in the late eleventh and early twelfth centuries. It was that epoch that gave birth to the modern Western belief in the autonomy of law, its professional character, its integrity both as a system of institutions and as a body of learning, and its capacity for organic growth over generations and centuries. It was then that consciously integrated systems of law came to be formed, first in the church and then in the various secular polities – kingdoms, cities, feudal domains, and mercantile communities. It was then that various branches of law, within each of those systems, were first given structure: criminal law, family law, corporation law, mercantile law, and others.[2]

Starting in the last two decades of the eleventh century, the glossators of Roman law began to construct out of Justinian's massive texts, newly discovered after more than five hundred years of virtual oblivion, a coherent *corpus juris* that had only been adumbrated in the original writings. (Justinian had not called his texts a *corpus juris*.) Equally important, the canon lawyers began to create, partly with the help of the new Romanist legal science, a consciously integrated legal system to be applied in the newly created hierarchy of ecclesiastical administrative and judicial agencies, culminating in the papal curia. Eleventh- and twelfth-century Roman law, as contrasted with the earlier Roman law whose vocabulary and rules it selectively adopted and transformed, was not as such the positive law of any jurisdiction. It was law taught as *ratio scripta* in the emerging universities of Europe, and it was drawn upon selectively by every jurisdiction, ecclesiastical and secular, as a subsidiary law, to fill gaps, to interpret, and sometimes to correct the positive law. Canon law, on the other hand, after 1075, was the positive law of the church, replenished by papal decrees and decretals and by the legislation of church councils. It was directly applicable throughout Western Christendom to most aspects of the lives of the clergy and to many aspects of the lives of the laity.[3]

To say that modern contract law was gradually formed in the late eleventh and the twelfth centuries is not to say that there were not, before then, contracts, in the sense of legally binding agreements. In the year 1000, however, there was no general principle that a promise or an exchange of promises may in itself give rise to legal liability among the inhabitants of Western Europe. Legal liability attached to promises only if they were embodied in formal religious oaths, which were almost always secured by some kind of pledge. The obligation that was enforced was not the mutual contractual obligation of the parties but the oath, that is, the obligation to God (or, before Christianity, to the gods); the legal liability that was imposed was the forfeiture of the pledge. Originally, the pledge might consist of the surrender of the oath-taker's own person, symbolized in the formal transfer of his faith (*fides facta*) through the ritual of shaking hands. Alternatively, other persons could be pledged as hostages, and eventually property could also be

---

[2] This is the main theme of Harold J. Berman, *Law and Revolution: The Formation of the Western Legal Tradition* (Cambridge, MA: Harvard University Press, 1983).

[3] See further chapters by R. H. Helmholz, Mathias Schmoeckel, and Brian Tierney herein.

pledged as security.[4] A sharp distinction was made between the oath-taker's obligation (*Schuld*) and his liability (*Haftung*). The breach of obligation triggered liability but was not itself a basis of liability. In itself it had no legal consequences, though it had spiritual consequences and could be punished as a sin in the penitential processes of the local monastic order or parish priesthood. The legal consequences were wholly interwoven with the pledge and consisted simply of its forfeiture. If forfeiture was resisted, resort was had either to conciliation or to blood-feud.

Germanic law (including Frankish, Anglo-Saxon, Burgundian, Lombard, and other varieties of clan or tribal law) also recognized a duty of restitution arising from a half-completed exchange: a party who had transferred property to another was entitled to receive from the other the purchase price or other equivalent. This also was not a contractual remedy in the modern sense of the word "contractual."

The older Roman law of contracts, reflected in Justinian's compilation, was, to be sure, much more sophisticated than the Germanic law. Names were provided for various ways of forming contracts and for various types of contracts that fell within those forms. Thus, certain named ("nominate") contracts were formed by following a prescribed verbal formula, others by formal entry in certain account books, a third category by delivery of the object covered by the contract, and a fourth by informally expressed consent. The fourth category included sale, lease, partnership, and mandate (a form of agency). Unnamed ("innominate") contracts included a gift for a gift, a gift for an act, an act for a gift, and an act for an act. Innominate contracts were actionable only after one party had performed his promise. In addition to an elaborate classification of categories and types of contracts, the Justinian texts included hundreds of scattered rules – opinions of jurists, holdings in decided cases, decrees of emperors, and so forth – concerning their operation.

Nowhere, however, did the texts of Justinian contain a systematic explanation of the reasons for the rules of contract law or for the classification of types of contracts. Nowhere was there stated a theory or even a general concept of contractual liability as such. Law in the Justinian texts, including those parts of it which we think of today as "contract" law, was not only unsystematized but casuistic in the extreme; its rules were sometimes classified, but the taxonomy was not explained in theoretical terms.

The glossators of the late eleventh and the twelfth centuries, in indexing the Roman texts, collected the various statements of the older Roman

---

[4] See Raoul Berger, "From Hostage to Contract," *Illinois Law Review* 35 (1940): 154–281 and literature cited therein; Johannes Bärmann, "Pacta sunt servanda: Consideration sur l'histoire du contrat consensual," *Revue Internationale de droit comparé* 13 (1961): 18.

jurists on contracts and, in glossing them, elaborated general concepts and principles that they found to be implicit in them. The canonists went even farther, offering a general theory of contractual liability and applying that theory to actual disputes litigated in the ecclesiastical courts.

For the first time, the canonists developed the general principle that an agreement as such – a *nudum pactum* – *may* give rise to a civil action. Drawing partly on the texts of Justinian but also on the Bible, on natural law, on the penitentials, on canons of church councils and of bishops and popes, and on Germanic law, the canonists drew a conclusion which none of those sources, taken individually, had ever before drawn: that consensual obligations as such are, as a general principle, binding not only morally but also legally, even though they were entered into without any formalities. By legally binding, the canonists meant that the promisee had a right against the promisor, enforceable in an ecclesiastical court, to the performance of the promise or else to compensation for losses. This general principle was in sharp contrast to the then prevailing Germanic law, under which a contractual obligation (*Schuld*) was in itself unenforceable, and a pledge accompanying such an obligation (*Haftung*) was only enforceable if its transfer had been carried out with the proper formalities. This new principle of canon law erased the Germanic distinction between obligation and liability. It was also in sharp contrast to the rules of the earlier Roman law set forth in Justinian's texts, under which formalities were essential to the validity of most types of contracts, partial performance was essential to the validity of innominate contracts, and special requirements existed for the limited class of contracts that could be concluded informally.

The general principle of contractual liability arising from agreements, developed by the canonists, rested, in the first instance, on the theory that to break a promise is a sin. A sin, however, in and of itself, gave rise not to legal liability but to penitential discipline; it was to be confessed and repented in the internal forum of the church following the rules and procedures of the sacrament of penance. Legal liability, imposed in the external forum, that is, in the bishop's court, was based not only on the sin of the obligor but also on the protection of the rights of the obligee.[5] This required a new development in moral theology, which was closely connected with new developments in political, economic, and social life.

The twelfth century witnessed an enormous expansion of commerce, including economic transactions between ecclesiastical corporations. In

---

[5] On the internal and external forum, see further the chapter by Mathias Schmoeckel herein.

addition, the ecclesiastical courts sought and obtained a large measure of jurisdiction over economic contracts between laymen, where the parties included in their agreement a pledge of faith. The faith that was pledged, it was now said, created an obligation not only to God but also to the church. To justify enforcement of contracts in the external forum of the church, it was necessary to add to the theory that to break a promise is a sin the theory that the claim of the party who has suffered from such breach is morally justified. The canonists developed the two theories together. They concluded that a morally binding promise should also be legally binding if it is part of an agreement (a *pactum,* or consensual *obligation*) that is itself morally justified. The object or purpose (*causa*) of the contract had to be reasonable and equitable.

Based on the theory that contracts should be legally binding if they serve a reasonable and equitable cause, the twelfth-century canonists, with the help of their contemporary Romanists, developed a whole series of principles which, taken together, justify the characterization of "general contract law." Some of these principles were the following: that agreements should be legally enforceable even though they were entered into without formalities (*pacta sunt servanda*), provided that their purpose (*causa*) was reasonable and equitable; that agreements entered into through the fraud of one or both parties should not be legally enforceable; that agreements entered into through duress should not be legally enforceable; that agreements should not be legally enforceable if one or both parties were mistaken concerning a circumstance material to its formation; that silence may be interpreted as giving rise to inferences concerning the intention of the parties in forming a contract; that the rights of third-party beneficiaries of a contract should be protected; that a contract may be subject to reformation in order to achieve justice in a particular case; that good faith is required in the formation of a contract, in its interpretation, and in its execution; that in matters of doubt, rules of contract law are to be applied in favor of the debtor (in *dubiis pro debitore*); and that contracts that are unconscionable should not be enforced.[6]

The last point, relating to unconscionability, deserves further elaboration. Equity, for the twelfth-century canonists and Romanists alike, required, in contracts, a balancing of gains and losses on both sides. This principle took form in the doctrine of the just price. Both the Romanists and the canonists started with the premise that normally the just price is the common estimate, that is, the market price; a sharp deviation from the

---

[6] See Bärmann, "Pacta sunt servanda," 18–25; Berman, *Law and Revolution,* 245–50.

market price was prima facie contrary to reason and equity. Usury, which was defined as a charge for the loan of money in excess of the normal rate of interest, was also condemned by both Romanists and canonists as a breach of market norms.

The canonists, however, in contrast to the Romanists, were more concerned with another aspect of a sale in excess of the just price, or a charge for money in excess of normal interest, namely, the immoral motive that often underlay such practices. Profit-making in itself – contrary to what has been said by many modern writers – was not condemned by the canon law of the twelfth century. To buy cheap and sell dear was considered to be proper in many types of situations. What was condemned by the canon law was "shameful" profit (*turpe lucrum*, "filthy lucre"), and that was identified with avaricious business practices. Thus, for the canonists, rules of unfair competition, directed against breach of market norms, were linked also with rules of unconscionability, directed against oppressive transactions.

In subsequent centuries, many of the basic principles of the canon law of contract were adopted by secular law and eventually came to be justified on the basis of the will-theory and party autonomy. It is important to know, however, that originally they were based on a theory of sin and a theory of equity. Our modern Western contract law did not start from the proposition that every individual has a moral right to dispose of his property by means of making promises, and that in the interest of justice a promise should be legally enforced unless it offends reason or public policy. Our contract law started, on the contrary, from the theory that a promise created an obligation to God, and that for the salvation of souls God instituted the ecclesiastical and secular courts with the task, in part, of enforcing contractual obligations to the extent that such obligations are just.

THE PURITAN CONCEPT OF CONTRACT AS COVENANT AND OF STRICT LIABILITY FOR BREACH

If we jump from Roman Catholic Christendom in the late eleventh, twelfth, and thirteenth centuries to Anglican and Puritan England in the seventeenth and eighteenth centuries, we confront a startling paradox. On the one hand, the political, economic, and social situation has changed drastically. On the other hand, the terms of the debates concerning law and government have remained remarkably stable; that is, the same issues continue to be addressed, although the emphasis is different and the answers are different. Brian Tierney has shown the remarkable continuity of Western constitutional theory from the twelfth to the seventeenth centuries – from

Gratian and John of Salisbury to Althusius and Locke. Tierney writes that "the juridical culture of the twelfth century – the works of the Roman and canon lawyers, especially those of the canonists where religious and secular ideas most obviously intersected – formed a kind of seedbed from which grew the whole tangled forest of early modern constitutional thought."[7] Tierney's study is a challenge to legal historians to show that continuity existed in the realm not only of constitutional theory but also of criminal and civil law, including the law of contracts.

Prior to the sixteenth century, the law in England governing what we would today call contractual liability had been divided among various jurisdictions, each with its own procedures and its own legal rules. The English ecclesiastical courts, which had a wide jurisdiction over contract disputes involving not only clerics but also laymen, applied the canon law of the Roman Church. In the numerous cities and towns of England, as well as at fairs, mercantile courts applied a customary commercial law, sometimes called the law merchant, whose general features were more or less uniform throughout Europe. English county courts, as well as feudal and manorial courts, enforced various types of agreements, applying chiefly local and feudal or manorial custom. The royal courts of Common Pleas and King's Bench resolved contract disputes chiefly through the common law actions of debt, detinue, account, deceit, covenant, and trespass on the case. In the fourteenth and fifteenth centuries the chancellor also acquired a wide jurisdiction over contracts in cases which fell outside the common law (such as many types of parole promises, uses, and actions by third-party beneficiaries) or which the common law courts were unable to decide fairly (for example, because of pressures exerted by powerful persons or because of inadequacy of common law remedies). The chancellor's "court of conscience" (as it was often called in those centuries) drew upon canon law, mercantile law, common law, and the chancellor's own ingenuity and sense of fairness.

All the diverse types of law applicable to contracts were strongly influenced by the religious beliefs that prevailed during those centuries in England as in the other countries of Western Christendom. In the canon law, as we have seen, contractual liability was based ultimately on the sin of the defaulting promisor and the right of the promisee to require performance or compensation insofar as the agreement served a reasonable and equitable purpose. The law merchant stressed the element of trust among merchants and, in the event of dispute, their need for a speedy, informal procedure and for decisions based on mercantile reasonableness.

---

[7] Brian Tierney, *Religion, Law and the Growth of Constitutional Thought, 1150–1650* (Cambridge: Cambridge University Press, 1982), 1. See further the chapter by Brian Tierney herein.

The chief common law actions relating to agreements were founded on the concept of moral wrong as expounded in Roman Catholic theology: debt, detinue, and account presupposed the wrongfulness of retaining money or property that was due to the other party in a half-completed exchange; deceit presupposed an intentional wrong; covenant presupposed the wrongfulness of violating a solemn oath; assumpsit – more accurately, trespass on the case upon an assumpsit – developed in the fifteenth century to permit recovery for the wrongful act ("trespass" is, of course, law French for the Latin *transgressio*, "sin") of negligently performing an undertaking (misfeasance). In Chancery, the influence of moral theology was even more apparent, if only because the chancellor, in those centuries, was almost invariably an archbishop or bishop, quite familiar with the basic features of the canon law, and his decisions were often grounded expressly in Christian teaching. Indeed, his jurisdiction may be said to have rested on three principles that were attributed to Christian faith: the protection of the poor and helpless, the enforcement of relations of trust and confidence, and the granting of remedies that "act on the person" (injunctions, specific performance, and the like).

In the sixteenth and early seventeenth centuries, the English law applicable to contracts underwent significant development. After the Act of Supremacy (1534), that established the monarch as "supreme head" of the church and commonwealth of England, the ecclesiastical courts lost a substantial part of their jurisdiction over matters of property and commerce. The Tudor monarchs created an array of new "prerogative" courts, including the Court of Star Chamber, the High Court of Admiralty, the Court of Requests, and others, and also transformed the chancellor's court into the High Court of Chancery. With the rapid growth of both domestic and overseas trade, these courts exercised an enormously expanded commercial jurisdiction, applying to commercial cases the traditional law merchant as well as many rules and concepts derived from canon law and from Romanist legal science. Partly, no doubt, in order to meet the new competition, and in the spirit of the times, the common law courts also began to reform the action of assumpsit, making it available in certain types of cases of nonfeasance, and simplifying procedures in order to make the action a less unwieldy instrument for settling commercial disputes. In *Slade's Case* (1602), assumpsit was made available in cases of half-performed contracts and half-performed sales of goods, which previously had been subject to the archaic remedies of debt and detinue. By that time, the common law courts had also elaborated a doctrine of consideration, similar to that of chancery and of the canon law, by which the validity and enforceability of an undertaking – whether in the case of the half-completed exchange or in the case of a simple promise – was tested in terms of the circumstances which caused or motivated it.

Despite the significant changes in the law of contracts which took place in the sixteenth and early seventeenth centuries, in all the legal systems that prevailed in England, including the common law, the underlying presuppositions of contractual liability remained what they had been in the earlier period. Breach of promise was actionable, in the first instance, because (or if) it was a wrong, called a tort, and in the second instance, because (or if) the promisee had a right to require its enforcement in view of its reasonable and equitable purpose. With some qualifications, the common lawyers accepted these premises no less than the canon lawyers. Prior to the latter part of the seventeenth century, assumpsit was essentially an action for breach of (a unilateral) promise, not breach of (a bilateral) contract in the modern sense, and the required consideration was conceived in terms of the moral justification and purpose of the promise. The action of covenant, on the other hand, was not seen to be a contractual remedy; duress was a defense but fraud in the inducement was not, although relief might be obtained from the chancellor. The fact that the common law courts used distinctive procedures in enforcing promises, applied distinctive technical rules (often required by the different procedures), and gave only limited contract remedies, reflected the division between the ecclesiastical and the secular spheres and the subdivision of the secular sphere into plural jurisdictions. These divisions and subdivisions were themselves associated with the specific religious worldview that had emerged in the eleventh and twelfth centuries.

The Puritan Revolution of 1640 to 1660 established the supremacy of the common law over its rivals. In 1641, the parliament, dominated by Puritans, abolished the prerogative courts. Eventually, a separate admiralty jurisdiction survived, but it was greatly restricted in its scope and was subordinated to the common law. Chancery also survived but it, too, suffered a reduction of jurisdiction and was no longer able to assert its superiority over Common Pleas or King's Bench. Under the Puritans, the common law courts heard cases of breaches of promise to marry, actions for legacies, and other ecclesiastical causes, on the ground that the ecclesiastical courts were not sitting. After 1660, some of that jurisdiction was retained, and the ecclesiastical courts, like the others, were ultimately bound by the common law as interpreted by Common Pleas and King's Bench.

With respect to commercial matters, the vast increase in the amount and variety of cases that came before the common law courts required an expansion and revision of their remedies and doctrines. Especially after 1660, when some of the most important reforms of the Puritan period were confirmed under a restored, chastened, and limited monarchy, the common law courts gradually adopted a great many of the remedies and rules that had been elaborated in the previous hundred years by the prerogative courts and by Chancery.

Other changes, however, in the common law of contracts, as it developed in the later seventeenth and eighteenth centuries, cannot be attributed to the adoption or adaptation of doctrines previously elaborated in rival jurisdictions. There was, in fact, a shift in some of the basic presuppositions of contract law that had developed over the previous five centuries. This shift may be summarized in three interrelated propositions.

First, the underlying theory of liability shifted from breach of promise to breach of a bargain. The emphasis was no longer placed primarily on the sin, or wrong, of the defaulting promisor but rather on the binding character of an agreement as such and the disappointment of the expectations of the promisee. This change raised more acutely than before the question whether the promises of the two sides were to be treated as independent or interdependent. The tendency of the courts in the century from 1660 to 1760 was to treat them increasingly as interdependent.

Second, the emphasis on bargain was manifested in a new conception of consideration. The older conception of consideration as purpose, or motive, or justification for a promise (analogous to the canonists' conception of *causa*) gave way to a conception of consideration as the price paid by the promisee for the promise of the promisor. This change raised more acutely than before the question of the adequacy or inadequacy of the consideration. The tendency of the courts in the century after the Puritan Revolution was increasingly to enforce agreements regardless of the inadequacy of the consideration.

Third, the basis of liability shifted from fault to absolute obligation. The promisee was entitled to compensation for non-performance with the terms of the bargain itself; excuses for non-performance were to be confined, generally speaking, to those provided for within those terms.

The shift from a *moral* theory to what may be called a *bargain* theory of contract is well illustrated in the famous case of *Paradine v. Jane*, decided in 1647, at the height of the Puritan Revolution. A lessor sued a tenant for non-payment of rent. The tenant defended on the ground that, due to the occupation of the leased premises by Prince Rupert's army, it was impossible for him to enjoy the benefit of his contract and therefore he should be excused from liability. He cited in his defense canon law, civil (i.e., Roman) law, military law, moral law, the law of reason, the law of nature, and the law of nations. Disregarding these authorities, the court held that by the common law of England a lessee for years is liable for the rent, even though the land be impossible to occupy. Although as an action of debt for rent the case could have been decided solely on the basis of the law of leasehold tenure, the court enunciated a broad principle of strict contractual liability. It said that where a duty is created by law, the party will be excused if he is not at fault, "but when the party by his own contract creates a duty or charge upon himself he is bound to make it good, if he may, notwithstanding accident or inevitable necessity, because he might have provided against it by his contract."[8]

One may find earlier cases that suggest a doctrine of strict contractual liability. Indeed, one may show that all the doctrinal ingredients of the modern action for breach of contract were present, in embryo, in the action of assumpsit as it developed in the late 1500s and early 1600s. In the history of legal doctrine, it is usually not difficult to find in some earlier decision or text a source for every new development. Yet it is fair to say that before *Paradine v. Jane*, no English court had ever laid down the theory of absolute obligation for breach of a bargained exchange, namely, that obligation in contract is distinguished from obligation in tort by the fact that the parties to a contract set their own limits to their liability. Moreover, that after *Paradine v. Jane*, that theory was never effectively challenged.

The moral theory of contractual liability, which linked legal liability closely with the sin or wrongfulness of a breach of promise, on the one hand, and the equitable purpose of the promise or exchange of promises, on the other, was attacked in the seventeenth century in England by Puritans, including both lawyers and theologians. The attack was part of a revulsion against the discretionary justice of the chancellor. In the words of the great seventeenth-century Puritan legal scholar and practitioner John Selden: "Equity in law is the same as the spirit is in religion, what everyone pleases to make it", and again: "Equity is a roguish thing . . . equity is according to the conscience of him that is chancellor . . . It is all one as if they should make the standard for the measure a chancellor's foot."[9] The distrust of equity was linked with a strict view of contractual liability. Of contracts Selden wrote:

We must look to the contract; if that be rightly made, we must stand to it; if we once grant [that] we may recede from contracts upon any inconveniency that may

---

[8] Style 47, 82 *English Reports* 519 (1647); Aleyn 26, 82 *English Reports* 897 (1647).

[9] John Selden, *Seldeniana; or, The Table Talk of John Selden, Esq.* (London, printed for E. Jeffrey, 1789), 45–46. Selden's *Table Talk* was first compiled in 1654 and first published in 1689.

afterwards happen, we shall have no bargain kept . . . [H]ow to make our contracts is left to ourselves; and as we agree upon the conveyance of this house, or this land, so it must be. If you offer me a hundred pounds for my glove, I tell you what my glove is – a plain glove – I pretend no virtue in it – the glove is my own – I profess not to sell gloves, and we agree for an hundred pounds – I do not know why I may not with a safe conscience take it.[10]

It was not the lawyers, however, but the theologians, who articulated the underlying premises of the new bargain theory of contractual liability. Three basic tenets of seventeenth-century Puritan theology may be identified as bearing directly on that theory. The first was the belief in a sovereign God of order, who requires obedience and self-discipline of his people, on pain of eternal damnation. As John Witte, Jr. has put it: "The austere ethical demands of the Puritan, frugality of time and money, severe church discipline, vocational ambition, and reformist zeal were all tied to theological assumptions. Because the Puritan was a part of the divine unfolding of the providential plan of the world, he viewed his work as holy and he sought to perform as God's agent impeccably." By the same token, "rules and laws were essential not only to arouse people to obedience to God and to guide them in the paths of virtue but also to bring English society to good order and discipline and to reform it."[11]

The second was the belief in the total depravity of man and total dependence for salvation on God's grace. The belief in the total depravity of man – his inborn lust for power, the corruption not only of his will but also of his reason – reinforced the Puritan's emphasis on strict adherence to rules, including rules agreed upon by parties to a contract. As evidenced in Selden's caustic remarks, quoted above, about the untrustworthiness of the chancellor's conscience, the Puritan view of human nature (including the human nature of judges) did not encourage a resort to general ideas of equity or fault for the resolution of conflict. The Puritans preferred to rely upon something that seemed to be more objective and certain, namely, the will of the parties as manifested in the words of the contract, just as they preferred in matters of personal morality to rely on the words of Scripture rather than on the ratiocinations of moral philosophers.

The third was the belief in a contractual ("covenantal") relationship between God and man, whereby God has bound himself to redeem his

---

[10] *Ibid.*, 37–38.
[11] John Witte, Jr., "Blest Be the Ties that Bind: Covenant and Community in Puritan Thought," *Emory Law Journal* 36 (1987): 579–601; see expansion in John Witte, Jr., *The Reformation of Rights: Law, Religion, and Human Rights in Early Modern Calvinism* (Cambridge: Cambridge University Press, 2007).

people in return for their voluntary undertaking to submit to his will. The emerging theological doctrine of covenant was perhaps the most direct link between the legal doctrine of absolute contractual obligation. As Witte has written:

In the late sixteenth and seventeenth centuries, English Puritan theologians radically expanded the doctrine [of covenants] with two major innovations. First, they transformed the covenant of grace as a merciful gift of God into a bargained contract, voluntarily negotiated and agreed upon, and absolutely binding on both sides . . . Second, Puritan theologians added parties to the covenant. The covenant of grace between God and "man" was now understood as a covenant not only with the elected individual Christian but also with the "elect nation" of England, which was called to reform its laws and legal institutions according to God's word. Moreover, within the Biblical covenants the Puritans advocated political and institutional covenants of all kinds: covenants to form families, communities, associations, churches, cities, and even commonwealths, each of which was deemed absolutely binding.[12]

SUMMARY AND CONCLUSIONS

The canonists and Romanists of the late eleventh and twelfth centuries and thereafter based the enforceability of contracts on two principles: first, that to break a promise is a sin, an offense against God, or, more fundamentally, an act of alienation of oneself from God; and second, that the victim of the breach ought to have a legal remedy if the purpose of the promise, or exchange of promises, was reasonable and equitable. These principles served as part of the foundation for the systematization of contract law, that is, the construction of an integrated set of concepts and rules of contract law. Many of these concepts continue to be taught today in law school courses throughout the world – concepts and rules concerning fraud and duress and mistake, unconscionability, duty to mitigate losses, and many other aspects of contract law that link it directly with moral responsibility. It would contribute enormously, I believe, to our understanding of modern contract law if teachers and writers were to trace its formation to the canon law of the church as it developed in a pre-capitalist, pre-individualist, pre-rationalist, pre-nationalist era. There is more "mythology" in the law of contract than Grant Gilmore chose to discuss, and more "rationalization" than its current critics on the left seem to realize.

---

[12] Witte, *The Reformation of Rights*, 277–320. Cf. John D. Eusden, *Puritans, Lawyers, and Politics in Early Seventeenth Century England* (Hamden, CT: Archon Books, 1968), 28ff.; J. W. Gough, *The Social Contract: A Critical Study of Its Development*, 2nd edn (Westport, CT: Greenwood Press, 1978), 82–99.

The bargain theory of contract was, in its inception, a moral theory, which started from the premise that God is a God of order, who enters into contracts with his people by which both he and they are absolutely bound. Its second premise was that the people of God, in entering into contracts with each other, whether social contracts or private, are also absolutely bound by the contract terms, and that non-performance is excused only to the extent that those terms permit. However, the Puritan stress on bargain and on calculability ("order") should not obscure the fact that the bargain presupposed a strong relationship between the contracting parties within the community. These were not yet the autonomous, self-sufficient individuals of the eighteenth-century Enlightenment. England under Puritan rule and in the century that followed was intensely communitarian.

As in the case of the canon law, the underlying principles of the English law of contracts, as it developed in the late seventeenth and early eighteenth centuries, brought that law into close contact with other branches of English law. In particular, English contract law was not separated from commercial law. There was therefore no independent integrated *body* of rules governing all kinds of contracts; in that special sense, there was no "general theory of contract." Only in the late eighteenth and early nineteenth centuries were efforts made to synthesize "contract" as an independent branch of law. Instead, English contract law in the late seventeenth and eighteenth centuries remained a law of different *types* of contracts. The parties who entered into a contract of bailment, or of lease, or an insurance contract, or a conditional sale, or a transportation contract, or the sale of land, or a contract of personal services, were bound by the rules applicable to the particular type of contract, except to the extent that they varied them by express terms. What was involved in the first instance was the will of the parties to enter into a type of relationship.

In the late eighteenth and nineteenth centuries, these older theories of contract law were secularized, in the sense that their religious foundations were replaced by a conception based not on faith in a transcendent reason and a transcendent will, from which human reason and will are derived and to which they are responsible, but rather on the inherent freedom of each individual to exercise his own autonomous reason and will, subject only to considerations of social utility. This secular theory drew heavily on contract doctrines and rules that had originally been developed on the basis of the earlier religious theories, but it subjected those doctrines and rules to a new rationalization and a new systematization. It broke many of the links not only between contract law and moral theology but also between contract law and the communitarian postulates which had informed both Catholic and Protestant legal traditions. The new secular theory also tended to isolate contract law from other branches of civil law, such as the law of torts and of unjust enrichment, whose moral and communitarian aspects were less easy to suppress.

With the decline of individualism and rationalism, it was inevitable that the prevailing nineteenth-century theory of contract law would come under attack. Both its attackers and its defenders need to be aware, however, of its historical background, and especially of the religious sources from which it was derived and against which it reacted. In the absence of such an awareness, the issues become distorted. We are given a choice between the prevailing theory of general contract law – without its historical roots – and no theory at all. We may learn from history, however, that there is a third possibility: to build a new and different theory on the foundation of the older ones.

RECOMMENDED READING

Bärmann, Johannes. "Pacta sunt servanda: Consideration sur l'histoire du contrat consensual." *Revue internationale de droit comparé* 13 (1961): 18–53.

Berger, Raoul. "From Hostage to Contract." *Illinois Law Review* 35 (1940): 154–281.

Berman, Harold J. *Law and Revolution: The Formation of the Western Legal Tradition.* Cambridge, MA: Harvard University Press, 1983.

  Law and Revolution II: The Impact of the Protestant Reformations of the Western Legal Tradition. Cambridge, MA: Harvard University Press, 2003.

  Faith and Order: The Reconciliation of Law and Religion. Grand Rapids, MI: Wm. B. Eerdmans Publishing, 1993.

Dawson, John P. *The Oracles of the Law.* Ann Arbor, MI: University of Michigan Law School, 1968.

Eusden, John D. *Puritans, Lawyers, and Politics in Early Seventeenth Century England.* Hamden, CT: Archon Books, 1968.

Fried, Charles. *Contract as Promise: A Theory of Contractual Obligation.* Cambridge, MA: Harvard University Press, 1981.

Gilmore, Grant. *The Death of Contract.* Columbus, OH: Ohio State University Press, 1974.

Hill, Christopher. *Puritanism and Revolution: Studies in Interpretation of the English Revolution of the 17th Century.* New York: Schocken Books, 1958.

Noonan, John T., Jr. *The Scholastic Analysis of Usury.* Cambridge, MA: Harvard University Press, 1957.

Schulz, Fritz. *The History of Roman Legal Science.* Oxford: Clarendon Press, 1946.

Simpson, A. W. B. *A History of the Law of Contract: The Rise of the Action of Assumpsit.* New York: Oxford University Press 1975.

Stoljar, S. J. *A History of Contract at Common Law.* Canberra: Australian National University Press, 1975.

Tierney, Brian. *Religion, Law and the Growth of Constitutional Thought, 1150–1650.* Cambridge: Cambridge University Press, 1982.

Walzer, Michael. *The Revolution of the Saints: A Study in the Origins of Radical Politics.* Cambridge, MA: Harvard University Press, 1968.

Witte, John, Jr. "Blest Be the Ties that Bind: Covenant and Community in Puritan Thought." *Emory Law Journal* 36 (1987): 579–601.

The Reformation of Rights: Law, Religion, and Human Rights in Early Modern Calvinism. Cambridge: Cambridge University Press, 2007.

CHAPTER SEVEN

Procedure, proof, and evidence

Mathias Schmoeckel

Legal procedure and rules of evidence set the notion of justice into motion. While today, Western state laws of procedure and evidence proceed largely without an explicitly Christian orientation, a number of the basic modern rules of procedure and evidence are grounded in biblical and Christian sources. Both the Roman lawyers and the Church Fathers of the fourth through sixth centuries developed some of these rules and procedures based on Jewish and biblical teachings. The canonists and moralists of the ninth through fourteenth centuries added more rules and wove them into an intricate moral theology and jurisprudence that dominated church courts and secular courts for centuries. After the sixteenth-century Reformation, some of these rules and procedures persisted in the civil courts of Protestant lands, and remained in place, with ample reforms and simplifications, in Protestant church tribunals. While the eighteenth-century French Revolution and subsequent codification movements eventually reformed most state laws of procedure and evidence, some of these basic assumptions, grounded in the Christian tradition, persist still today. This chapter recounts briefly a few of the major developments of the law of procedure, proof, and evidence from biblical to modern times, with a focus on the *ius commune* tradition.

JUSTICE BY MEANS OF PROCEDURE: THE JEWISH HERITAGE

A number of basic Western concepts of procedure are rooted in biblical Judaism, including the understanding of what is just. The Semitic word ṣ*dq* is the root of such words as ṣ*addīq* (the righteous), ṣ*addæq* (the fair order), and ṣ*ᵉdāqām* (the just deed). This is not the only Semitic notion of justice, but it shows that this basic notion applies to the state of public order involving persons and actions.

In the ancient Jewish world, the king was seen as a representative of the God of justice, with power to pass judgment on deviations from the

8 "The Judicial Duel" (litho), from Paul Lacroix, *Le Moyen Age et la Renaissance*
(Paris, 1847).

traditional just order and to protect persons who were socially weak.[1] As a
consequence, the king passed divine righteousness and justice to the people
(Psalm 72:1ff.). In honoring the just and condemning the wrongdoer, the
king re-established divine peace (ŝalôm) in the community. The Hebrew
Bible makes clear that God does not let the guilty win his case in
court (Exodus 23:7), and that God wants the innocent set free (Exodus
21:1–3; 6–8; Psalm 7:8). King Solomon, therefore, asked God to ensure that
the kings of Israel always condemn the wicked and justify the righteous
(1 Kings 8:32; 2 Chronicles 6:23).

---

[1] Josef Scharbert,"Gerechtigkeit," in *Theologische Realenzyklopädie*, ed. Gerhard Krause and Gerhard
Müller (Berlin/New York: De Gruyter, 1984), XII:404–11. See further the chapter by David Novak
herein.

Justice is thus a basic quality of the ruler (Genesis 18:19) in the ancient Jewish world, and it refers explicitly to the ruler's central duty to preside over trials and to give just judgments. A ruler's judgment even helps the culprit to become just again in the eyes of God and of the community. But the king must take great care in exercising this power of judgment, for "He who says to the wicked, 'You are innocent,' will be cursed by peoples, abhorred by nations" (Proverbs 24:24). It is further a great sin to condemn the righteous without a trial, and an unjust sentence is considered a menace to society (2 Samuel 4:11; 1 Kings 2:32). The king who does not render justice deprives his subjects of the chance to lead their lives in fundamental concordance with God and his order. Justice, therefore, is a divine way to preserve a man in community with God, neighbor, and self; it gives each person a right and duty to live properly. Priests are to help the king in rendering such justice (Psalm 132:9). The task of the trial is to decide who is just ("ṣaediq") and who is not. God helps the process of discovering the truth by showing righteousness "bright as the light of the noonday sun" (see Psalm 37:5ff).

In the ancient Jewish world, justice ultimately remained an act of God, who is the righteous judge (Psalm 7:11; Jeremiah 12:1). Behind all human procedures, God judges each man according to his merits (1 Kings 8:32). If the king does not judge and punish the sins committed in his realm, God will take the king's place and render his own judgment. And in his anger, God will send devastation, war, diseases, and hunger upon the land for its failure to do justice – just as he had condemned Sodom and Gomorrah in earlier days (Deuteronomy 29:15–27; Leviticus 26).

Trial before a judge is a central means to re-establish the God-given status of peace and justice. The judicial procedure cannot be merely formulaic; it must be carried out in an equitable way in order to achieve a just result. The laws of procedure and evidence are central to this pursuit of justice. These laws legitimate the ruler and the maintenance of a just order that pleases God. This basic Jewish understanding continued with the New Testament Greek term *dikaiosunē*. St. Paul did not use this term in its Greek philosophical sense of justice as a human virtue but in the Jewish sense of a just relationship between God and man. A just man is one who longs to be just before God, that is, to be approved of by God (1 Corinthians 1:30).

Much of the influence of this ancient thinking can also be seen in early Roman law. The Roman Stoic philosopher, Cicero, defined justice (*iustitia*) as "giving to each his due" (*reddens unicuique quod suum est*). Unlike Jewish scholars, however, Cicero did not mean by justice the divine act of allowing a person to come back into harmony with God. He referred, instead, to a human action alone by which a person must be rewarded for his merit or punished for his sin. This idea of justice helped to take the art of procedure out of the exclusive competence of priests, the *pontifices*, and place it with a developing secular profession of lawyers. But even these lawyers still sometimes called themselves "priests of justice" with responsibility to define what is right by proper criminal procedures and to offer the promise of awards in civil cases.[2] In ancient Israel, as later in the Roman Empire, judicial trials remained a central means to ensure justice and order. Since the Emperor could not personally sit in judgment in all cases throughout the Empire, he established a hierarchy of judges who depended on him and acted with his authority to help stabilize the Roman Empire. While they acted on the basis of imperial authority, however, these judges were free to judge according to their own consciences. Their judgments could be overruled by higher-ranking judges, and by the Emperor himself in the last instance.

It was this Roman system of judging and judgment that was at work with the trial of Jesus Christ by Pontius Pilate, the governor of Judea. The Bible's detailed description of the process is well known to Christians (Matthew 27:11–16; Mark 15:2–15; Luke 23:3–25; John 18:28–19:16). Despite the tragic outcome of this pivotal trial, the early Christian church was not hostile to legal procedures in general. For a time after the ascension of Christ, Christians believed in the imminence of the Return of Christ and God's Last Judgment, and thus thought that punishment might be better left to God (cf. I Corinthians 4:5).[3] But they soon agreed on the need for a legal order and for proper procedures, and they accepted the authority of the Emperor to be as "of God." The apostle Paul instructed Christians to "honor" and "obey" the Emperor and other authorities, and to accept their rules and judgments as a matter of conscience (Romans 13:1–7; Titus 3:1). Peter added that all Christians were to be subject to the secular order so that wrongdoers could be pursued and punished (1 Peter 2:13–14).[4]

Yet early Christians were divided on the question whether human wrongs themselves would trigger the end of the world, or at least bring the kind of divine punishment and destruction that the sins of Sodom and Gomorrah had earlier occasioned. The fourth-century Church Father, Lactantius, settled this question dispositively in his famous tract,

---

[2] *The Digest of Justinian*, trans. and ed. Alan Watson, 2 vols., rev. edn (Philadelphia: University of Pennsylvania Press, 1988) 1:bk. 1, ch.1, tit (hereafter "Dig.")
[3] See further chapter by Luke Timothy Johnson herein.
[4] See further discussion of this text in the chapter by Kent Greenawalt herein.

De mortibus persecutorum. He argued that God would not in his anger immediately punish all of humanity for their sins, but would give them time to reform themselves. But God would interfere in an individual person's life according to his sins or merits, and would reward the faithful and punish the unjust. In Lactantius' view, God not only controlled all human deeds, especially legal procedures, but also reserved the ultimate power to act as a supreme judge himself and to correct unjust human judges when necessary. Lactantius' view was thus parallel to that of ancient Judaism, namely, that God is the supreme judge who now presides through and over the hierarchy of Roman judges.[5]

THE DEVELOPMENT OF LEGAL PROCEDURE IN THE WESTERN CHRISTIAN TRADITION

In the Western Christian tradition, just as in the Jewish tradition, legal procedure was viewed as necessary to do justice. But it remained a highly risky task for the judge, since he would be judged by God as he himself had judged others (Matthew 7:2). Christ said that judges were not to act superficially "by appearances," but had to give righteous judgments (John 7:24). A certain number of such basic precepts of judging can be found in the Gospel, reflecting common beliefs of the day in the basic standards of procedure. Neither the passion of Christ nor the persecution of the Christian martyrs by the Roman authorities persuaded Christians to question the basic need for legal procedures. Even though these procedures were sometimes unjust, Christians regarded such injustice as a divine test to prove the strength of their faith.

Early in the Christian tradition, the ruler was already seen as essential to establishing public order, guaranteeing peace, and letting justice prevail. For this reason, when the monarchic government of the first bishops was established in the Christian communities, these bishops were given the power to judge controversies between the members of the parish. By a law of June 23, 318, enacted almost immediately after Christianity was officially tolerated, Constantine obliged his secular judges to accept the jurisdiction of bishops (*audientia episcopalis*).[6] This was the beginning of the tradition of bishops serving as judges, with competence not only in spiritual matters, but in some civil and criminal matters as well. Bishops were

[5] L. Caelii Firmiani Lactantii, *De ira Dei liber*, ed. H. Kraft and A. Wlosok, Texte zur Forschung, 4, (Darmstadt: Wissenschaftliche Buchgemeinschaft, 1971), lib. 21, tit. 10, cap. 71.
[6] Jean Gaudemet, *L'Église dans l'Empire Romain (IV–V siècles)*, Histoire du Droit et des Institutions de l'Église en Occident, (Paris: Sirey, 1958), 498, 230ff.

thereafter incorporated into the hierarchy of imperial judges, and they learned to yield to higher tribunals if and as needed. This was also the beginning of a hierarchy of ecclesiastical judges within the church, which the pope, after the eleventh century, took over from the emperor.[7]

All bishops were expected to act skilfully as judges. This was possible in the later Roman Empire, because most bishops came from upper-class families and were brought up according to the educational ideals of the day (*paideia*). Their education included a basic training in law and (legal) rhetoric. After the merger of the early church law and Roman law in the fourth century, the church leaders themselves issued many procedural rules for centuries. For example, the prohibition on giving judicial sentences in dubious matters was a Roman law principle; Roman judges could leave matters unsolved as *non liquet*. In the early sixth century, Pope Gregory I upheld this principle but to the effect not of ordering that judgments be suspended but rather that judges ascertain the facts of the case in order to render a judgment.

A decisive influence for European history came from newly evangelized Ireland, where the kings were seen as sources and guarantors of justice. Due to the essential influence of Old Testament examples and the new monastic theology, justice was no longer viewed as something provided by God according to his will; it was rather an essential human task to be done on God's behalf. A hierarchy of judges, with the king as highest authority, had to determine that all judgments accorded with the truth and the principles of Christian piety. Human verdicts would inspire compunction, which would induce God to forgive the sinner in the Last Judgment. For this reason, royal justice would help subjects find their salvation.

The Carolingian ecclesiastical reformers of the ninth century sought to free the church from the rule of secular powers. Procedural law became a primary device for this purpose. Clerics were now to be judged only by ecclesiastical courts, not by secular courts; this was the so-called "privilege of forum" (*privilegium fori*). Other privileges were invented as well, such as the *actio spolii*, by which land taken by violence first had to be restored to the prior possessor before any litigation on the right to possess the land could begin. This rule was designed for bishops, who could not afford litigation when a rival had deprived them of their diocese and all financial and political means.

The ninth-century reformers also reinterpreted the nature of the judiciary and the purpose of judgment. More radical than their ancestors, these

---

[7] See further the chapter by Harold J. Berman herein.

Carolingian reformers understood that God's Last Judgment of the world was to be the last instance of all litigation. Furthermore, they understood that all litigation was a means of punishing committed sins. As everybody could only be judged legitimately according to his sin, nobody could be sentenced twice for the same sin or crime. This exclusion of double jeopardy (*ne bis in idem*) applied also to God, they argued. God could only punish sins which had not been punished by any human court. The just sanction of a judge, therefore, would exclude purgatory and eternal punishment.

This new understanding of the nature of judgment required that the function of legal procedure be redefined in a specifically Christian way. Just like the omniscient God who would sit in the Last Judgment, so the worldly judges who presided over individual cases here and now were obliged to render their judgments in accordance with the true facts. The danger of a sentence disproportionate to the defendant's actual guilt was regarded as a higher risk for the judge than for the accused. Whereas excessive criminal punishment by government would be credited to the accused in the Last Judgment, the judge who imposed this excessive punishment had committed a crime and a sin, which could cost him his own salvation.[8] With this new understanding of the relation between human and divine judgment, all human judges, whether ecclesiastical or secular, were understood to sit subject to the highest court of the Last Judgment. All legal procedures in turn were interpreted to be a means of salvation.

This had two implications. First, it was necessary to draft rules for judges to guarantee the lawful and effective development of procedures. Though they restricted the judges, these rules were ultimately for the judges' own protection against ultimate divine sanction for judging unjustly. Judges had to learn these procedural rules and to prove their compliance with them by keeping written court records. Traditional forms of judicial discretion operating in accordance with the judge's conscience were now replaced by the idea of a just order to be realized and implemented by a rule-bound judiciary. Higher judges, sitting on appeal, could check the written record of the tribunal below them to see whether lower court judges had followed proper rules of procedure, and they could issue remedies or reversals if these procedural rules were breached. Second, the right of appeal to a higher judge and court became increasingly important as a means of doing justice in individual cases. In the last instance, only the pope, as head of the church and representative of God, was competent to dispense final human

---

[8] Capitula Angilramni, *Cor. Sal.* xi, ed. Karl Georg Schon, Projekt Pseudoisidor, 2005, 35, www.pseudoisidor.de/pdf/CA-Text.pdf (accessed May 31, 2007).

justice. This had powerful political implications in the Middle Ages. As the highest judge in all of Christendom, the pope claimed the suzerainty of all secular princes, including the emperor, and established the standards for justice which all princes had to obey in their territories. In cases of disobedience, the pope could intervene and depose and replace these disobedient rulers.

From the ninth century onward, clerics established the rules of procedure in order to meet these new Christian standards of justice. These reformers felt remarkably free from earlier secular laws. Archbishop Hincmar of Reims, for example, argued that all Christians would know that God would not judge according to Roman, Salic, or Burgundian law, but rather according to divine and apostolic law.[9] Henceforth, the church was to create a whole new legal order of procedure in order to ascertain justice and a truly Christian order. The laws of procedure, in turn, developed a central eschatological dimension. One effect of this was that there could be no sharp distinction between civil and criminal matters. Criminal law dealt with cases of possible criminal punishment by the authorities; civil cases obliged guilty defendants to pay damages to their victims. But there was no real difference in the ultimate treatment of civil and criminal cases: just a warning for the judge to handle "criminal cases" with greater care due to the higher risk of permanent harm to the parties.

A central maxim of the emerging Roman–canon law of procedure was that a trial is an act that involves three persons: the judge, the actor or plaintiff, and the accused party. Nobody else needed to attend the trial. Only the accused had the right to involve an advocate. In cases in which he could not afford one, the tribunal was obliged, by a decision of Pope Honorius III, to provide legal counsel.[10] The judge alone was responsible for ensuring a fair and just procedure in the individual case. In contrast to earlier Germanic procedures, Roman–canon procedures were not public. Trials of adultery, for example, could be carried out against a husband without his wife ever knowing about the case. It was up to the judge to decide how secret the sentence should remain. At minimum, the people were told of the trial only after the judgment was rendered. In an important case, a great crowd would be gathered on a given date, and the judgment pronounced publicly in order to ensure its proper execution in

---

[9] Hincmar of Reims, *De divortio Lotharii Regis et Theutbergae reginae*, MGH Conc. IV.I, (Hannover: Hahn, 1992), 145.

[10] *Decretales Gregorii IX*, lib. I, tit. 23, cap. I, in Emil Friedberg, *Corpus Iuris Canonici* 2 vols. (Leipzig: Tauchnitz, 1879) (hereafter, following convention, x.). See further Franck Roumy, "Le développement du système de l'avocat commis d'office dans la procédure romano-canonique (XIe–XIVe siècle)," *Tijdschrift voor Rechtsgeschiedenis* 71 (2003): 359–86.

or outside the town. This "theatre of justice," as it was called, could also include a public confession of the criminal to show his or her repentance. Especially in medieval France, this tradition, called the *amende honorable*, was carried out in front of the cathedral to ensure reconciliation of the sinner with God and the community. But most trials were carried out without ever making the process or judgment public.

The assumption at work in this secret procedure was that the judge was not to be controlled by the public but rather by procedural rules and by a higher appellate judge. Only in cases involving notorious crimes did the process have to end with a public execution in order to prove the effectiveness of the tribunal and the justice of its lord. But in order to make a statement on the legitimacy of the judgment, the procedure had to be documented in writing. The Fourth Lateran Council (1215) made the keeping of court records compulsory, although it did not introduce compulsory written procedure. The sentence could consist of a notice in the records as being "the consequence of law" (*von Rechts wegen*), without stated reasons.

In most cases, judges were not left alone to find out the facts – although there was no regular police force to assist them until the seventeenth century. Both parties were compelled to help to find the truth. Prior to the establishment of a trial (*litis contestatio*), both parties had to swear an "oath of calumny" to hide nothing and to speak the truth only. The plaintiff had to prove his accusation, and if he failed he could be punished with the verdict destined for the guilty party. But even the accused had to search for evidence to prove his innocence.

Since the plaintiff was charged with proving the accused guilty, the task of the judge was made simpler. This accusation procedure was accordingly named a *processus ordinarius*. But no one dared to accuse or even denounce an important person, for fear of reprisal. Thus, in cases involving important people, including notably the clergy, the function of accusation often fell to the courts themselves. Already in the ninth-century Carolingian period, itinerant episcopal courts (*Sendgerichte*) could investigate matters that had become public scandals, and could file accusations against parties when appropriate. In the later twelfth century, Pope Innocent III allowed ecclesiastical courts to proceed against clerics, even without a formal accusation, in cases of public scandal in order to maintain discipline in the church.[11] In the early thirteenth century, this disciplinary practice led to an independent form of criminal procedure

---

[11] Markus Hirte, *Papst Innozenz III., das IV. Lateranum und die Strafverfahren gegen Kleriker* (Tübingen: Diskord, 2005).

called the *processus extraordinarius*. This was an inquisitorial procedure that became a common practice in the later Middle Ages. Its rules and procedures were documented in detail by the great thirteenth-century jurist, Albertus Gandinus.

Given its eschatological function, the judge's judgment in an individual case served not only to reconcile the sinner with God but also to reestablish justice in the community. But if the case could not be proved by the facts, judges were to adjourn the procedure until further evidence was found (*absolutio ab instantia*). In rendering such an *absolutio* or similar judgment, the judge had discretion to order some disciplinary punishment in order to ensure public order. Such judgments were increasingly left to the arbitrary power of judges, so that by the later twelfth century every judgment came to involve what was called literally "arbitrary punishment" (*poena arbitraria*). This punishment did not depend on an enacted statute, and the form of punishment could follow customary laws or the judge's own discretion. In order to save the judge, a common saying demanded benevolent treatment of the accused in cases of doubt (*in dubio pro reo*).

These rules of regular legal procedure, with their safeguards for the defendant, could be waived in individual cases, especially those that involved abominable offenses, such as heresy or treason. According to a maxim by Pope Innocent IV, normal procedural rules could be waived in such cases (*ordo est ordinem non servare*). In the later thirteenth century, in fact, treatises were developed for the special procedures to follow in cases of suspected heresy. The most popular of these was the *Practica officii inquisitioni* of Bernardo Gui, which introduced the ex officio procedure of the Inquisition. This medieval procedure against heretics was the model for later inquisitorial procedures against "witches" formulated in the papal bull *Summis desiderantes affectibus* (1484) of Pope Innocent VIII. In 1487, the two Dominicans, Jacob Sprenger and Heinrich Institoris, developed the *Mallus Maleficarum* (literally "the witchcraft hammer"), the basic manual for the examination of "sorcerers" and "witches" in many parts of the Empire.

In order to offset the repressive power of some of these procedural laws and their exceptions, the decretalists from the mid thirteenth century forward began to formulate minimum guarantees of procedural justice. Particularly important were the decree *Pastoralis cura*,[12] and the *Constitutio Saepe* of 1314, in which Pope Clement V mandated immediate application of minimum procedural requirements for every case, even in cases of

---

[12] *Constitutiones Clementinae*, in Friedberg, *Corpus Iuris Canonici*, lib. 2, tit. 11, cap. 2.

interim "summary" jurisdiction.[13] These laws became starting points for canonists and legists to determine limits on the power of even the highest human judge.

Given the important role of the medieval church in Western society, the Roman–canon law of procedure became the archetype for Continental European law, and it even influenced English law at an early stage. Medieval English churches and monasteries appealed to the pope, who sent a "delegated judge" and instructed them how to decide the case depending on the findings. This delegate's decrees were later often cast in more generic form and incorporated into the books of canon law to become standard procedural guides for ecclesiastical and secular courts alike. The instruments of the "delegated judge" secured the uniformity of procedural law in Europe. Similar decrees issued by bishops or deans, and backed by threats of excommunication, were also accepted all over Western Europe – unlike deeds by secular authorities of distant countries which could be disregarded without great risk. Furthermore, the pope claimed a general competence to decide any cases involving a denial of justice. Every prince, whose jurisdiction did not meet the standards established by Roman–canon law, therefore, risked possible interference by the Holy See. Even in the Holy Roman Empire, after 1346, the emperor granted the electoral prince bishops jurisdiction free from his imperial intervention, save in extreme cases of denial of justice.

In the sixteenth century, Protestant countries in particular drew in part on the Old Testament to call for reforms of the medieval system of justice and punishment. Every criminal act that was not punished by the prince, they argued, could cause God in his anger to punish the unjust country with war, diseases, and misery. This was one reason, why, beginning in the sixteenth century, many important codes of criminal procedure, such as the *Constitutio Criminalis Carolina* of 1532, were enacted. These codes not only secured common procedural standards for the community, but also limited judicial discretion and thereby ultimately spared the community divine sanction for the injustice being committed. Reformers in this period also debated the equity of some common criminal procedures inherited from medieval times. Sixteenth-century Spanish reformer, Juan Luis Vives, for example, argued in his commentary on Augustine's *City of God* that, considering the standards of modern Christianity, especially the obligation of fraternal love and commiseration with the poor, brutal practices of investigation and punishment rising to torture should not be tolerated. Humanists like Thomas More and Michel de Montaigne declared that

[13] *Ibid.*

many other barbarous forms of medieval procedure were cruel and ill-advised. How could people be expected to refrain from violence if the state used violence to such a great extent, especially in meting out public punishments? The delinquent could be made more useful, they argued, by putting them to mandatory labor in the community and by tending to the repair of their souls. Protestant authors, drawing especially on the Lutheran theorist, Philipp Melanchthon, pressed natural law arguments for fair procedures, arguing that the natural right of self-defense should also apply to the rights of the accused to defend themselves in court.[14]

Some reformers took particular aim at the traditional practice of torture, which was commonly used to extort confessions and extract information in criminal cases, as we shall see in a moment. They argued that it was better for a judge in case of uncertainty not to render judgment rather than use torture to find evidence; it was better to leave all such uncertainties to the court of ultimate resort at the Last Judgment. These main reform ideas were later summarized in the famous work of Cesare Marchese Beccaria, *On Crimes and Punishments* (1764).

When the judiciary became independent, under modern constitutional systems of separation of powers, the executive task of investigation and the administration of the police were left to a *ministère public*, who had to ensure that all crimes were prosecuted according to the law. This reduced the role of the judge within the scope of the inquisition procedure. He became free to judge after his own conviction (*intime conviction*). Also important for protecting the accused was the rise of constitutional guarantees of the traditional privilege against self-incrimination (*nemo tenetur se ipsum accusare*). In the seventeenth century, this principle was grounded in the natural law idea of English philosopher Thomas Hobbes that everybody has the right to use all means of self-preservation – now including procedural means as well. Though Hobbes taught this as a principle of natural law, he still regarded natural law as the law of God.[15]

THE DEVELOPMENT OF LAWS OF EVIDENCE AND PROOF

In ancient Roman law as well as in medieval canon law, the evaluation of evidence of a fact had to make that fact *manifestum*. A case was manifest

---

[14] Matthaeus Wesembecius, *In Pandectas Iuris Civilis et Codicis Iustiniani Libros IIX Commentarii olim Paratitla dicti* (Basel 1606), De Iust.&Iure, tit. I, n.15, 27.
[15] See Thomas Hobbes, *On The Citizen*, ed. and trans. Richard Tucker and Michael Silverthorne (Cambridge/New York: Cambridge University Press, 1998), ch. 4. See also the discussion of Hobbes in the chapter by Brian Tierney herein.

when the proof against the defendant was considered sufficient. In 382, just after the establishment of Christianity as the official faith of the Empire, the Roman emperors ruled that a verdict should only be admitted based on "indubitable evidence" (*indiciis indubitatis*), and that such evidence had to be brighter than light.[16] Echoing this rule, St. Augustine regarded simple suspicion as an insufficient basis for conviction. Pope Gregory the Great, too, declared famously the maxim that it is improper for a judge to give a judgment in a case of doubt.

Beginning in the ninth century, canon lawyers asked for more certain proof. Only the evidence that was as "clear as the noon-day sun" (*luce meridiana clarior*) (cf. Matthew 13:43), they argued, was sufficient for a legitimate judgment in a *poena ordinaria* procedure. Whatever remained less clear had to be left to God's Last Judgment (1 Corinthians 5:12–13). These ideas of the ninth century remained in place even during the two dark centuries that followed, and were staples in the renewed jurisprudence of the later eleventh century forward. Theologians, too, increasingly understood them as principles of moral theology. Particularly Thomas Aquinas, in his *Summa theologiae*, explained these rules of proof thoroughly, which added to their authority.

There were some exceptions to the high standards of evidence and proof. Again, in grave cases of heresy and high treason, these formalities of proof could be waived. A prince, as the highest judge in the realm, had the authority to sentence a party suspected of such serious offences, even without having complete evidence and full proof. An even more decisive exemption was the possibility of issuing a sentence not only without complete evidence of a crime, but even without a law criminalizing the act (*poena extraordinaria*). This exception was first introduced during the prosecution of heretics around 1200 by Vincentius Hispanus. It became a standard part of canon law thereafter by a decree of the Fourth Lateran Council of 1215. A century later, Pope Innocent IV adopted and approved this rule, too, in his commentary on the book of canon law called *Liber Extra*. The judge, Innocent argued, should have discretion to mete out a disciplinary punishment in such cases, but the death penalty was excluded absent full proof.

A common feature of the Western Christian tradition from late antiquity to modern times was the belief in miracles, wrought by God and his saints. Augustine, for example, commented on a case in which two priests cleared themselves of incrimination by swearing on their innocence at the

---

[16] *The Theodosian Code and Novels*, trans. Clyde Pharr (Princeton, NJ: Princeton University Press, 1952), lib. 9, tit. 37, lex 3 and lib. 4, tit. 19, lex 25.

tomb of St. Felix of Nola. As they remained sound and thriving after their oath, they were regarded as innocent.[17] Although such ordeals were not practiced in North Africa, Augustine concluded that some saints had special miraculous powers. Later Christians drew on this early example to justify the use of ordeals to collect evidence – a practice already known in Roman Gaul and various Germanic kingdoms. These practices were eventually supported by various biblical texts. Peter and Paul had both asked their communities to pray to God for just sentences (1 Peter 2:13–17; 1 Timothy 2:1 and 4). And the Old Testament gave several examples of true ordeals, such as the ordeal of the bitter water (Numbers 5:11–18) or the combat of David and Goliath (1 Samuel 17:45–50). Believing in the immediate punishment of the guilty as well as in the remuneration of the just in their lifetime in the tradition of Lactantius, Western Christians increasingly resorted to ordeals in order to solve evidentiary disputes. Especially in the context of Frankish procedure, with its characteristically weak judge, ordeals proved to be exceedingly useful evidentiary techniques.

While earlier Christians accepted ordeals as consistent with the church's teachings on miracles, theologians, such as the ninth-century Archbishop Agobard of Lyon, criticized this practice as a direct challenge to God's omnipotence. They argued that it was an attempt to force God to intervene in a trial, and that the Bible had too many examples where God accepted unjust human judgments without interfering immediately. This criticism carried weight. Though it retained its belief in miracles, the church increasingly fought against the ordeal as an improper method for collecting evidence. The Fourth Lateran Council of 1215 decreed that priests should not participate in the bloodiest ordeals, and, eventually, the Council of Trent of 1563 banned all forms of ordeal and combat without exception.[18]

In ancient Roman law, the praetors and other imperial judges acted on the authority of the Roman Empire and were thus free to evaluate the proof and to decide whether the evidence collected was sufficient. As an exception, a defendant's guilty plea was regarded as sufficient proof for a judge to give a sentence according to the law.[19] With such a plea, the judge could judge the case without further delay, just as if the defendant were caught

---

[17] Augustinus Hipponensis, *Epistolae LVI-C*, ed. D. D. Daur (Turnhout: Brepols, 2005), epistle 78, ch. 5, 83–91.

[18] Decrees of the Fourth Lateran Council (1215), session 25.19, in *Decrees of the Ecumenical Councils*, ed. Norman P. Tanner, 2 vols. (London: Sheed & Ward, 1990), vol. 1.

[19] Paulus in Dig. bk. 42, ch. 2, tits. 1, 3; Ulpian in Dig. bk. 42, ch. 2, tit. 6; *The Institutes of Gaius*, trans. W. M. Gordon and O. F. Robinson (London: Duckworth, 1988), bk. 4, ch. 24; *Code of* (Hildesheim: Weidmann, 1989–1993), vol. II, bk. 7, ch. 59 (hereafter cod.)

red-handed.[20] Medieval canon law reformers stressed more distinctly the importance of proper rules of procedure and evidence to guarantee justice in individual cases, even those involving such confessions and pleas. Ninth-century church lawyers sought to establish a set of rules, which had to be respected by a judge in all cases in order to achieve a just sentence. Benedictus Levita and Ansegis in particular collected detailed rules to determine the evidence necessary for a guilty verdict. No judge acting in accordance with these rules could be held responsible for wrong judgments.

In 862, however, Pope Nicolas pronounced a judgment without follow-ing any prior procedure; he did not even give the condemned a chance to argue the case. Based on the authority of St. Paul (1 Corinthians 5) and the authoritative commentary on Paul called the *Ambrosiaster*, Nicholas argued that an immediate judgment prevented culprits from hiding the truth and using a judicial audience to publish their lies. This stood in sharp contrast to the general assertions of the canon law of the day that proper procedures were needed to evaluate all evidence, even if false. In the twelfth century, the great medieval canonist Gratian explained this famous case, which vio-lated all other canon law statements on procedure and evidence, as a "noto-rious" case. It was based on the scholastic epistemology of the day that considered it possible to have perfect knowledge of a case. Generally known facts of cases, which the accused could not deny, came to be regarded as "notorious." The twelfth- and thirteenth-century canonists added to such cases of "notorious facts" (*notorium facti*), cases of "notorious laws" (*noto-rium iuris*), of which the singular example was a defendant's guilty plea – a presumption that followed the Roman principle *confessus pro iudicato habetur*. They added further cases of "notorious presumptions" (*notorium praesumptionis*), involving legal fictions and legal presumptions. In all such cases, the evidence was considered perfect, rendering further procedural steps, including appeals, superfluous and thus dispensable. The medieval doctrine of "notoriety" remained an important exception to the usual canon law rules that judges collect and evaluate evidence in a formal trial. Although cases of notoriety were probably rare, they constituted a consid-erable threat – especially in cases of political importance.

Moreover, in the developed Roman–canon law of proof, the confession itself remained an important case of notoriety (*notorium iuris*), with not only legal but also theological significance. Confession and other acts of penitence, in public or private, were part of a long tradition in the church and were considered to be essential to one's salvation (Romans 10:10). The

---

[20] See Cod. bk. 9, ch. 13, tit. 1; Cod. bk. 1, ch. 3, tit. 53. (both from Justinian in 533 CE).

confession not only revealed one's submission to God (2 Corinthians 9:13), but also contained a revelation of God's glory (1 Timothy 3:16). The confession was seen as medicine for the soul; everybody should repent of his sins and praise the Lord before his death (Ecclesiasticus 17:26). After the ninth century, the church developed the principle that every Christian should confess at least once a year before Easter. This principle was established as a rule by the Fourth Lateran Council in 1215; failure to do annual confession could lead to charges of heresy.[21]

This common practice and eventual canon law of annual confession had two important consequences for the Roman–canon law of evidence and proof. First, confessions before a confessor and a church court were rendered equivalent – with the penitentiary called the *forum internum* and the court trial the *forum externum*. Both confessions helped to reconcile the sinner with God and the community. Second, because the annual duty of confession could be discharged in the *forum externum*, the failure of an accused party to appear in court and confess his sin could lead to charges not only of contumacy, but also of heresy. If a year passed before the defendant appeared to justify himself, he faced double condemnation.

In medieval Roman–canon law, a free, unforced confession was considered the most valuable evidence of all other proofs; it was called the "queen of proof" (*regina probationum*). The accused party could be forced to confess by torture, as well, a practice earlier maintained by both Roman law and Germanic law, though temporarily suspended during the ninth-century Carolingian reforms. In the later Middle Ages, torture came to play an important role in demonstrating the prince's power and effectiveness in achieving justice, though the citizens of some privileged countries and cities were not subjected to torture except in cases of heresy and high treason. The confession given in torture was not regarded to be perfect proof, however, but only an indication of guilt. The judge was expected to interrogate the accused some days after the torture to establish the truth. If a defendant persisted in his denials, he could legally be submitted to torture two more times. Without any legal confession, but with other strong evidence of guilt, the accused could only be condemned to what was called "extraordinary punishment" (*poena extraordinaria*).

Other forms of proof were grounded in biblical teachings. The Bible, for example, often called the evidence of two or three certain witnesses sufficient for proving an act (Deuteronomy 6:2; 19:17; 2 Corinthians 13:1).

---

[21] X 5.38.12.

Medieval canonists, therefore, established the rule that any verdict based on two credible witnesses was almost as sound as one based on the confession of the accused. The problem remained to determine when a witness was credible and when his testimony was believable. Canonists required that the witness have a good, undiminished observation of the accused and that he be unbiased toward the accused. Starting in the fourteenth century, copious books set out detailed rules for determining the credibility of witnesses.

In cases involving grave crimes, even improper witnesses could be examined by the judge. To be sure, their testimony was only probative of guilt and could not constitute a sound basis for a guilty verdict. But, in such grave cases, many traditional immunities against testimony could be relaxed – including the immunity that protected spouses from testifying against each other, and even the immunity of the confessor from giving evidence gathered in the sacrament of penance.[22] This latter relaxation was unusual, for the secrecy of the confessional was an ancient church teaching. Medieval canon law did not require confessors to denounce criminals,[23] but it did require them to impel criminals to denounce themselves. If necessary, confessors could even refuse a criminal absolution until such voluntary confessions were made. Thomas Aquinas allowed further that a confessor could reveal facts about the confessed sinner in cases where those facts proved a candidate to be inappropriate for an important position within the church. In late medieval France, the state introduced "monitors" (*monitoires*) by which the priests were forced to look out for crimes and evidence. The same idea was later at work in Protestant Prussia, where the revelation of the confessor entitled the royal courts to use torture.[24] Only in 1682 did Pope Innocent XI issue a prohibition on all use of evidence gathered in confession. Thereafter, with increasing rigor, the Catholic Church defended the secrecy of the confessional. In secular law, priests unwilling to give evidence were no longer punished.[25]

In order to improve the credibility of the testimony, a judge could order a party to confirm his testimony by swearing an oath. This had been a common practice in the Germanic kingdoms, just as it had been in biblical

---

[22] B. Karitzky, "Die Geschichte der Zeugnisverweigerungsrechte. Ihre Entwicklung aus den Zeugen-Ausschlüssen und Privilegien des älteren Rechts," Diss. jur. Heidelberg 1959, (Düsseldorf: Zentral Verlag für Dissertationen Triltsch, 1959).   [23] Honorius III, Po 7844, a.1216–1227, X 5.31.13.

[24] Carl Christoph Stockmayer, Praeses: Johann Gottlieb Gonne, *Dissertatio inauguralis de tortura confessi*, (Erlangen: Becker, 1744).

[25] See, e.g., the first prohibition in the Prussian Allgemeines Landrecht of 1794 (II.II §.81), discussed in Bertrand Kurtscheid, *Das Beichtsiegel in seiner geschichtlichen Entwicklung* (Freiburg im Breisgau: Herder, 1912).

Israel (1 Kings 8:31; 2 Chronicles 6:22). While Jesus forbade any swearing of oaths (Matthew 5:33–37; James 5:12), this prohibition found no place in Western courts. The church even argued for a frequent use of oaths in order to diminish the application of ordeals. Indeed, whereas use of the ordeal to purify oneself of an accusation was called "vulgar purgation" (*purgatio vulgaris*), use of the oath was called "canonical purgation" (*purgatio canonica*). Such canonical purgation was considered credible because, in a case of perjury, the party was risking damnation at the Last Judgment. In order to enhance reliability, the judge could ask a party to collect other people as compurgators who could swear on his trustworthiness. This common practice of taking oaths was only slowly diminished in the later Middle Ages. Gregory XI condemned it in 1374 at the Council of Basel, but without immediate success.

In medieval laws of evidence, documents played a smaller role, for this was still a mostly illiterate world. But documents could establish perfect proof for a verdict, and in such cases, theoretically, judges were no longer free to decide on guilt or innocence. Instead, they had to obey the rules of evidence, stating which kinds of evidence permitted a guilty verdict or an acquittal. For this reason, historians usually call the Roman law of evidence a legal theory of proof. Only full proof (*probatio plena*) was sufficient for a verdict, whereas "less than full" (*semiplena*) evidence legitimized only a *poena extraordinaria*. But the judge retained the discretion to decide whether the confession or the witness were trustworthy, and he thus at least indirectly determined the outcome of the trial.

A guilty verdict could not be rendered on grounds of indictment, presumption, or suspicion alone. If a poor man, for example, was discovered to have stolen objects in the vicinity of his house, he could not be convicted on those facts alone. He could easily claim that he had just found or purchased these items, and absent further proof of his unlawful acquisition, the man would need to be exonerated.

With the introduction of the jury into Continental procedure during the French Revolution, many of these traditional binding rules of evidence had to be abolished. Lay jurors could not be expected to know the intricate rules of evidence. They were instead asked to decide cases according to their "free conscience" (*intime conviction*). According to Beccaria, the French reformers saw the long-practicing English juries, which had already operated for centuries, as a model for the new administration of criminal justice. Laymen, Beccaria argued, would be less prejudiced than judges, who belonged to a certain social sphere, and who routinely betrayed bias against members of the lower classes. The experiments with laymen, mixed courts with learned and lay judges, and the slow reintroduction of the only competent learned judges starting in 1808, remained true to the basic principle that all litigation should lead to a perception of the truth. And yet, in spite of all possible scientific ways of proving people guilty, such means as the polygraph illustrate to what degree the confession remains important for a "just" verdict.

Some essential vestiges of the old eschatological dimensions of procedure are still preserved in the reformed criminal procedure of modern Europe. Most people think that justice lies not only in a fair trial but also in the correct assertion of the facts. But even for those philosophers who now argue that justice is a function of fair procedure only, the Christian heritage is still manifest, for this was a Western conviction first fully developed by canon lawyers in the ninth century and expanded in subsequent centuries. Although the theological dimension of trials has been mostly forgotten, the task of the judge and the parties is still influenced by it.

When in modern times large courtrooms were designed to accommodate the public, they were decorated in many countries, except France, with Christian symbols. And they featured many formulaic words and rituals that echoed centuries of earlier Christian beliefs and practices. This was meant to remind the public and the court of the common ethical standards and the obligation of the judges to achieve justice. The removal of such symbols, which is currently occurring in such countries as Germany, does not solve the problem of determining the function of the legal procedure and the ethics which guide the court.

RECOMMENDED READING

Assmann, Jan. *Herrschaft und Heil. Politische Theologie in Ägypten, Israel und Europa.* Darmstadt: Wissenschaftliche Buchgemeinschaft, 2000.

Brundage, James A. *The Profession and Practice of Medieval Canon Law.* Aldershot: Ashgate Publishing, 2004.

van Caenegem, Raoul. "Methods of Proof in Western Medieval Law," in *Legal History: A European Perspective.* London: Hambledon Press, 1991, 71.

Carbasse, Jean-Marie. *Introduction historique au droit pénal et de la justice criminelle.* Paris: Presses Universitaires de France, 2006.

Cordero, Franco. *Procedura penale.* Milano: Giuffrè, 1987.

Gillissen, John, ed. *La Preuve.* Recueils de la Société Jean Bodin, XVI.1 and 2, XVII,1 and 2., 4 vols. Brussels: Librairie Encyclopédique, 1965.

Helmholz, R. H. *The Spirit of Classical Canon Law.* Athens, GA: University of Georgia Press, 1996.

Litewski, Wiesław. *Der römisch-kanonische Zivilprozeß nach den älteren ordines iudiciarii.* 2 vols. Krakau: Jagiellonian University Press, 1999.

Mausen, Yves. *Veritas adiutor. La procédure du témoigage dans le droit savant et la pratique française (XIIe–XIVe siècles).* Università degli studi di Milano, 35. Milan: Giuffrè, 2006.

Noonan, John T., Jr. *Power to Dissolve. Lawyers and Marriages in the Courts of the Roman Curia.* Cambridge, MA: Harvard University Press, 1972.

Salvioli, Giuseppe. *Storia del diritto Italiano, III.2: Storia della procedura civile e criminale.* Milano: Giuffrè, 1927.

Tomás y Valiente, Francisco. *El Derecho Penal de la Monarchia absoluta.* Madrid: Ed. Tecnos, 1969.

CHAPTER EIGHT

Family law and Christian jurisprudence

Don S. Browning

Christianity has had an enormous influence on Western family law. But it has not had this influence all by itself. It is best to think of Christian marriage and family theories as special twists brought to a variety of other folk, philosophical, legal, and economic perspectives on marriage and family. Christian marriage and family traditions have mixed with influences from Judaism, Greek philosophy, Roman law, and Germanic law. Christianity massively influenced the formal legal theories and practices of medieval and early modern Europe, but it did so through its unique packaging of a complex range of sources. These sources had logics, values, and traditions that were given new meaning by Christian narratives and metaphors.

But in modern times the influence of Christianity has weakened, and there are powerful intellectual forces that object to its continuing presence in contemporary legal codes. Many present-day scholars believe in the autonomy of law from all religious influence. This observation leads to the central normative questions of this chapter: Should Christianity continue to contribute to secular family law of the state as it often did in the past? Can legal arguments shaped by Christian sensibilities pass the so-called rationality test that all legal positions must meet – a test many scholars believe excludes the influence of religious faith?

I argue that Christianity can and should continue contributing to secular family law. It can do this, however, only if it rejects the view that Christian teachings on marriage, family, and children are pure revelation through and through, and devoid of other forms of thinking. Instead, it should understand itself as a carrier of forms of practical rationality applied to marriage and family that its sacred narratives reinforce but neither fully create nor completely dominate. Only when its rational core is detected and advanced in legal deliberations can the confessional narratives of the Christian tradition be understood to enhance, rather than to disqualify, its contributions to contemporary law. Legislators, judges, and jurists alike should examine Christianity's rational core and

9 "A Proposal," by Otto Erdmann (1834–1905): German private collection (nineteenth century).

assess the way its metaphorical and narrative surround support law's inner logics.

Present-day theories of family law are not monolithic. On the whole, however, they are all coping with sociological trends pertaining to marriage and family brought about by the dynamics of modernization and the accompanying rise of the culture of expressive individualism and personal choice. As Max Weber predicted, the rise and spread of technical rationality, that is, the quest for increasingly efficient means to achieve short-term satisfaction,[1] has had a major impact on all social experience in modern societies, including the spheres of marriage and family. The spread of technical rationality has stimulated the differentiation and autonomy of social systems such as market, government, law, medicine, and science from the integrating values of religion and family. These increasingly autonomous institutional spheres have gradually developed logics and practices of their own and gained increasing independence from the guidance of religion and the rhythms of family life.

Technical rationality, in the form of social-systemic differentiation, has been accompanied by the emergence of *techné* in birth control and assisted reproductive technology (ART). Together, these forces have introduced a variety of separations into human sexuality – separations of love from sexual exchange, sexual intercourse from marriage, marriage from conception, marriage from childbirth, childbirth from parenthood, sex from parenthood, child-rearing from marriage, child-rearing from biological parenthood, and economic viability of individuals from marriage – goods previously held together in the legal and religious institution of the marriage-based family.

To amplify, in many advanced Western cultures, economic activity became separated from the home, as men in the nineteenth century and women in the twentieth moved their sources of income from the family farm or craft to the wage economy. Sexual exchange more frequently became separated from marriage through the hoped-for protections of birth-control technology. Parenthood became increasingly separated from marriage and sexual intercourse through the spread of ART, the increasing economic independence of women, and the advent of welfare assistance for single mothers in affluent modern societies. These social-systemic transformations are now spreading around the world and even into areas shaped by the family-cohesive values of Hinduism and Confucianism. Social theorist

---

[1] Max Weber, *The Protestant Ethic and the Spirit of Capitalism* (New York: Charles Scribner's Sons, 1958), 182.

Anthony Giddens, in *The Transformation of Intimacy* (1992), provides a compelling account of the decline of marriage, the disconnection of sexual intimacy from child-rearing, and the "sequestering" of sexual intimacy in the nooks and crannies between increasingly autonomous social systems. This sequestering of sexuality ends in the quest for the "pure relationship" of love unencumbered by responsibility for either children or the constraint of the law.[2]

This social-science description of the emerging condition of marriage and family in modernity is relevant to the major concern of this chapter – the possible contribution of religion (specifically Christianity) to law governing this social sphere. I am assuming that the reader is aware of social-science reports on the consequences of these separations since the mid 1960s – for example, the increase of non-marital births, the rise in divorce rates, the decline of marriage rates, the increase of cohabitation, the increased use of ART by single mothers and alternative family forms, and the increased likelihood that children in American and other Western societies will both unintentionally and intentionally be born outside marriage and raised by individuals who are not their parents of conception.[3] I also assume the reader is acquainted with the significant amount of social science research which gives discouraging evaluations of the consequences of these trends for children, society, and even adults.[4]

My purpose for summarizing these social facts is to ask the following questions: How is contemporary American legal theory on marriage and family interpreting and evaluating these trends and determining the best response of the law? Does it use the law to counter these trends or is it accommodating, if not actively exacerbating, the social trends of modernization in the sexual field? I believe that, for the most part, contemporary family law theory both accommodates and encourages these trends. Some of its accommodations are positive adaptations, but many are capitulations that close the legal mind to alternative responses. I believe that a critical retrieval of a Christian jurisprudence of marriage and family can offer alternatives that are just, imaginative, and beneficent, without being reactionary.

---

[2] Anthony Giddens, *The Transformation of Intimacy* (Stanford: Stanford University Press, 1992), 94–96, 134–56.

[3] For a review of evidence supporting these generalizations, see James Q. Wilson, *The Marriage Problem* (New York: Harper Collins, 2002).

[4] For authoritative reviews of the consequences of these changes, especially for children, see Sara McLanahan and Gary Sandefur, *Growing up with a Single Parent* (Cambridge, MA: Harvard University Press, 1994); Paul Amato and Alan Booth, *A Generation at Risk: Growing up in an Era of Family Disruption* (Cambridge, MA: Harvard University Press, 1997).

Stanford law professor Lawrence Friedman summarizes the majority response of contemporary family law in the following words:

More and more, law, like the broader society, focuses on the wishes, desires, and needs of individual people, freely chosen, within a broad band of possibilities. Each person is felt to have the right to select his or her own lifestyle, to craft his or her marriage and divorce, even to make basic decisions about family affiliation in general . . . [T]he *ideology* of choice is an important social fact.[5]

Friedman is saying that the response of law to modernization's separations in the sexual sphere is basically to mirror, accommodate, or adapt to these social trends. As we shall see toward the end of this chapter, however, this is not true of all the leading theorists of contemporary American family law.

Some illustrations will demonstrate how contemporary civil law, in an effort to adapt to the dislocations of modernity, may be in reality encouraging its separations in the sexual realm. No-fault divorce, for example, acknowledged the strains of modern marriage. In facilitating adult happiness, however, it inadvertently encouraged the separation of marriage and parenthood. Most observers affirm the separation of sexual intercourse from uncontrolled conception that resulted when the Supreme Court decision in *Griswold vs. Connecticut* (1965)[6] freed birth control from state interference. But many people question the wisdom of the Court's subsequent decision in *Eisenstadt v. Baird* (1972)[7] that legalized birth control for unmarried persons, thereby indirectly encouraging the separation of sexual intimacy from marriage. Leading legal theorists carry these separations even further. Critical feminist legal scholar Martha Fineman proposes separating parenting from legal marriage by delegalizing marriage (what she calls the "sexual family") and using the legitimations of law and government to support care-givers and their dependents, principally single parents and their vulnerable children.[8] Legal theorist June Carbone does not advocate delegalizing marriage but does, in effect, disestablish it by giving the bulk of legal supports to parenthood rather than marital partnerships, thereby abetting the separation of parenting from the marital state. Many legal theorists agree with the proposal of the American Law Institute's (ALI) *The Principles of the Law of Family Dissolution* (2002) that mutually dependent cohabiting partners should be given a legal status equivalent to marriage

---

[5] Lawrence Friedman, *Private Lives: Families, Individuals, and the Law* (Cambridge, MA: Harvard University Press, 2004), 146.   [6] 381 US 479 (1965).   [7] 405 US 438 (1972).
[8] Martha Fineman, *The Autonomy Myth: A Theory of Dependency* (New York: The New Press, 2004), 134.

with the same supports and responsibilities.[9] Liberal feminist legal scholar
Linda McClain concurs with ALI's recommendation to develop a functional equivalence in law between marriage and cohabitation, but she goes
even further. She does not recommend the delegalization of marriage, as
does Fineman. But she does recommend adopting a system of legal registration for various unmarried family-like living arrangements that would
give them marital-type governmental protections and supports, thus using
a matrimony look-alike as a system for distributing general welfare
benefits.[10]

Finally, the growing use of ART – possibly the most extreme example of
Weber's technical rationality in the family sphere – may be the greatest
force for the separation of parenting from conception and of marriage from
parenting. There are very few legal barriers in the United States to the
extensive use of ART within and outside of marriage or within a variety of
emerging family experiments. However, the growing public complaints by
young people born through anonymously donated eggs and sperm expose
the increasing likelihood of children intentionally being born and raised by
people other than their genetic parents and the need for legal review of this
situation from a children's rights point of view.[11]

THE CONCERN OF CHRISTIAN JURISPRUDENCE

A jurisprudence informed by the historic Christian concern to integrate the
goods of the sexual field for the benefit of both children and adults cannot
be happy with these new divisions in human sexuality. As we shall see
below, it is precisely the concern to integrate the field of sexuality – sex and
marriage, marriage and childbirth, parenting and marriage – into a mutually reinforcing and self-renewing whole that has been at the core of
Christian marriage theory, both within the churches and in its influence on
the wider society. It has done this through the way its doctrines of God's
creation, governance, and redemption have further qualified, defined, and
shaped the natural realities and rhythms of human sexuality and the
possibility of offspring. Building on these metaphors of God's action in
the world, this tradition has viewed marriage as either a sacrament (as
in Roman Catholicism and Orthodox Christianity) or a covenant (as in

---

[9] *The Principles of the Law of Family Dissolution* (New York: The American Law Institute, 2002).
[10] Linda McClain, *The Place of Families: Fostering Capacity, Responsibility, and Equality* (Cambridge, MA: Harvard University Press, 2006), 197–201.
[11] Elizabeth Marquardt, *The Revolution of Parenthood: The Emerging Global Clash between Adult Rights and Children's Needs* (New York: Institute for American Values, 2006).

Protestantism) that recapitulates the enduring and redemptive love of God expressed through the life and death of Jesus Christ (Ephesians 5:25).

Until recently, Western law absorbed many of the values of this tradition. This has been reflected most pointedly in the idea that law, for the most part, has treated marriage as a status defined by society, tradition, and even religion. The institutional status of marriage has traditionally functioned as a legal covenant defining the mutual rights and obligations that contracting couples freely chose but did not themselves create or define.[12] Although marriage as status, in contrast to a mere contract created by the couple, is still visible in some modern Western legal systems, no-fault divorce and other changes have put this view on the defensive in both legal practice and current theory. There are exceptions to this trend, however, which I review at the conclusion of this chapter.

MAIN FEATURES OF A CHRISTIAN JURISPRUDENCE OF MARRIAGE AND FAMILY

As indicated, it is best to understand early Christianity as developing a complex spin or twist on Jewish, Greek, and Roman perspectives on sex, marriage, and family. This twist led early Christianity (1) both to appropriate and relativize aspects of Judaism, and (2) both to use and critique the Aristotelian aristocratic paternalism of Roman and Hellenistic civic life by introducing a new image of servant fatherhood and a new love ethic of equal regard. Subsequent interpretations of these early Christian trajectories gradually emphasized more and more the integrative purpose of the family – the integration of sexual exchange, marriage, procreation, and child-rearing within the context of a love ethic of equal regard for both family and society.

The two most central scriptural texts influencing Jesus from his Hebrew heritage are Genesis 1:27 and Genesis 2:24. The first reads: "So God created man in his own image, in the image of God he created him; male and female he created them." The second reads: "Therefore a man leaves his father and his mother and cleaves to his wife, and they become one flesh." Jesus refers to these two passages in his response to a Pharisee's question as to whether it was "lawful to divorce one's wife for any cause" (Matthew 19:3). Jesus' answer has probably influenced Western marriage patterns and law more than any other words ever spoken or written:

---

[12] John Witte, Jr., *From Sacrament to Contract: Marriage, Religion, and Law in the Western Tradition* (Louisville, KY: Westminster John Knox Press, 1997), 13.

Have you not read that he who made them from the beginning made them male
and female, and said, "For this reason a man shall leave his father and mother and
be joined to his wife, and the two shall become one flesh"? So they are no longer
two but one flesh. What therefore God has joined together, let not man put
asunder. (Matthew 19:4–6)

In subsequent centuries, Roman Catholic canon law, the civil law of both
Protestant and Roman Catholic countries, and the Anglo-American
common law of marriage and the family have been influenced by Jesus'
reflection on these ancient passages from the Hebrew Scriptures.

But what do these words mean? Modern scholarship has taught us much
about the importance of context for understanding a text. Unfortunately,
these biblical texts have been interpreted for centuries without these new
insights into their cultural context. New Testament scholar Warren Carter
points out how these few words should be interpreted when read within the
surrounding structure of Matthew 19 and 20.[13] He demonstrates that they
assume an audience that has been shaped since the fourth century BCE con-
quests of Alexander the Great by Roman Hellenism and the hierarchical
Aristotelian family codes that came with this cultural conglomerate. Jesus'
listeners would have known the peripatetic customs sanctioning the male
householder's aristocratic rule over his wife, royal rule over children, and
tyrannical rule over slaves – ideals outlined in Aristotle's *Nicomachean
Ethics* and *Politics* and disseminated throughout the Mediterranean world
by his philosophical followers.[14]

Carter believes that this passage attributed to Jesus functioned to question this ancient Hellenic pattern and promote an equality of discipleship
in both household and economic life. He sees this in the Scripture's strictures against ancient practices of arbitrary patriarchal divorce at the expense
of women. It also appears in Jesus' giving centrality to the principle of
neighbor love in a neighboring verse: "You shall love your neighbor as yourself" (Matthew 19:19), a teaching given in response to the rich man's question about how to earn eternal life. And finally, in Matthew 20:1–16, we
read the parable of the generous landlord who paid laborers the same wages
no matter how long they worked – a story that illustrates the economic
equality of the kingdom of God and ends with the words: "So the last will
be first, and the first last" (Matthew 20:16). If Carter's perspective is correct,
we should interpret Jesus' teaching on marriage and family as countering

---

[13] Warren Carter, *Households and Discipleship: A Study of Matthew 19–20* (Sheffield, UK: Sheffield
Academic Press, 1994), 31, 46, 49–55.
[14] Aristotle, *Nicomachean Ethics* (New York: Random House, 1941), bk. 8, ch. 10.

the hierarchies of economic and family life of the Greco-Roman world. Doing this opens a more egalitarian trajectory of meaning in Christian family theory than has generally been appreciated.

This trajectory – that is, the meaning "in front of the text" to use a phrase by Paul Ricoeur[15] – occurs not only within a hierarchical social context but one also defined by the honor/shame codes of Roman Hellenism. This is what anthropologists have called an agonistic or conflictual cultural system that celebrated male public honor expressed through dominance and female shame – that is, a form of female honor that protects mothers, wives, and daughters by more or less restricting their lives to the domestic realm.[16] Not only did early Christianity conflict with the Aristotelian aristocratic family model of Roman Hellenism but also with the honor/shame gender codes often associated with it.

Grasping this cultural context helps us understand the second most influential New Testament text on Western cultural and legal family theory, a famous passage from Ephesians 5:21–33. Although these verses are ambiguous, three points of enduring jurisprudential significance, for both ecclesial and civil law, were made. One concerned the husband's role in marriage as modeled after Christ's unbreakable and sacrificial love for the church: "Husbands, love your wives, as Christ loved the church and gave himself up for her" (Ephesians 5:25). Recent New Testament scholarship now sees this view of male servanthood as a striking contrast to the aristocratic male honor codes of the surrounding civic society. Second, the ethic of neighbor love or equal regard, as I call it, is brought directly into the marital relationship: "husbands should love their wives as they do their own bodies" (Ephesians 5:28). Finally, there is a reaffirmation of the Genesis 2:24 understanding of marriage as a one-flesh union: "For this reason a man shall leave his father and mother and be joined to his wife, and the two shall become one flesh" (Ephesians 5:31).

The passage ends with an extremely important addition that became a great point of controversy in later ecclesial and civil law. With reference to the analogy of marriage as a one-flesh union and Christ's covenantal love for the church, the writer of Ephesians adds: "This mystery (*mysterion*) is a profound one, and I am saying that it refers to Christ and the church" (Ephesians 5:32). Translations of words are crucial and the debate over whether *mysterion* should be translated by the words "mystery" or "sacrament" (*sacramentum)* gets to the heart of one of the great divisions between Protestant and Roman Catholic jurisprudence and the traditions

---

[15] Andre LeCocque and Paul Ricoeur, *Thinking Biblically* (Chicago: University of Chicago Press, 1998), xi–xii.　[16] Halvor Moxes, "Honor Shame," *Biblical Theology Bulletin* 23:4 (Winter, 1993): 164–76.

of civil and common law in countries influenced by these two divisions of Christianity.

However this controversy is resolved, this pivotal passage suggests that Christian marriage should be enduring, if not unbreakable. In addition, it suggests that the male headship so prevalent in ancient families should be tempered if not absent. Marital relations should be characterized by a love ethic of equal regard, energized and renewed by openness to sacrificial love. These elements gave rise to the idea in both later canon and civil law that marriage should be a status with covenantal features – a predefined set of mutual and enduring obligations – as well as a freely chosen contract.

But traditions never unfold smoothly, and the spin or trajectory that early Christian teachings gave to ancient marital customs was often misinterpreted. For instance, later interpretations of these teachings in the so-called Pastoral Epistles (such as Colossians, 1 and 2 Timothy, and Titus) often seemed to retreat to the hierarchies of the Greco-Roman civic culture in which the early church tried to establish itself.

AUGUSTINE AND AQUINAS

Early Christianity continued the idea that marriage was a one-flesh union that in principle was open to the trinity of the embodied mother–father–child relationship. Because of its eschatological expectations, the earliest stages of Christianity followed St. Paul's personal preference for celibacy expressed in I Corinthians 7:7 – a preference he did not propose as binding on all Christians. Nonetheless, his teachings functioned to elevate the celibate state and to make marriage and childbearing more a matter of permission than a religious vocation. By the time of St. Augustine in the fifth century, and the writing of his pivotal tract, *On the Good of Marriage*, the classic forms of the integration model of Christian marriage had begun to emerge.

Augustine saw Christian marriage as integrating three fundamental goods – the good of the procreation and education of children (*proles*), the good of faithfulness and chastity (*fides*), and the good of a permanent union (*connubi sacramentum*).[17] In speaking of the goods of marriage, Augustine advanced an early Christian formulation of the explicit teleological ends or aims – the human goods – of this institution. He gave a Christian twist to a form of thinking found in Greek philosophy – in this case the thought of Plato, who influenced Augustine so profoundly. Plato, like other Greek and

---

[17] Augustine, "The Good of Marriage," in *The Fathers of the Church* (New York: Fathers of the Church, 1955), XXVII:4.

Roman thinkers, understood marriage as a natural institution that was simultaneously beneficial to the couple, to their children, and to the wider community. Of course, procreation for Augustine was more than the brute fact of bringing warm bodies into the world; it was a matter of conceiving human infants made in the image of God who also should be raised to be disciples in the kingdom of God. Marriage as sacrament meant for Augustine that it should be permanent and not as such a source of supernatural grace as the concept of sacrament came to mean later in medieval Roman Catholicism.

Sexual exchange between husband and wife and mutual rights to each other's body were part of this view of marriage, but less as a source of pleasure and intimacy, and more as a way of integrating sex into the good of conception and child-rearing. Augustine brought together what philosophers call a *teleological* language (a language about goods) with what they call a *deontological* language (a language of obligation), all designed to convey an integrational or one-flesh view of marriage that unified love, sex, procreation, and child-rearing into an enduring relation between husband and wife in the mother–father–infant union. Augustine, more than any other Christian writer, established the terms, if not always the details, of the Western canon and civil view of marriage. He formulated the idea that marriage as an institution should function to channel the natural energies and goods of sexuality, procreation, and parental investment into this enduring union.

Several centuries later, Christian views of marriage selectively incorporated and creatively interpreted aspects of two additional traditions: (1) Roman family law, and (2) Aristotle's rediscovered bio-philosophical views on the importance of kin altruism for parental investment in their children, particularly paternal investment. These combined traditions came together most powerfully in the thought of the thirteenth-century Dominican friar, Thomas Aquinas. Aquinas accepted much of Peter Lombard's synthesis of Roman law and Christian sensibilities, developed a century before, especially his view that mutual consent to a conjugal life together stated by the couple in words of the present tense, even if without witnesses, made for a valid marriage. Aquinas also accepted the emerging view, articulated by Peter Lombard, that marriage is a sacrament – a supernatural source of grace that overcomes the taint of sin and provides the capacity for forgiveness.[18] Aquinas followed the Latin Vulgate translation of the New Testament and rendered Ephesians 5:32 as

---

[18] Peter Lombard, *Book of Sentences*, in *Sex, Marriage, and Family in the World Religions*, ed. Don Browning, M. Christian Green, and John Witte, Jr. (New York: Columbia University Press, 2006), 110–11.

saying Christian marriage is "a great sacrament" (*sacramentum*) rather than "a great mystery" (*mysterium*), which sixteenth-century Protestant reformer Martin Luther would later offer as the better translation of the Greek word *mysterion*.[19]

On the other hand, Aquinas made a remarkable synthesis between the biblical narrative and another aspect of Aristotle that can be appreciated independently of the great Greek philosopher's patriarchy, namely, his understanding of the naturalistic elements in marriage. Aquinas made theological use of two of Aristotle's ideas: (1) the naturalistic observation that humans, like other animals, have a natural tendency to leave behind "an image of themselves,"[20] and (2) the belief that natural parents, who have bodily continuity with their offspring, are likely to care more for their children than alternative caregivers, especially the state nurses that Plato proposed should replace parents in order to overcome the injustice of nepotism. Aquinas combined Lombard's emphasis on consent with an Aristotelian interpretation of the Genesis and Ephesians one-flesh understanding of marriage. When he wrote: "And they shall become two in one flesh,"[21] he meant that the spouses consent to become one flesh and embody this in their sexual relations and in their love for and identification with their children, who are part of their very substance.

Aquinas believed matrimony arose among humans because, in contrast to other mammals, the human infant takes a long time to mature; in species where infants mature rapidly, long-term bonding between male and female does not occur. He wrote: "In man, however, since the child needs the parents' care for a long time, there is a very great tie between male and female, to which tie even the generic nature inclines."[22] The long period of infant dependence and altruistic inclinations toward infants who come forth from our very bodily existence – these are the naturalistic springs of marriage in the Thomistic tradition. But there is more. Aquinas also used a primitive theory of kin altruism as a trope to symbolize the wife–husband relation who in marriage treat each other as blood kin – "bone of my bones and flesh of my flesh" (Genesis 2:23) – even though, as a matter of fact, they are not. Hence, in Aquinas' Christian view of marriage and family, the marital relationship both

[19] Thomas Aquinas, *Summa Theologica*, trans. Fathers of the English Dominican Province (New York: Benzinger Brothers, 1948), vol. III, "Supplement," q. 42, a. 1.
[20] Aristotle, *Politics*, in *The Basic Works of Aristotle* (New York: Random House, 1941), bk. I, i.
[21] Thomas Aquinas, *Summa Contra Gentiles*, trans. The English Dominican Fathers (London: Burns, Oates and Washbourne, 1928), lib. 3, 2, cap. 124 (quoting Genesis 2:24 [Vulgate]).
[22] Aquinas, *Summa Theologica*, vol. III, "Supplement," q. 42, a. 1.

symbolically builds on, transforms, and analogically generalizes the basic solidarities of kin altruism.

Finally, Aquinas' use of the real and symbolic attachments of kin altruism is further consolidated by a narrative of marital commitment as recapitulating the unbreakable covenantal love of Christ for the church. He believed that this enactment by spouses of the enduring love of Christ was necessary to meet the physical and educational needs of the slowly developing human infant and to protect the vulnerabilities of the couple themselves, especially the wife and mother. Although Aquinas regarded the mystery (*mysterion*) of this enduring commitment as a sacrament (*sacramentum*), it is instructive to notice how the narrative of Christ's sacrificial love functioned to consolidate the one-flesh union of spouses and their offspring. Aquinas says it this way: "Although Matrimony is not conformed to Christ's passion as regards to pain, it is as regards charity, whereby He suffered for the church who was to be united to Him as His spouse."[23]

PROTESTANT FAMILY JURISPRUDENCE

I have tried to illustrate the core of practical rationality that can be found within the Christian theology of marriage and family. I have done this to suggest that this core is identifiable independently of surrounding Christian metaphors and narratives. Yet this core is also informed by these narratives and metaphors. The enduring solidarity of mother–father–infant one-flesh union enacted primarily to meet the dependency needs of the slowly developing human infant captures the heart of this rational core. In this sense, this religious tradition was a carrier of an insight into what many strands of the social sciences, especially evolutionary psychology, today identify as the natural conditions, in ways absent in other mammalian species, for the formation of the long-lasting marital unions at the level of *homo sapiens*.[24] Marriage is an institution designed to increase the probability that the adults who conceive a child will channel and integrate their sexuality, affections, and labor to meet the child's long-term dependency needs. In its Christian context, this human good of marriage is perceived as a very important, finite good that is not itself a condition for redemption or salvation. A Christian's status before God did not depend at any time throughout Christian history on his or her marital or parental condition. In addition, the justice of the

---

[23] *Ibid.*
[24] Martin Daly and Margo Wilson, "The Evolutionary Psychology of Marriage and Divorce," in *The Ties that Bind: Perspectives on Marriage and Cohabitation*, ed. Linda J. Waite (New York: Aldine de Gruyter, 2000), 91–110.

kingdom of God and one's discipleship to Jesus were always seen as having priority over marital or family standing. Nonetheless, as Augustine had said, there were many goods associated with marriage, and these goods could and should be integrated and given Christian theological meaning. Furthermore, as important as one's own children were, the obligation to extend analogically the solidarities of kin altruism to needy or orphaned children, possibly even through the act of lawful adoption, was viewed as a worthy expression of Christian *agape*, or self-giving love.

The sixteenth-century Protestant Reformation altered important aspects of the Roman Catholic canon law tradition of marriage and family. Luther rejected, as indicated, the sacramental view of marriage. He also rejected, as did Genevan reformer John Calvin, the belief that celibacy was a higher religious status than marriage and family life. Luther reversed this ranking and elevated family formation, marriage, child-rearing, and the education of offspring to the level of a religious vocation. But, as legal historian John Witte, Jr. has pointed out, even though the early Luther railed against Roman Catholic canon law as a condition for salvation, later he, Philip Melanchthon, and the jurists working with them incorporated much of it into the civil law of the Protestant German state.[25] They did this in a social theory that distinguished between the earthly kingdom of this world and the heavenly kingdom of salvation that itself was only visible in finite life through various hints, glimmers, or masks. The earthly kingdom was the realm of the social institutions of family, government, and the visible manifestation of the church. The norms of family and government were to be drawn from the natural law revealed in the Ten Commandments and elsewhere in Scripture, natural law discerned by practical reason, and even the wisdom of the Roman Catholic canon law tradition.[26] Much of the Catholic blend of the Genesis "one-flesh" view of marriage and the Aristotelian–Thomistic kin altruism model found its way into the civil law and common law of Protestant states. This was a view of marriage as a social and legal status that was both good for the modern state and permeable to the blessings of the church and its portrayal of marriage as a sacred covenant.

The Protestant Reformation, both its Lutheran and Calvinist wings, gave rise to the idea of marriage and family as a twofold institution governed by a double language with complementary but differentiated rationales. One provided a secular justification that saw marriage and

---

[25] John Witte, *Law and Protestantism: The Legal Teachings of the Lutheran Reformation* (Cambridge: Cambridge University Press, 2002), 120–24.   [26] *Ibid.*, 114–15.

family as natural institutions useful for the common good, and the other saw them as covenantal institutions recapitulating Christ's faithfulness to the church. Before the Protestant Reformation, the legal and religious dimensions of marriage had both been administered for centuries by the clergy and tribunals of Roman Catholic Church. After the Reformation, the legal registration, public witness, and certification of valid marriage became a function of the state, even though the church blessed it and gave it additional meaning and sanctity. Since marriage for Protestants was no longer a sacrament, the conditions of divorce were broadened to include desertion in addition to adultery. Because family law was primarily the obligation of the state, combinations of scriptural interpretation and practical rationality led Protestant jurists to revise older canon law traditions by lowering the number of impediments to marriage, permitting remarriage after legitimate divorce, softening the distinction between the future promise and the present consent to marry, and requiring marriage vows to be made in public before witnesses and with parental consent. Seldom, however, did the Reformation totally reject the older canon law tradition.

Calvin may have been even more influential than Luther on the civil law of marriage in Protestant countries. This was due to his extensive influence on both church law and civil law in the city of Geneva and the spread of these legal frameworks into countries influenced by Calvinism such as Scotland, Holland, England, the United States, and their respective spheres of influence. His contributions both built on and revised the Catholic canon law tradition in which Calvin had been trained as a law student. His legal teachings on marriage found a place for practical reason and natural law, and even used these forms of thought to harshly judge such practices as polygamy by the patriarchs of the Old Testament.[27] Calvin and his associates, Theodore Beza, Pierre Viret, and François Hotman, retained and amplified the distinction between the earthly and heavenly kingdoms and thereby developed an elastic double language of practical reason and religious metaphor to order the life of both secular society and the church.

RECENT INFLUENCE OF CHRISTIAN JURISPRUDENCE

Roman Catholic canon law continued to influence the civil law in Catholic regions such as France, Spain, Italy, South America, parts of Germany, and the southern and western parts of the United States. It has

---

[27] John Witte, Jr., and Robert M. Kingdon, *Sex, Marriage, and Family in John Calvin's Geneva* (Grand Rapids, MI: Wm. B. Eerdmans Publishing, 2005–), I:xxiv, 181–182, 224–226.

also had considerable influence on modern human rights thinking, especially as it pertains to the rights of children and the place of marriage and family. Beginning with Pope Leo XIII, Aristotelian–Thomistic influences on Roman Catholic marriage theory had a powerful revival, especially as manifest in his important encyclical *Rerum Novarum* (1891). Leo's social teachings reaffirmed the importance of kin altruism in the one-flesh union of husband, wife, and child.[28] This view was extended by Pope Pius XI in a full-blown theory of subsidiarity – the idea that care radiates outward from the family and kin relations to the wider society and that neither the state nor the market should undermine the family although both should stand ready to support it (*subsidum*) when it is weakened or endangered by poverty, war, or economic stress.[29] Through the influence of Charles Malik and his advisor, Roman Catholic theologian Jacques Maritain, subsidiarity theory significantly influenced ideas about the role of the family and the rights of children in the *Universal Declaration of Human Rights* (1948) and many successor declarations, including the *UN Convention on the Rights of the Child* (1989). In a series of international human rights documents, we find variations on the words of the Universal Declaration that: "The family is the natural and fundamental group unit of society and is entitled to protection by society and the State."[30] This statement gave priority to the family in matters of child-care, the rights of the child to a family, the rights of the child to protection from abuse whatever the source, and the obligations of state parties to guarantee these rights and protections.

A CASE STUDY IN A DOUBLE LANGUAGE OF FAMILY LAW

Does this double language of covenant and bio-philosophical forms of practical reason offer a model for the practice of Christian jurisprudence today, both within the churches and for influencing the laws of the modern state? To address this question, I want to discuss the work of legal theorist Margaret Brinig, who preserves in fresh terms some of the accomplishments of the older Christian jurisprudence without, however, advocating Christianity as such. Her work resists the emerging multiple separations in the sexual field, exposes the self-deception in law's alleged neutrality, and works to restore law's capacity to help channel sexual intimacy into more durable one-flesh covenants.

---

[28] Leo XIII, *Rerum novarum* (May 15, 1891).   [29] Pius XI, *Quadragesimo anno* (May 15, 1931).
[30] "Universal Declaration of Human Rights," Article 16.3, reprinted in Mary Ann Glendon, *A World Made New* (New York: Random House, 2001), 311–14.

She does this by first beginning with a phenomenology of covenant – a thick description of the cultural model of marriage that historically has dominated Western thinking in both law and religion. She then makes use of the new institutional economics and evolutionary psychology, in ways analogous to Aquinas's use of Aristotle. She does this to illustrate what covenant thinking means in the realm of the hard procreative, economic, and health realities of marriage and family – the things that the law and the state rightly believe are their principal concerns.[31]

In contrast to most of contemporary family law theory, Brinig begins her legal thinking something like the great sociologist Emile Durkheim, although she never discusses him. She does this by giving us a phenomenological description of the dominant normative understanding of marriage that has been delivered to us by our religio-cultural heritage. She says that the contractual model of marriage that sees it as a freely chosen agreement is inadequate both to our experience of marriage and the ideals forming legal understandings in the past. Marriage, she insists, historically has been viewed as a solemn agreement to a union of "unconditional love and permanence" through which the "parties are bound not only to each other but also to some third party, to God or the community or both."[32] This phenomenological description of the inherited normative understanding of marriage is not presented by Brinig as a confessional religious statement. It is, rather, an effort simply to state the culturally received meaning associated with marriage and then give a further account of its concrete institutional implications.

In order to understand the social implications of covenant, Brinig turns to what is today commonly called the "new institutional economics."[33] This perspective both builds on yet goes beyond the rational-choice view advocated by Nobel Prize winning economist Gary Becker and law and economics theorist Judge Richard Posner. Marriage, she argues, is more like a firm than it is an individualistically negotiated contract. A firm is an association organized to perform a specific function, achieve economies of scale, capitalize on special talents of individual participants, and relate to external parties as a collective unit. A firm is based on a prior agreement between the parties involved and the surrounding community – something like a covenant – about the purpose of the corporate unit. Brinig says this about the analogy between firms and covenantal marriage: "This agreement does not purport to anticipate all future transactions among the firm members. In fact, one of the goals of the firm is the elimination of explicit

---

[31] Margaret Brinig, *From Contract to Covenant: Beyond the Law and Economics of the Family* (Cambridge, MA: Harvard University Press, 2000). [32] *Ibid.*, 6–7. [33] *Ibid.*, 6.

interparty contracting and account keeping."[34] The new institutional economics helps us see things in the firm, and in marriages (especially marriages with children), that the older individualistic rational-choice economic model missed. It helps us see the "channeling," "signaling," and "reputational" aspects of firm-like marriages. The firm model helps us understand how marriages formed by settled public commitments (covenants) between the couple, potential children, and society develop identifiable social patterns that convey trusted information, dependable access to known and valued goods, and esteemed reputations both within the marriage and before the wider community.

Marriages that result in children, however, are more like a particular type of firm called franchises. A set of imposed responsibilities come from the child and from outside expectations that cannot be totally dissolved even with legal divorce. The inextricable one-flesh union and the shared family history do "not disappear" when the marriage ends or the child turns eighteen. Brinig points out something that the ancient "one-flesh" model of marriage profoundly understood, that "divorcing couples never completely revert to a pre-marriage state. Nor do children leaving home entirely free themselves from their parents or siblings."[35] Brinig's twofold account of marriage conveyed through a phenomenology of covenant and an institutional-economics analysis of the goods that this covenant organizes leads her to assert that "marriage persists to a certain degree in spite of divorce. To the extent that it persists, the family still lives on as what I call the franchise."[36]

Brinig uses the analogies of firm and franchise to give partial accounts of the social work accomplished by marriage understood as covenant. These analogies do not fully comprehend the unconditional love associated with the traditional idea of covenant. But they help amplify the rationality of the covenant concept. Her contributions help illustrate how religion and law can still have fruitful interaction and beneficial consequences for modern theories of family.

Her position has many concrete implications, more than I can discuss in detail. In contrast to the recommendations of the ALI's *Principles of the Law of Marital Dissolution*, she believes rendering cohabitation and marriage largely equivalent before the law would undermine the signaling and channeling functions of marriage – a significant loss for guiding men into aligning and integrating their sexuality, affection for sexual partner, and commitment to children. Brinig is fully aware, as was Aquinas before her

---

[34] *Ibid.*, 5.   [35] *Ibid.*, 8–9.   [36] *Ibid.*, 9.

and evolutionary psychology today, that a man is more likely to commit to a child if the man knows the child is his, spends time with the child, and has a satisfying relation with the mother of the child. She accepts the massive witness of both the tradition and the contemporary social sciences that, on average, children do much better, on a host of measures of well-being, when raised by their own married, biological parents. She contends that law should not hesitate to do what it can, in cooperation with other sectors of society, to encourage the marital franchise with children as the defining center of the marital institution. Marriage can be encouraged through the law, she suggests, by not recognizing cohabitation, not protecting it except with respect to the children involved, and by greatly increasing the social and cultural rewards of marriage. She believes that it is worth taking seriously the Louisiana, Arkansas, and Arizona experiments in what they call "covenant marriage" – the provision of offering couples both the present no-fault marriage option ("marriage lite") or a marriage with higher standards of commitment (covenant marriage) which demands more preparation as well as counseling and a waiting period before divorce.

Brinig rejects efforts by Martha Fineman to delegalize marriage and place legal and social supports behind various caring relationships. She also is skeptical of Fineman's proposal to end the practice of joint custody in favor of a presumed preference for custody by the mother. Brinig accepts social-science evidence showing that divorced fathers remain more involved with their children when awarded a role in custody. Since Brinig's covenant or franchise view of marriage, especially when children are involved, holds that even in divorce there is no "clean break," joint custody provides a way for separated parents to deal with the one-flesh union that remains after the marriage officially ends. Brinig, like Fineman, is a feminist legal scholar interested in the equal treatment of women in advanced modern societies. But she is a "difference feminist" who also holds that equality for women and mothers can be best maintained in a world where men relate to their children and sexual partners in marriage, and where both men and women in principle work out equal (not necessarily identical) privileges and responsibilities in the public world of paid work and the private world of domestic obligations and pleasures. Although she does not use the term, she is for a love ethic of equal regard. Brinig also shows the implications of her views for several other issues in family law – same-sex marriage, surrogacy, divorce, care for the elderly, and the emancipation of children, but the illustrations above give a taste of the direction of her thinking.

As I indicated above, I make no claim that Brinig has a full theology of Christian marriage. A richer Christian theology would develop a fuller account of marriage as willed by God in creation, a more explicit equal-regard ethic of marital love, an understanding of the role of self-sacrificial love in the wider view of love as equal regard, and a theology of forgiveness so crucial for the renewal of marital commitment. These latter elements will rightly be of more interest to the church than the state. But in Brinig's perspective, we have glimpses of a jurisprudence of marriage that meets the rationality test of legal theory yet is both influenced by and broadly compatible with the outlines of the integrated view of marriage so central to a Christian jurisprudence.

RECOMMENDED READING

Amato, Paul and Alan Booth. *A Generation at Risk: Growing up in an Era of Family Disruption.* Cambridge, MA: Harvard University Press, 1997.

Aquinas, Thomas. *Summa Contra Gentiles.* Translated by the English Dominican Fathers. London: Burns, Oates and Wasbourne, 1928.

Aquinas, Thomas. *Summa Theologica,* 3 vols. Translated by the Fathers of the English Dominican Province, vol. III, "Supplement." New York: Benzinger Brothers, 1948.

Aristotle. *Politics,* in *The Basic Works of Aristotle.* New York: Random House, 1941.

Augustine. "The Good of Marriage," in *The Fathers of the Church.* Vol. XXVII. Translated by T. Wilcox. Edited by Roy J. Deferrari, New York: Fathers of the Church, 1955.

Brinig, Margaret. *From Contract to Covenant: Beyond the Law and Economics of the Family.* Cambridge, MA: Harvard University Press, 2000.

Browning, Don. *Equality and the Family: A Fundamental Practical Theology of Children, Mothers and Fathers in Modern Societies.* Grand Rapids, MI: Wm. B. Eerdmans Publishing, 2007.

Marriage and Modernization: How Globalization Threatens Marriage and What to Do about It. Grand Rapids, MI: Wm. B. Eerdmans Publishing, 2003.

Browning, Don, M. Christian Green, and John Witte, eds. *Sex, Marriage, and Family in the World Religions.* New York: Columbia University Press, 2006.

Browning, Don, Bonnie J. Miller-McLemore, Pamela D. Couture, K. Brynoff Lyon, and Robert M. Franklin. *From Culture Wars to Common Ground: Religion and the American Family Debate.* Edited by Don S. Browning. Louisville, KY: Westminster John Knox Press, 1997, 2000.

Carter, Warren. *Households and Discipleship: A Study of Matthew 19–20.* Sheffield, UK: Sheffield Academic Press, 1994.

Daly, Martin and Margo Wilson. "The Evolutionary Psychology of Marriage and Divorce," in *The Ties That Bind: Perspectives on Marriage and Cohabitation.* Edited by Linda Waite. Hawthorne, NY: Aldine de Gruyter, 2000. 91–110.

Fineman, Martha. *The Autonomy Myth: A Theory of Dependency.* New York: The New Press, 2004.

Friedman, Lawrence. *Private Lives: Families, Individuals, and the Law.* Cambridge, MA: Harvard University Press, 2004.

Giddens, Anthony. *The Transformation of Intimacy: Sexuality, Love, and Eroticism in Modern Societies.* Stanford: Stanford University Press, 1992.

LeCocque, Andre and Paul Ricoeur. *Thinking Biblically.* Chicago: University of Chicago Press, 1998.

Marquardt, Elizabeth. *The Revolution of Parenthood: The Emerging Global Clash between Adult Rights and Children's Needs.* New York: Institute for American Values, 2006.

McClain, Linda. *The Place of Families: Fostering Capacity, Responsibility, and Equality.* Cambridge, MA: Harvard University Press, 2006.

McLanahan, Sara and Gary Sandefur. *Growing up with a Single Parent.* Cambridge, MA: Harvard University Press, 1994.

Moxes, Halvor. "Honor and Shame." *Biblical Theology Bulletin* 23:4 (Winter 1993): 164–76.

Weber, Max. *The Protestant Ethic and the Spirit of Capitalism.* New York: Charles Scribner's Sons, 1958.

Wilson, James Q. *The Marriage Problem.* New York: Harper Collins, 2002.

Witte, John, Jr. *From Sacrament to Contract: Marriage, Religion, and Law in the Western Tradition.* Louisville, KY: Westminster John Knox Press, 1997.

  Law and Protestantism: The Legal Teachings of the Lutheran Reformation. Cambridge: Cambridge University Press, 2002.

Witte, John, Jr. and Robert M. Kingdon. *Sex, Marriage, and Family in John Calvin's Geneva.* 3 vols. Grand Rapids, MI: Wm. B. Eerdmans Publishing, 2005–.

10 "The Good Samaritan," from Christoph Weigel, *Biblia ectypa: Bildnussen auss heiliger Schrifft Alt und Neuen Testaments* (Augsburg, 1695), s.v. Luke 10.

CHAPTER NINE

Poverty, charity, and social welfare

Brian Pullan

In 1427, the eloquent Franciscan Bernardino of Siena reminded his congregation that the laws of the Old and New Testament commanded them to give alms to the poor. So did the law of nature: "man possesses reason; on this account alone man must and is bound by nature to give alms to a rational creature like himself."[1] Deuteronomy and other sacred texts urged open-handedness to poor people and strangers, kindness to widows and orphans (Deuteronomy 10:18–19, 15:7–11; Sirach 3:30–31, 4:1–10). The New Testament obliged Christians, on pain of mortal sin, to do all they could to assist fellow creatures in extreme and perhaps also in "very grave need" (see Matthew 25:31–46; Luke 16:19–31).[2] There were worthy but less essential forms of almsgiving. Popular in Bernardino's day and long afterwards was the practice of contributing to the dowries of virtuous young women, a life-changing rather than life-saving form of charity. Such acts, in the words of Thomas Aquinas, were advisable rather than essential, a "better good," matters for counsel rather than precept, but important for the acquisition of religious merit and earthly happiness.[3]

The natural law which Bernardino invoked was a universal moral law implanted in the hearts of human beings, the inclination of reasonable people (unless corrupted by passions) to do as they would be done by, to do good and avoid evil.[4] In Catholic doctrine, the greatest rewards for compassion and the heaviest penalties for callous indifference were eternal rather than earthly penalties, although the righteous could expect some more immediate rewards. Preachers would point out, with suitable anecdotes, that generous givers would enjoy health and prosperity in this life. The worldly-wise doubtless knew that a seat on the board of a prominent

---

[1] Bernardino of Siena, *Le prediche volgari*, ed. Piero Bargellini (Milan/Rome: Rizzoli, 1936), Sermon XL, 921–22.

[2] See further the chapters by Luke Timothy Johnson and Frank S. Alexander herein.

[3] Thomas Aquinas, *Summa theologiae*, II–II, 32.5, in *Summa Theologiae*, vol. XXXIV, *Charity*, trans. English Dominicans, ed. R. J. Batten (New York: Blackfriars-McGraw Hill, 1975), 254–55.

[4] See further the chapter by Brian Tierney herein.

charitable foundation would improve a citizen's standing in the community, perhaps further his political career, and that the distribution of largesse was a means (not always wholly respectable) of securing influence and patronage.

This chapter focuses on some of the enduring questions of the Christian tradition which arise from Bernardino's sermons. How did divine, natural, and human law interact with each other, and how far did the care of the poor depend on legal protection and coercion? To what extent was almsgiving an internal matter for individual consciences or for penitents and confessors rather than an external matter for courts of bishops and civil magistrates? Were these religious and political authorities obliged to do more than encourage it? Should people be compelled to relieve the poor, or should they at most be exhorted to do so? Did they look for guidance to private rules rather than public laws? At what point, if ever, did the main responsibility for poor relief and welfare shift from the private and voluntary to the public sphere?

THE TERMINOLOGY OF CHARITY

Words such as "almsgiving," "charity," "mercy," and "pity" ruled the vocabulary of poor relief and entered the names of hospitals and institutions in early modern Europe. More secular terms such as "philanthropy," "welfare," and "*bienfaisance*" came into more general usage from the seventeenth century onwards. Almsgiving, as the term was used by earlier Catholic writers, denoted assistance given to people less fortunate than oneself through material gifts or services or advice and comfort, from avowedly religious motives. Its simplest form was a personal, mutually beneficial transaction between giver and receiver. Givers would acquire merit in the sight of God and obtain disproportionate rewards ("God is obliged to pay one hundred for one"; see Luke 8:5–15) if they gave cheerfully, compassionately, and without ostentation – so long as they drew on goods legitimately acquired and not, say, on the proceeds of theft or usury. Receivers, acting as God's representatives and his agents for the transfer of temporal wealth to eternity, would undertake to pray for their benefactors. More elaborately, it was possible by last will and testament to endow permanent foundations which would be administered by executors, trustees, or persons appointed by them, such as the wardens of hospices or almshouses. By that means testators could win for their souls the support of generations of grateful beneficiaries, witnesses to their good deeds, perhaps wearing their livery, perhaps selected at solemn commemorative ceremonies on the anniversary of the benefactor's death.

By the fourteenth and fifteenth centuries, bishops and magistrates acknowledged a duty to protect such arrangements against fraud and abuse – against the negligence of executors or administrators or the tricks of the idle poor. The fear was not that false beggars and malingerers would deprive almsgivers of their merit but that, as "thieves of pity," they would misappropriate the rightful possessions of the poor of Christ. Most effective, perhaps, were measures which encouraged clergy and laity to collaborate in the hope of avoiding jurisdictional disputes, since both could legitimately claim an interest in pious foundations. Their religious purpose made them matters for the bishops, who as "fathers of the poor" insisted at intervals on their right to visit, scrutinize accounts, and ensure respect for testators' wishes.

In 1311, Pope Clement V's Council of Vienne made the bishops responsible for the efficiency of hospitals; over two centuries later, several German provincial councils asserted episcopal control over charities, as did the general Council of Trent of 1545–1563. Lay authorities felt entitled to rejoin that many charities were lay foundations whose founders had expressly sought to exempt them from clerical interference, and that they themselves had an interest both in taxing these charitable properties and in forestalling subversive moves on their part. (The government in Renaissance Florence, for example, was notoriously suspicious of its religious brotherhoods.) Cooperation between bishop and magistrate could, however, be established through joint schemes to merge hospitals and subject them to public boards of management, or other kinds of commission. Charged with collecting improperly withheld legacies to poor people, the *Ufficio di Pietà dei Poveri*, established in Milan in 1405, consisted of twelve clerics and twelve laymen. Similarly, after the Protestant Reformation, county commissions appointed to consider breaches of charitable trust in England included the diocesan bishop or his chancellor and associated them with representatives of the local gentry, thereby acknowledging the time-honoured position of the ecclesiastical judge. The task of policing the undeserving poor became a major concern of the civil magistrate.

Beyond almsgiving lay the broader virtues of charity and mercy. Theologically, charity denoted the love of God and neighbors, a divine fire which consumed the love of self and could pass between people of equal standing as much as between rich and poor or strong and weak. Those who hardened their hearts to the poor would betray their indifference to God. Charity, in its widest sense, pronounced an English judge in 1804–1805,

meant "all the good affections men ought to bear towards each other."[5] By
that time the legal definition of a charitable foundation in England, by
virtue of the Charitable Uses Act of 1601, depended on objectives which the
Elizabethan government and its successors had recognized as laudable.
These objectives included not only relief of the indigent, but also advancement of learning, of religion, and of "objects of general public utility."
These latter objects included "repair of bridges, ports, havens, causeways,
churches, seabanks and highways" – undertakings which benefited poor
persons among others.[6] Law courts could privilege legacies within those
areas, for example by saving defectively worded bequests from failing for
technical reasons and directing them toward uses deemed to be as close as
possible to the testator's intentions. Secular authorities in any country
could encourage charities by subsidies or tax exemptions or by instructing
notaries to bring them to the attention of testators. They could, on occasion, order the conversion of obsolete charities such as leper asylums to new
uses. To force subjects to practice charity, to feel the affection on which it
ideally rested, was in the strict sense impossible, though they could be made
to contribute to poor relief. In theory, to go back in time to the thirteenth-
century canonist Johannes Teutonicus, it was possible for a poor person to
denounce a rich one who refused him alms and for a church court to apply
spiritual censures. How many skinflints were brought to book by this procedure is not known.

Arguably, both charity and mercy were essential to maintaining the
social order established by divine providence, which rested on an unequal
distribution of wealth and ability. There should, wrote Muratori of Modena
in the early eighteenth century, be "a fine exchange of charity" between
human beings "that God might in the name of the poor and needy bestow
a priceless reward upon their benefactors."[7] A conservative force, respect-
ful of property and rank, charity took it for granted that the "natural"
poverty of those born to labor (the kind which resulted neither from bad
habits nor from bad laws) could be alleviated but not abolished. Outcasts
such as vagrants and prostitutes could perhaps be taught godly, sober, and
laborious habits and thereby made part of the social structure, but few contemplated altering the structure itself or redistributing wealth on a large
scale. Moralists, preachers, theologians, and canon lawyers only required

---

[5] Sir William Grant in *Morice v. Bishop of Durham*, discussed in Gareth Jones, *History of the Law of
  Charity 1532–1827* (Cambridge: Cambridge University Press, 1969), 122–27.
[6] Jones, *ibid.*, 22–33, 120–27.
[7] Ludovico Antonio Muratori, *Trattato della carità cristiana e altri scritti sulla carità*, ed. Piero G. Nonis
  (Rome: Edizioni Paoline, 1961), 516–17.

the well-to-do to share with the poor those things that were surplus to meeting their natural needs and to living in the style expected of them without undue luxury and ostentation. Property could be owned, but the use of it should not be reserved entirely to oneself. "[N]obody should live unbecomingly," pronounced Thomas Aquinas, "and hence it would not do for a man so to impoverish himself by almsgiving that he could no longer live in decency on the residue according to his position and business com-mitments." But when the poor were in danger of dying of want, attach-ment to possessions ought to dissolve. As Aquinas put it, "In a case of extreme necessity everything becomes common property." That doctrine might possibly justify the use of taxation to raise relief funds in crises, though Aquinas himself was more anxious to insist on a starving man's right to help himself to food.[8]

In medieval and early modern Christianity, the words "mercy" and "charity" were often used interchangeably, although "mercy" referred more specifically to exchanges between superior and inferior. Compilers of cate-chisms found it easier to reduce merciful acts to numbers: they listed seven works addressed to the body and seven others directed to the spirit. Six works of "corporal" mercy – to the hungry, the thirsty, the naked, the sick, the homeless and the prisoner – derived from the vision of the Last Judgment offered by Christ in Matthew 25, and the condemnation of all reprobates who had failed to minister to Christ in the persons of the poor. A seventh act of corporal mercy, the burial of the dead, was subsequently added. All such acts of mercy, explained the seventeenth-century Jesuit, Jerome Drexel, were the most God-like deeds within the power of human beings. They could hardly imitate God's wisdom, power, or justice or "the vast, blazing fire of his love," but they were "often inspired to imitate his mercy," and God could be expected to show special favor to those most like himself.[9] Evidence of merciful deeds, produced in the final court of all, was the best if not the only sure defense against damnation at the Last Judgment.

Unlike corporal mercy, spiritual mercy addressed both the souls of the living and those of the departed. It could be urged that souls in purgatory, beyond the grave but not beyond human help, deserved pity as the living poor did: that the pious should aid them by prayer, by having masses said or sung for them, and by performing good works which could be credited to their accounts. Furthermore, spiritual mercy included the instruction of

---

[8] Aquinas, *Summa theologiae*, II–II, 32.6 and 32.7, in vol. XXXIV, *Charity*, 256–59, 262–63.
[9] Heremias Drexelius [Jerome Drexel], *Gazophylacium Christi; sive, De Eleemosyna*, III.v., in *Opera Omnia*, vol. III, ed. Petrus de Vos (Lyons: Huguetan, 1647), 199.

the ignorant and the admonition of sinners. In the sixteenth and seventeenth centuries especially, Catholic evangelists campaigned to redeem the souls of seemingly sinful, misbelieving, and ignorant people, using poor relief as a means to this end. The works most eagerly advocated included the rescue of prostitutes and girls exposed to acute moral danger, the education of the poor and their children in the elements of Christian doctrine and ritual, and the conversion of Jews, Muslims, pagans, and heretics to the Catholic faith.

Almsgiving, charity, and mercy pursued at least three objectives which made them subjects for both ecclesiastical and secular law: the salvation of souls, the promotion of social harmony, and the appeasement of divine wrath, given that the merciful acts of a community were a form of sacrifice which compensated for its sins and injustices, a defense (not always successful) against catastrophe. It was the duty of governments both to please God and to advance the common good of their subjects, thereby promoting the power and prosperity of the state. Some of them attempted to curb practices which offended against charity in the broad sense of the word, such as lavish spending and usurious lending. In extreme situations, where charity broke down, public authorities resorted to drastic measures and legal coercion, spending lavishly on precautions and poor relief in the hope of saving lives. Arguably, they had a natural duty to preserve subjects against the assaults of famine and pestilence as against those of human enemies; the belief that these events were God-ordained penalties for collective sin did not diminish the prince's responsibility to his poorest and most vulnerable subjects. Disasters tended to bring out uncharitable impulses of self-seeking and self-preservation which only the police powers of government could attempt to control. Fluctuating food prices tempted hoarders and speculators to make quick fortunes at the expense of starving people. The terror of plague, often deemed no less lethal than the disease itself, suspended normal feelings of mutual obligation and put well-to-do citizens to flight from the towns and their public duties, leaving their abandoned territory to the poor, the sanitary police, and the gravediggers. Draconian quarantine regulations paralyzed the economy and forced governments to distribute relief to thousands of poor subjects who were isolated in their homes.

By the sixteenth and seventeenth centuries, some governments were asserting their right to levy taxation to finance emergency measures, but representing it as a last resort. People should be exhorted to give, the voluntary principle preserved, for as long as might be possible. For example, in Rouen, France, during the famines of the 1590s, the government sent officials from house to house to make personal appeals; only if these failed to raise the necessary funds would the authorities levy taxes "according to property and means." During the plague of the 1630s, the Medici Grand Duke in Florence justified a possible resort to taxation by openly invoking reason of state, declaring: "[N]ecessity justifies any kind of impost. For everything vital to the state is just, and everything profitable to it is necessary, and nothing is of greater profit than the safety of subjects."[10]

DESERVING AND UNDESERVING POOR

Lawyers and legislators, judges and magistrates were unwilling to ignore altogether the social consequences of almsgiving. Perhaps it should not involve moral judgements. Since one was giving to God, not to an individual of good or bad character, there was no need to conduct an inquisition for the sake of a penny; the act derived its value from the donor's state of mind. At least from the twelfth and thirteenth centuries, however, canon lawyers were arguing that some poor were worthier than others, that an order of charity ought to be laid down, and that giving to the undeserving poor would endanger the social order. A popular image was that Christ's poor and the Devil's lay at two poles – the meek and the rebellious, sufferers unable to work and shirkers bent on avoiding labor. Magistrates were particularly concerned with disciplining the unruly poor, who were depicted both as sinners and as petty criminals, offenders against both divine commandments and human laws. Missionaries to the lower depths of society, particularly in the sixteenth and seventeenth centuries, dreamed of reforming beggars and prostitutes and saving souls from eternal death.

"Christ's poor" in Catholic countries and the "impotent poor" of Protestant England had much in common. Both categories included the very young (especially orphans and foundlings), and the aged, the physically and mentally impaired, and the victims of sickness and accident. In Catholic countries they also included pilgrims and the religious poor whose poverty came not from misfortune but from renunciation. Widows headed a large proportion of the households designated by fiscal assessors as "miserable," unable to pay direct taxes. Poverty was also seen not only as destitution, but also as "lacking those things required to live rightly."[11]

---

[10] Dante Catellacci, "Curiosi ricordi del contagio del Firenze del 1630," *Archivio storico italiano*, 5th ser., 20 (1897): 384.
[11] As the Perugian lawyer Cornelio Benincasa put it in 1562, cited in Christopher F. Black, *Italian Confraternities in the Sixteenth Century* (Cambridge: Cambridge University Press, 1989), 148–49.

Most communities showed special consideration for persons of standing who had fallen into straitened circumstances. These were the hidden or "shamefaced" poor who, unlike beggars, did not parade themselves publicly and had to be sought out and discreetly helped. Over time, between the fourteenth and the eighteenth centuries, there was growing recognition of "labouring persons not able to live off their labour,"[12] and some sympathy for poorly paid, insecure workers, subject to spells of underemployment or prolonged industrial stoppages, often blessed (or burdened with) young children not yet able to contribute to family income. Able-bodied they might be, but if judged rightly they were neither lazy, nor improvident, nor socially inadequate. In the interests of enabling a labor force to survive spells of forced inaction, it was advisable to organize systematic relief for essential workers. Even if societies jibbed at supporting adults, they could pay child allowances to parents or allow children to be temporarily relinquished to institutional care in hard times.

If the poor in the broadest sense of the word were those people who had to work for a living, and if Christ had his own poor, consisting in part of those who could not, the Devil, it seemed, had others who were fraudulent, dissolute, and, worst of all, idle. Drunkards, blasphemers, gamblers, evil-livers, vagrants, tricksters, bogus pilgrims, and prostitutes: all such reprehensible characters began to trouble church and state officials before the end of the twelfth century and perhaps provided excuses for reluctant almsgivers. In the late Middle Ages, visions of the unworthy poor developed into fantasies about a conspiracy of professional beggars who exploited the generosity of decent society. Sanitary authorities traced the plague to contagion as well as to poisonous miasma, and their theories concentrated suspicion on vagrants who might well be coming from infected places or even, allegedly, plotting to spread disease. Ritual purifications of cities by periodic expulsions of vagrants and prostitutes became a common practice in medieval times and continued well into the early modern period on both sides of the Atlantic.

During the twelfth century, canon law commentators agreed on the need to establish priorities: give to the just before the unjust, to the sick before the healthy, to neighbors before strangers, to the modest before the importunate. But should Christians give to everyone if they had the means to do so, or should they on principle withhold assistance from unworthy people? About 1190, the canonist Huguccio advised refusing alms to one who is

---

[12] From parish surveys of the poor in England in the 1590s, cited in Paul A. Slack, *Poverty and Policy in Tudor and Stuart England* (London: Longmans, 1988), 27–29, 65–66.

"capable of working and earning his bread but does not want to do so, and spends the whole day in gambling and rolling the dice."[13] Legislation designed to set all idle people to work attempted to remedy the labor shortages of the thirty-year period after the great mortality of the mid fourteenth century caused by the plague. By the later Middle Ages, laws were set out to control wages, to mobilize the labor force, to forbid almsgiving to sturdy beggars, to prevent even bona fide "impotent" beggars from wandering. This was the start to a long tradition of ascribing destitution not to general social or economic causes but rather to the feeble character of individuals, who could, allegedly, always help themselves if they chose. Willingness to work, unless prevented by infirmity or inhibited by gentility, became a crucial test of entitlement to relief. Other social legislation, likewise directed against the related inconveniences of loose almsgiving and disorderly begging, was to follow after 1520 and to have more lasting effects.

RULES AND INSTITUTIONS

Almsgiving was often a collective enterprise, shaped by private rules rather than public laws. Particularly important were the statutes and ordinances of non-profit associations or corporations such as hospitals or fraternities. These were half private and half public bodies, entitled to hold property and engage in litigation, usually subject to oversight by bishops or magistrates or both. Some of these institutions, indeed, had magisterial powers of their own, and could be charged with arresting beggars or administering prisons.

Especially versatile institutions in Catholic countries were the multitudes of religious fraternities established in almost every town and in many villages between the thirteenth and eighteenth centuries. Practicing charity and mercy in general and dedicated to Christ, the Trinity, the Virgin, the saints, and other cults such as the Blessed Sacrament, they existed at almost every social level from nobles to beggars. These religious fraternities were often connected with crafts or professions, and could undertake almost any task, including the administration of hospitals and orphanages. The most reputable fraternities were often called upon to act as trustees, carrying out the wishes of pious testators and celebrating masses for their souls. The largest recruited from all parts of a city, the smaller from particular parishes or wards. An ardent Christian, wishing to practice all the works

---

[13] Cited in Brian Tierney, "The Decretists and the 'Deserving Poor'," *Comparative Studies in Society and History* 1 (1958–59): 369–70.

of mercy, or an ambitious citizen eager to form useful social connections and ensure a good turn-out at his funeral, could belong to several fraternities at once. They were generally managed by laymen rotating offices among themselves and advised by clergymen acting as their chaplains or spiritual directors, but a few were confined to women and some to the clergy alone. These fraternities bore some resemblance to artificial extended families, formed not by blood or marriage but by subscribing to a simple religious rule designed for persons leading active lives in the world. This fraternity rule was usually a formal, written code of conduct which would make the task of pursuing salvation more finite and manageable. It prescribed essential devotions and good deeds, and laid down regulations for the election of officers and the examination of accounts. The ruling principle was that all members should strive by performing good works to build up spiritual capital, to accumulate a treasury of religious merit for the use of all members in good standing. Gross neglect or violation of the rule would lead to expulsion from the fraternity and loss of benefits. Works of corporal and spiritual mercy were not their sole concerns, but were often among their largest undertakings. The poorest fraternities tended to turn inwards upon themselves, acting in a modest way as mutual insurance societies. The most prosperous turned outwards, devoting much of their income to relieving the house poor in their cities, and sometimes running general almonries as well. Their records suggest that, although they might distribute tiny sums in a haphazard, almost purely symbolic fashion, they were much more careful in bestowing more substantial benefits, such as marriage portions, small regular pensions, or the right to occupy almshouses. No doubt favoritism, corruption, and patronage sometimes influenced the distribution, but at least they knew to whom they were giving.

After the Protestant Reformation, sixteenth-century English parliaments established by statute a national system of poor relief. It used Church of England parishes as administrative units, employing territorial entities rather than voluntary associations, but permitting variations in local practice. In some Catholic countries, parishes entered the field of social action later than fraternities and in a sense became their competitors. In most societies, parish relief depended on collaboration between local clerics and lay persons. Parish priests, churchwardens, elected lay deputies sometimes called overseers, and assemblies of parishioners were entitled to vote on "voluntary taxes." All these parties could be charged with raising funds, identifying deserving cases, finding work for the capable, and even (in England) running workhouses. Like fraternities, parishes were commonly used as trustees of charitable bequests. The practice of taxing the owners and occupiers of property, rather than relying on their voluntary contributions, was permitted by statute in England from 1572 onwards, although it took hold only gradually and became general only by about 1700. In any country, the effectiveness of parishes depended on their size, the social range of their residents, and the extent to which their revenues had been left intact. Much would depend on the institution – as in eighteenth-century and even more in nineteenth-century England – of statutory arrangements for creating unions of parishes to manage expensive amenities such as workhouses, or at least for providing cross-subsidies. Parochial relief in England was seldom equal to dealing with major crises such as famines and plagues, which called for intervention by the central government.

In Catholic Europe, bishops, suspicious of the fraternities' independence but seeing in their structure and functions a device too useful to neglect, strove to bring parishes and fraternities together. They found ways of taming the fraternities by printing model statutes, subordinating them to parish clergy rather than elected lay presidents, and introducing into all parishes in their dioceses fraternities dedicated to distributing alms systematically to the local poor and to teaching the essentials of Christian doctrine to adults and children. Some "enlightened" rulers of the late eighteenth century, such as Pietro Leopoldo of Tuscany, looking askance at the superstitious antics of their all-too-numerous local fraternities (Florence in *c.* 1780, for example, had 253), threatened to dissolve them all. But he allowed a remnant to survive, so long as they tied themselves to parishes, cast away their uniforms, and concentrated on their most laudable activity, the relief of the poor.

POOR LAWS AND REORGANIZATION

Between about 1520 and 1580 some sixty European towns and a few states issued comprehensive legislation, in the form of statutes, church ordinances, and council decrees, designed to direct and control poor relief. Their schemes were often syntheses of measures and reassertions of principles acknowledged, if not acted upon, in previous centuries. The magistrates of the Flemish city of Ypres, for example, invoked canon law in their defense, and some of the legislation seemed to reflect the order of charity outlined by the medieval canonists.

The new poor laws were designed to suppress vagrancy, to repel strange beggars, to concentrate attention on local people whose claims to assistance would be carefully examined through censuses compiled by official visitors. Begging, if partially tolerated (as it often had to be), would in theory be confined to licensed "impotent" poor who could do nothing else. Schemes attempted to coordinate almsgiving, sometimes by establishing central almonries or bureaus under boards of prominent citizens (as in Lyons, Rouen or Antwerp) or by establishing common chests (as in Germany and the Netherlands), through which donations and revenues from endowments were supposed to pass. Overseers, superintendents, or visitors of the poor were now officially in charge of "outdoor" relief (assistance was administered in domestic surroundings rather than in institutions). Some of these poor relief officials were municipal officers, others church functionaries; some were universal in their distribution, others more targeted. In sixteenth-century Holland, for example, the Calvinist deacons of Amsterdam sometimes ministered only to members of their own congregations, while their counterparts in Delft attended to the city poor in general. Occasionally, magistrates would invite deacons to join the city bureau of charity to serve alongside other almoners or "regents." Willingness to work, required of all but the feeble and the genteel, became a crucial qualification for eligibility for this relief. From this principle it often followed that local authorities felt some obligation to put work in the way of capable people and, if need be, force them to do it in closed workhouses or labor gangs. Private charity, collections, and self-assessment for donations and subscriptions were still the financial mainstay of most schemes. But taxation could be contemplated, making poor relief a matter for the community rather than the individual – either through additional levies of existing direct taxes such as the Venetian property tax, or through specific poor taxes. Luther's ordinance of 1523 for Leisnig in Electoral Saxony specified that, should the resources of the common chest prove inadequate, all householders and participants "in the use and enjoyment of our parish rights" should be required to pay a flat-rate tax – which should be tolerable, he suggested, because it would prove to be a lighter burden than the exactions of the Romish clergy.[14]

Many of the new schemes coincided with the coming of religious revolution; the poor laws' progress from town to town began in Lutheran Germany in the early 1520s. Protestant theology opposed the belief that one vital function of almsgiving was to accumulate spiritual merit; rejecting an ethos founded on spiritual rewards and punishments, it argued that

---

[14] Martin Luther, "Ordinance of a Common Chest," in *Luther's Works*, vol. XLV, ed. Walther I. Brandt (Philadelphia: Muhlenberg Press, 1962), 192.

salvation depended on faith in Christ's sacrificial death. Good works, including almsgiving, were the fruits of faith, a way of exercising it in the world, not a means of earning divine favours. It may have opened ways to more effective social action, ideally a manifestation of God's love, directed toward establishing a well-ordered Christian commonwealth on earth. But Catholic civil authorities, and those hesitating between different Christian persuasions, also enacted poor laws, with certain differences. Most schemes were, to some extent, adopted for social and economic reasons connected with immigration controls, the need for cheap labor in the textile industries, and the fear of famine and epidemic disease. But the laws were generally designed to nurture godly communities founded on sobriety, thrift, and hard work, and religious arguments were potent forces that supported such laws. To live in idleness was to rebel a second time against the Creator, to shuffle off Adam's burden by defying the commandment: "In the sweat of your face you shall eat bread till you return to the ground" (Genesis 3:19). It was also to ignore the Pauline instruction, "If any one will not work, let him not eat" (2 Thessalonians 3:10). Discriminating charity, which would reward docility, piety, and sound morals, could become a powerful weapon in the hands of reformers and disciplinarians of any religious faith and provide a pretext for inquiring into poor families' way of life. The "prefects of the poor" of Ypres, instructed to gather information about candidates for relief, were "by certain tokens and conjectures to get the knowledge of their condition, their health, their homely and secret griefs, their manners and (as near as can be) their merits, and to write these in a book or tables ordained by the same purpose."[15] No doubt the attractions of new churches would be even greater should they be known, as were the Calvinist congregations, to provide systematically for poor members and refugees for the sake of religion, neither leaving relief in the hands of their adversaries nor abandoning their followers to hospital wards which administered Catholic sacraments to the sick and dying.

Protestant societies redefined the objects of charity, and it often fell to godly princes as instruments of reformation to redirect funds. Neither chantries (foundations to maintain priests to sing masses for departed souls) nor religious fraternities accorded with the new Protestant theology, although the dissolution of religious brotherhoods did not mean the abolition in perpetuity of all organizations for mutual help. Their distant, secularized descendants were some of the friendly societies of the nineteenth

---

[15] See William Marshall's translation of the Ypres scheme of poor relief in Frank R. Salter, ed., *Some Early Tracts on Poor Relief* (London: Methuen, 1926), 56.

and twentieth centuries. Protestant leaders no longer deemed it worthy to support the voluntary poverty of monks, friars, and nuns, let alone the self-imposed hardships of pilgrims. By virtue of a parliamentary statute of 1547, King Edward VI of England and his council were to convert the endowments of chantries from "superstitious" and "erroneous" to "good and godlie uses, as in erecting of Gramer Scooles to the education of Youthe in virtue and godlinesse, the further augmenting of the Universities and better provision for the poore and nedye."[16] In some Protestant societies, monasteries became hospitals or schools. For example, the German Landgrave Philip of Hesse, holding that secularized monastic property ought to serve the common weal, devoted about 60 percent of appropriated monastic revenues to charity and the rest to the needs of the court and the administration. He strove to create hospitals so self-evidently governed by Christian discipline that monastic orders would have had great moral difficulty in reclaiming them even if the opportunity arose. Revenues diverted from so-called "superstitious" uses did not, however, always benefit poor people or scholars. Most confiscated chantry wealth in sixteenth-century Lutheran Denmark, for example, passed to the crown and to the nobles and aspiring gentry.

Catholic measures in the sixteenth and seventeenth centuries proved to be less radical than in Protestant lands, but Catholic authorities joined in the general condemnation of vagrancy, idleness, and disorderly begging. They also shared the general desire to reorganize almsgiving. Begging was obnoxious to them partly because beggars haunted churches and interrupted services, especially at the elevation of the host during the Eucharist. Despite their addiction to using sacred places as pitches, these beggars neglected the sacraments and thereby sank to the level of beasts. Catholic authorities taught that these poor could aspire to the human condition only by practicing Christianity, rather than by exploiting other Christians' piety.

There were significant differences between early modern Catholic and Protestant approaches to poverty and charity, however – some of an organizational kind. Since funds for financing masses for the dead, religious fraternities, and religious orders continued to multiply until well into the eighteenth century, the institutional structure in Catholic societies generally remained more complicated and less amenable to central control. Furthermore, Catholic societies were more given to a kind of disapproving, pragmatic tolerance of certain sinful practices, which involved permitting lesser, seemingly unavoidable evils for the sake of avoiding greater ones and

---

[16] Jones, *History of the Law of Charity*, 10–13.

bringing sin to the surface the better to control it. Foundling hospitals, public pawn offices in Jewish or Christian hands, and institutions for the care and discipline of penitent prostitutes were commoner in Catholic than in Protestant realms. Child abandonment might be evil, but it was preferable to infanticide or the public disgrace of young women who had given birth to bastards; it was legitimate, therefore, to provide facilities for it. Lending upon usury might be evil, but it could be better to entrust it to Jews, whose law permitted them to take interest from strangers and who could be legally regulated, than to allow Christians to endanger their souls by exploiting the needy. If Christian pawnshops were established, let them charge moderate interest to pay staff and cover their administrative costs, this being a realistic concession to the shortcomings of human beings who would never perform efficiently unless they were paid. Public prostitution might be evil, but it was preferable to the seduction of respectable women by lechers and philanderers. Though Catholic societies tolerated these practices, however, they also used the law to ghettoize and stigmatize Jews and prostitutes and, through organized charity, provide for their conversion and the protection of their children.

Catholic charity tended to broaden its scope during the sixteenth and seventeenth centuries and to become redemptive as well as supportive. It was more obviously concerned with the reclamation of outcasts and undesirables from the consequences of ignorance and sin. Redemption could only be achieved by altering a person's way of life, by remolding the character, and this, some would argue, could only be effected through the austere regime of a closed, authoritarian, quasi-monastic institution, marked by long hours of regular work, pious exercises, and sometimes frequent confession.

Reformers of all persuasions, Catholic or Protestant, outlined and debated during the sixteenth and seventeenth centuries most of the principles which were to govern public relief and private charity until well into the nineteenth century. Much of the argument over time was about the application of those principles and about which agencies – central or local, public or private, clerical or lay – ought to control relief. Many of the questions remained the same. To what extent was the freedom to seek alms and wander wherever one chose a natural right of which poor laws could not justly deprive beggars? Or were these things squalid burdens of which Christian kindness ought to relieve them by "remedial" charity? Such kindness might well take the form of tough love, in the name of charity toward the body politic. "I do not avenge wickedness; I compel goodness. My hand is heavy but my heart is full of love," declared a notice at the door of a female workhouse in Amsterdam in 1667.[17] Was it right to eliminate face-to-face relationships, at best humane and sympathetic, between the giver and the receiver and substitute impersonal, bureaucratic procedures? Would these not stifle generosity, and would the poor really be able to help themselves if they did? Endlessly debated was the question whether poor relief should only be administered in closed institutions, in hospices or workhouses under various names, where loss of liberty, segregation of the sexes, and a degrading regime would deter malingerers. Or might it be possible to dispense allowances to families in their own homes without destroying their self-reliance and somehow rendering the condition of (in nineteenth-century language) a "pauper" preferable to that of an independent laborer? The staff of an institution would be able to discriminate, it was often argued, where an ordinary citizen could hardly assess the credentials of a beggar in the street.

In the nineteenth century, some imaginative schemes promoted domestic relief as an alternative to institutional confinement by entrusting it to visitors who would each handle a few cases only, establish a personal relationship with clients, and encourage self-help, sobriety, and saving. One influential scheme was developed in Elberfeld (later called Wuppertal) in Rhenish Prussia about 1800 and was recast in the 1850s. A total force of over 500 almoners, ideally one for every four recipients of relief, shared the task of visiting "needy but capable" persons on the relief roll, advising them and reporting to the central poor administration of the town. Qualified citizens were not entitled to decline civic service as almoners, nor were "capable" poor persons allowed to refuse work allotted to them. Other German cities took up the scheme, and it influenced some organizations in late Victorian and Edwardian England, including both the Charity Organization Society and the Guild of Help. Founded in Bradford in 1904, the Guild set out "[t]o provide a friend for all those in need of help and advice, and to encourage them in efforts towards self-help." It also adopted the time-honored aim of discouraging "indiscriminate almsgiving by private persons" and devising "methods whereby the generosity of such persons may be wisely directed and enabled to secure results of permanent benefit."[18]

---

[17] Cited in Bronislaw Geremek, *Poverty; a History*, trans. Agnieska Kolakowska (Oxford: Blackwell, 1994), 215.

[18] Keith Laybourn, *The Evolution of British Social Policy and the Welfare State, c. 1800–1993* (Keele: Ryburn Publishing and Keele University Press, 1995), 283.

In several Western European countries – Bismarck's Germany was the first – the half-century from the 1880s to the 1930s saw a tilting of the balance between state provision for the poor and voluntary action by charities and mutual aid societies. States began to do more than intervene in emergencies and supplement the initiatives of voluntary associations. They attempted by degrees to establish a safety net strong enough to save all citizens from sinking into utter destitution and to release them from dependence on the judgments or whims of charities. "It is no use letting the poor come and go as they think, to be helped or not as the charitable choose," wrote Beatrice Webb in the Minority Report of the English Poor Law Commission of 1905–1909. Charity, it was often urged, could only palliate. In Lloyd George's rhetoric, heralding the People's Budget of 1909, the state, empowered to impose redistributive taxation, would "wage implacable warfare against poverty and squalidness." Arguably the state alone had the coercive powers to provide, through taxation or compulsory contributions to insurance, against income loss through the death of breadwinners, sickness, accident, disability, and even (most ambitiously) long spells of unemployment. Only the state, it might seem, could transform the recipients of benefit into citizens claiming rights, rather than petitioners for charity or social inadequates stigmatized as "paupers." A number of factors contributed to an extension of state power over income protection and elementary education: concern for national efficiency and competitiveness, which depended on a reasonably healthy and educated work force (to say nothing of one fit to perform military service); the extension of the franchise; the desire of central governments to promote through elementary education a national, generally understood language at the expense of local dialects; the eagerness of astute politicians to forge ties with industrial workers, if need be outmanoeuvring socialist parties and trade union leaders; the desire of employers for industrial harmony; the relative weakening in some countries of the lesser bourgeoisie, who were often the most stubborn defenders of private property against taxation; increasing longevity, which made it impossible for mutual aid societies to provide old age pensions; and the moral obligation to meet the expectations of war veterans.

"Welfare states," as they emerged in Western Europe and North America in the twentieth century, were not equally generous or comprehensive. Their triumph was not inevitable, nor was their full survival guaranteed, especially in the face of flagging economic performance. Not all succeeded in eliminating poverty, especially if this were defined in relative rather than absolute terms. It may be that the British version, less thoroughgoing than the Scandinavian, was still, as charity had been, an instrument for taking the sting out of inequality by reducing desperation. In the words of *Tribune*'s critique of the Beveridge Report of 1942: "Sir William has described the conditions in which the tears might be taken out of capitalism." Charities and voluntary associations might be reduced to the rank of handmaiden or junior partner to the state. But where the state's principle was to provide "help according to need at a basic level," charities, ready to fill gaps in the state system, meeting specialized needs and rising a little above basics, could still compensate for the bureaucratic and insensitive tendencies of public machinery.[19]

RECOMMENDED READING

Aquinas, Thomas. *Summa theologiae*. II-II 22–33. Reprinted and translated in *Summa Theologiae*. Vol. XXXIV, *Charity*. Translated by the English Dominicans. Edited by R. J. Batten. New York: Blackfriars-McGraw Hill, 1975.

Bernardino of Siena. *Le prediche volgari*. Edited by Piero Bargellini. Milan/Rome: Rizzoli, 1936.

Black, Christopher F. *Italian Confraternities in the Sixteenth Century*. Cambridge: Cambridge University Press, 1989.

Critchlow, Donald T. and Charles H. Parker, eds. *With Us Always. A History of Private Charity and Public Welfare*. Lanham, MD: Rowman and Littlefield, 1998.

Dorwart, Reinhold A. *The Prussian Welfare State Before 1740*. Cambridge, MA: Harvard University Press, 1971.

Geremek, Bronislaw. *Poverty; a History*. Translated by Agnieska Kolakowska. Oxford: Blackwell, 1994.

Grell, Ole Peter, and Andrew Cunningham, eds. *Health Care and Poor Relief in Protestant Europe 1500–1700*. London: Routledge, 1997.

Grell, Ole Peter, Andrew Cunningham, and Jon Arrizabalaga, eds. *Health Care and Poor Relief in Counter Reformation Europe*. London: Routledge, 1999.

Jones, Gareth. *History of the Law of Charity 1532–1827*. Cambridge: Cambridge University Press, 1969.

Jütte, Robert. *Poverty and Deviance in Early Modern Europe*. Cambridge: Cambridge University Press, 1994.

Laybourn, Keith. *The Evolution of British Social Policy and the Welfare State, c. 1800–1993*. Keele: Ryburn Publishing and Keele University Press, 1995.

Luther, Martin. "Ordinance of a Common Chest." In *Luther's Works*. Vol. XLV. Edited by Walther I. Brandt, 162–94. Philadelphia: Muhlenberg Press, 1962.

---

[19] For the quotations in these last two paragraphs, see *ibid.*, 166, 176–77, 256–57, 295.

Mollat, Michel. *The Poor in the Middle Ages.* Translated by Arthur Goldhammer. New Haven, CT: Yale University Press, 1986.

Muratori, Ludovico Antonio. *Trattato della carità cristiana e altri scritti sulla carità.* Edited by Piero G. Nonis. Rome: Edizioni Paoline, 1961.

Pullan, Brian. *Poverty and Charity: Europe, Italy, Venice 1400–1700.* Aldershot: Variorum, 1994.

"Catholics, Protestants and the Poor in Early Modern Europe." *Journal of Interdisciplinary History* 35 (2005): 441–56.

Salter, Frank R., ed. *Some Early Tracts on Poor Relief.* London: Methuen, 1926.

Slack, Paul A. *Poverty and Policy in Tudor and Stuart England.* London: Longmans, 1988.

Swaan, Abram de. *In Care of the State: Health Care, Education and Welfare in Europe and the USA in the Modern Era.* Cambridge: Polity Press, 1988.

Tierney, Brian. "The Decretists and the 'Deserving Poor'." *Comparative Studies in Society and History* 1 (1958–59): 360–73.

Medieval Poor Law. A Sketch of Canonical Theory and its Application in England. Berkeley/Los Angeles: University of California Press, 1959.

Zamagni, Vera, ed. *Povertà e innovazioni istituzionali in Italia. Dal Medioevo ad oggi.* Bologna: Il Mulino, 2000.

11 "Lazarus Begging for Scraps from the Rich Man's Table," from Julius Schnorr von Carolsfeld, *Die Bibel in Bildern* (Leipzig, 1853), s.v. Luke 16.

CHAPTER TEN

Property and Christian theology

Frank S. Alexander

THE THEOLOGICAL CONTEXT FOR PROPERTY

Few concepts are more challenging for Christian theology than that of property. Property is often viewed as fundamentally inconsistent with the proclamation of the Gospel, yet it is proclaimed as evidence of God's bountiful reward. It is neither evidence of salvation nor a means to redemption, yet it is used to create personal identity and to define interpersonal relationships. Property is that which is to be gathered up, yet it is that which is to be shared with others and held in common. It is a resource to be appropriated and consumed, yet it is God's creation and it is *"very good."*

Property is an analogy for the human condition theologically understood. The multitude of the types of property, of the functions of property, and of the ways of dividing property all can be understood in light of the theology of the human condition. It makes little sense to speak of "a theology of property," for property is not essentially sacramental in nature. It makes a great deal of sense, however, to speak of a theological understanding of property because the nature of being human reflects, refracts, and refines the nature and function of property.

The core Christian doctrines of creation, fall, and redemption provide the context for a multifaceted conception of property. The doctrine of creation provides the foundation for understanding that all that exists is created by God, and is in its essence "very good" (Genesis 1:31). This doctrine establishes three propositions about the nature and function of property. First, all forms of property are a result of God's creation and are divine gifts. Because they are gifts, we cannot and must not use them as a source of our own righteousness, as "we all drink from cisterns we did not hew" (Deuteronomy 6:11). Second, creation stands as a radical rejection of a conception of *private* property as Western law has come to know it – at least in the face of the never-ending assertion that all that is held is held individually or collectively by humankind only as a gift of God. There can be no such thing as private property as against God, for all that is, is God's (1 Chronicles 29:11). Human appropriation of finite things is always to be understood with reference to the antecedent grace of God. Third, the vocation of being human is, in part, to care for the property which God created. As humans, we are called to be stewards of the land, to have dominion over it and to keep it (Genesis 1:28, 2:15), and never to defile it (Numbers 35:34).

The doctrine of the fall describes the human condition as we know it and in so doing it indicates the use and abuse of property. The theology of the fall mirrors the theology of creation in reverse image. The things we have, the things we acquire, the things we make define our success and (in vain) our own righteousness. The refusal to heed God's word in the insistence on eating the forbidden fruit is the assertion of the self as independent of God and against God. Self-interestedness is the fall as it blinds us to the primacy of God who created us and all things around us. The claim from our earliest years that something "is mine" is a manifestation of fallen human nature. Property becomes subservient to the human will for exploitation.

Redemption is the Gospel narrative of the incarnation, crucifixion, and resurrection of Christ. It is the word by which God unconditionally reaches out once again to the human and permits the possibility through faith of knowing grace. Because property in itself is not "fallen," it is not the object of redemption. The nature and function of property, however, transform as redemption transforms the individual and the community. Just as redemption permits us to see through "a mirror dimly" (1 Corinthians 13:12), we can begin to recall and reclaim the reality that property is never fully "mine," that it is not to be exploited, and that it is not a means of justification nor evidence of sanctification. As simultaneously fallen sinners and redeemed children of God, we construct laws of property that are mirrors of the fall yet hold open the promise of redemption.

In its first two millennia, the Christian church has had a profound ambiguity about the role of property in the human condition and in society at large. Many mendicants and monastic orders, especially the Franciscans and Dominicans in the thirteenth and fourteenth centuries, presented in stark form the assertion that property and possessions stand as barriers to the grace of God. Giving primacy to Christ's exhortations to "go, sell what you possess and give to the poor" (Matthew 19:21), and to "[t]ake nothing for your journey, no staff, nor bag, nor bread, nor money" (Luke 9:3), they pressed for a Christian theology that acknowledged the manifold ways in which property became indicative of fallen human nature and an obstacle to the imperative call of redemption. Counterpoising "God and Mammon" (Matthew 6:24), they stressed Christ's admonition that "it is easier for a camel to go through the eye of a needle than a rich man to enter the kingdom of heaven" (Mark 10:25).[1]

But despite these texts and tendencies toward renunciation of property, the Western church has never rejected property, even if it was to be generously shared in the communion of saints (Acts 4:35). The Western church held to the belief that property was part of the "natural law" and "created order."[2] But, since property was part of the natural order, the church left most of its regulations to the secular authorities. It was not until the high Middle Ages that the church developed a sophisticated body of canon law governing aspects of family property, ecclesiastical foundations, and personal inheritance – laws which sometimes stood in an awkward relationship if not outright tension with existing Western property laws.[3] Most Western laws of real property (land and fixtures) and of personal property (tangible and intangible items not attached to land) were more heavily dependent on Roman civil law with its complex rules of private and public property and English common law with its feudal tenure origins, and only marginally derived from explicit ecclesiastical concepts.

Western Christian theology and Western laws of property are wonderful matches not so much because of doctrinal connections but because of the conceptual correlation between them. There are certainly many concepts and terms that appear in both Christian theology and in property law. We can think of "covenants" (God's covenant with Abraham, and the American law of real covenants running with the land), "redemption" (redemption from the fall and the equity of redemption during the life of a mortgage), "grace" (God's grace and the law of a grace period prior to default in real estate finance), and many more. While today these parallels are at best semantic coincidences, they contain conceptual overlaps that reflect the analogy of property to the human condition theologically understood. Property is an analogy for the human condition precisely because our use of property, our relationship to it, and the ways in which we use it to determine our relationships one to another, all mirror the doctrines of creation, fall, and redemption.

Property is not just a thing, and property law is rarely just about the legal relationships between a person and a thing. Property is identity, power, and

---

[1] See further chapter by Brian Pullan herein.   [2] See further chapter by Brian Tierney herein.
[3] See generally Harold J. Berman, *Law and Revolution: The Formation of the Western Legal Tradition* (Cambridge, MA: Harvard University Press, 1983) and chapters by Luke Johnson and R. H. Helmholz herein.

control; property is that which defines relationships between persons with respect to a thing. Property is identity because we use it to symbolize, define, and express who we are as individuals and as communities. Property is power because it lies at the essence of survival (consumption) and is the subject matter of exchange. Property is control because it allows the property "owner" the right to consume it, dispose of it, and – most importantly – to exclude others from it.

Property rights do not exist in the absence of the potential claims of others. Theologically there is the human vocation of keeping the land and not defiling it, but legally the nature of property laws is to define the relationships between persons with respect to a thing (or a right to a thing). In Western law, property and property rights can be divided conceptually and legally in five ways: (1) by physical location; (2) by owners; (3) by item; (4) by use; and (5) by time. Property (most particularly land) can be divided geographically, separated by vertical or horizontal boundaries. It can be divided among one or more concurrent owners (joint tenancies, tenancies in common, partnerships). It can be divided according to item (timber rights, mineral rights, rights to the surface of land). It can be divided according to use and activities (non-exclusive easements, restrictive real covenants). Finally, it can be divided according to time (life estates, tenancies). These multiple divisions of property and property rights reflect and refine, in part, our many roles and relationships in life – as a child of God, a child of parents, a sibling, a parent, a member of a series of ever larger concentric communities. Though Western law does, from a positivist perspective, define property rights in formal categories within all of the forms of "ownership," every delineation of a property right is a normative conclusion about the relationship between the actors, the activity, and the thing in question.

Christian theology allows one to understand the differing claims, and different rules, of property in a far deeper and richer context while at the same time insisting that no single positivist, normative, or economic claim dominates. The human experience of property begins with the fall and humanity's assertion of self-awareness as against God. This is the experience of "property as mine." The necessary corollary to this is an understanding of "property as yours." But both in theology and in law the recognition of the identity and claims of the other person is fraught with ambiguity. A theological affirmation of another person as a child of God, the one we are to love as we love ourselves, invites the affirmation through law of the property of that person, the things that form the identity, power, and control of the other. At the same time, however, the creation of boundaries between us and other persons and their property can become the creation of barriers, and the distinction between the self and the other can become a source of distance, of alienation, and of estrangement. Both "property as mine" and "property as yours," in turn, prompt a conception of "property as ours." When property is "ours" we quickly confront both the positive conception of shared ownership and the economic reality of the imposition of external costs on others. The area where Christian theology and Western property law encounter the strongest disconnection is in the movement from property as defining relationships between persons and entities to the concept of a shared human duty to the land itself. The theological grounding of dominion as stewardship may be clear, yet the expression of environmental laws as something other than homocentric priorities remains an unfinished task.[4]

The following sections take up these understandings of property as "mine," "yours," and "ours," underscoring the parallels, tensions, and possibilities of new understanding between the teachings of Christian theology and Western property law.

PROPERTY AS MINE

If you ever wonder about essential human instincts regarding property, just take a toy, a bottle, or really any item away from the firm grasp of a one-year-old child. The intensity of the non-verbal response makes it abundantly clear that the child is not pleased with the affront to her or his possession, indeed her or his dignity. By the age of two the child has usually learned to place the label "mine" on any item that is desired, whether held, or seen, or – even more poignantly – held by another. Theologically, this primal claim that something is "mine" is simply the doctrine of the fall. The fall is the elevation of individual human self-centeredness over and against the omnipotent creator. The initial human tendency is to supplant an experience of dependency with an assertion of autonomy and to form one's identity by possession and control.[5]

The American law of property – even more than the English common law – affirms and reifies the legitimacy of these instinctual claims to ownership. We see it in the early legal doctrines for the capture of wild animals and in the rules protecting the first possessor of land ("I was here first"). The myopia of this self-interested formulation of property claims is revealed

---

[4] Laurence Tribe, "Ways Not to Think About Plastic Trees: New Foundations for Environmental Law," *Yale Law Journal* 83 (1974): 1315.
[5] Margaret Jane Radin, "Property and Personhood," *Stanford Law Review* 34 (1982): 957.

most clearly in the hegemonic arrogance of the positive laws of discovery and conquest used to wipe aside virtually all recognition of the tribal claims of Native Americans in the history of the United States. We see the dominance of the self-interested formulation in the protected legal categories of intellectual property ("It's mine because I made it") and in the rules protecting the first to exploit natural resources ("The stream is mine because I used it first"). Often justified philosophically by reference to John Locke, Thomas Hobbes, or William Blackstone, the explanatory stories are not the only options available. Other narrative or anthropological perspectives suggest that the primacy of the claim that "property as mine" is but one approach and one that is inadequate.[6]

In the United States the laws of property take a curious turn at times in overriding the claim of a first possessor and affirming the claim of a subsequent possessor. This occurs in the doctrine of adverse possession, which affirms the right of a current possessor to prevail over a prior "owner" of land. The adverse possessor prevails if she has been in actual physical possession of the land for a statutory period of time in a manner that would put the prior possessor on notice and which manifests dominion and control over the land. Two theories are used to explain these laws of adverse possession, neither of which is inconsistent with the doctrine of the fall. One theory focuses on the manner in which the adverse possessor has, over time, developed a relationship – an identity – with the land and correspondingly the prior possessor (by taking no action to protect her claim) has indicated that such relationship as may once have existed is no longer a vital part of her identity.[7] The law is protecting the role of property in the formation of identity. A second theory focuses on the use of the property as the concept of primary importance, demonstrating a preference for active use and control over passive claims.

If Western laws affirming the primal assertion that "property as mine" are a direct analogy to the theological depiction of human condition in light of the fall, then the doctrine of redemption stands as a strong rebuke to any sense that "it is mine and therefore I am good." The parables of the laborers in the vineyard (Matthew 20:1–16) and the servants' rewards (Luke 17:7–10) are a direct rejection of an entitlement to salvation, and to the possibility of righteousness through one's works or one's property accumulation.

---

[6] Carol M. Rose, "Property as Storytelling: Perspectives from Game Theory, Narrative Theory, Feminist Theory", *Yale Journal of Law and Humanities* 2 (1990): 37.

[7] Carol M. Rose, "Possession as the Origin of Property," *University of Chicago Law Review* 52 (1985): 73.

PROPERTY AS YOURS

If "property as mine" is the legal counterpart to the fall, "property as yours" rests on the theological ambiguity of the relationship between the self and the other. Christian theology contains the affirmation of the other person and the call to serve, care for, and love the other.[8] It also contains the recognition that the other person is different, is distant, and often in disagreement. If the price paid for the knowledge of good and evil is estrangement from God and from the other person, the redemption of the Gospel is a call to move beyond the self and toward the other.

The property of the other person is assumed in Christian theology, as five of the Ten Commandments are declarations against violating that of another person (see Deuteronomy 6:17–21), and boundary lines are not to be moved and are to be respected (Deuteronomy 19:14). Property laws of trespass, of private nuisance (and in earlier centuries trespass on the case), of conversion, and of landlord–tenant evictions are all legal declarations of the rights of one to hold property free from interference by another. Classic descriptions of property rights include the right to exclude others. An act of attempted self-preservation is not an affirmation of the dignity of the other person.

The dilemma for understanding "property as yours" as an analogy to Christian theology of the human condition is that the Gospel narrative is far more than a proclamation (in Robert Frost's terms) that "good fences make good neighbors." Theologically this is accurate insofar as the fence or boundary requires one to acknowledge the identity and dignity of the other person. It is also accurate insofar as Christians are called to love their neighbors and to serve and assist the other. Boundary lines, however, can also become dividing lines that separate and segregate. The metaphor of "law as a bulwark" is never more true than in the context of Western laws of property,[9] for the right to exclude becomes a rejection rather than an affirmation of the other.

Christian theology calls us to give all to others (Mark 10:21; Matthew 16:24; Luke 12:33; Acts 2:45, 4:34–35), to know that those who have the least shall be first (Luke 6:20), to provide for those who have little (Matthew 25:40), and to give what you have whenever another seeks it (Luke 6:30).[10] With this powerful ethic, Christian theology moves from a bulwark conception of "property as yours" to a counterintuitive transformation of

---

[8] See further chapters by Jeffrie Murphy and Michael J. Perry herein.
[9] Milner S. Ball, *Lying Down Together: Law, Metaphor, and Theology* (Madison, WI: University of Wisconsin Press, 1985).   [10] See further the chapter by Brian Pullan herein.

boundaries as a medium, a line to be crossed in giving unselfishly to the other person. To give to the other who seeks to exclude is to undermine the power of exclusion. The act of giving, of sharing, sets aside both for oneself and for the other the assertion of power and control in gaining property. To this doctrine of redemption the Western law of property has no answer.

PROPERTY AS OURS

The ownership of most real property is shared in some sense. Both English and American law recognize in theory the possibility of the "fee simple absolute" form of ownership in which a single person or entity possesses all of the possible rights and privileges in the property together with absolute dominion and control over it. This fee simple absolute, however, exists only in theory. Even when one person or entity possesses all rights, and no other has any affirmative right in or to the land, this "owner" does not possess absolutely the right to use the land as she pleases. The use of property in all jurisdictions is subject to two key limitations. First, one is not permitted to use property in a manner that harms others. Enforced through the legal doctrines of private and public nuisances, this affirms the often interrelated if not interdependent consequences of use of property. Second, the public at large (by and through the appropriate governmental entities) has the right to regulate, define, and limit the permissible uses of property. Grounded in implicit constitutional police power doctrines, public land use controls are experienced primarily in the form of zoning, housing and building codes, and environmental regulations.

The fact that the law of property never confers absolute rights of control and that all forms of ownership are subject to some degree to shared control by the larger community is, in a very small way, directly analogous to the theological premise that what we have, we have been given by God. The theoretical fee simple absolute and the tendency to believe – at least in American culture – of the absolute nature of private property rights are contrary both to law and to the theology of the human condition.

On a more pragmatic level, Western law recognizes concurrent ownership in multiple forms. American property law permits joint tenancies, tenancies in common, and marital estates, in each instance the multiple owners having simultaneously full and complete rights over the entire property. It also recognizes the ability to have defeasible fees, life estates, and long-term tenancies, all of which can be transferred as security for a debt (a mortgage relationship). Concurrent ownership necessarily means that multiple owners must find ways to allocate costs and burdens and agree upon their respective rights. In the absence of private agreements, the law defines default positions for allocation of the benefits and burdens of concurrent ownership. These property regimes are also – again in a small way – analogous to the theological doctrine that we are all interrelated and bear responsibility one for another.

What is far more problematic for theology and property are the twin propositions that some land can be owned by everyone in common, and that some land is not subject to ownership by anyone. The former is characterized as "the problem of the commons,"[11] and it is used as the economic explanation for the origin of private property rights. The latter is the agreed-upon exclusion of governmental and private rights in certain geographic areas such as the polar continents, the open seas, and outer space.

When multiple parties all have rights to use a given area of land and no one has the right to exclude others from its use, each individual actor has strong incentive to maximize her or his own use largely because the costs of such use are imposed upon all concurrent owners (external costs), while the benefits of the use belong to the actor (internal benefits). This misallocation of costs and benefits leads to over-consumption of the land and long-term losses to the community as a whole. The response, at least in theory, was the emergence of private property rights with the ability to exclude others and thereby internalize all of the costs and benefits of one's actions. Buttressed by the rise of theoretical work in the field of law and economics, such an analysis is largely accurate from a descriptive perspective, and led to the focus on the "rational self-interested utility maximizer" as the quintessential human actor.

On the descriptive level, the paradigm of the self-interested person as a basis for defining property rights is entirely consistent with the theological doctrine of the fall. In both instances the individual self is primary and all else is secondary unless and until it is defined as important to the individual. Western capitalism does precisely the same thing. The premise is that the human condition innately seeks to maximize self-interest. In Christian theology, however, the fall is not the last word, and the self-interested person is not the paradigm for normative behavior. Because "all have sinned and fall short of the glory of God" (Romans 3:23), the doctrine of redemption offers a new paradigm through the incarnation, crucifixion, and resurrection.

Christian theology presents not just an alternative to property rules based on individual self-interest; it provides challenges to the conception

---

[11] Garrett Hardin, "The Tragedy of the Commons," *Science* 162 (1968): 1243.

of private (individual or entity) ownership and control of property. The ancient Hebrew practice of Jubilee stands as a dramatic recurring redistribution of all property and possessions (Leviticus 25). From the mendicant orders of the thirteenth century to the contemporary Hutterite communities, Christians have proclaimed in a strong voice that property does not belong to the individual but rather that the community holds "all things in common" (Acts 4:32–35).

Though the theological perspective of property held purely in common is troublesome for Western laws of real property (and most especially for economists), in recent years property regimes in American jurisdictions have begun to experiment with a variety of forms of shared ownership. Condominiums and cooperatives are examples of ownership of property in which some, if not all, of the underlying real property is held in common and governed by agreements on use and control. In similar fashion, residential communities are increasingly governed by extensive "covenants, conditions, and restrictions" created and imposed at the time of the initial development of the community. These "CC&Rs," as they are called by property lawyers, significantly narrow the degree of individual rights and individual control, all in the name of the common good of the community, and common control.

"Property as ours" reflects both the descriptive human condition as revealed in the fall, and the promise of an alternative vision as revealed by redemption. As humans we are innately resistant to yielding control and are frightened by holding all things in common. Yet, we are reminded that what we have has been graciously given to us, "for the land is mine, for you are strangers and sojourners with me" (Leviticus 25:23).

DOMINION AS STEWARDSHIP

Theology demonstrates that the fall makes it quite difficult for us to see our relationship to the land except through the context of subduing and of sharing, of exploitation and exchanges of the land with others. What has been missing in our property law regimes is any sense of the normative relationship of humans to the land. On this the word of theology is quite clear, though we may not have heard it and do not reflect it in our laws.[12]

Property laws as an analogy of the human condition are challenged to acknowledge the doctrine of creation. All that has been created in heaven

---

[12] John Copeland Nagle, "Christianity and Environmental Law," in *Christian Perspectives on Legal Thought*, ed. Michael W. McConnell, Robert F. Cochran, Jr., and Angela Carmella (New Haven, CT: Yale University Press, 2001): 435.

and in earth belongs not to humans but to God (Deuteronomy 10:14; 1 Chronicles 29:11), and all that has been created is "very good." The doctrine of the fall reveals that humans define their world in their own terms, with themselves as the center, and not as part of God's creation. This homocentric approach is what has characterized the nature of human obligation to the non-human environment in Western laws of property.[13]

Property laws affirm the right of an owner to consume and to alter, to destroy and to exploit, her or his property in any manner. This is limited only by the common law injunction not to use it in a matter that harms others – the law of private and public nuisances. Environmental laws as they began to emerge at the end of the second millennium of Christianity were a recognition that certain uses of property and acts toward the environment have long-term adverse consequences for other humans. Pollution of the land with hazardous chemicals, dumping of sewage into waterways, and emission of noxious and poisonous fumes into the air are increasingly understood as harmful to others, to future generations if not to the present generation. The limitation of this expanded conception of environmental responsibility is that it is, at base, only an enlightened expression of the traditional common law maxim to use your property in a manner that does not harm others. What has been missing is an understanding that all of property has value not because we as humans value it, but because, as a creation of God, "it is very good."

At the core of the theological context for human obligations to the land is the meaning of dominion set out in the creation mandate: "Be fruitful and multiply, and replenish the earth and subdue it, and have dominion over the fish of the sea, and over the fowl of the air, and over every living thing that moves upon the earth" (Genesis 1:28). In light of the fall, the human tendency is to experience dominion as superiority and control, as hierarchy and subservience, understanding the call to subdue the earth as treating the earth as subordinate to human needs, desires, and wishes. Theology, however, suggests that dominion is more than power and control. It carries with it a responsibility of stewardship. The challenge is to perceive that the environment has value and significance independent of its value to the human.

Stewardship is a conception of dominion which imports a sense of obligation. Dominion as stewardship rests first on the premise that what has been created belongs ultimately to another. It rests second on the duty to protect and affirm the inherent value of that which is controlled. Christians

---

[13] Tribe, "Ways Not to Think About Plastic Trees."

are called to be stewards of the mysteries of God (1 Corinthians 4:2), and to do so by knowing that what has been received has been given as a gift (1 Corinthians 4:7).

In our legal history are two parallel concepts of property rights which contain this multilayered sense of duty. The first is that of the *usufruct*; the second is the *trust*. While both may be found in American law today, they rarely reflect their original meanings. A usufruct is a right to use the property of another. Grounded more in Roman law and civil law than in English common law, the holder of a usufruct is entitled to limited rights of use of the property, at all times being required to acknowledge that the property is that of another. The holder of the usufruct may use and consume the property, but never to the detriment of the primary "owner." The holder may transfer the right of use, but never transfer all rights to the property. Similarly, church property was property owned by one yet held in trust for the use and benefit of another. The Franciscans reconciled their rejection of individual private ownership by positing a trust relationship in which property was held by the order, or the church, for the use and benefit of others, yet at all times belonging ultimately to God.[14]

Christian theology unequivocally calls us not to pollute the land, for God lives in its midst (Numbers 35:33–34). Environmental laws, however, continue to be a clearer image of the fall than of the creation or redemption as we struggle to transcend the homocentric use of property for our own benefit. What remains to be done is to recall and to reclaim the belief that the land is not ours but is given for our use and benefit, and to hold for the use and benefit of others.

CONCLUSIONS

From the perspective of law, property is not a thing. Property is that which defines relationships between persons with respect to a thing. Property is a means of creating identity of an individual and of a community. It is a form of power not just over a thing, but far more importantly it is an expression of power over others. It is a method of control, not just control over a thing but a desire for control over others. The Western law of property reifies concepts of use and of relationship into specific formal rights and in so doing obscures the richness of property properly understood. A diamond is a rock, but diamond is also an instrument for the transformation of light. The facets of a diamond each serve to reflect, refine, and refract light into

---

[14] Berman, *Law and Revolution*, 239.

rays of color, each presenting new combinations of the rainbows present within every ray of light.

So it is with the human condition theologically understood. Laws of property are an analogy of this humanity. They reflect the primal experience of the doctrine of the fall in the desire to view all "property as mine." They refine the experience of the fall as they come to grips with correlative rights of others in "property as yours" and the duality of the call to love the neighbor as one's self. They refract the great complexities of holding all things common as they struggle with "property as ours." In "dominion as stewardship," we see the word of creation and the promise of redemption, yet understand always our fallen nature.

RECOMMENDED READING

Ball, Milner S. *Lying Down Together: Law, Metaphor, and Theology*. Madison, WI: University of Wisconsin Press, 1985.

The Word and the Law. Chicago: University of Chicago Press, 1993.

Berman, Harold J. *Law and Revolution: The Formation of the Western Legal Tradition*. Cambridge, MA: Harvard University Press, 1983.

Law and Revolution II: The Impact of the Protestant Reformations on the Western Legal Tradition. Cambridge, MA: Harvard University Press, 2003.

Ellickson, Robert C., Carol M. Rose, and Bruce A. Ackerman. *Perspectives on Property Law*, 2nd edn. Boston: Little, Brown and Co., 1995.

McConnell, Michael W., Robert F. Cochran, Jr., and Angela Carmella, eds. *Christian Perspectives on Legal Thought*. New Haven, CT: Yale University Press, 2001.

Merrill, Thomas W. and Henry E. Smith. "The Morality of Property." *William and Mary Law Review* 48 (2007): 1849.

Peters, Victor. *All Things Common: The Hutterian Way of Life*. Minneapolis, MN: University of Minnesota Press, 1965.

Radin, Margaret Jane. "Property and Personhood." *Stanford Law Review* 34 (1982): 957.

Rose, Carol M. "Possession as the Origin of Property." *University of Chicago Law Review* 52 (1985): 73.

"Property as Storytelling: Perspectives from Game Theory, Narrative Theory, Feminist Theory." *Yale Journal of Law and Humanities* 2 (1990): 37.

Tribe, Laurence. "Ways Not to Think About Plastic Trees: New Foundations for Environmental Law." *Yale Law Journal* 83 (1974): 1315.

12 "Jesus Forgiving the Adulteress," from Julius Schnorr von Carolsfeld, *Die Bibel in Bildern* (Leipzig, 1853), s.v. Luke 7.

CHAPTER ELEVEN

Christian love and criminal punishment

Jeffrie G. Murphy

What would law be like if we organized it around the value of Christian love, and if we thought about and criticized law in terms of that value? Christian love as a divine command is, of course, not identical with either *philia* (friendship love) or *eros* (erotic love), although it may incorporate elements of both. Christian love is rather that kind of universal (that is, nonparticular) love called *agape* or love of neighbor. American philosopher John Rawls claimed that justice is the first virtue of social institutions. But what if we considered *agape* to be the first virtue? What would social institutions – law in particular – be like?

My primary focus in this chapter will be to explore criminal law and the practice of criminal punishment from a perspective of Christian love. Why should anyone really care about such an exploration? Almost everyone would acknowledge that Christianity's emphasis on the moral and spiritual significance of the inner life exercised great influence on the development of a comparable emphasis on this in Western criminal law – for example, the idea that *mens rea* (intention, for instance) is generally required for conviction of any serious crime. But this general rejection of strict liability, one might think, has more to do with justice than with love, and this may still leave one with the question of why one should care about the value of love in thinking about criminal law.

One might begin to answer this question by noting that one does not have to choose between love and justice and that, indeed, justice (properly understood) may be entailed by love (properly understood). Former Archbishop of Canterbury William Temple put it this way: "It is axiomatic that love should be the predominant Christian impulse and that justice is the primary form of love in social organization."[1] To say that one is acting in a loving way while subjecting a person to unjust oppression can only be seen as a sick joke.

---

[1] Quoted in Lord Denning, *The Influence of Religion on Law* (Alberta, Canada: Canadian Institute for Law, Theology, and Public Policy, 1997), 3.

In addition to welcoming Archbishop Temple's invitation to think of justice as a part of love, I also have some personal reasons for caring about the issue of love and punishment. Because of my upbringing, I have always been someone whose moral sensibilities are grounded – even when in the past I called myself an atheist – in the Christian tradition, a religious tradition that makes love of neighbor central. When a person brought up a Christian becomes an atheist, he tends to become a Christian atheist. The questions he chooses to make central and many of the answers that tempt him are often framed, even if he does not realize it, by the very set of beliefs he claims to reject. I suspect that this is true for other religions as well. I suspect, for example, that my Protestant upbringing had a great deal to do with the fact that I was early in my studies so drawn to the moral philosophy of German philosopher Immanuel Kant, a philosopher who has been interpreted, with some justice, as seeking a secular and rational defense for what is essentially a Protestant moral vision. The child is father of the man, as Wordsworth reminded us.

Of course, even those outside the Christian tradition generally celebrate some version of the value of love. We know from popular culture and music that "love makes the world go round," that "love conquers all," and that "all we need is love." One might thus find it both interesting and puzzling to consider how, if at all, that value can consistently sit with law – particularly criminal law, which often seems a very harsh and unloving institution.

Finally, there is a great deal of public sermonizing from politicians these days – far too much for my taste – that purports to draw the basic tenets of Christianity into political decision-making. It might be useful to examine what the actual legal consequences of Christianity properly interpreted would be, consequences that could turn out to be quite different from those represented in much current political posturing. As the bloody record of historical Christianity clearly reveals, those in power who speak the language of love do not always act in loving ways but can instead be vessels of intolerance, persecution, hatred, and cruelty.

I realize that I cannot speak for all Christians or survey Christian scholarship in a brief chapter, but I can, at most, give my own "take" on what Christianity has to offer on the topics of crime and punishment. Neither can I explore every aspect of the relationship between criminal law and love. So I shall focus on only one aspect: the nature of *forgiveness* – often seen as a paradigm Christian virtue – and its relation to criminal law and criminal justice. I focus on this aspect because many people seem to think that forgiveness is at odds with criminal punishment, that to the degree we are forgiving then to that degree we will oppose punishment. Indeed, in a recent provocative essay, Notre Dame law professor Thomas Shaffer goes even farther than this. In developing what he calls a "jurisprudence of forgiveness," Shaffer argues that forgiveness is not simply incompatible with criminal punishment but with the very idea of law itself. Speaking of those prisoners securely imprisoned on death row, he writes:

There is no rational argument any longer to kill them – much less the common good argument Caiaphas had for killing Jesus. Legal power, it seems, has to kill them anyway, if only because it would not be legal power if it didn't. Law here cannot take the risk of forgiveness. Forgiveness would remove the fear, the accountability, and the responsibility that law provides – and this, as law sees it, would invite chaos [because] . . . forgiveness disrupts legal order.[2]

Shaffer's claim strikes me as deeply wrong – confused all the way down, if I may say so. I think that he misunderstands both forgiveness and love and thus misunderstands the relationship that forgiveness and love bear to law and punishment. I realize that this is a strong claim made against a distinguished academic who has produced much admirable work, and I will have an uphill fight making a case for it. Since many people share some version of this confusion, however, unmasking it is worth a shot.

THE LOVE COMMANDMENT

Before getting into the details of a law-versus-loving forgiveness debate, however, let me begin with a bit of background, and remind you of the Christian love commandment itself. It occurs most famously in Luke 10:25–37 when a lawyer – yes, a lawyer – interrogates Jesus and asks him how one might gain eternal life. Jesus answers that the lawyer knows the answer to this question already, for it is found in Jewish law: "You shall love the Lord your God with all your heart, and with all your soul, and with all your strength, and with all your mind; and your neighbor as yourself." Continuing his cross examination, the lawyer then asks: "And who is my neighbor?" Jesus replies not with a definition of "neighbor" but with the parable of the Good Samaritan.

Two things relevant to the present chapter are worth noting about this scriptural passage. First, it must be emphasized that, for the Christian, what happens to the human soul – in this life and the next – is of primary concern. Note that the love commandment is endorsed by Jesus as the

---

[2] Thomas L. Shaffer, "The Radical Reformation and the Jurisprudence of Forgiveness," in *Christian Perspectives on Legal Thought*, ed. Michael W. McConnell, Robert E. Cochran, Jr. and Angela C. Carmella (New Haven, CT: Yale University Press, 2001), 325–26.

correct answer to the question "What must I do to inherit eternal life?" Thus a central question for the Christian with respect to punishment must be, not simply what will happen to the body, but what will happen to the soul. (Those who prefer a less metaphysically rich term might provisionally – but only provisionally – here substitute "character" for "soul.") One who is impatient with this concern must necessarily be impatient with Christianity at its core and thus with much of what Christianity will have to say about punishment.

Second, and intimately related to the first point, is the importance of not mistakenly interpreting the role played by the parable of the Good Samaritan in this scriptural passage. If one mistakenly sees this parable as primarily an answer to the question "What is love?" one might be led to see *agape* as nothing more than what could be called liberal compassion – helping the sick, the despised, and the poor. The love commandment surely involves that, as it involves justice, but I think that it also involves much more. The actual question answered through the parable, however, is not "What is love?" but is rather "Who is my neighbor?" The answer that seems to emerge from the parable is that *all human beings* are to be seen as neighbors. As Danish theologian and philosopher Søren Kierkegaard puts it: "when you open the door that you shut in order to pray to God and go out the very first person you meet is the neighbor whom you *shall* love"[3] – regardless of whether that person is your enemy, a member of some despised group, your king, a criminal, or someone who strikes you as intrinsically and grotesquely unlovable.[4] This is a doctrine of universalism, in contrast to tribalism, with respect to loving concern. Some Christians like to claim that it is unique to the moral outlook of Christianity, but in fact a similar kind of moral universalism can be found in some aspects of Stoicism and Judaism, and I suspect elsewhere as well.[5]

There are, of course, many fascinating questions that could be raised about the love commandment. Does it command love as an emotion or simply that we act in a certain way? Kant, convinced that we can be morally bound only to that which is in our control and believing (hastily in my view) that emotions are not in our control, called emotional love *pathological love* and claimed that it could not be our duty to feel it. What is actually commanded he called *practical love*, which is simply acting morally as Kant conceived it. In the century after Kant, Kierkegaard in

---

[3] Søren Kierkegaard, *Works of Love*, ed. and trans. Howard V. Hong and Edna H. Hong (Princeton, NJ: Princeton University Press, 1995), 51.   [4] *Ibid.*, 17–90.
[5] See further the chapters by David Novak and Brian Tierney herein.

his *Works of Love*, famously raised a variety of additional puzzles about Christian love of neighbor. He assumed that we would all agree that most human beings seem to be anything but lovable. (If you think it is possible to love everyone, just look around in a supermarket as Ayn Rand once suggested.) Given the apparent unlovability of those Kierkegaard called "your very unpoetic neighbors," would it be possible to love them absent a divine command to do so? Kierkegaard thought not.[6] And to what degree, if at all, is the command of love of neighbor compatible with those particular loves of lovers, spouses, children, parents, friends, and one's own country that Kierkegaard calls "preferential"? This was a question of great concern to Kierkegaard. Such loves seem to many of us among the crowning glories of human life and thus most of us will not look with favor upon Jesus' teaching that "any one [who] comes to me and does not hate his own father and mother and wife and children and brothers and sisters, yes, and even his own life . . . cannot be my disciple" (Luke 14:26). Even most devout Christians will seek some way of interpreting this remark to keep it from having the unhappy consequence it seems to have upon first reading.

Given my limited purposes to explore the place of agapic forgiveness in the context of law, particularly criminal punishment, I think that all I will need to say about love here is the following, what I hope most interpreters of Christianity would find non-controversial: *agape* is not simply a matter of being nice and cuddly – of giving everyone a warm hug, saying "have a nice day," and sending them on their way. In spite of what the secular mind and even some religious believers might wish, the full doctrine of *agape* is to be found not simply in the social gospel films of Frank Capra but also in the grim stories of Flannery O'Connor and in the hard and demanding theologies of Augustine and Kierkegaard. "God loves you whether you like it or not," as the bumper sticker says.

One of the things that is manifestly not cuddly about *agape*, at least as I understand it, perhaps shows the influence of ancient Greek thought on love and friendship (*philia*). It is this: such love is concerned not simply with satisfying preferences, alleviating distress, providing for people's material well-being, and thereby making their lives more pleasant – what I earlier called liberal compassion. It is also centrally concerned with promoting their moral and spiritual good – helping their souls or characters to grow in *virtue*. (Recall Aristotle's discussion of what he calls "the perfect form of friendship."[7]) In this way, a legal order dominated by *agape* would

---

[6] *Ibid.*   [7] Aristotle, *Nichomachean Ethics*, 1156b.2f, and generally bks. 8–9.

almost certainly be more paternalistic than would be acceptable to the more value neutral and libertarian versions of political liberalism of, say, John Rawls or Ronald Dworkin. Those motivated by *agape*, as a basic principle, will (subject no doubt to some major side-constraints of a prudential nature) seek to design legal practices and institutions with a view to the moral and spiritual improvement in virtue of affected citizens.

In the area of free expression, just to give one example, such persons will probably seek greatly to restrain the corrupt and corrosive availability of pornography – refusing to see its production, distribution, and consumption as an important human liberty. They might very reluctantly allow pornography for practical or instrumental reasons – if they think that it is impossible to design a legal prohibition that would not constrain legitimate expression. But they would never seek to protect it in principle under the general heading of a fundamental right of personal autonomy. Rather than seeing basic rights as rights to exercise unrestrained "do your own thing" autonomy, they would tend to see such rights (as some perfectionist liberals see them) as rights to choose only among options that could all be part of a good life. Thus they would see conversation about the good life as being central to law and politics, not as in principle a "private" matter that should be left out of the political and legal domains. This suggests that there may be some interesting tensions between some forms of political liberalism and *agapic* love as I have conceptualized it – tensions that might force some choices that many would find hard and unattractive.

For the law of crime and punishment, those motivated by *agape* will seek punitive practices that contribute to, or at least do not retard, the moral and spiritual rebirth of criminals. It is perhaps regrettable but true that there may be little that the state can do actively to promote virtuous character. This might be because the state is sometimes nothing but a collection of inept apparatchiks who cannot even deliver the mail. Or it could be because, even at its best, the state must be very cautious about using state power to encourage a particular vision of the good life, in an environment of religious pluralism and free exercise of religion. For such a vision may capture the moral view from only one segment of those with deep and serious commitments to seeking what they deem to be the good life. I, for one, am less concerned about those who are indifferent to the good life and want only to revel under an uncritical "do your own thing" conception of liberty.

But surely, even under these constraints, it ought to be possible to do *something* for prisoners that is potentially character-building. If Aristotle is right, then virtue is often acquired through a process of *habituation* – becoming by doing – and encouraging certain habits might promote, for example, a virtuous kind of empathetic kindness often absent or greatly limited in criminal wrongdoers. A small start in this direction might involve something as simple as the Prison Dog Project, a program in which prisoners care for dogs and thereby perhaps develop some of the virtues that come from the receiving and giving of love they have been missing in their prior lives. This program is only one small thing, but great things often consist of many small things.

Even those who remain skeptical of all positive programs of character reform, however, should still at the very least seek to create a prison environment where opportunities for positive character development are not radically minimized or even extinguished by unspeakable conditions. For example, those who claim to champion agapic love should be on the forefront of any movement to eliminate those current aspects of criminal punishment and prison life such as gang rape, that – to put it mildly – are hardly likely to encourage the reflection, repentance, and spiritual rebirth that should be hoped for from those culpable of serious wrongdoing. In this case, religious believers and traditional secular liberals should find, and have found, themselves united. The Prison Rape Elimination Act, for example, enacted by Congress in 2003, was supported by such diverse agencies and individuals as Amnesty International, Human Rights Watch, Senator Ted Kennedy, the Southern Baptist Ethics and Religious Liberty Commission, and Charles Colson's Prison Fellowship Ministries.

Of course, none of this is even worth thinking about if Shaffer is correct that (1) the duty to forgive is mandated by the love commandment and (2) forgiveness is incompatible with criminal punishment. I think he is right about (1) but dead wrong about (2), and so I will now move to a discussion of forgiveness, its nature, and value, and relation to punishment.

FORGIVENESS AND PUNISHMENT

What is forgiveness? I think that one of the most insightful discussions of forgiveness ever penned is to be found in Bishop Joseph Butler's 1726 sermon "Upon Forgiveness of Injuries" and its companion sermon "Upon Resentment."[8] These sermons are long and carefully reasoned philosophical essays on the character of forgiveness, and they must have greatly tried the patience of his congregation. According to Butler, forgiveness is a moral virtue (a virtue of character) that is essentially a matter of the heart, the

---

[8] Both sermons are collected in *Works of Joseph Butler*, vol. ii, *Sermons*, ed. W. E. Gladstone (Oxford: Clarendon Press, 1896), 136–67.

inner self, and involves a change in inner feeling more than a change in external action. The change in feeling is the overcoming, on moral grounds, of the intensely negative and reactive attitudes that are quite naturally occasioned when one has been wronged by another – the passions of resentment, anger, even hatred, and the desire for revenge. We may call these the vindictive passions. A person who has forgiven has overcome those vindictive passions and has overcome them for a morally creditable motive – for example, being moved by repentance on the part of the person by whom one has been wronged. Of course, such a change in feeling often leads to a change of behavior – reconciliation, for example. But, as our forgiving of the dead illustrates, change in feeling does not always change behavior. Forgiveness, so understood, is often a good thing because it may allow us to reconcile and restore relationships of value, free us from the inner turmoil that may come from harboring grudges, and free us from an overly narcissistic involvement with our own unjust victimizations, for it seems that the common human tendency is often to magnify such victimizations out of all reasonable proportion.

None of this shows, however, that forgiveness – particularly hasty and uncritical forgiveness – is *always* a good thing. Sometimes forgiveness mistakenly tempts us into restoring relationships that would be better left permanently ruptured. Also, hasty overcoming of anger and resentment through forgiveness may sometimes show insufficient self-respect, since feeling such reactive emotions when wronged is a characteristic sign of self-respect. This is no doubt the point of S. J. Perelman's famous quip: "to err is human; to forgive, supine." The popular self-help literature on forgiveness tends to stress only its benefits, but I think it is important to note at least some of its potential costs.[9]

On my Butler-inspired analysis of forgiveness as a victim's change of heart toward culpable wrongdoing, it is useful initially to distinguish forgiveness from four other responses to wrongdoing with which forgiveness is often confused: justification, excuse, mercy, and reconciliation. Although these concepts are to some degree open-textured and can bleed into each other, clarity is served if one at least starts by attempting to separate them. I discuss each of them briefly.

---

[9] Butler believed the benefit of forgiveness is a God-given check on the valuable passions of resentment and anger, which are necessary to defend one's own rights, the rights of others, and the moral order itself. For uncannily similar observations, see Reinhold Niebuhr, "Anger and Forgiveness," in *Discerning the Signs of the Times – Sermons for Today and Tomorrow* (London: SCM Press, 1946), 26–39.

Justification

To regard conduct as justified (as in lawful self-defense, for example) is to claim that the conduct, though normally wrongful, was the right thing to do in the given circumstances and all things considered. In such cases, there is nothing legitimately to resent and thus nothing to forgive.

Excuse

To regard conduct as excused (as in the insanity defense, for example) is to admit that the conduct was wrong but to claim that the person who engaged in the conduct was not a fully responsible agent. Responsible agency is, of course, a matter of degree. But to the degree that the person who injures me is not a responsible agent, resentment of that person would make no more sense than resenting the wasp that stings me. Again, there is nothing here to forgive.

Mercy

To accord a wrongdoer mercy is to inflict a less harsh consequence on that person than allowed by institutional (usually legal) rules. Mercy is less personal than forgiveness, since the one granting mercy (a sentencing judge, say) typically will not be a victim of wrongdoing and thus will not have any feelings of resentment to overcome. (There is a sense in which only victims of wrongdoing have what might be called *standing* to forgive.) Mercy also has a public behavioral dimension not necessarily present in forgiveness. I can forgive a person simply in my heart of hearts, but I cannot show mercy simply in my heart of hearts. I can forgive the dead, but I cannot show mercy to the dead.

This distinction between mercy and forgiveness allows us to see why there is no inconsistency in fully forgiving a person for wrongdoing but still advocating that the person suffer the legal consequence of criminal punishment. Here you see one of my primary disagreements with Professor Shaffer. To the degree that criminal punishment is justified in order to secure victim satisfaction, then of course the fact that the victim has forgiven will be a relevant argument for reducing the criminal's sentence and the fact that a victim still resents will be a relevant argument for increasing that sentence. It is highly controversial, of course, that criminal punishment should to *any* degree be harnessed to a victim's desires. Such considerations are generally considered only in assessing damages in a private suit in tort. Even if the criminal punishment is partly calibrated by the victim's desires, however, it must surely be admitted that the practice of punishment serves other values as well, such as crime control and justice. With respect to these values, a victim's forgiveness could hardly be dispositive. In short, it would indeed be inconsistent for a person to claim that he has forgiven the wrongdoer and still advocate punishment for the wrongdoer in order to satisfy his personal vindictive feelings. If he still has those feelings, he has not forgiven the wrong or the wrongdoer. It would not be inconsistent, however, to advocate punishment for other legitimate reasons – for example, crime control and just deserts. Of course, the possibilities for self-deception are enormous here. As Friedrich Nietzsche reminded us, our high-sounding talk about justice and public order is often simply a rationalization for envy, spite, malice, and outright cruelty – the cluster of emotions for which Nietzsche used the loaded French term *ressentiment*.[10]

But what about mercy itself as a virtue independent of forgiveness? Is it not also required, as an aspect of Christian love, to exhibit mercy in dealing with wrongdoers? And would this not involve mercy to criminals? I think that the answer to this question is yes. Yet it is important to see that the requirement to exhibit mercy is best understood not as a requirement never to punish but rather as a requirement to develop a character that is not hardened and rigidly formalistic – a requirement that leaves room for considering relevant features of a criminal (remorse, repentance, or apology, for example) that might legitimately incline one to favor a reduced sentence for that criminal. This is most appropriately done in an executive clemency decision rather than at the time of sentencing.

Reconciliation

The vindictive passions (those overcome in forgiveness) are often a major barrier to reconciliation. Since forgiveness often leads to reconciliation, it is thus easy to confuse the two concepts. I think, however, that it is

---

[10] As I have argued in my "Legal Moralism and Retribution Revisited," *Proceedings of the American Philosophical Association* 80:2 (2006): 45–62, one must be careful about how one understands the idea of criminal just desert. This idea legitimately focuses our attention on the criminal's act, the intentionality of that act, and the degree of responsibility for that act. However, if one employs the concept of just desert to target deep character, ultimate evil, or what Kant called "inner viciousness," then one is presuming to judge what no human being should presume to judge. For "thou, [God] thou only, knowest the hearts of all the children of men" (1 Kings 8:39). It is hard enough for us to discern the shallows of intentions to surmise the utter futility of probing the depths of character – for whether, to use some language from American homicide law, the criminal has "a hardened, abandoned, and malignant heart" or a character that is "cruel, heinous and depraved."

important also to see how they may differ – how there can be forgiveness without reconciliation, and how there can be reconciliation without forgiveness.

For an example of forgiveness without reconciliation, imagine a battered woman who has been repeatedly beaten and raped by her thuggish husband or boyfriend. This woman – after a religious conversion, perhaps – might well come to forgive her batterer (for example, stop being angry with him) without a willingness to resume her relationship with him. "I forgive you and wish you well" can, in my view, sit quite consistently with "I will never allow you in this house again." In short, the fact that one has forgiven does not mean that one must also trust or live again with a person.

For an example of reconciliation without forgiveness, consider the example of the South African Truth and Reconciliation Commission. In order to negotiate a viable transition from apartheid to democratic government with full black participation, all parties had to agree that there would in most cases be no punishment for evil acts that occurred under the previous government. Politically motivated wrongdoers, by making a full confession and accepting responsibility, would typically be granted amnesty. In this process the wrongdoers would not be required to repent, show remorse, or even apologize. I can clearly see this process as one of reconciliation (although I might prefer the term cooperation) – a process that will allow all to work toward a democratic and just future. I do not so easily see this process as one of forgiveness, however. No change of heart was required or even sought from the victims – no overcoming of such vindictive feelings as anger or resentment or hatred. All that was hoped of them was a willingness to accept this process as a necessary means to the future good of their society.

It should now be obvious why I reject Shaffer's claim that agapic forgiveness is incompatible with legal punishment. On my view, following Bishop Butler, forgiveness is mainly a matter of a change of heart, not of external practice.

So can forgiveness of a person, so understood, still be compatible with the continued demand that the person be punished – perhaps even executed? In my view the answer to this question is yes. It all depends on the *motive* or *reason* for the demand. If the motive or reason is to satisfy one's vindictive passions, then of course there is immediate inconsistency. If one still retains those passions, one has not forgiven. Thus an appeal to *agapic* forgiveness does constitute a powerful attack on legal punishment to the degree that such punishment is driven by vindictive passions, particularly by hatred.

Of course, if one is doing something truly horrendous to another human being, the chance that hatred and cruelty are behind it should not be too quickly dismissed. In fact, many present penal practices in America are, alas, hard to understand on any other terms. To return to my earlier example of prison conditions, Mary Sigler has recently written on such terrible conditions as subjecting inmates to repeated acts of forced sodomy that are generally tolerated by prison officials and the public. She notes that the popular media freely makes jokes about this. For example, there was a soft drink commercial in which someone is handing out cans to prison inmates, drops one on the floor, and notes that in this environment it probably would not be a good idea to bend over and pick it up. The commercial closes with a scene in which the soft drink huckster is shown sitting at a table with a large inmate who has an arm around him. The voice over says that this drink makes friends, the inmate tightens his arm, and the huckster says in dismay "not that kind of friend." What kind of a society is it that knows about forced sodomy in prison and feels comfortable making jokes about it? In trying to answer this question, the words "hatred" and "cruelty" certainly come to my mind.[11]

I think that callous indifference also deserves a place next to hatred as something that is ruled out by *agape* – something that should be guarded against in the realm of punishment. Recall the New Testament parable in which a servant, forgiven his debt out of compassion from his master, is blind to the suffering of one of his own servants and shows no compassion when that servant cannot pay a debt to him (Matthew 18:23–35). The sin of the forgiven servant inflicting harsh treatment on his own servant was not based on any hatred he felt toward his servant. It was, rather, a radical failure of compassion, a total indifference to the adverse life circumstances that caused the servant to become indebted and to fear harsh punishment for failing to pay the debt – the very kind of life circumstances that the master, out of compassion, had taken account of in showing mercy to the unforgiving servant for the non-payment of his own debt. As Raimond Gaita, drawing on Simone Weil, argued in his book, *A Common Humanity*, our indifference to the suffering of those whom we regard as outsiders – an indifference that makes them, as Weil said of the poor, invisible to us – often flows from an incapacity to see anything that could *go deep* in their inner lives, a failure to find it even intelligible that someone could love them. This is, I think, at least part of what Weil meant when she said that "love sees what is invisible."[12]

[11] See Mary Sigler, "By the Light of Virtue: Prison Rape and the Corruption of Character," *Iowa Law Review* 91(2006): 561–607.
[12] Quoted in Raimond Gaita, *A Common Humanity: Thinking About Love and Truth and Justice* (London: Routledge, 2000), 84.

Suppose, however, that the motive or reason for punishment is not grounded in any vindictive passion or in callous indifference of the kind just noted. Suppose, rather, that it is grounded in the sincere belief that punishment of the kind prescribed is necessary to control crime and thereby promote the common good. Or suppose that it is required by justice (what the criminal deserves for his wrongdoing), or that it will be instrumental in the moral and spiritual transformation of the criminal. Then, even if one has doubts about one or more of these justifications, those doubts cannot legitimately be grounded in the claim that they are inconsistent with the demands of Christian love.

The main point, then, is this: *agape* does not forbid punishment. What it forbids is *punishment out of hatred or other vindictive passions*. What Jesus counseled, it will be recalled, is that we visit and comfort those in prison; he did not counsel the abolition of prisons (Matthew 25:36). To visit and comfort those in prison – even those justly there – is a way of saying that they are still loved and not hated, that their essential humanity is still being acknowledged, and that we have not presumed to banish them from the domain of loving concern. Such loving concern is quite consistent, however, with thinking that it is proper that they be in prison – because they deserve it or for the common good, for example.

As stated above, the possibilities of self-deception here are enormous – particularly the possibility that, as Nietzsche warned, we use the rhetoric of justice and the common good in order to hide from ourselves the fact that our actual motives are instances of *ressentiment* – spite, malice, envy, and cruelty. Thus, although I think that Shaffer overreaches when he uses the virtue of forgiveness to condemn all law and punishment, he has offered an important corrective to much of what we are *actually* doing in contrast to what we say and think we are doing, a contrast dramatically illustrated when we consider the actual conditions present in many of our jails and prisons. For this he deserves our gratitude.

LOVE AND THE DEATH PENALTY

In closing, let me briefly say something about *agape* and capital punishment. The death penalty is so extreme that many might think that, even if much punishment is consistent with *agape*, this punishment cannot be. This was certainly the view of Catholic theologian Bernard Häring. He acknowledged that the Old Testament is filled with what appear to be robust defenses of capital punishment, but then claimed that "it would not be in harmony with the unique fullness of salvation and its loving kindness to apply drastic [Old Testament] directives without any qualification as obligatory in the present order of salvation and grace."[13]

Not all Christians would agree with Häring, of course, and the fact that so many prominent Christian philosophers and theologians have through the ages been supporters of capital punishment should make us pause before hastily assuming that the practice is inconsistent with *agape*. However, the enthusiasm expressed by these thinkers for capital punishment has often been radically overstated by supporters of the death penalty. The radio show host and newspaper columnist Dennis Prager, for example, has cited Augustine as a Christian authority to support his belief in the legitimacy of capital punishment. He quoted this passage from *The City of God*: "It is in no way contrary to the commandment 'thou shalt not kill' to put criminals to death according to law or the rule of natural justice."[14]

Augustine did indeed make this claim, but it takes a great deal of creative free association to turn this into a statement of support for the death penalty. And getting Augustine right is a matter of some importance, since, after Jesus and Paul, he has probably done more than anyone else to set what might be called "the moral tone" of Christianity, at least among educated people. I read Augustine – and here I impose on him a modern distinction – as asserting the *right* of the state to execute but also arguing that *it is almost always wrong for the state to exercise that right*. The state may not be denied to have, in the abstract, the right to execute if this promotes the common good or gives the criminal the punishment that he in justice deserves or promotes the personal repentance and rebirth of the wrongdoer – the only three objectives that could justify it. (And, before you laugh dismissively at the idea of capital punishment as personal reform, recall Samuel Johnson: "Depend upon it, Sir, when a man knows he is to be hanged in a fortnight, it concentrates his mind wonderfully."[15]) One can hold this view of capital punishment's three possible justifications, however – common good, just deserts, and personal rebirth – and also consistently hold that in every particular case that one knows of or can imagine, that execution either does not promote these goals or does not promote

---

[13] Bernard Häring, *The Law of Christ*, 3 vols. (Westminster, MD: The Newman Press, 1966), III:124.

[14] Quoted in Dennis Prager, Editorial, "There's A Moral Reason That McVeigh Must Die," *Los Angeles Times* (June 8, 2001): B-17.

[15] Quoted in *Boswell's Life of Johnson*, 2nd edn, 6 vols., ed. George Birkbeck Hill, revised by L. F. Powell (1934; Oxford: Clarendon Press, 1964), III:167 Or, as Flannery O'Connor's Misfit said of his victim: "She would of been a good woman if it had been someone there to shoot her every day of her life." Flannery O'Connor, "A Good Man is Hard to Find," in *Collected Works* (New York: Library of America, 1988), 153.

them any better than less drastic means. Augustine sometimes argues in this way and indeed, for all his reputation to the contrary, offers some of the most eloquent objections to capital punishment ever given in our culture. For example, in a letter to Marcellinus, the special delegate of the Emperor Honorious to settle the dispute between Catholics and Donatists, Augustine is concerned with the punishment to be administered for what must have, to him, seemed the most vicious of crimes: the murder of one Catholic priest and the mutilation of another by members of a radical Donatist faction. He wrote:

I have been prey to the deepest anxiety for fear your Highness might perhaps decree that they be sentenced [to death]. Therefore, in this letter, I beg you by the faith which you have in Christ and by the mercy of the same Lord Christ, not to do this, not to let it be done under any circumstances . . . We do not wish that the martyrdom of the servants of God should be avenged by similar suffering, as if by way of retaliation . . . We do not object to wicked men being deprived of their freedom to do wrong, but we wish it to go just that far, so that, without losing their life or being maimed in any part of their body, they may be restrained by the law from their mad frenzy, guided into the way of peace and sanity, and assigned some useful work to replace their criminal activities. It is true, this is called a penalty, but who can fail to see that it should be called a blessing rather than a chastisement when violence and cruelty are held in check, but the remedy of repentance is not withheld?[16]

Of course capital punishment is far too complex an issue and too dependent on a variety of contested empirical claims to be settled here. And philosophy, an *a priori* discipline, is certainly in no position simply to pronounce finally on whether the fear of death as a punishment could ever promote the common good or could ever provoke spiritual rebirth on the part of the criminal. So let me close by making a claim that I can in conscience endorse: to the degree that our willingness to support the death penalty is based on the thoughtless cruel hatred or indifference to the humanity of criminals (and I suspect that much of it is), then it manifestly is not consistent with *agape*, a love that teaches that all human beings, even the worst among us, are precious because created in the image of God. And thus Christians, Jews, and those from many other religions should, I think, be willing to join in endorsing these words of Ezekiel 33:11: "I have no pleasure in the death of the wicked; but that the wicked should turn from his way and live."

---

[16] Quoted in Donald X. Burt, *Friendship and Society: An Introduction to Augustine's Practical Philosophy* (Grand Rapids, MI: Wm. B. Eerdmans Publishing, 1999), 195–96.

RECOMMENDED READING

Brugger, E. Christian. *Capital Punishment and Roman Catholic Moral Tradition.* Notre Dame, IN: University of Notre Dame Press, 2003.

Burtt, Donald X. *Friendship and Society: An Introduction to Augustine's Practical Philosophy.* Grand Rapids, MI: Wm. B. Eerdmans Publishing, 1999.

Butler, Joseph. "Sermons VIII and IX," in *Works of Joseph Butler.* Vol. II, *Sermons.* Edited by W. E. Gladstone. Oxford: Clarendon Press, 1896, 136–67.

Denning, Lord. *The Influence of Religion on Law.* Alberta, Canada: Canadian Institute for Law, Theology, and Public Policy, 1997.

Gaita, Raimond. *A Common Humanity: Thinking about Love and Truth and Justice.* London: Routledge, 2000.

Gorringe, Timothy. *God's Just Vengeance.* Cambridge: Cambridge University Press, 1996.

Griswold, Charles L. *Forgiveness: A Philosophical Exploration.* Cambridge: Cambridge University Press, 2007.

Häring, Bernard. *The Law of Christ.* 3 vols. Westminster, MD: The Newman Press, 1966.

House, H. Wayne and John Howard Yoder. *The Death Penalty Debate.* Dallas, TX: Word Publishing Company, 1991.

Kant, Immanuel. *Practical Philosophy.* Translated by Mary Gregor. Cambridge: Cambridge University Press, 1996.

Kierkegaard, Søren. *Works of Love.* Edited and translated by Howard V. Hong and Edna H. Hong. Princeton, NJ: Princeton University Press, 1995.

Murphy, Jeffrie G. "Repentance," In *Repentance.* Edited by Amitai Etzioni. Totowa, NJ: Rowman and Littlefield, 1997, 143–70.

"Moral Epistemology, the Retributive Emotions, and the 'Clumsy Moral Philosophy' of Jesus Christ," in *The Passions of Law.* Edited by Susan Bandes. New York: New York University Press, 1999, 49–167.

Getting Even: Forgiveness and its Limits. Oxford: Oxford University Press, 2003.

"Legal Moralism and Retribution Revisited." *Proceedings of the American Philosophical Association* 80:2 (2006): 45–62. This essay has also appeared in *Criminal Law and Philosophy* 1 (January 2007): 5–20.

"Remorse, Apology, and Mercy." *Ohio State Journal of Criminal Law* 4 (2007): 423–53.

Murphy, Jeffrie G. and Jean Hampton, *Forgiveness and Mercy.* Cambridge: Cambridge University Press, 1988.

Murphy, Jeffrie G., Stephen P. Garvey, R. A. Duff, Joseph Vining, John Witte Jr., and Patrick McKinley Brennan. "Religion and the Criminal Law: Legal and Philosophical Perspectives." Special issue, *Punishment and Society* 5:3 (2003).

Niebuhr, Reinhold. "Anger and Forgiveness," in *Discerning the Signs of the Times – Sermons for Today and Tomorrow.* London: SCM Press, 1946, 26–39.

O'Connor, Flannery. "A Good Man is Hard to Find," in *Collected Works.* New York: Library of America, 1988, 136–67.

Owens, Eric C., John D. Carlson, and Eric P. Elshtain, eds. *Religion and the Death*

Penalty: A Call for Reckoning. Grand Rapids, MI: Wm. B. Eerdmans Publishing, 2004.

Sigler, Mary. "By the Light of Virtue: Prison Rape and the Corruption of Character." *Iowa Law Review* 91 (2006): 561–607.

Shaffer, Thomas, L. "The Radical Reformation and the Jurisprudence of Forgiveness," in *Christian Perspectives on Legal Thought.* Edited by Michael W. McConnell, Robert E. Cochran, Jr. and Angela C. Carmella. New Haven, CT: Yale University Press, 2001, 321–39.

13 Eleanor Roosevelt holding a poster of the Universal Declaration of Human Rights, November 1949.

CHAPTER TWELVE

Christianity and human rights

Michael J. Perry

The emergence of the law of human rights – especially the international law of human rights – is one of the most important and heartening developments of the twentieth century. In this chapter I discuss the relationship of Christianity, understood as a particular theological worldview, both to the *morality* of human rights and, then, to the *law* of human rights to which the morality of human rights has given rise in the period since the end of World War II.[1] It bears emphasis that the relationship of Christianity to human rights I discuss here is not historical but, for want of a better term, conceptual.[2]

THE MORALITY OF HUMAN RIGHTS

Although it is only one morality among many, the morality of human rights – that is, the morality that grounds the law of human rights – has become the dominant morality of our time; indeed, unlike any morality before it, the morality of human rights has become a truly global morality. Relatedly, the language of human rights has become the moral *lingua franca*. Nonetheless, the morality of human rights is not well understood.

What does the morality of human rights hold? The International Bill of Rights, as it is informally known, consists of three United Nations documents: the Universal Declaration of Human Rights (1948), the International Covenant on Civil and Political Rights (1966), and the International Covenant on Economic, Social, and Cultural Rights (1966). The Universal Declaration refers, in its preamble, to "the inherent dignity . . . of all members of the human family" and states, in Article 1, that "[a]ll members of the human family are born free and equal in dignity and rights . . . and

---

[1] See elaboration in Michael J. Perry, *Toward a Theory of Human Rights: Religion, Law, Courts* (Cambridge: Cambridge University Press, 2007), 3–13, 33–36.

[2] For related historical perspectives, see the chapters by Luke Timothy Johnson, Brian Tierney, and David Little herein.

should act towards one another in a spirit of brotherhood." The two covenants each refer, in their preambles, to "the inherent dignity . . . of all members of the human family" and to "the inherent dignity of the human person" – from which, the covenants insist, "the equal and inalienable rights of all members of the human family . . . derive."

According to the International Bill of Rights, then, and also according to the constitutions of many liberal democracies,[3] the morality of human rights consists of a twofold claim, the first part of which that each and every human being has equal inherent dignity. To say that every human being has "inherent" dignity is to say that the fundamental dignity every human being possesses, she possesses *not* as a member of one or another group (racial, ethnic, national, religious, etc.), *not* as a man or a woman, *not* as someone who has done or achieved something, and so on, but simply as a human being. To say that every human being has "equal" inherent dignity is to say that having inherent dignity is not a condition that admits of degrees. Just as no pregnant woman can be more – or less – pregnant than another pregnant woman, no human being can have more – or less – inherent dignity than another human being. According to the morality of human rights, "[a]ll members of the human family are born . . . equal in dignity." Hereafter, when I say "inherent dignity" I mean "equal inherent dignity." The second part of the twofold claim is that the inherent dignity of human beings has a normative force for us, in this sense: we should live our lives in accord with the fact that every human being has inherent dignity; that is, we should respect – we have conclusive reason to respect – the inherent dignity of every human being. I say that the morality of human rights consists of a *twofold* claim, rather than that it consists of two claims, as a way of emphasizing that according to the morality of human rights, the claim that every human being has inherent dignity is not an independent claim but is inextricably connected to the further claim that we should lives our lives in a way that respects the inherent dignity of every human being.

There is another way to state the twofold claim: every human being has inherent dignity *and is "inviolable,"* not-to-be-violated. According to the morality of human rights, one can violate a human being either explicitly or implicitly. One violates a human being *explicitly* if one explicitly denies that she has inherent dignity. The Nazis, for example, explicitly denied that

---

[3] See, e.g., David Kretzmer and Eckart Klein, eds., *The Concept of Human Dignity in Human Rights Discourse* (New York: Springer, 2002); Vicki C. Jackson, "Constitutional Dialogue and Human Dignity: States and Transnational Constitutional Discourse," *Montana Law Review* 65 (2004): 15.

the Jews had inherent dignity. One violates a human being *implicitly* if one treats her as if she lacks inherent dignity, either by doing her what one would not do to her, or by refusing to do for her what one would not refuse to do for her if one genuinely perceived her to have inherent dignity. Even if the Nazis had not explicitly denied that the Jews had inherent dignity, they would have implicitly denied it. The Nazis did to the Jews what no one person would have done to them, had that person genuinely perceived the Jews to have inherent dignity. In the context of the morality of human rights, to say that (1) every human being has inherent dignity and we should live our lives accordingly (i.e., in a way that respects that dignity) is to say that (2) every human being has inherent dignity and is inviolable – not-to-be-violated, in the sense of "violate" just indicated. To affirm the morality of human rights is to affirm the twofold claim that every human being has inherent dignity and is inviolable.

If it is true, *why* is it true – in virtue of what is it true – that every human being has inherent dignity and is inviolable? That the International Bill of Rights is famously silent on that question is not surprising, given the plurality of religious and non-religious views that existed among those who bequeathed us the Universal Declaration and the two covenants.[4] But it is precisely on that question that various religious traditions, not least Christianity, offer distinct grounding and perspective.[5]

CHRISTIANITY AND THE MORALITY OF HUMAN RIGHTS

There is a serious question whether any secular worldview can ground – can embed, can make sense of – the claim that every human being has inherent dignity and is inviolable.[6] The Christian worldview, however, can and does ground the claim. I want to elaborate the Christian ground of the morality of human rights by imagining an advocate of human rights named Sarah, who, as a Christian, affirms that every human being has inherent dignity and that we should live our lives accordingly. For a reason that will soon be apparent, Sarah prefers to say that every human being "is sacred." Nonetheless, for Sarah each predicate – "has inherent dignity", "is sacred" – is fully equivalent to the other; Sarah translates each predicate into the other without remainder. In affirming the inherent dignity and

---

[4] Jacques Maritain, "Introduction," in *UNESCO, Human Rights: Comments and Interpretation* (London, New York, A. Wingate 1950), 9–17.
[5] See, e.g., Robert Traer, *Faith in Human Rights: Support in Religious Traditions for a Global Struggle* (Washington, DC: Georgetown University Press, 1991).
[6] See Perry, *Toward a Theory of Human Rights*, 14–29.

inviolability of every human being, Sarah affirms the morality of human rights.

Predictably, Sarah's affirmation provokes this question: "Why – in virtue of what – does every human being have inherent dignity?" Sarah gives a religious explanation. Speaking the words of The First Letter of John, Sarah says that "God is love." "He who does not love does not know God; for God is love" (1 John 4:8). "God is love, and he who abides in love abides in God, and God abides in him" (1 John 4:16).[7] Moreover, God's act of creating and sustaining the universe is an act of love, and we human beings are the beloved children of God and sisters and brothers to one another. Every human being has inherent dignity, says Sarah, because, and in the sense that, every human being is a beloved child of God and a sister/brother to every other human being. (Other Christians prefer to say, equivalently, that every human being is created in the image of God.) Sarah is fully aware that she is speaking analogically, but that's the best anyone can do, she insists, in speaking about who God is – as in "Gracious God, gentle in your power and strong in your tenderness, you have brought us forth from the womb of your being and breathed into us the breath of life."[8]

Sarah's explanation provokes a yet further question about the source of the normativity – of the "should" – in the claim that we *should* live our lives in a way that respects the inherent dignity of every human being: "Let's assume, for the sake of discussion, that every human being has inherent dignity because, and in the sense that, every human being is a beloved child of God and a sister/brother to every other human being. So what? Why should it matter to me – to the way I live my life – that every human being has inherent dignity, that every human being is a beloved child of God and a sister/brother to me? Why should I respect – why should I want to be a person who respects – the inherent dignity of every human being?" In responding, Sarah – who "understands the authority of moral claims to be warranted not by divine dictates but by their contribution to human flourishing"[9] – states her belief that the God who loves us has created us to love one another. (We are also created, Sarah believes, to love God.) Given our created nature – given what we have been created *for* – the most fitting way of life for us human beings, the most deeply satisfying way of life of

---

[7] See John D. Caputo, "The Experience of God and the Axiology of the Impossible," in *Religion after Metaphysics*, ed. Mark A. Wrathall (Cambridge: Cambridge University Press, 2004), 123: "There is no name more closely associated in the Christian Scriptures with 'God' than love. That is what God is, and this comes as close as the New Testament does to a 'definition' of God . . ."

[8] *United Church of Christ, Book of Worship* (New York: United Church of Christ, 1983), 111.

[9] Stephen Pope, "The Evolutionary Roots of Morality in Theological Perspective," *Zygon* 33 (1998): 545, 554.

which we are capable, as children of God and sisters and brothers to one another, is one in which we embrace Jesus' "new" commandment to "love one another . . ." For Christians, the basic shape of the good life is indicated by the instruction given by Jesus at the Passover Seder on the eve of his execution: "A new commandment I give to you, that you love one another; even as I have loved you, that you also love one another" (John 13:34). By becoming persons of a certain sort – persons who discern one another as bearers of inherent dignity and love one another as such – we fulfill our created nature. "We know that we have passed out of death into life, because we love the brethren. He who does not love abides in death" (1 John 3:14). Indeed, Sarah believes that in some situations, we love most truly and fully – and therefore we live most truly and fully – by taking the path that will probably or even certainly lead to our dying. "Greater love has no man than this, that a man lay down his life for his friends" (John 15:13).

The "love" in Jesus' counsel to "love one another" is not *eros* or *philia*, but *agape*.[10] To love another in the sense of *agape* is to see her (or him) in a certain way, as a child of God and a sister/brother to oneself, and, therefore, to act toward her in a certain way. The "one another" in Jesus' counsel is radically inclusive:

You have heard that it was said, "You shall love your neighbor and hate your enemy." But I say to you, Love your enemies and pray for those who persecute you, so that you may be sons of your Father who is in heaven; for he makes his sun to rise on the evil and on the good, and sends rain on the just and on the unjust . . . You, therefore, must be perfect, as your heavenly Father is perfect. (Matthew 5:43–48)

As it happens, Sarah embodies Jesus's extravagant counsel to "love one another even as I have loved you." She loves all human beings. Sarah loves even "the Other." She loves not only those for whom she has personal affection, or those with whom she works or has other dealings, or those among whom she lives; she loves even those who are most remote, who are unfamiliar, strange, alien, those who, because they are so distant or weak or both, will never play any concrete role, for good or ill, in Sarah's life. Sarah loves even those from whom she is most estranged and toward whom she feels most antagonistic – those whose ideologies and projects and acts she judges to be not merely morally objectionable, but morally abominable. "[T]he language of love . . . compels us to affirm that even . . . the most radical evil-doers . . . are fully our fellow human beings."[11] Sarah loves even

---

[10] See further the chapter by Jeffrie Murphy herein.
[11] Raimond Gaita, *A Common Humanity: Thinking about Love and Truth and Justice* (London: Routledge, 2000), xviii–xix.

her enemies; indeed, Sarah loves even those who have violated her, who have failed to respect her inherent dignity. Sarah is fond of quoting Graham Greene to her incredulous friends: "When you visualized a man or a woman carefully, you could always begin to feel pity . . . When you saw the corners of the eyes, the shape of the mouth, how the hair grew, it was impossible to hate. Hate was just a failure of imagination."[12]

Such love – such a state of being, such an orientation in the world – is, obviously, an ideal. Moreover, it is, for most human beings, an extremely demanding ideal; for many persons, it is also an implausible ideal. Why should anyone embrace the ideal? Why should anyone want to be (or to become) such a person – a person who, like Sarah, loves even the Other? This is, existentially if not intellectually, the fundamental moral question for anyone: why should I want to be the sort of person who makes the choices, and who does the things, I am being told I should make or do? And, in fact, Sarah's interlocutor presses her with this question: "Why should I want to be the sort of person who, like you, loves the Other? What reason do I have to do *that*?" Because that is essentially the question about the source of the normativity in the claim that we should live our lives in a way that respects the inherent dignity of every human being, Sarah is puzzled. She thought that she had already answered the question. Sarah patiently rehearses her answer, an answer that appeals ultimately to one's commitment to one's own authentic well-being: "The most deeply satisfying way of life of which we are capable is one in which we 'love one another even as I have loved you.' By becoming persons who love one another, we fulfill – we perfect – our created nature and thereby achieve our truest, deepest, most enduring happiness." It is now Sarah's turn to ask a question of her interlocutor: "What further reason could you possibly want for becoming (or remaining) the sort of person who loves the Other?"

A clarification may be helpful here. Does Sarah do what she does for the Other – for example, does she contribute to Oxfam as a way of feeding the hungry – for a *self-regarding* reason? Does she do so, say, because it makes her happy to do so? No. Although feeding the hungry does make Sarah happy, that's not why she does it. Given the sort of person she is, the reason – the *other-regarding* reason – Sarah feeds the hungry is this: "The hungry are my sisters and brothers; I love them." And, indeed, Sarah as a Christian ultimately sees Christ in the Other, and sees loving and offering charity to the Other as a way of serving Christ. As Jesus said it to his followers:

---

[12] Graham Greene, *The Power and the Glory* (New York: Penguin Books, 1940), 131.

Come, O blessed of my Father, inherit the kingdom prepared for you from the foundation of the world; for I was hungry and you gave me food, I was thirsty and you gave me drink, I was a stranger and you welcomed me, I was naked and you clothed me, I was sick and you visited me, I was in prison and you came to me . . . Truly, I say to you, as you did it to the least of these my brethren, you did it to me. (Matthew 25:34–40)[13]

Now, a different question: why is Sarah committed to being the sort of person she is, and why does she believe that everyone should want to be such a person? Sarah's answer to that question *is* self-regarding: "As persons who love one another, we fulfill our created nature and thereby achieve our truest, deepest, most enduring happiness." According to Sarah, it is not individual acts of love that necessarily make one happy; it is, rather, becoming a person who loves the Other "even as I have loved you." "[S]elf-fulfillment happens when we are engaged from beyond ourselves. Self-fulfillment ultimately depends on self-transcendence. This is essentially the claim that is made by religion, that the meaning of our lives is to be found beyond ourselves."[14]

It bears emphasis that Sarah does not believe that she should be the sort of person she is because God has issued a command to her to be that sort of person – a command that, because God is entitled to rule, to legislate, she is obligated to obey. For Sarah, God is not best understood in such terms. A theistic religious vision does not necessarily include, though some conventional theistic religious visions do include, a conception of God as supreme legislator, issuing directives for human conduct. For Sarah (for whom God is love, not supreme legislator), some choices are good for us to make (or not to make) – and, therefore, we ought (or ought not) to make them. We do this not because God commands (or forbids) them, but because God is who God is, because the universe created and sustained by God who is love in an act that is an expression of God/love is what it is, and, in particular, because we human beings are who we are. For Sarah, "[t]he Law of God is not what God legislates but what God is, just as the Law of Gravity is not what gravity legislates but what gravity is."[15] Sarah believes that because God is who God is, because the universe is what it is, and because we are who we are, and not because of anything commanded by God as supreme legislator, the most fitting way of life for us human beings – the most deeply satisfying way of life of which we are capable – is one in which we children of God, we sisters and brothers, "love one another even as I have loved you."

---

[13] See further the chapter by Brian Pullan herein.
[14] Colin Grant, *Altruism and Christian Ethics* (Cambridge: Cambridge University Press, 2001), xix.
[15] John Dominic Crossan, "Case Against Manifesto," *Law Text Culture* 5 (2000): 129, 144.

Again, there is a serious question whether any secular worldview can ground (embed, make sense of) the claim that every human being has inherent dignity and is inviolable. Listen, in that regard, to Raimond Gaita, Australian philosopher and atheist:[16]

We may say that all human beings are inestimably precious, that they are ends in themselves, that they are owed unconditional respect, that they possess inalienable rights, and, of course, that they possess inalienable dignity. In my judgment these are ways of trying to say what we feel a need to say when we are estranged from the conceptual resources we need to say it. Be that as it may: each of them is problematic and contentious. Not one of them has the simple power of the religious way of speaking.

Where does this power come from? Not, I am quite sure, from esoteric theological or philosophical elaborations of what it means for something to be sacred. It derives from the unashamedly anthropomorphic character of the claim that we are sacred because God loves us, his children.[17]

FROM MORALITY TO LAW

Because, as I just explained, Christianity is one way of grounding the morality of human rights, and because the morality of human rights is the morality that grounds the law of human rights, it follows that Christianity can also ground the law of human rights. The morality of human rights grounds the law of human rights in this sense: Christians and others who affirm the morality of human rights, *because* they affirm it, have conclusive reason to establish and protect, as legal rights, certain claims – rights-claims – about what may not be done to, or about what must be done for, human beings. Let me explain.

The morality of human rights holds that every human being has inherent dignity and is "inviolable," not-to-be-violated. So we who affirm the morality of human rights, *because* we affirm it, should do what we can, all things considered, to prevent human beings, including government officials, from doing things (or from failing to do things) that violate human beings either explicitly or implicitly – explicitly, by denying that they have inherent dignity, or implicitly, by doing to them what no one would do to them, or by refusing to do for them what no one would refuse to do for them, who perceived their inherent dignity. Of course, the "all things considered" will be, in many contexts, indeterminate. As Amartya Sen has remarked, "[t]he perfectly specified demand not to torture anyone

---

[16] See John Haldane, "The Greatest of These Is Love, As an Atheist Reminds Us," *The Tablet* [London] (December 9, 2000): 1678 (reviewing Gaita's book).   [17] Gaita, *A Common Humanity*, 23–24.

is supplemented by the more general, and less easily specified, requirement to consider the ways and means through which torture can be prevented and then to decide what one should, thus, reasonably do."[18]

Moreover, we who affirm the morality of human rights, *because* we affirm it, have conclusive reason to do what we can, all things considered, to *do more than* prevent human beings from doing things that violate human beings. We also have conclusive reason to do what we can, all things considered, to prevent human beings from doing things that, even if they do not violate human beings, even implicitly, nonetheless cause them unwarranted suffering (or other harm). I am referring here to serious, not trivial, human suffering. In Germany during World War II, Lutheran ethicist Dietrich Bonhoeffer observed that "[w]e have for once learned to see the great events of world history from below, from the perspective of the outcast, the suspects, the maltreated, the powerless, the oppressed, the reviled – in short, from the perspective of those who suffer."[19] If we refuse to do what we can (all things considered) to prevent human beings from violating human beings or otherwise causing them unwarranted suffering – and by "we" I mean here primarily the collective we, as in "We the People," acting though our elected representatives – we refuse to do what we can to protect the victims and thereby violate them. We treat "those who suffer" as if they lack inherent dignity by refusing to do for them what no one would refuse to do for them who genuinely perceived them to have inherent dignity. Sometimes we violate a human being not by doing something to hurt her but by refusing to do something to protect her. "Sins against human rights are not only those of commission, but those of omission as well."[20]

To say, in the present context, that an instance of human suffering is "unwarranted" is to say that the act that causes the suffering – even if the act is a refusal to act, a refusal to intervene to diminish the suffering – is not warranted, that it is not justified. Not justified from whose perspective? It is scarcely surprising that the act, and therefore the suffering it causes, may be justified from the perspective of those whose act is in question. But theirs is not the relevant perspective. The relevant perspective belongs to those

---

[18] Amartya Sen, "Elements of a Theory of Human Rights," *Philosophy & Public Affairs* 32 (2004): 315, 322.

[19] Dietrich Bonhoeffer, "After Ten Years: A Letter to the Family and Conspirators," in Dietrich Bonhoeffer, *A Testament to Freedom*, ed. Geoffrey B. Kelly and F. Burton Nelson, rev. edn (San Francisco: HarperSanFrancisco, 1995), 482, 486. "After Ten Years" bears the date "Christmas 1942."

[20] Charles L. Black, Jr., *A New Birth of Freedom: Human Rights, Named and Unnamed* (New Haven, CT: Yale University Press, 1999), 133.

of us who, in coming face to face with the suffering, must decide what, if anything, to do, or to try to do, about it; in making that decision, we must reach our own judgment about whether the suffering is warranted.

I said that the morality of human rights grounds the law of human rights – that Christians and others who affirm the morality of human rights, *because* they affirm it, have conclusive reason to establish and protect, as legal rights, certain rights-claims about what may not be done to, or about what must be done for, human beings. We can now see how this is so: we who affirm the morality of human rights, *because* we affirm it, should press our elected representatives not to do anything that would violate human beings or otherwise cause them unwarranted suffering. But we should *also* press them to establish and protect these principles, as legal rights, certain claims about what may not be done to, or about what must be done for, human beings. As Christians and others have learned in the period since the end of World War II, the law of human rights is an important way of trying to prevent government officials and others from violating human beings or otherwise causing them unwarranted suffering.

The papacy of John Paul II was richly illustrative of the relationship of Christianity to the law of human rights. In 1989, the UN General Assembly adopted the Second Optional Protocol to the International Covenant on Civil and Political Rights, Article 1 of which provides: "1. No one within the jurisdiction of a State Party to the present Protocol shall be executed. 2. Each State Party shall take all necessary measures to abolish the death penalty within its jurisdiction." In 2002, the Council of Europe adopted Protocol No. 13 to the European Convention for the Protection of Human Rights and Fundamental Freedoms, Article 1 of which provides, without exception, that "[t]he death penalty shall be abolished. No one shall be condemned to such penalty or executed." Two years earlier – in December 2000 – the European Union adopted the Charter of Fundamental Rights, Article 2 of which proclaims: "1. Everyone has the right to life. 2. No one shall be condemned to the death penalty, or executed." As one who affirmed the inherent dignity and inviolability of *every* human being, even the most depraved criminal, John Paul II applauded these legal developments; indeed, he had pled with the nations of the world to abolish capital punishment.[21] In a 2005 statement calling for abolition of the death penalty in the United States, the United States Conference of Catholic Bishops,

---

[21] For the most careful and thorough discussion of John Paul's position on capital punishment, see E. Christian Brugger, *Capital Punishment and Roman Catholic Moral Tradition* (Notre Dame, IN: University of Notre Dame Press, 2003). I discuss capital punishment as a human rights issue, and discuss John Paul's position, in Perry, *Toward a Theory of Human Rights*, 37–51.

following John Paul's lead, wrote:

Each of us is called to respect the life and dignity of every human being. Even when people deny the dignity of others, we must still recognize that their dignity is a gift from God and is not something that is earned or lost through their behavior. Respect for life applies to all, even the perpetrators of terrible acts. Punishment should be consistent with the demands of justice *and* with respect for human life and dignity.[22]

SUMMARY AND CONCLUSIONS

Some recent Christian thinkers have been wary or even skeptical about "rights-talk" understood as an idiom of *moral* discourse.[23] However, no Christian should be wary about rights-talk understood as an idiom of *legal* discourse. Whatever one thinks about the propriety or utility of *moral*-rights-talk, *legal*-rights-talk is undeniably proper and useful.[24] It bears repetition: the morality of human rights is the morality that grounds the law of human rights, and, as we have learned in the period since the end of World War II, the law of human rights is an important way of trying to prevent government officials and others from violating human beings or otherwise causing them unwarranted suffering.

I said at the beginning of this chapter that I would discuss the conceptual relationship of Christianity both to the morality of human rights and to the law of human rights. I want to conclude with this a brief comment about the *moral* relationship of Christianity to human rights – that is, to the law of human rights. We can now see that to live as a faithful Christian in the contemporary world requires that one take human rights very seriously indeed. As the eminent Catholic philosopher Charles Taylor has correctly argued, the "affirmation of universal human rights" that characterizes "modern liberal political culture" represents an "authentic development[] of the Gospel."[25]

---

[22] *A Culture of Life and the Penalty of Death: A Statement of the United States Conference of Catholic Bishops Calling for an End to the Use of the Death Penalty* (Washington, DC: USCCB, 2005), 6.

[23] See, e.g., Alasdair MacIntyre, *After Virtue: A Study in Moral Theory* (Note Dame, IN: University of Notre Dame Press, 1984), 69–70; Mary Ann Glendon, *Rights Talk: The Impoverishment of Political Discourse* (New York: Free Press, 1991). For my commentary on Glendon's position, see Michael J. Perry, *The Idea of Human Rights: Four Inquiries* (New York: Oxford University Press, 1998), 48–54. See also John Witte Jr., *God's Joust, God's Justice: Law and Religion in the Western Tradition* (Grand Rapids, MI: Wm. B. Eerdmans Publishing, 2006), 110–13.

[24] Elsewhere I have expressed some skepticism about *moral*-rights-talk, as distinct from *legal*-rights-talk. See Perry, *Toward a Theory of Human Rights*, xii–xiii.

[25] Charles Taylor, *A Catholic Modernity?* (New York: Oxford University Press, 1999), 16.

RECOMMENDED READING

An-Na'im, Abudullahi A., Jerald D. Gort, Henry Jannsen, and Hendrick M. Vroom, eds. *Human Rights and Religious Values*. Grand Rapids, MI: Wm. B. Eerdmans Publishing, 1995.

Brugger, E. Christian. *Capital Punishment and Roman Catholic Moral Tradition*. Notre Dame, IN: University of Notre Dame Press, 2003.

Gaita, Raimond. *A Common Humanity: Thinking about Love and Truth and Justice*. London: Routledge, 2000.

Glendon, Mary Ann. *Rights Talk: The Impoverishment of Political Discourse*. New York: Free Press, 1991.

Hollenbach, David. *Claims in Conflict: Retrieving and Renewing the Catholic Human Rights Tradition*. Mahwah, NJ: Paulist Press, 1979.

Justice, Peace, and Human Rights. New York: Crossroad, 1988.

Kohen, Ari. *In Defense of Human Rights: A Non-Religious Grounding in a Pluralistic World*. London: Routledge, 2007.

Küng, Hans and Jürgen Moltmann, eds. *The Ethics of World Religion and Human Rights*. London: SCM Press, 1990.

Perry, Michael J. *The Idea of Human Rights: Four Inquiries*. New York: Oxford University Press, 1998.

Toward a Theory of Human Rights: Religion, Law, Courts. Cambridge: Cambridge University Press, 2007.

Rouner, Leroy S., ed. *Human Rights and the World's Religions*. Notre Dame, IN: University of Notre Dame Press, 1988.

Ruston, Roger. *Human Rights and the Image of God*. London: SCM Press, 2004.

Sen, Amartya. "Elements of a Theory of Human Rights." *Philosophy & Public Affairs* 32 (2004): 315–56.

Stackhouse, Max L. *Creeds, Society and Human Rights: A Study in Three Cultures*. Grand Rapids, MI: Wm. B. Eerdmans Publishing, 1984.

Taylor, Charles. *A Catholic Modernity?* New York: Oxford University Press, 1999.

Tinder, Glenn E. *The Political Meaning of Christianity*. San Francisco: HarperCollins, 1991.

Traer, Robert. *Faith in Human Rights: Support in Religious Traditions for a Global Struggle*. Washington, DC: Georgetown University Press, 1991.

CHAPTER THIRTEEN

Religious liberty

David Little

Religious liberty as currently understood is the condition in which individuals or groups are permitted without restraint to assent to and, within limits, to express and act upon religious convictions and identity free of coercive interference or penalty imposed by outsiders, including the state. So conceived, the topic is an explosive one, both historically and at present. Severe theoretical disputes surround it, and have for a long time. Why do religious convictions and identity deserve special protection? Where, exactly, do we draw the line between religious and other sorts of conviction and identity? What are the limits of proper expression and practice, and what constitutes "coercive interference" or penalty as imposed by the state or others?

In addition, violations of religious liberty have, throughout history, "brought, directly or indirectly, wars and great suffering to mankind," in the words of the 1981 *UN Declaration on the Elimination of All Forms of Intolerance and Discrimination Based on Religion or Belief.* Though examples involve more than just religious oppression, the inquisition and the religious wars of post-medieval Europe, together with the practices of Western colonialists and the Ottomans, especially in the Armenian case, as well as of fascists, state socialists, and ultra-nationalists in the twentieth century and after, all illustrate the fearsome effects of punishing and degrading individuals or groups because of their religious convictions and identity.

In fact, just because of such baleful circumstances, the human rights system, adopted as a consequence of fascist malefactions in the middle of the last century, includes elaborate provisions for the protection of religious liberty. Since these provisions, as expressed in the relevant documents, especially the *Universal Declaration of Human Rights*, the *International Covenant on Civil and Political Rights* (ICCPR) and the *Declaration on the Elimination of Intolerance and Discrimination*, are considered binding by fully three-fourths of the nations of the world, they constitute

14 "Decree Instituting the Freedom of Worship, November 1799" (colored engraving)
French School (eighteenth century).

the appropriate starting point for a contemporary approach to religious liberty.

Accordingly, the first task of this chapter is to exposit the prevailing human rights provisions in the light of relevant jurisprudence, particularly the "general comments" of the United Nations Human Rights Committee, which is authorized to interpret the ICCPR. We may do that by identifying salient features and highlighting important points of controversy. The second task is to excavate the historical background, mainly in the West, out of which the human rights understanding has emerged. The objective in both cases is mainly descriptive. The elucidation of existing standards, as well as the explanation of where they came from, leaves open, for the most part, the subject of how the standards ought to be construed and implemented, though it is not always possible to abstain completely from suggesting preferences.

HUMAN RIGHTS UNDERSTANDING OF RELIGIOUS LIBERTY[1]

Context and exposition

The whole edifice of human rights standards is based on the imperative to protect individuals against collective domination and the license for arbitrary abuse thereby entailed. Such was the basic lesson after World War II of the effects of fascist pathology, whose root is the absolute subjection of the individual to the will of the state. As Hitler put it, National Socialism gives priority neither to the individual nor humanity, but to protecting *das Volk*, "even at the expense of the individual."[2] Revulsion against such views gave rise to the human rights revolution, and to what Mary Ann Glendon, in her book on the subject, calls, "A World Made New."[3]

At the heart of fascist ideology was the impulse to prevent by all means necessary any dissent or independence in matters of religious conviction and identity. Together with their notorious policies of liquidating millions of Jews and "undesirable" religious minorities, like the Jehovah's Witnesses, the Nazis harassed Catholics, curtailing and suppressing most of their

---

[1] This section is drawn from my "Culture, Religion, and National Identity in a Post-Modern World," *Anuario del Derecho Eclesiastico del Estado* 22 (2006): 19–35, and "Religion, Human Rights, and Secularism: Preliminary Clarifications and Some Islamic, Jewish, and Christian Responses" in *Humanity Before God: Contemporary Faces of Jewish, Christian, and Islamic Ethics*, ed. William Schweiker, Michael A. Johnson, and Kevin Jung (Philadelphia: Fortress Press, 2006), 256–85.

[2] Cited in Alan Bullock, *Hitler* (New York: Harper and Row, 1962), 401.

[3] Mary Ann Glendon, *A World Made New: Eleanor Roosevelt and the Universal Declaration of Human Rights* (New York: Random House, 2001).

practices, and eventually came to dominate the Protestant Church by means of "terroristic methods."[4] In particular, fascism, especially in its German and Japanese versions, constituted a direct, comprehensive, and systematic assault on the four categories of the right to religious liberty that were subsequently guaranteed in the documents, and that were explicitly formulated against the background of fascist offenses.

1. "Everyone shall have the right to freedom of thought, conscience and religion. The right shall include freedom to have or to adopt a religion or belief of his choice . . . No one shall be subject to coercion which would impair his freedom to have or to adopt a religion or belief of his choice."[5] This is a liberty right. It does not allow "any limitation whatsoever" in regard to harboring thoughts of any kind or choosing and holding beliefs, either religious or not, that have the same fundamental or "conscientious" status that a religious belief has for a believer. This conclusion may be inferred from the fact that the right to freedom of thought, conscience, and religion "protects theistic, nontheistic and atheisitic beliefs," as well as "the right not to profess any religion or belief." Furthermore, fundamental or conscientious beliefs, as distinct from other thoughts and beliefs, appear to be privileged in a special way. They may serve as the basis for legal exemptions, as, for example, in the case of conscientious objection to military service. Accordingly, human rights law may be said to be especially deferent to conscientious belief.[6]

Also guaranteed is the freedom, "either individually or in community with others and in public and private, to manifest . . . religion or belief in worship, observance, practice and teaching." "The observance and practice of religion or belief may include not only ceremonial acts but also such customs as the observance of dietary regulations, the wearing of distinctive clothing or head covering," among other practices. The only allowable limitations are those that governments may impose on manifesting, or overtly expressing or acting on, a religion or belief, for the purpose of protecting "public safety, order, health, or morals or the fundamental rights and freedoms of others."[7]

---

[4] Arcot Krishnaswami, "Study of Discrimination in the Matter of Religious Rights and Practices," in *Religion and Human Rights: Basic Documents*, ed. Tad Stahnke and J. Paul Martin (New York: Center for the Study of Human Rights, Columbia University, 1998), 10.

[5] *International Covenant of Civil and Political Rights*, art. 18, pars. 1 and 2 (hereafter ICCPR). For similar wording, cf. *Declaration on the Elimination of Intolerance and Discrimination*, art. 1, par. 1 (hereafter DEID).

[6] United Nations Human Rights Committee General Comment No. 22 (48) (Article 18), par. 2, 11 in *Religion and Human Rights: Basic Documents*, 92, 94 (hereafter UNHRC General Comment No. 22). See further David Little, "Studying 'Religious Human Rights': Methodological Considerations," in *Religious Human Rights in Global Perspective: Legal Perspectives*, ed. Johan D. van der Vyver and John Witte, Jr. (The Hague: Martinus Nijhoff Publishers, 1996), 50–52, including n.12.

[7] ICCPR, Article 18, par. 1, 3; cf. DEID, art. 1, par. 3; UNHRC General Comment No. 22, par. 4, p. 92.

At the same time, the burden of proof clearly rests with the government in regard to such actions. For one thing, what constitutes a "manifestation" of religion or belief should be left primarily to believers, and not to the state. For another, the government must show that any limitation on the manifestation of conscientious belief is both "necessary" and "proportionate"; that is, the limitation must be designed and administered so as to impose the least restrictive burden consistent with protecting a truly compelling state interest. It should be noted that limitations on the freedom of religion or belief are *not* permitted for unspecified considerations, such as national security.[8] Since fascists justified the abridgement of any and all rights on grounds of national security, this is an important exclusion.

2. "No one shall be subject to discrimination by any State, group of persons or person on the grounds of religion or other beliefs."[9] This is an equality right, which also includes provisions against "intolerance based on religion or belief." Discrimination has a clear legal meaning in the documents, namely, "any distinction, exclusion, restriction or preference based on religion or belief and having as its purpose or as its effect nullification or impairment of the recognition, enjoyment or exercise of human rights and fundamental freedoms on an equal basis." While intolerance is sometimes equated with discrimination in certain sections of the documents, elsewhere it is not, leaving the concept open to interpretation.[10]

According to the right against intolerance and discrimination, a state or official religion is not ruled out as such; nevertheless, its existence may not be used as a basis for "any discrimination against adherents of other religions or non-believers." For example, any "measures restricting eligibility for government service to members of the predominant religion or giving economic privileges to them or imposing special restrictions on the practice of other faiths," are prohibited. Moreover, this right is broadly inclusive and not limited to protecting "traditional" or majority religions. It prohibits discrimination against "any religion or belief for any reasons, including the fact that they are newly established, or represent religious minorities that are the subject of hostility by a predominant religious community."[11]

---

[8] Asma Jahangir, *Report of the Special Rapporteur on Freedom of Religion or Belief,* E/CN.4/2006/5 (January 9, 2006), par. 41, p. 13; UNHRC General Comment No. 22, par. 8, p. 93.

[9] DEID, art. 2, par. 1.

[10] DEID, art. 2, par. 2, art. 4, par. 2. Cf. ICCPR, arts. 2 and 27; and *Universal Declaration of Human Rights*, arts. 2 and 7 (hereafter UDHR). See David Little, "Rethinking Religious Tolerance: A Human Rights Approach," in David Little and David Chidester, *Religion and Human Rights: Toward An Understanding of Tolerance and Reconciliation* (Atlanta, GA: Emory Humanities Lectures, No. 3, 2000-01), 9ff.   [11] UNHRC General Comment No. 22, par. 9, p. 94; *ibid.* par. 2, p. 92.

3. "Persons belonging to [ethnic, religious or linguistic] minorities shall not be denied the right, in community with other members of their group, to enjoy their own culture, to profess and practice their own religion, and to use their own language."[12] Authoritative interpretation of this right by the Human Rights Committee has gone some way toward overcoming the weakening of this provision that took place at the time of the drafting of the UDHR, mainly at the urging of representatives of the United States, Canada, and Australia, who were concerned to reduce the scope of cultural autonomy for minorities in favor of a policy of assimilation. The recent pronouncements by the Committee suggesting that in the interest of "correcting conditions which prevent or impair the enjoyment" of minority rights, "positive measures by States may . . . be necessary to protect the identity of a minority and the rights of its members to enjoy and develop their culture and language and to practice their religion . . .," recall more robust formulations of the right of minority protection that were rejected at the time of drafting.[13] It is also worth mentioning that in the 1990s the UN has produced a number of documents aimed at substantially expanding minority protection, such as the *Declaration on the Rights of Persons Belonging to National or Ethnic, Religious and Linguistic Minorities* (1993) and the *Draft Declaration on the Rights of Indigenous Peoples* (1994).

4. The right against "religious . . . hatred that incites to discrimination, hostility or violence."[14] Considerable perplexity surrounds this right. Against the background of fascist practice, it makes good sense to "prohibit by law" actions aimed at and capable of producing discrimination and violence against religious and other groups and individuals. There is no lack of vivid examples of impermissible behavior from the Nazi time. Moreover, bringing about discrimination (as defined above under right no. 2) is by now indisputably a violation of human rights, as is inciting violence (except as an expression of "the sovereign right of self-defense or the right of peoples to self-determination"[15]).

On the other hand, it is particularly difficult, for legal purposes, to specify the meaning of "religious hatred" and "hostility," as referred to in the provision. Hatred and hostility, which are largely matters of attitude and emotion, are notoriously hard to police, and, because of that, invite

---

[12] ICCPR, art. 27; cf. UDHR, art. 27, par. 1.

[13] See Johannes Morsink, *The Universal Declaration of Human Rights: Origins, Drafting, and Intent* (Philadelphia, University of Pennsylvania Press, 1999), 269–80; Stahnke and Martin, *Religion and Human Rights: Basic Documents*, par. 6.2., p. 99; Morsink, *The Universal Declaration of Human Rights*, esp. 272–74.   [14] ICCPR, art. 20, par. 1. Cf. UDHR, art. 7.

[15] Stahnke and Martin, eds., *Religion and Human Rights: Basic Documents*, par. 2, p. 96.

conflicts with the rights of free speech and expression, as was already clear from the debates surrounding the drafting of this provision. It is predictable that this right, however indispensable, will continue to generate considerable debate around the edges.[16]

Controversial points of interpretation

Among the States Parties to the 1966 ICCPR, there are, currently, two highly sensitive examples of disagreement concerning the interpretation of religious liberty rights. One concerns minority protection, which touches on the first three rights, and the other is hate speech, which touches, of course, on the fourth right, but also on the first two.

The French law banning the wearing of Muslim headscarves and other visible religious symbols in state schools was adopted by parliament in March 2004, and upheld by the European Court of Human Rights in June, as a measure believed to be necessary for several reasons. Lawmakers contended that displaying religious attire or symbols in public schools violates the principle of *laïcité*, or the idea of the French secular state, according to which public life, in the interest of separating church and state, must be shielded from "conspicuous" forms of religious expression. In addition, supporters argued that the law upholds public order and the human rights of children, and thus constitutes a legitimate limitation on the right to free exercise. The law at once guards the state against the threat of Islamic fundamentalism, and protects Muslim girls against undue family or community coercion regarding their attire.

In opposition, human rights groups and others have vigorously challenged the law as a violation of the right to manifest religion or belief free of coercion. They argue that the government fails to prove that there exists a state interest compelling enough to override the strong presumption in favor of the freedom to manifest one's religion or belief in public, including "the wearing of distinctive clothing or head covering." Moreover, the government, it is claimed, has not given adequate evidence that Muslim girls are, in large numbers, being compelled against their will to wear head coverings. Opponents also describe the law as discriminatory, and, by implication, to be a violation of the right of minorities "to profess and practice their own religion," since the impact of the law, however neutrally

[16] Morsink, *The Universal Declaration of Human Rights*, 69–72; Natan Lerner, *Religion, Beliefs, and International Human Rights* (Maryknoll, NY: Orbis Books, 2000), ch. 3; Little, "Rethinking Religious Tolerance."

phrased, "will fall disproportionately on Muslim girls," and leave them no choice but to bear the extra financial burden of attending private school. In partial support of the opposition, a recent report of the UN Special Rapporteur for Freedom of Religion or Belief cites with approval concerns that the law banning religious symbols in public schools "may neglect the principle of the best interests of the child and the right of the child to access to education." It also supports a proposal that the French government consider "alternative means" to law, such as mediation and student participation in policy-making, as a way of balancing state interests with the rights of children to religious liberty. [17]

A landmark decision in 1990 by the United States Supreme Court, *Employment Division, Department of Human Resources of Oregon v. Smith*, represents a second example of conflicting interpretation over minority protection in the light of a human rights understanding of religious liberty. The Court denied unemployment compensation to two members of the Native American Church, who had been fired from their jobs with a private drug rehabilitation center because they ingested peyote for sacramental purposes in a religious ceremony. Under the religious free exercise clause of the First Amendment to the US Constitution, the defendants claimed a right of exemption from a state law that criminalized all use of controlled substances, including peyote, except if prescribed by a physician. The Court majority argued that there is absolutely no constitutionally required protection from generally applicable laws. Whatever religious exemptions are allowed must be left to state legislatures, who are fully entitled to ignore and override any conscientiously held beliefs of citizens, so long as the laws passed do not specifically single out one individual or group for discriminatory treatment. There is an admission that failing to give constitutional protection to "religious practices that are not widely engaged in" – namely, by minority religions like the Native American Church – "will place them at a relative disadvantage." Nevertheless, that is an "unavoidable consequence," since otherwise "anarchy" would result from a system where "each conscience is a law unto itself or in which judges weigh the social impact of all laws against the centrality of all religious beliefs."[18]

A storm of protest from religious groups, as well as from other non-governmental organizations and civil libertarians, arose over the *Smith*

---

[17] For example, Human Rights Watch, "France: Headscarf Ban Violates Religious Freedom. By Disproportionately Affecting Muslim Girls, Proposed Law is Discriminatory" hrw.org/english/docs/2004/02/26/france7666_txt.htm; see Jahangir, *Report of the Special Rapporteur*, par. 46, p. 14.

[18] 494 US 872, 881, 888–890 (1990) (rehearing denied 496 US 913 (1990)).

decision. Opposition forces gathered momentum and eventually coalesced around the Religious Freedom Restoration Act (RFRA), passed by Congress in 1993. The act declared that the government "may substantially burden a person's exercise of religion only if it demonstrates that application of the burden to the person, (1) is in furtherance of a compelling governmental interest; and (2) is the least restrictive means of furthering that compelling governmental interest." The act held until 1997 when the Court partially overturned it in *City of Boerne v. Flores* for exceeding Congress's authority by trying to tell the Court how to rule on religious freedom issues. Still, widespread disagreement with *Smith* continues to exist, and there is some indication the Court may be moving away from it.[19]

The dissenters in the *Smith* case took strong exception to the majority arguments. They held that the twofold test of RFRA – determining the least restrictive means in support of a compelling state interest – epitomizes "the First Amendment's command that religious liberty is an independent liberty, and that it occupies a preferred position," and that it is the responsibility of the Court "to strike sensible balances between religious liberty and a compelling state interest." The dissenters also added that were the protection of religious liberty rights left to the legislative process, that would contradict the clear purpose of the First Amendment, which is "precisely to protect the rights of those whose religious practices are not shared by the majority, and may be viewed with hostility." They concluded: "The history of our free exercise doctrine amply demonstrates the harsh impact majoritarian rule has had on unpopular or emerging religious groups such as the Jehovah's Witnesses or the Amish," and, it might be added, the Native American Church.[20]

Hate speech laws are another highly sensitive subject of controversy bearing on the interpretation of a human rights understanding of religious liberty. Restricting hate speech is directly addressed by the fourth religious liberty right, though the subject also prompts conflicting opinions concerning the ranking of the rights to liberty and equality of religion or belief (rights nos. 1 and 2). Countries like South Africa, Canada, Hungary, the Netherlands, Germany, Austria, France, and the United Kingdom, to mention a few, have all adopted laws against utterances or publications that slander, insult, or threaten a group of persons on the basis of their nationality, color, race, or religion. Such laws have generally been upheld by the European Court of Human Rights so long as they are necessary to protect

---

[19] *Religious Freedom Restoration Act, US Code* 42 (1993) § 2000bb-1; Garrett Epps, *To An Unknown God: Religious Freedom on Trial* (New York: St. Martin's Press, 2001), 239–40.

[20] 494 US 904–913.

a democratic society and are proportionate to the threat. By contrast, the United States, while experimenting in its history with hate speech laws, including campus speech codes, has eventually tended to turn away from them, thereby creating considerable tension between the USA and the Europeans and others over the meaning of religious liberty in this matter.

One vexing problem as between the two sides focuses, as mentioned, on the difficulty of specifying for purposes of legal enforcement the meaning of "religious hatred" and "hostility," including the link between them, implied in article 20.2 of the ICCPR. Generally speaking, both sides agree that it is permissible to prohibit the expression of religious and other forms of hatred that constitute incitement to discrimination or violence. But proponents of hate speech laws argue that, however delicate the task, failing to place legal restrictions on the free exchange of religious beliefs and attitudes has the effect of undermining equal protection. To subject individuals or groups to spoken, written, or symbolic expressions of religious hatred that insult them, "whether by suggesting they are inferior in some respect or by indicating that they are despised or not welcome for any other reason," is to discriminate against them, and is, in effect, to violate the religious right to equality.[21]

For their part, opponents object that expanding the regulations on free expression in the name of equality produces an ominous and potentially unlimited threat to the rights of free expression and tolerance, a threat that may well, in fact, double back and undermine equality. That happens when, repeatedly, the very minorities who are presumably protected against the incitement of hostility are themselves held liable under such laws for employing abusive language. These problems are caused, as the opponents see it, because of the insuperable difficulty of framing coherent, consistent, and reliable laws capable of governing attitudes or communications that are disconnected from an explicit act of inciting discrimination or violence.

RELIGIOUS LIBERTY IN THE WESTERN TRADITION

The Enlightenment setting

The prevailing view that human rights language, and in particular the emphasis on "freedom of conscience, religion or belief," is a simple product

---

[21] Eric Neisser, "Hate Speech in the New South Africa: Constitutional Considerations for a Land Recovering from Decades of Racial Repression and Violence," *South African Journal on Human Rights* 10: 3 (1994): 337.

of the Western Enlightenment, is at best a half-truth. For one thing, such a conclusion overlooks the historical context in which the human rights instruments were adopted. The fascist experiment of the last century, vivifying as it did the ominous imbalance in modern life between the technology of force and the institutions of restraint, was global in character, enveloping not just Europe and environs, but also the Far East. The worldwide catastrophe caused by the doctrine of collective domination gave urgent impetus everywhere to the cause of individual protection, starting with personal conviction and identity, no matter which country or culture was involved.

That common experience helps explain the universal resonance of human rights ideas, despite the strong traces of culture-specific language, as well as why human rights documents were, in fact, open both to significant intercultural influence, and to continuing efforts to anchor the documents in a variety of cultural settings.[22] Beyond that, and just as consequential, the Western cultural roots of a human rights understanding of religious liberty (as well as of other provisions), go back well before the Enlightenment, and can only adequately be understood when looked at against a broader tradition.

To be sure, there is clear evidence in Enlightenment literature of the crucial conjunction between the idea of a "subjective right" – the existence of a sovereign sphere of individual authority protected from coercive interference – and religious liberty. The contributions of English and American Enlightenment figures, like John Locke, Thomas Jefferson, and James Madison are unmistakable, even though here and there, particularly in Locke's case, there is some ambiguity in their writings on religious liberty.

Representatives of the French Enlightenment, like Pierre Bayle and Jean-Jacques Rousseau, were also proponents in their own way of religious liberty, even though, among Enlightenment figures, the balance of influence on modern human rights language must go to the Anglo-American tradition. While Bayle, for example, developed a view of the freedom of conscience and the importance of tolerance based on his experience of the persecution of French Huguenots, he was nevertheless deeply fearful of "the great concepts of law, liberty, and the limitations of the king's sovereignty"[23] so central to the development of modern human rights ideas. Similarly, Rousseau's belief in the omnipotence of the general

---

[22] See Glendon, "Universality Under Siege," in *A World Made New*, ch. 12.
[23] Walter Rex, *Essays on Pierre Bayle and Religious Controversy* (The Hague: Martinus Nijhoff, 1965), 252.

will threatens to undercut the priority of individual rights.[24] Two provisions in the *French Declaration of the Rights of Man and Citizen* of 1789, which bear Rousseau's stamp, raise deep questions about the compatibility of French conceptions of religious liberty with the individualistic assumptions of human rights language: "3. The source of all sovereignty resides essentially in the nation; no group, no individual may exercise authority not emanating expressly therefrom." "6. Law is the expression of the general will; all citizens have the right to concur personally, or through their representatives in its formation."[25]

Many of Jefferson's views are consonant with a human rights understanding of religious liberty, as is made clear in his Statute for Religious Freedom passed by the Virginia legislature in 1786. "No man shall be compelled to frequent or support any religious worship, place or ministry whatsoever, nor shall be enforced, restrained, molested, or burdened in his body or goods, nor shall otherwise suffer on account of his religious opinions or belief." It goes on to state "that all men shall be free to profess, and by argument to maintain, their opinions in matters of religion, and that the same shall in nowise diminish, enlarge, or affect their civil capacities," and that "the rights hereby asserted are of the natural rights of mankind." "It is time enough for the rightful purposes of civil government, for its offices to interfere when principles break out into overt acts against peace and good order." When magistrates intrude on matters of religion they invariably corrupt both religion – "by bribing, with a monopoly of worldly honors and emoluments those who will externally profess and conform to it," and state – by permitting public officials to abuse their office by making their opinions "the rule of judgment, and approve or condemn the sentiments of others only as they shall square or differ" from that rule.[26]

The underlying idea is the sovereignty of conscience. "Our rulers can have no authority over such natural rights, only as we have submitted to them. The rights of conscience we never submitted, we could not submit." Accordingly, the "legitimate powers of government extend to such acts only as are injurious to others. But it [should do] me no injury for my neighbor to say there are twenty gods, or no God. It neither picks my pocket nor

---

[24] Georg Jellinek, *The Declaration of the Rights of Man and of Citizens: A Contribution to Modern Constitutional History* (New York: Henry Holt and Co., 1901), 11–12. Jellinek also argues convincingly that the French Declaration of Rights drew much of its language from the state declarations of rights of the American colonies.

[25] *The Declaration of the Rights of Man* (approved August 26, 1789), trans. Avalon Project at Yale Law School.www.yale.edu/lawweb/avalon/rightsof.htm (accessed June 18, 2007).

[26] "An Act for Establishing Religious Freedom," in *The Life and Selected Writings of Thomas Jefferson*, ed. Adrienne Koch and William Peden (New York: Modern Library, 1944), 312–13.

breaks my leg."[27] Uniformly enforced religion is neither necessary nor desirable since human beings share a common moral capacity independent of religious conviction or identity. "Some have made the love of God the foundation of morality . . . [But] if we did a good act merely from the love of God and a belief that it is pleasing to him, whence arises the morality of the Atheist[s]?. . . Their virtue must have some other foundation." These sentiments should be emphasized, even though Jefferson, in these as in other opinions, was not altogether consistent.[28]

The doctrine of the sovereignty of conscience, so central to Jefferson's thinking, is forcefully supplemented in the writings of James Madison. In his famous Memorial and Remonstrance, published in 1785 in defense of Jefferson's proposed Statute for Religious Freedom, Madison puts the doctrine with unforgettable clarity: "Man's duty to his Creator is precedent both in order of time and degree of obligation to the claims of civil society." Moreover, in the subsequent debates in 1789 over the proposed Bill of Rights, Madison's suggested draft of the First Amendment included the following wording: "nor shall the full and equal rights of conscience be in any manner, or on any pretext, infringed . . ." He even went so far as to propose additional wording to what became the Second Amendment in favor of an exemption from military service for "religiously scrupulous" persons.[29]

In most respects, John Locke is the major proximate inspiration for Jefferson and Madison's views on religious liberty. The most important similarity, of course, is the belief, as Locke put it, "that liberty of conscience is every man's natural right, equally belonging to dissenters as to themselves; and that nobody ought to be compelled in matters of religion either by law or force." There is also the common emphasis on the distinction between what Locke calls "the outward and inward court," or "the magistrate and conscience," with the magistrate's jurisdiction being confined to the "civil interest," or "bodies and goods" – namely, "life, liberty, health and indolency of the body" [by which Locke meant freedom from arbitrarily inflicted pain]; and the possession of outward things, such as money, lands, houses, furniture, and the like."

Locke's doctrine of what may be called "the sovereignty of conscience," according to which, "every man . . . has the supreme and absolute

---

[27] Thomas Jefferson, "Notes on Virginia," in *ibid.*, 275.

[28] "Jefferson to Thomas Law, June 13, 1814," in *ibid.*, 637; see David Little, "Religion and Civil Virtue in America," in *The Virginia Statute for Religious Freedom: Its Evolution and Consequences in American History*, ed. Merrill D. Peterson and Robert C. Vaughan (New York: Cambridge University Press, 1988), 238–41.

[29] Cited in *Conscience in America: A Documentary History of Conscientious Objection in America, 1757–1967*, ed. Lillian Schlissel (New York: E. P. Dutton, 1968), 47.

authority of judging for himself," illuminates the position of Jefferson and Madison.

Such is the nature of the understanding that it cannot be compelled to the belief of anything by outward force. Confiscation of estate, imprisonment, torments, nothing of that nature can have any such efficacy as to make men change the inward judgment that they have framed of things . . . The magistrate's power extends not to the establishing of any articles of faith or forms of worship by force of his laws. For laws are of no force at all without penalties, and penalties in this case are absolutely impertinent, because they are not proper to convince the mind.

The key point for Locke, as for Jefferson and Madison, is that "to believe this or that to be true does not depend on our will." That is why "the business of laws is not to provide for the truth of opinions, but for the safety and security of the commonwealth, and of every particular man's goods and person." It follows that while the magistrate may rightfully punish behavior that violates "the public good" and the rights of others, as, for example, the sacrifice of infants even on grounds of conscience, citizens are not obliged to obey laws "against their consciences," "concerning things that lie not within the [limits] of the magistrate's authority (as, for example, that the people, or any party amongst them, should be compelled to embrace a strange religion and join the worship and ceremonies of another church)." The affairs of conscience stand above the affairs of state, except where the dictates of conscience violate a compelling public interest, including the rights of equal freedom.

To be sure, Locke was not totally consistent on these matters. The most striking anomaly in his writings on religious liberty concerns his argument against tolerating atheists. "Promises, covenants, and oaths, which are the bonds of human society, can have no hold upon an atheist. The taking away of God, though but even in thought, dissolves all." Here Locke forsook his critical distinction between inward belief and outward action, and attacked atheists for their beliefs, however they may behave. This conclusion, however at odds with other things Locke said, appears to rest on a divine law conception of ethics, according to which morality necessarily presupposes a belief in a divine lawgiver.

As regards other groups, like Muslims and Roman Catholics against whom he also preached intolerance, Locke's views are somewhat more understandable. Insofar as they harbor allegiance to a foreign power, whether the mufti of Constantinople or the pope in Rome, and thus intend, if able to take power, to incite violence and discrimination against others, they cannot be accommodated. But in those cases, it is the threat of sedition that is the reason for intolerance, not the beliefs themselves. Even here, of course, it is fair to wonder whether Locke was sufficiently sensitive to the need for safeguards against unwarranted attribution. Still, except for the atheist, the conscience, religion, or belief of everyone is, at least in theory, to be protected against undue coercive interference or penalty.[30]

The seventeenth-century moment

The decisive historical locus of the idea of a right to religious liberty generally consonant with a human rights understanding was not the Enlightenment, however, but mid-seventeenth-century England and America.[31] Around the time of the English Civil War (1642–1648), claims for expanding the scope of religious liberty were widely heard. But it was mainly the more radical voices of the period, and, most prominently, that of Roger Williams, by then transplanted to the New World, that definitively filled out the foundations of the modern view. Locke's ideas, and by extension Jefferson and Madison's, derived from Williams and from the supporting figures of the period.

Roger Williams was one of the founders in 1635 of the Rhode Island colony, an experiment rightly called "the first commonwealth in modern history to make religious liberty . . . a cardinal principle of its corporate existence and to maintain the separation of church and state on these grounds."[32] Williams wound up in Rhode Island in the first place because, with the help of some Native American friends, he escaped there after being officially banished from Massachusetts Bay and condemned to punishment in England.

He affirmed an array of offending beliefs, which eventually provoked his expulsion. One was his challenge to the right of the English monarch to allocate colonial land, a conclusion apparently inferred from his belief in the "natural and civil rights and liberties" of all human beings. Since, according to a presumed "natural right," Native Americans, and not the king, are the true owners of the lands of the new world, it is from the natives

---

[30] John Locke, *Letter Concerning Toleration* (New York: Liberal Arts Press, 1955), 17–18, 39, 45–48, 52. See David Little, "A Christian Perspective on Human Rights," in *Human Rights in Africa*, ed. Abdullahi Ahmed An-Na'im and Francis M. Deng (Washington, DC: Brookings Institution, 1990), esp. 51–56, 71.

[31] Brian Tierney, "Religious Rights: An Historical Perspective," in Witte and Van der Vyver, eds., *Religious Human Rights in Global Perspective*, 35ff.

[32] See Edwin S. Gaustad, *Sworn on the Altar of God: A Religious Biography of Thomas Jefferson* (Grand Rapids, MI: Wm. B. Eerdmans Publishing, 1996), 72; David Little, "Roger Williams and the Separation of Church and State," in *Religion and the State*, ed. James E. Wood, Jr. (Waco, TX: Baylor University Press 1985), 7ff.

alone that land must be acquired. Another was his claim that the English flag should be shorn of the prominent red cross at its center because, as a religious symbol, its presence serves to confuse civil and spiritual spheres. Related to that was his opposition to public oaths, particularly when imposed on unbelievers, together with his belief in a very stringent restriction of the jurisdiction state to the "bodies and goods" of human beings, namely, to their "outward state," and *not* to their spiritual affairs.

These and other highly controversial views all touched on Williams's radical commitment to the right of "soul liberty," as he called it. His position was simply an elaboration and reinterpretation of a distinction in the Christian tradition between the internal forum and external forum, or conscience and civil authority, which are parallel in some ways, if differently administered and enforced. The one is governed by the "law of the spirit," and the other by the "law of the sword."

There are, in Williams's mind, several grounds on which to draw this distinction. One is clearly religious. He spent considerable time interpreting Christian Scripture, and particularly the image and impact of Jesus, to prove that authentic Christianity favors a distinction between spirit and sword. But he also relied on reason and experience. To try to convince a person of the truth of something by threatening injury or imprisonment is to make a mistake about how the mind and spirit work. It is futile, wrote Williams, to try "to batter down idolatry, false worship, and heresy" by employing "stocks, whips, prisons, swords" because "civil weapons are improper in this business and never able to effect anything in the soul." Civil efforts to coerce conscience lead either to defiance and thus the probability of extensive bloodshed and suffering, or to hypocrisy, neither of which advances the cause of conscience.

There are various compelling reasons, then, for believing in the existence of an internal forum and its right to freedom: "Only let it be their soul's choice, and no enforcing sword, but what is spiritual in their spiritual causes . . . I plead [on the part of the civil authority] for impartiality and equal freedom, peace, and safety to [all] consciences and assemblies, unto which the people may as freely go, and this according to each conscience," in keeping of course with the requirements of civil order.

Williams invoked the idea of a universal moral law available to all, regardless of religious identity, as the proper basis for protecting the "common rights, peace and safety" of all citizens, which is, he said "work and business, load and burden enough" for political officials without presuming "to pull down, and set up religion, to judge, determine and punish in spiritual controversies." There exist common moral standards that are available to all sorts of people other than Christians, so that "civil places need not be monopolized [by] church members, (who are sometimes not fitted for them), and all other [people] deprived of their natural and civil rights and liberties." Indeed, Williams's theory of government is remarkably modern. Particular governments, he said, "have no more power than fundamentally lies in the [body of people who appoint them], which power, might or authority is not religious, Christian, etc., but natural, humane and civil." In addition, he was as concerned with the corruption caused in the civil order by confusing temporal and spiritual matters as he was with the corruption such confusion produced in religious communities: It is "against civil justice for the civil state or officers thereof to deal so partially in matters of God . . ."

These common and naturally available moral standards place important limits on tolerable religious practices. Williams held that civil magistrates are entitled to punish religiously authorized behavior that violates what he took to be the fundamental conditions of public safety and order. For example, he approved of the outlawing of human sacrifice, even though practiced for conscience's sake. But beyond the protection of the "common rights, peace and safety" of all citizens, Williams exhibited a remarkable degree of religious and cultural tolerance. So long as Jews, Roman Catholics, and "Mohammedans" were willing to accept citizenship on Williams's terms of equal freedom, they were all welcome. It is "known by experience," he said, that "many thousands" of Muslims, Roman Catholics and Pagans "are in their persons, both as civil and courteous and peaceable in nature, as any of the subjects in the state they live in."

Despite his own fervent Christian convictions, he resolutely refrained from evangelizing Native Americans because, among other reasons, they mostly lived under colonial legal systems which denied them genuine freedom in matters of religion and conscience. Based on his commitments to "impartiality and equal freedom," as well as "peace and safety" for all "consciences and assemblies," he attempted to deal honestly and equitably with Native Americans, seeking unsuccessfully to achieve what one historian has called a "bicultural" solution to the relations between colonists and Native Americans.

Also worth mentioning in this connection was Williams's extraordinary willingness not only to promote freedom *of* religion, but freedom *from* religion as well. Even atheists and people altogether indifferent or hostile to religion, should be equally respected. He considered the objection, undoubtedly widespread at the time, that if the state does not enforce religion, people are likely to drift away from religion and "turn atheistical and irreligious," as he put it. Such an outcome, he conceded, is a risk that must be run; "however it is infinitely better, that the profane and loose be unmasked, than to be muffled up under the veil and hood as of traditional hypocrisy, which turns and dulls the very edge of all conscience either toward God or man."[33]

Earlier Christian foundations

As to what would come after, Williams's theory of religious liberty – its elements and the way they were assembled – was clearly formative. But Williams hardly invented those elements, nor did he weave them together without regard to where they came from. Throughout their history, Christians had disagreed, sometimes violently, over the meaning and application of religious liberty. Williams knew that well enough. What he could not understand was why they had such difficulty choosing the right side.

The idea of conscience and its freedom was important to the early Christian church, particularly as expressed in the Pauline literature. The influential notion of conscience as a private, internal tribunal, adjudicating the probity of an individual's religious and moral beliefs and practices, is referred to in Romans 2:14–15. The passage speaks of non-Jews possessing "by nature" a moral law "written on their hearts," to which their "conscience" (*syneidesis*) "bears witness," and in relation to which their "conflicting thoughts accuse or perhaps excuse them," all under the authority of God who "judges the secrets of everyone." The idea that this moral law is universal, according to which "the whole world may be held accountable," is affirmed in Romans 3:19–20. In the context of a discussion in First Corinthians about tolerating conscientious differences, there is the additional suggestion that the conscience is fundamentally free, since one person's conscience cannot control anyone else's.[34]

Furthermore, given that God is understood to be the ultimate judge of conscience, the conviction arises in early Christian experience that an

---

[33] Roger Williams, *Complete Writings of Roger Williams*, 7 vols. (New York: Russell and Russell, 1963), III:148, 363, 398; IV:251; VII:154–55, 181; Roger Williams, *A Key into the Language of America* (Bedford, MA: Applewood Books, 1936) (originally published in 1643), 95. See further quotes and discussion in Edward S. Gaustad, *Liberty of Conscience: Roger Williams in America* (Grand Rapids, MI: Wm. B. Eerdmans Publishing, 1991), 31–44; James C. Davis, *The Moral Theology of Roger Williams: Christian Conviction and Public Ethics* (Louisville, KY: Westminster John Knox Press, 2004), 94; Russell Bourne, *The Red King's Rebellion: Racial Politics in New England, 1675–1678* (New York: Oxford University Press, 1990); Sydney E. Ahlstrom, *A Religious History of the American People* (New Haven, CT: Yale University Press), 1972), 182.

[34] 1 Corinthians 10:29: "For why should my liberty be determined by another's conscience?" (my translation).

important part of the freedom of conscience is its independence from and superiority to human judgments, including those of the civil authority. Some have even interpreted Paul's words in Romans 13:5, enjoining political obedience "for the sake of conscience," to imply a right to stand in judgment concerning the behavior of governments, particularly in the light of his preceding claim that "rulers are not a terror to good conduct, but to bad" (Romans 13:3).

Classical texts used to support what later came to be known as the doctrine of the "sovereignty of conscience" are Acts 5:29: "We must obey God rather than human beings," and Mark 12:17: "Render unto Caesar the things that are Caesar's, and to God the things that are God's." Conflicting opinions of how to interpret and apply these ideas would punctuate the life of the church ever after.[35]

The interpretations of these fundamental ideas by thirteenth-century Catholic theologian Thomas Aquinas and sixteenth-century Protestant reformer John Calvin were particularly important in paving the way for Williams's definitive articulation in the seventeenth century. Though Thomas did not work out a developed notion of a right to the freedom of conscience, he elaborated some significant features. Since unwilling belief is, he said, an impossibility, the idea of trying to compel belief by force is disallowed. If force is excluded in such matters, then "the state is guilty of injustice if it interferes with a person's [obeying] conscience in matters of religious choice, profession and worship."[36] Conversely, the state would appear to be acting justly by enforcing the free exercise of conscience. This is, in effect, to argue for a subjective right of conscience – that is, an enforceable title, individually claimable, against coercive interference with conscience.

Thomas proceeded to develop an elaborate and very influential theory of conscience, which thereafter kept reappearing in discussions of religious liberty in the Western tradition. Nevertheless, in keeping with general attitudes of the medieval Roman Catholic Church, he applied his theory in a way that drew the limits of religious liberty very narrowly, compared to Williams and his successors. Thomas drew a sharp distinction between uninitiated unbelievers and apostates and heretics. Since the latter at one time accepted Christian faith in the act of baptism, they are subject to civil punishment upon their defection. According to Thomas, since the state has the authority to enforce contracts, it may properly intervene when a religious pledge of faith is broken.

[35] See further chapters by Luke Johnson, Brian Tierney, and Kent Greenawalt herein.
[36] Eric D'Arcy, *Conscience and Its Right to Freedom* (London: Sheed and Ward, 1961), 153–54.

Calvin made a great deal of the doctrine of the sovereignty of conscience, even if he, like Thomas, extensively narrowed its scope. On the one side, he proclaimed a sharp distinction between the "spiritual power" and the "power of the sword," notions linked to the idea of two forums or tribunals so important to Williams and the Anglo-American tradition, and he, like them, gave pride of place to the conscience. In addition, he supported the idea of the superiority of conscience. Conscience, he said, is "higher than all human judgments," and "human laws, whether made by magistrate or church, even though they have to be observed (I speak of good and just laws), still do not of themselves bind conscience."

On the other side, Calvin veered in the opposite direction. Speaking both as a theologian, and as a community organizer frustrated with widespread insubordination and religious dissent, he assigned to the Genevan authorities the right to impose on the unruly masses "the outward worship of God" and "sound doctrine of piety and the position of the church." And then, having declared that the "church does not have the right of the sword to punish or to compel, not the authority to force, not imprisonment, nor the other punishments, which the magistrate commonly inflicts," he contrived an arrangement with Genevan officials to use none other than the "sword, force, and imprisonment" to enforce his doctrines across the city.[37]

CONCLUSIONS

A central part of the social and political devastation caused by a grim succession of collectivist ideologies, beginning in the middle of the last century, was the systematic and world-wide assault on religious belief and identity. As a result, the protection of religious liberty as a universal and fundamental human right took on new urgency. The equal right to hold and express religious and other conscientious beliefs has been authoritatively elaborated in a series of broadly ratified international documents, which now set the stage for understanding and applying that right.

The natural rights tradition provided, often against strong resistance, much of the terminology and some critical parts of the rationale for human rights, including religious liberty. Although the tradition was nurtured and conveyed by certain segments of Western Christianity, a key assumption – also essential for human rights language – is that the rights of individual

---

[37] John Calvin, *Institutes of the Christian Religion*, ed. John T. McNeill, trans. Ford Lewis Battles, 2 vols. (Philadelphia: Westminster Press, 1960), bk. 3, ch. 19, par. 15, pp. 847–48; bk. 4, ch. 10, pp. 1183–84; bk. 4, ch. 20, par. 2, p. 1487, par. 3, p. 1215

conscience neither depend on nor require prior religious or other comprehensive commitments, just as they neither depend on nor require being born in one place or another, or having this or that gender, culture, or ethnic identity. That such rights are believed to be independent of such considerations is what it means to call them "natural," or in the human rights idiom, "inherent" or "inalienable."

What was distinctive about the Christian contribution was the disposition of figures like Roger Williams to foreswear any special claim by Christians or others to civil authority in regard to enforcing religious belief and action. Instead, Christian proponents of natural rights, in varying degrees, held everyone, including fellow Christians, accountable to a common human standard of political order, a proposition believed to be thoroughly consonant with their faith.

This principle of what might be called self-abnegation in regard to the religious control of civil and political life, one partially based on theological conviction, constitutes a compelling model for the implementation of religious liberty. The principle is of course highly controversial, within Christianity as well as other religions, but there is evidence that it is finding increasing resonance in religions around the world, as it has found resonance, historically, in at least one segment – often a besieged minority – of Western Christianity.

RECOMMENDED READING

Boyle, Kevin and Juliet Sheen, eds. *Freedom of Religion and Belief: A World Report.* London: Routledge, 1997.

Danchin, Peter G. and Elizabeth A. Cole, eds. *Protecting Human Rights of Religious Minorities.* New York: Columbia University Press, 2002.

Evans, Carolyn. *Freedom of Religion under the European Convention on Human Rights.* New York: Oxford University Press, 2001.

Evans, Malcolm D. *Religious Liberty and International Law in Europe.* Cambridge: Cambridge University Press, 1997.

Gaustad, Edwin S. *Liberty of Conscience: Roger Williams in America.* Grand Rapids, MI: Wm. B. Eerdmans Publishing, 1991.

Horton, John and Susan Mendus, eds. *John Locke, A Letter Concerning Toleration, in Focus.* London; New York: Routledge, 1991.

Lerner, Natan. *Religion, Beliefs, and International Human Rights.* Maryknoll, NY: Orbis Books, 2000.

Lindholm, Tore, W. Cole Durham, Jr., and Bahia G. Tahzib-Lie, eds. *Facilitating Freedom of Religion or Belief: A Deskbook.* Leiden: Martinus Nijhoff, 2004.

Little, David. "A Christian Perspective on Human Rights," in *Human Rights in Africa,* ed. Abdullahi Ahmed An-Nai'm and Francis M. Deng. Washington, DC: Brookings Institution, 1990, 51–76.

"Rethinking Religious Tolerance: A Human Rights Approach," in David Little and David Chidester, *Religion and Human Rights: Toward an Understanding of Tolerance and Reconciliation* (Atlanta, GA: Emory Humanities Lectures, Academic Exchange, 2001).

"Culture, Religion, and National Identity in a Postmodern World." *Anuario del Derecho Eclesiastico del Estado* 22 (2006): 19–35.

"Religion, Human Rights, and Secularism: Preliminary Clarifications and Some Islamic, Jewish, and Christian Responses," in *Humanity Before God: Contemporary Faces of Jewish, Christian, and Islamic Ethics*, ed. William Schweiker, Michael Johnson, and Kevin Jung. Philadelphia: Fortress Press, 2006, 256–85.

Peterson, Merrill D. and Robert Vaughan, eds. *Virginia Stature for Religious Freedom: Its Evolution and Consequences in American History*. Cambridge: Cambridge University Press, 1988.

Reynolds, Noel B. and W. Cole Durham, Jr., eds. *Religious Liberty in Western Thought*. Atlanta, GA: Scholars Press, 1996.

Stahnke, Tad and J. Paul Martin, eds. *Religion and Human Rights: Basic Documents* New York: Center for the Study of Human Rights, Columbia University, 1998.

Symposium. "The Permissible Scope of Legal Limitations on the Freedom of Religion or Belief." *Emory International Law Review* 19 (2005): 456–1320.

Taylor, Paul. *Freedom of Religion: UN and European Human Rights Law and Practice*. New York: Cambridge University Press, 2005.

Tierney, Brian. "Religious Rights: An Historical Perspective," in *Religious Rights in Global Perspective: Religious Perspectives*. ed. John Witte, Jr. and Johan van der Vyver. The Hague: Martin Nijhoff Publishers, 1996, 17–46.

The Idea of Natural Rights: Studies on Natural Rights, Natural Law and Church Law, 1150–1625. Atlanta, GA: Scholars Press, 1997.

Witte, John, Jr. *Religion and the American Constitutional Experiment*, 2nd edn. Boulder, CO/London: Westview Press, 2005.

The Reformation of Rights: Law, Religion, and Human Rights in Early Modern Calvinism. Cambridge: Cambridge University Press, 2007.

CHAPTER FOURTEEN

Modern church law

Norman Doe

In recent years, there has been a renewed interest in the study of church law (ecclesionomology), that is, the exploration of the internal laws and other regulatory instruments of Christian churches (as distinct from state laws on religion). Not only do learned societies study the internal rules of churches (including their relation to civil law), in Europe, the Americas, and elsewhere, but also universities now have courses in the field following the example of continental European universities which for generations have studied church law systematically. However, one gap in modern scholarship of this field is the study of comparative church law.

The purpose of this chapter is to explore the feasibility of comparative religious law from a Christian perspective. The following chapter outlines five issues: (1) the sources and forms of church law; (2) the subject matter and scope of church law; (3) the purposes of church law in theology and law; (4) the effect and enforcement of church law; and (5) church law and civil law. It does so in relation to (principally) the Roman Catholic, Eastern Catholic, Old Catholic, Orthodox, Anglican, Lutheran, Presbyterian, Reformed, Methodist, and Baptist churches.

THE SOURCES AND FORMS OF CHURCH LAW

The ecclesial communities studied here employ laws and other regulatory instruments at two levels: international and local. These instruments represent the formal sources of regulation. They exist under a variety of titles appropriate to the tradition in question (from canon law to church order). This section sketches their forms and makers as well as the juridical formulae (rules, principles, and the like) appearing in them.

I am very grateful to colleagues at the Centre for Law and Religion, the Law School, Cardiff University, Russell Sandberg, Professor Mark Hill, and Eithne D'Auria, for their assistance in commenting on this study in draft.

15 "Christ Giving the Keys to St. Peter," from a Psalter of Don Appiano from the Church of the Badia Fiorentina, Florence, 1514–1515.

The international level

The instruments of global ecclesial communities fall into three basic categories: (1) codes of canon law (Roman Catholic and Eastern Catholic); (2) customs (Orthodox, canonical tradition, and Anglican, informal bonds of affection); and (3) constitutions (Lutheran, Reformed, Methodist, and

Baptist) and statutes (Old Catholics). First, the twentieth was the century of *codification* for the Catholic Church. Its principal sources of law are the Code of Canon Law (1983) for the Latin Church and the Code of Canons of the Eastern Churches (1990). In the Latin or Roman Catholic Church, which sees the church as both sacrament and visible organization with a central papacy, the Code of Canon Law of 1983, replacing that of 1917, was promulgated by Pope John Paul II after a revision process following the Second Vatican Council. The 1983 Code distinguishes "universal law" and "particular law" (see further below). Universal law is applicable to the Latin Church in all parts of the world; it includes the Code itself, papal decrees, and authentic interpretations of a legislator, but judicial decisions do not generate law (Canons 12, 16, 29). Similarly, the twenty-one oriental Catholic churches, reunited with Rome and acknowledging the supremacy of the Roman Pontiff, have a code: the Code of Canons of the Eastern Churches promulgated by Pope John Paul II in 1990. This 1990 Code, in which "the ancient law of the Eastern Churches has been mostly received or adapted," represents their "common law." It embraces "the laws and legitimate customs" of the entire Church and those common to all the Eastern Churches (Canons 1, 1493). Pope John Paul II saw the Eastern Code of 1990 and the Latin Code of 1983 as "one *Corpus Iuris Canonici*" for the Catholic Church, and called for comparative studies of them.

Secondly, in contrast, the Orthodox Church is a family of self-governing churches with no centralized organization. It has no universal code (though whether Orthodox law should be codified is the subject of debate). The "law of the church" globally is, rather, "her canonical tradition," "an outgrowth of the holy canons."[1] The holy canons stem from three main sources: ecumenical synods (representing the universal church), local synods (subsequently ratified by the ecumenical synods as representing the tradition of the universal church), and the Fathers of the church. These are contained in several collections; the most widely used today in Greek-speaking Orthodox churches is the *Pedalion* (first edition 1800). Nevertheless, some Orthodox churches may at the inter-church level organize themselves on the basis of a *constitution*, such as that of the Standing Conference of Canonical Orthodox Bishops in the Americas (Greek, Antiochian, Serbian, Romanian, Bulgarian, Carpatho Russian, Ukrainian, Albanian), which preserves the jurisdictional autonomy of the member churches.

---

[1] L. Patsavos, "The Canonical Tradition of the Orthodox Church," in *A Companion to the Greek Orthodox Church*, ed. F. K. Litsas (New York: Greek Orthodox Archdiocese of North and South America, 1984), 145.

Similarly, the Anglican Communion has no formal body of law applicable globally to its forty-four member churches in communion with the See of Canterbury; each church is autonomous with its own legal system. The Communion is held together by "bonds of affection" – shared loyalty to Scripture, creeds, baptism, eucharist, historic episcopate, and its institutional instruments of unity (the Archbishop of Canterbury, Primates Meeting, Lambeth Conference, and Anglican Consultative Council). But the institutional instruments cannot make decisions binding on churches. However, in 2001, work began on a statement of principles of canon law common to the churches of the Anglican Communion induced from the similarities between their legal systems.[2] Moreover, the Communion is currently debating adoption by each church of a common Anglican Covenant to regulate relationships between the member churches. The proposal (of the Lambeth Commission's *Windsor Report* 2004) is that this could bind each church juridically. The covenant would be similar to the Statute 2000 of the Old Catholic Bishops United in the Union of Utrecht, which defines the communion between its autonomous churches and superseded the Agreement between the Old Catholic Bishops and the Regulations of the International Old Catholic Bishops' Conference 1974.

Other global ecclesial communities employ *constitutions* enabling worldwide collaboration in matters of common concern while preserving the autonomy of member churches. The Lutheran World Federation, "a communion of churches which confess the triune God, agree in the proclamation of the Word of God and are united in pulpit and altar fellowship," is "organized under" its constitution (and supplementary bylaws) as an "instrument of its autonomous member churches," which helps them collaborate (Arts. I–IV). Similarly, the World Alliance of Reformed Churches, "a fellowship of Congregational, Presbyterian, Reformed and United churches," adopted its present Constitution in 1970, and this protects the autonomy of its member churches (Arts. I and IV). The World Methodist Council, a manifestation of a "fellowship" of Methodists worldwide, has a constitution, but the Council has no legislative authority over member churches. Likewise, the Baptist World Alliance, "extending over every part of the world, [is] an expression of the essential oneness of Baptist people in . . . Christ." Its constitution "recognizes the traditional

---

[2] In 2001, the Primates Meeting endorsed suggestions in Norman Doe, "Canon Law and Communion," *Ecclesiastical Law Journal* 6 (2002): 241. Tested at a Consultation of Legal Advisers, its conclusions were endorsed by the Primates in 2002. See Doe, "The Common Law of the Anglican Communion," *Ecclesiastical Law Journal* 7 (2003) 4. A draft was agreed in 2006 and awaits final approval by the Anglican Communion Legal Advisers Network.

autonomy and interdependence of Baptist churches and member bodies" (Art. 11). Finally, the ecumenical World Council of Churches has a constitution and rules.

The local level

Within each of these global ecclesial communities, there are member churches (mostly pre-existing the global entity). Each institutional church has its own regulatory system. Their instruments fall into three broad categories: canon law, constitutions, and instruments of church order. The Code of Canon Law of the Roman Catholic Church provides that whereas universal law applies to the whole church, "particular laws" apply to a specific territory (a particular church, such as a diocese) or a group of people (such as a religious community). Particular laws include diocesan legislation (made by a bishop in consultation with the diocesan synod), laws promulgated by national episcopal conferences, or the special or proper laws created for and by institutes of religious life. Particular laws are abrogated by universal law only by express repeal; custom also has the force of law (Canons 13, 20, 23–26). A similar position pertains in the Eastern Catholic Churches. Each church is *sui juris* (not a concession of the Latin Church) with its own juridical system operative within the common law of the Code of 1990. The churches differ in terms of "rite," their liturgical, theological, spiritual, and disciplinary heritage; and custom has the force of law (Canons 28, 1506). The common law does not derogate from particular laws unless it expressly provides for this (Canon 1502). In Orthodoxy, each local church is either autocephalous (one which elects its own primate) or autonomous (one which elects its primate with the participation of the primate of an autocephalous church), in communion with its sister churches, episcopal and eucharistic, catholic, and sometimes national, with a constitutional foundation (as with the autocephalous Greek Orthodox Church, and the autonomous Orthodox Church of Crete, each with its own "statutory charter"). The Greek Orthodox Archdiocese of America, for example, an eparchy under the canonical jurisdiction of the Ecumenical Patriarchate of Constantinople, has a charter according to which the church is "governed by the Holy Scriptures, the Holy Canons, this Charter, and the regulations promulgated by it; and, as to canonical and ecclesiastical matters not provided therein, by the decisions thereon of the Holy Synod of the Ecumenical Patriarchate" (Art. 1). Its eparchial synod may make regulations (to implement the charter) on specified subjects; all regulations must conform to the holy canons, sacred tradition, and practice of Orthodoxy. Others, to be operative, must be approved by the Ecumenical Patriarchate (Arts. 10, 22).

Similarly, each autonomous church in the Anglican Communion has its own central system of general law (typically provincial law created by a synod or other assembly representative of bishops, clergy, and laity) and laws made at more localized levels (such as diocesan law created by the diocesan synod of bishop, clergy, and laity), which to be operative must be consistent with the general law. In terms of general law, some churches have a code of canons only. Most have a constitution, canons, and other regulatory instruments, including rules and regulations, ordinances, resolutions, and liturgical rubrics found in the service books. Alongside written laws are less formal and sometimes unwritten sources, including customs or tradition, the decisions of church courts, the English Canons Ecclesiastical of 1603, or pre-Reformation Roman canon law.[3]

Lutheran churches generally employ constitutions and bylaws. The Lutheran Church of Australia, for example, has a central constitution, bylaws, rules, and regulations (which may be amended by its General Synod representative of congregations and pastors), and it recognizes custom. In turn, each district of the church, and each congregation within a district, has its own constitution and bylaws, which must be consistent with the central constitution and by-laws; constitutional articles on its Confession are unalterable (Constitution, Arts. IV, VI–IX, XII). Some Lutheran churches have model congregation constitutions (such as the Evangelical Lutheran Church in Canada). By way of contrast, Presbyterian churches employ systems of "law" (as with the Church of Scotland), or of "church order." The constitution of the Presbyterian Church in America consists of its doctrinal standards set out in the Westminster Confession of Faith, the Larger and Short Catechisms, and its Book of Church Order. Amendment of the Book of Church Order is effected by the General Assembly with the consent of two-thirds of the Presbyteries. Amendment of the Confession of Faith and Larger and Shorter Catechisms requires a three-quarters vote of the General Assembly with the consent of three-quarters of the Presbyteries. The church also recognizes custom (Book of Church Order, 1.26, III.58). Other churches employ a plethora of regulatory instruments. In Great Britain, the Methodist Church has its Constitutional Practice and Discipline expressing "Methodist Law and Polity." The United Reformed Church has its Scheme of Union and Manual. The Quakers have Queries

---

[3] Norman Doe, *Canon Law in the Anglican Communion: A Worldwide Perspective* (Oxford: Clarendon Press, 1998).

and Advices, not laws, but the Quaker Faith and Practice is composed of "regulations." And the Baptist Union of Great Britain and Ireland has a Constitution.

The formal laws of churches employ standard juridical formulae: principles, rules, norms, dispensations, powers, rights, duties, privileges, and responsibilities appear in Roman and Eastern Catholic canon law, Orthodox instruments, Anglican laws, Methodist laws, Lutheran constitutions, and Presbyterian books of church order.[4] Finally, in addition to formal laws (appearing in charters, constitutions, canons, etc.), churches today increasingly use what may be styled "ecclesiastical quasi-legislation." These are informal administrative rules designed to supplement formal laws (to clarify or implement them). They resemble laws (with prescriptive language) but may not bind in the same way as laws properly so-called. This is the case in the Roman Catholic Church (e.g., directories), Orthodox churches (e.g., instructions), Lutheran churches (e.g., guidelines), and Anglican churches (e.g., codes of practice or policy documents).[5]

THE SUBJECT MATTER AND SCOPE OF CHURCH LAW

There is considerable but not exact convergence between churches as to the subjects treated by their regulatory instruments. What differs is the instrument by which subjects are treated. First, at the international level, the codes of the Latin and Eastern Catholic churches are comprehensive and cover all aspects of ecclesial life. The canons of the Latin code are organized in seven books: general norms; the people of God; the teaching office; the sanctifying office (the sacraments); temporal goods; sanctions; and processes. Liturgical law is to be found mainly outside the code, in the ritual books, their preambles, and their rubrics (Canon 2). The canons of the Eastern code are somewhat differently organized under thirty titles: those without obvious equivalents in the Latin code include: patriarchal churches; major archiepiscopal churches; metropolitan churches; eparchies, exarchies, and

---

[4] See Latin Code (1983), bk. I, bk. II, cc.208–223; Patsavos, "The Canonical Tradition"; the Anglican Province of the West Indies, Const., Art. 6.2; Methodist Church in Britain, Deed of Union, 9; Evangelical Lutheran Church in Canada, Const., V.1; and Presbyterian Church in America, Book of Church Order, I.12.

[5] For the Latin Church, see F. Morrisey, "Papal and Curial Pronouncements: Their Canonical Significance in the Light of the 1983 Code of Canon Law," *The Jurist* 50 (1990): 102. The Orthodox Archdiocese of Thyateira and Great Britain has Instructions (e.g. on marriage). The Lutheran Church of Australia has Pastoral Guidelines for Responsible Communion Practice (2001) and Guidelines for Inter-Church Marriages (2000). For Anglicanism, see Norman Doe, "Ecclesiastical quasi-legislation," in *English Canon Law*, ed. N. Doe, M. Hill, and R. Ombres (Cardiff: University of Wales Press, 1998), 93.

exarchs; assemblies of hierarchs; communion with the Catholic Church; and ecumenism.

While the canonical tradition in Orthodoxy has a comprehensive compass, Orthodox inter-church instruments have a more limited focus. The constitution of the Standing Conference of Orthodox Bishops in the Americas, for example, deals in seven articles only with membership; objectives; authority and structure; and committees and meetings. However, the draft statement of principles of canon law common to churches of the Anglican Communion treats church order; communion relationships; government; ministry; doctrine; liturgy; rites; property; and ecumenism. Moreover, the proposed Anglican covenant provides for common identity, communion relationships and commitments, the exercise of autonomy, and management of communion issues. The statute of the Old Catholic Bishops of the Union of Utrecht is similar. It has the ecclesiological foundations of the union (such as the duties of communion and the right of autonomy) and the international bishops' conference (composition, functions, and discipline). The instruments of Protestant global communities are minimalist in terms of subject matter. The constitution of the Lutheran World Federation (in fourteen articles) deals with: doctrinal basis; nature and functions; scope of authority; membership and affiliation; organization; the assembly; the council; national committees; officers and secretariat; finance; and amendments and by-laws. Likewise, the constitution and by-laws of the World Alliance of Reformed Churches address: membership; purposes; general council; executive committee; officers; departments; organization of areas; and amendments. Similar in terms of subject matter arrangements are the constitutions of the Baptist World Alliance (covering objective; method of operations; Church membership; Baptist World Congress; General Council; executive committee; officers; departments; regional fellowships; and amendments), and of the World Council of Churches. The seven articles of the constitution of the World Council of Churches treat basis; membership; purposes and functions; authority; organization; other ecumenical organizations; and amendments. Its rules deal with the responsibilities of membership, among other topics.

Secondly, at the local level, in the case of the Roman Catholic Church, particular laws treat a less extensive range of subjects than those of the Eastern Catholic churches. The focus of the Charter of the Greek Orthodox Archdiocese of America is solely on jurisdiction; mission; institutional organization; and the officers of the local church; leaving liturgy and sacraments under the regulation of canonical tradition. Like some Old

Catholic churches,[6] the subject matter of Anglican laws is extensive. Typically, Anglican *constitutions* treat matters of faith and doctrine; territorial, governmental, and institutional organization (legislative, administrative, and judicial); the appointment of bishops; discipline; and property. *Canons*, in turn, address functions of ordained and lay ministers, and liturgical and sacramental matters. The position in Lutheran churches is complex. In some (e.g., the Lutheran Church of Australia), the constitution deals with such topics as confession of faith; objects; membership; ministry; authority and powers; general synod; officers and administration; districts; discipline; adjudication and appeals; by-laws; and alteration of the constitution. In others, rights and duties of members, matters of worship, and the administration of rites are dealt with in congregational constitutions (as in the Evangelical Lutheran Church in Canada), or at the regional level (as is the case in the Evangelical Lutheran Church of Southern Africa, Natal-Transvaal). In the Presbyterian Church in America, the book of church order is very comprehensive, dealing with the form of government (the doctrine of government, courts, orders, and election); the rules of discipline (offenses, censures, procedure, and appeals); and worship (public worship, baptism, Lord's Supper, marriage, and burial). Methodist laws deal with similar subjects, as is the case in the *Laws and Discipline* (2000) of the Methodist Church in Southern Africa.

Thirdly, although an examination of the subjects treated by modern church laws reveals differences, it also reveals a wealth of substantive similarities between the churches. Some examples may be offered. In *government*, the principle that authority in the church is legislative, judicial, and administrative (though churches differ in the distribution of such functions) surfaces in the laws of the Roman Catholic (Canon 135), Old Catholic, Orthodox, Anglican, Lutheran, Presbyterian, and United Reformed churches.[7] In *ministry*, the principle that no minister may be disciplined except by due process (though disciplinary powers are assigned to different institutions) appears in the laws of the Roman Catholic, Old

---

6 For example, the constitution of the Polish National Church (USA) (2002) deals with: members' rights and duties; parishes; authority; legislative authority (general synod, diocesan synod); executive authority; bishops; clergy; and the judiciary. The church was suspended from the Union of Utrecht in 2003.

7 For example: Polish National Church (USA), Const., Art. VI.1: "The authority of this Church is vested in three branches, namely: legislative, executive and judicial"; Greek Orthodox Archdiocese of America, Charter: law-making vests in the eparchial synod (Art. 10); adjudication, in the spiritual courts (Art. 9); administration of monasteries, in a hierarch (Art. 21); Church of England: law-making vests in the General Synod (Synodical Government Measure 1969); administration of a parish, in the Parochial Church Council (Parochial Church Councils (Powers) Measure 1956); and adjudication, in the courts (Ecclesiastical Jurisdiction Measure 1963); Evangelical Lutheran Church

Catholic, Orthodox, Anglican, Lutheran, and Presbyterian churches.[8] In *doctrine*, the principle that the faithful must not publicly dissent from the ecclesiastical doctrine (though laws differ as to which members of the faithful are subject to this) is shared by the Roman Catholic, Orthodox, Anglican, Lutheran, and Presbyterian churches.[9] In *worship*, that the faithful must gather for worship regularly appears in the laws of the Roman Catholic, Anglican, Lutheran, and Presbyterian churches.[10] Finally, in relation to *rites*, that baptism (to which rights and duties attach) effects incorporation into the church universal appears in the instruments of the Roman Catholic,[11] Orthodox,[12] Anglican,[13] Lutheran,[14] Presbyterian,[15] and Methodist churches.[16]

THE PURPOSES OF CHURCH LAW: THEOLOGY AND LAW

The purposes of modern church law are shaped by the understandings that each church has about the nature of the church (its ecclesiology) and about

---

Footnote 7 (cont.)

in Canada, Const.: the Convention is "the highest legislative authority" (Art. X.1); the episcopal president of the National Church Council is "the chief executive officer" (Art. XII.5); and judicial functions vest in the Court of Adjudication (Art. XVIII); Church of Scotland: legislative, administrative and judicial functions vest in the court of General Assembly; and United Reformed Church (Britain), Manual, B: General Assembly is required to: make regulations; appoint moderators of synods; and "determine when rights of personal conviction are asserted to the injury of the unity and peace" of the URC.

[8] Code, Canon 221: the faithful have the right not to be punished except in accord with the norm of law; Polish National Church, Const. XXII; Greek Orthodox Archdiocese of America, Charter, 9: a hierarch who judged a case at first instance cannot hear an appeal; for Anglicanism, see Doe, *Canon Law in the Anglican Communion*, 86ff; Lutheran Church of Australia, Const., X: the judicial system of the church must uphold the "rules of natural justice." For the Church of Scotland, see J. L. Weatherhead, *The Constitution and Laws of the Church of Scotland* (Edinburgh: Board of Practice and Procedure, 1997), 42ff.

[9] Code, Canons 747–755; Archdiocese of Thyateira and Great Britain, Instructions: Apostasy and Restoration; (Anglican) Church in Wales, Const., XI.18 (clergy and laity are subject to the Disciplinary Tribunal for "teaching, preaching, publishing or professing doctrine or belief incompatible with that of the Church in Wales"; in the Church of England lay people are not subject to doctrinal discipline in church courts; Evangelical Lutheran Church in Canada, Approved Model Constitution for Congregations, Art. IV.6–9; Presbyterian Church in America, Book of Church Order, Preface, II.3; I.I.I.

[10] Code, Canon 214 (right to worship); Canon 920 (the duty to receive holy communion); Church of England, Canon B15: the duty of confirmed persons to receive holy communion; Evangelical Lutheran Church in Canada, Approved Model Constitution for Congregations, Art. III.a; Presbyterian Church in America, Book of Church Order, III.47.   [11] Code, Canon 849.

[12] Greek Orthodox Archdiocese of Australia, Handbook, Baptisms.

[13] Church of England, Canon B21.

[14] Evangelical Lutheran Church of South Africa (Natal–Transvaal), Guidelines, 1.10.

[15] Presbyterian Church in America, Book of Church Order, III.56: baptism is not to be delayed.

[16] Methodist Church in Great Britain, Constitutional Practice and Discipline, Deed of Union, 6; Standing Orders, 010A.

itself as an institutional church (its ecclesiality). Consequently, there is a distinct relationship between church law and theology. In this respect, the concept of divine law is one which surfaces to a greater or lesser extent in the laws of churches.

First, at the global level, the strategic objects of identity, unity, and witness are commonplace in the instruments of international ecclesial communities. The statute of the Old Catholics Bishops of Utrecht seeks "to promote and to realize" communion; it requires the churches, for example, to "maintain the catholicity, doctrine, and worship in apostolic succession" (B. Order, art.1), and no bishop may consecrate any person as a bishop for another church without approval of the conference. The constitution of the Standing Conference of Canonical Orthodox Bishops in the Americas enables the churches through the conference "to actualize . . . unity in all those fields in which a common effort is required" (Arts. 1 and v). One strategic goal of the constitution of the Lutheran World Federation is to unite the churches, strengthen them, and help them "to act jointly in common tasks" (Art. III). Similar goals appear in the constitutions of the World Alliance of Reformed Churches, World Methodist Council, and Baptist World Alliance. At the local level, the principal purposes of juridical instruments are to facilitate and to order the life and mission of the particular church. In the Roman Catholic Church, for Pope John Paul II, canon law "facilitates . . . an orderly development in the life of both the ecclesial society and of the individual persons who belong to it." Laws do not replace faith, grace, and charity (*Sacrae disciplinae leges*, apostolic constitution, 1983), and the supreme law is the salvation of souls (Canon 1572). Roman canonists stress the spiritual, pastoral, educative, protective, unifying, and ecclesiological purposes of canon law. Similarly, in the Orthodox tradition, canon law is "at the service of the Church . . . to guide her members on the way to salvation." Its main function is "the spiritual growth of the faithful."[17] For Anglican churches, typically, church law exists "to serve the sacramental integrity and good order of the Church and to assist its mission and its witness to the Lord Jesus Christ" (Church in Wales, Constitution, Prefatory Note).

The notions of facility and order sometimes surface explicitly in the regulatory instruments themselves. The constitution of the Lutheran Church of Australia, for example, enables it to "fulfil the mission of the Christian Church by proclaiming the Word of God and administering the Sacraments *in accordance* with the Confession of the Church." It

---

[17] Patsovos, "The Canonical Tradition."

unites the congregations and ensures that preaching, teaching, and practice conform to the Confession, and protects the performance of duties and maintenance of rights. In short, its rules are for "the administration of its affairs" (Arts. III, VI). In other Lutheran churches, such as the Evangelical Church of Southern Africa (Natal–Transvaal), "regulations" and "instructions" "are not to be understood legally, but rather in the freedom according to the Gospel." They represent "the guiding principle for the life of the Christian in worship, congregation and world which is realised in faith, love and responsible behaviour." The Gospel is "the binding foundation for faith and life and therefore also the basis of these guidelines" (Guidelines, Introduction). The Presbyterian Church in America understands that church order exists to administer a system of government which Christ himself appointed and to protect the doctrinal standards of the church. The law and discipline of the Methodist Church of Southern Africa is designed for "the good of the entire community" and represents the "minimum" required of the faithful (Law and Discipline, Foreword).

Secondly, there is an intimate relationship between church law and theology. For Roman Catholic canonists (such as Urresti), theology is a direct (material) source for canon law. Theology concerns judgment based on knowledge obtained through and reflection upon revelation, and canon law imposes a decision based on that judgment: "every single piece of law in the church must be in the service of values either defined or at least controlled by theological reflection."[18] Others (like Corecco) see canon law as *ordinatio fidei*, a legal system born of faith. By way of contrast, some Orthodox canonists (such as Patsavos) separate theology and canon law, and Anglican canonists have not yet developed a systematic theology *of* canon law but more often recognize theology *in* canon law. Indeed, in the Lutheran and Reformed tradition (as was said at the Barmen Synod 1934), "the external juridical order of the church should be at the service of the proclamation of the word." Consequently, "the external order must be tested ever anew by the confession of faith, and on no level of legal church life can juridical questions be solved without relation to the church's confession" (Statement, May 31, 1934). In short, church law is not a "constitutive," but a "consecutive" and "regulative" element of the reality of a church.[19] Consequently, theological ideas surface explicitly (particularly in descriptive provisions) in laws of the

---

[18] L. Örsy, *Theology and Canon Law: New Horizons for Legislation and Interpretation* (Collegeville, MN: Liturgical Press, 1992).

[19] M. Reuver, *Faith and Law: Juridical Perspectives for the Ecumenical Movement* (Geneva: World Council of Churches, 2000), 4.

Roman and Eastern Catholic, Old Catholic, Orthodox, Anglican, Lutheran, Presbyterian, and Baptist churches.[20]

Thirdly, therefore, modern church law is understood to have a relationship with divine law. This arises in the regulatory instruments in four ways: divine law is the foundation of church law; church law must conform to divine law; church laws may incorporate divine law; and church law in conflict with divine law may be invalid. For the Latin Church, "the highest norm of human life is the divine law itself – eternal, objective and universal," ascertained by the teaching authority of the church (*Dignitatis Humanae*, 1965). Commonly the code presents canons as derived from divine law (for example, the faithful *ex lege divine tenentur* to do penance: Canon 207), and "no custom which is contrary to divine law can acquire the force of law" (Canon 24). According to the constitution of one Old Catholic church, the Polish National Church, the authority of ordained ministers over faith, morals, and discipline is derived from God, whereas authority in administrative, managerial, and social matters derives from "the people" (Art. VI). Orthodox churches, such as the Greek Orthodox Archdiocese in America, present themselves as "governed by the Holy Scriptures" (Charter, Art. 1). For Anglican churches, Holy Scripture is presented juridically as the ultimate standard and rule in matters of faith (and according to the Thirty-Nine Articles of Religion, "it is not lawful for the Church to ordain any thing which is contrary to God's Word written": Art. 20), but there is no obvious legal evidence which indicates a general practice that divine law binds directly in a juridical sense, nor that divine law vitiates contrary canon law. Protestantism also distinguishes *ius divinum* and *ius humanum*. Thus "[b]ecause divine Church law is a law of the Spirit, a law of grace and love, the ecclesiastical lawgiver has a corresponding legal obligation to mirror this material structure in his human Church law in so far as he can," to provide "a model for the world". As such, Lutheranism distinguishes structures of human and divine institution.[21] Thus, for

---

[20] Latin Code, Canon 834: "In the liturgy . . . our sanctification is symbolised and . . . brought about"; Statute of the Old Catholic Bishops United in the Union of Utrecht (2000), Art. 3: each local church is "a representation" of the church universal; Greek Orthodox Archdiocese of America, Charter, Art. 2: the mission of the archdiocese is to proclaim the Gospel; Church of England, Canon B30.1: marriage is "in its nature a union permanent and lifelong"; Evangelical Lutheran Church in Canada, Constitution, II.2: "Congregations find their fulfilment in the universal community of the Church, and the universal Church exists in and through congregations"; Presbyterian Church in America, Book of Church Order, I.16: "Ordinary vocation to office in the Church is the calling of God by the Spirit"; the Church Constitution Guide, North American Mission Board, A Southern Baptist Convention Agency: a local church covenant should include the "one another passages" of Scripture.
[21] See W. Steinmuller, "Divine Law and its Dynamics in Protestant Theology of Law," *Concilium* 8 (1969): 13.

example, whereas baptism and preaching are divinely instituted, forms of ministry, church organization, or worship are of human institution (Confession of Augsburg, Art. v). In turn, the laws of some Lutheran churches (such as the constitution of the Lutheran Church of Australia) recognize, typically, "the Holy Scriptures . . . as the only infallible source and norm for all matters of faith, doctrine and life" (Art. II.I); and disciplinary process is governed by "scriptural principles." Again, the courts of the Presbyterian Church in America must "uphold the laws of Scripture." The constitution of the church is itself "subject and subordinate to the Scriptures of the Old and New Testaments, the inerrant Word of God," and the "ordinances established by Christ" are listed (such as prayer, praise, reading, expounding and preaching the word of God, administering the sacraments, fasting, thanksgiving, catechizing, making offerings to relieve the poor, exercising discipline, and ordination to sacred office: Book of Church Order, Preface, 1.4, II, III).

THE EFFECT AND ENFORCEMENT OF CHURCH LAW

The extent to which, and the ways in which, regulatory instruments are binding vary as between the different churches. At the international level, for Roman Catholics world-wide, the Code of 1983 affects only the Latin Church, but its provisions bind all the faithful directly in the particular churches, bishops, clergy, and laity alike (Canons I, II). The Eastern Catholic code is similar (cc.1489–91). In the Orthodox Church there is a lively debate as to whether the canonical tradition binds in the sense of letter or of spirit.[22] The principles of canon law common to the churches of the Anglican Communion do not bind those churches internationally, but they have persuasive authority. The instruments of other global ecclesial communities bind the institutional churches (rather than the faithful of each member church directly) on the basis of their formal acceptance by churches on admission to membership. For example, "acceptance" of its constitution is required for membership of the Lutheran World Federation. In turn, full members have voting rights in the governing bodies of the World Alliance of Reformed Churches, but associate members do not. Some instruments require member churches to take those instruments into account at the local level; this is the position under the Leuenberg Agreement of the Community of Protestant Churches in

[22] See John H. Erickson, *The Challenge of Our Past: Studies in Orthodox Canon Law and Church History* (Crestwood, NY: St. Vladimir's Seminary Press, 1992).

Europe (Arts. 42–46). With some instruments the decisions of the central body of the global community bind only that body; they do not bind as to matters within the competence of the autonomous member church, as is the case under the constitution of the Standing Conference of Orthodox Bishops in the Americas (Art. 11).

At the local level, in the Roman Catholic Church, while laws bind all the faithful (ordained and lay), provision exists for the dispensation of laws (Canons 85–93). Moreover, laws do not bind if they have not been promulgated (Canon 7), or if there a doubt about the law, a *dubium legis* (Canon 14). In Orthodox churches, laws bind, but ample scope is made for their relaxation in the principle of economy. In some churches of the Anglican Communion canon laws bind only ordained ministers (as is the case in the Church of England), but in others the laws bind both ordained and lay persons (as with the Church in Wales). Often laws provide for undertakings to be made by church members to assent to or comply with the law. In the Scottish Episcopal Church, for instance, clergy must declare: "I will give due obedience to the Code of Canons" (Canon 58). In Lutheran churches, a precondition to membership is acceptance of the constitution and by-laws (as in Australia), or else classes of member "covenant" compliance (as in Canada). The position is similar in some Presbyterian churches. In the Presbyterian Church in America, for example: "All baptized persons, being members of the Church, are subject to its discipline and entitled to the benefits thereof," but "[n]o judicatory may make laws to bind the conscience" (Book of Church Order, Preface, II.8).

The administration and enforcement of law is assigned to a variety of institutions within churches. Two approaches surface. On the one hand, compliance is effected by means of executive or quasi-judicial authority. In the Roman Catholic Church, enforcement is possible through hierarchical administrative recourse (Canons 1732–55), or oaths of fidelity (such as those of bishops to the Apostolic See (Canon 380)). Orthodox archbishops may enjoy executive authority to implement laws. Anglican clergy owe canonical obedience and undertake to obey the lawful and honest directions of their bishops. Lutheran pastors may administer discipline in their congregations, and in some Presbyterian churches (such as those in America) compliance may be effected by visitation (an institution also known in Anglicanism and Roman Catholicism). On the other hand, churches provide for formal judicial law-enforcement and resolution of conflict. Courts or tribunals are ordered hierarchically and their subject matter jurisdictions are prescribed in Roman Catholicism (from courts of first instance through to tribunals of the Apostolic See), Orthodoxy (e.g., the "Spiritual

Courts" of the Greek Orthodox Archdiocese of America deal with family matters and moral and disciplinary offenses), Anglicanism (where courts deal primarily with disciplinary cases), Lutheranism (e.g., the interpretations of law by the Court of Adjudication bind in the Evangelical Lutheran Church in Canada), and Presbyterianism (e.g., the hierarchically ordered Courts of Session, Presbytery and General Assembly in the Presbyterian Church in America). However, the interpretation of law is not necessarily carried out by courts and tribunals. In the Roman Catholic Church, only the legislator may give an authentic and binding interpretation of law. Interpretation may involve recourse to parallel passages, the purposes of the law, the mind of the legislator, and – if there is a gap in the law (*lacuna legis*) – to laws on similar matters, the jurisprudence of the Roman curia, opinions of learned authors, and the principles of law observed with canonical equity (Canons 16,17,19). In Anglicanism, alongside the courts, numerous bodies may be charged with the function of authoritative interpretation, typically constitutional committees of central church assemblies. Lutheran and United Reformed churches also make provision for authoritative extra-judicial interpretation.

Failure to comply with church law may result in proceedings for offenses and the imposition of sanctions. At the international level, the instruments of global ecclesial communities commonly contain disciplinary provisions. For example, in the Lutheran World Federation, the Assembly may suspend or terminate the membership of a church by a two-thirds vote of the delegates. The Federation suspended the memberships of two churches in 1977 (which have since been restored), as did the World Alliance of Reformed Churches in 1982 (though it was lifted conditionally in 1997). In the Union of Utrecht, the Bishops' Conference may ascertain whether a bishop has "gravely harmed" the Declaration of Utrecht, the catholicity of ministry, doctrine, and worship, its Statute, or the "moral order"; it may then deprive the bishop of membership. At the local level, elaborate systems of offenses, sanctions (typically conceived as medicinal and corrective, such as rebuke, suspension, and exclusion), and restoration operate in the Roman Catholic, Orthodox, Anglican, Lutheran, and Presbyterian churches. The Presbyterian Church in America provides extensive theological justification for its system of ecclesiastical discipline.

CHURCH LAW AND CIVIL LAW

Ecclesiastical regulatory instruments sometimes deal with the relationship between the institutional church and the law of the state in which that church exists. On the one hand, most churches see no problem with the use of secular legal facilities to promote the mission of the church. The Roman Catholic Church has some general norms on the matter. Civil law is deemed incorporated in canon law when a matter is not provided for by canon law (canonization), but only if civil law is consistent with divine law (Canon 22). In the Latin Church, canon law may not derogate from concordats entered between the Holy See and a Nation-State (Canon 3), and many concordats operative today enjoy status in international law. Indeed, concordats and other agreements have proliferated in church–state relations within national borders. In Europe, for example, agreements are entered to define church–state relations, to guarantee religious freedom, and to make provision for collaboration in matters of common concern. Protestant churches (Lutheran, Reformed, and Methodist) as well as the Roman Catholic Church are parties to these agreements. Orthodox churches, too, exploit civil law facilities; the Greek Orthodox Archdiocese of America, for example, is incorporated under and recognized by civil law, and in some countries such as Greece they enjoy a formal constitutional status. Agreements have also been established between alliances of churches and the state (such as that in Poland with the alliance of Lutheran, Orthodox, Polish Catholic, Evangelical Reformed, United Methodist, Old Catholic Mariavites, and Baptist Union of Poland). This mirrors the increase in formal ecumenical instruments, such as the *Charta Oecumenica* (2001) between the Conference of European Churches and the (Roman Catholic) Council of European Bishops' Conferences – "a common commitment to dialogue and co-operation" (Preamble). The charter, however, has no binding force in church law.

On the other hand, some churches eschew close links with the state. For instance, the Book of Church Order of the Presbyterian Church in America provides: "No religious constitution should be supported by the civil power further than may be necessary for protection and security equal and common to all others." The instrument presents its own theological foundation: the power of the church is spiritual, that of the state includes the exercise of force. The constitution of the church derives from divine revelation; the constitution of the state is determined by human reason and the course of providential events. "The church has no right to construct or modify a government for the State, and the State has no right to frame a creed or polity for the Church."

The complexities of the relationships between institutional churches and the states may be illustrated by the case of the United Kingdom. In England, the Church of England is "established according to the laws of

this realm under the Queen's Majesty" (Canon A1). The incidents of establishment are well known: the monarch has "supreme authority over all
persons in all causes, as well ecclesiastical as civil" (Canon A7). The
monarch is empowered by Act of Parliament (the Appointment of Bishops
Act 1533) to appoint bishops. The Measures of the General Synod (on parliamentary approval and royal assent) have the same force and effect as Acts
of Parliament, by virtue of the Church of England Assembly (Powers) Act
1919. People who are resident in its parishes have rights at common law to
baptism, holy communion, marriage, and burial. In Scotland, the relation
of the (Presbyterian) Church of Scotland to the state is regulated by the parliamentary Church of Scotland Act 1921. The church is "a national Church
representative of the Christian Faith of the Scottish people [which]
acknowledges its distinctive call and duty to bring the ordinances of religion to the people in every parish of Scotland through a territorial ministry." The aim of the Act is "to declare the right of the Church to
self-government in all that concerned its own life and activity," and its
courts are recognized as public forums.

Other churches function in civil law as voluntary associations, and their
internal regulatory instruments have the status in civil law of terms of a
contract entered into by the members. They do so under the common law
doctrine of consensual compact (as is the case with the Latin Church), or
also by virtue of statute. As with the Church of Ireland in Northern Ireland
(under the Irish Church Act 1869), in Wales, the (Anglican) Church in
Wales is often classified as a disestablished church (though technically it was
the Church of England in Wales that was disestablished). Its laws are part
of a statutory contract (which the church may modify) provided under the
Welsh Church Act 1914, and are enforceable in matters of property in State
courts. The foundational instruments of the Methodist, Baptist, and
United Reformed churches are protected by separate parliamentary statutes
(the Methodist Church Act 1976, Baptist and Congregational Trusts Act
1951, and United Reformed Church Act 2000) and are enforceable as such
(at least with regard to property matters) in the civil courts.

CONCLUSIONS

This study is an exploratory examination of modern church law. However,
three tentative conclusions may be drawn. First, it may be possible to construct a category of "Christian law" from the similarities between the regulatory systems of churches of different traditions. Clearly, there are profound
differences between their juridical systems, flowing most obviously from

their respective theological positions on the nature of church, ministry, and rites. This is perhaps most evident in governance. In the Catholic (Latin and Eastern) and Orthodox churches, the power of governance is reserved for a clerical hierarchy, while in Anglican, Methodist, Lutheran, Presbyterian, and Reformed churches, it vests in assemblies representative of ordained and lay persons. Nevertheless, there seem to be principles of law common to all churches. For all of them, law expresses a theological self-understanding of a church. Laws function predominantly in the public sphere of church life. Scripture is a key material source for church law. Law should reflect the revealed will of God. Ecclesiastical persons and bodies should act in accordance with law. Finally, law is the servant of the church in its mission.

Second, comparative study of the modern laws of churches may provide a rich resource for dialogue and for mutual understanding on two levels: ecumenical and inter-faith. Development of the category "Christian law" shows that (despite differences in doctrine) laws and other regulatory instruments of churches reveal, in concrete form, the inner and functional character of an ecclesial community. A clear understanding of modern church laws indicates ecumenical ways in which both separation and the potential for greater visible unity among churches are conditioned in practical ways by law.[23] It might also benefit inter-faith understandings and relations.

Third, there are numerous benefits for scholarship. Comparative church law allows scholars working within a single Christian tradition to contextualize their work. The category of "Christian law" also provides a point of comparison for scholars working in the fields of Islamic, Jewish, and Hindu law (for example). Furthermore, the study of the convergences and divergences between church laws stimulates a greater understanding of the concept and role of law and of debates concerning legal pluralism. Such study may also enable states and international bodies to comprehend better the common pressures of belief and law which churches experience. In an age of multiculturalism, religious resurgence, and uncertainty, it seems particularly timely to engage in study of modern church law.

RECOMMENDED READING

Bartholomaios, Metropolitan. "A Common Code for the Orthodox Churches." *Kanon* 1 (1973): 45–53.

---

[23] In 1974 the Faith and Order Commission of the World Council of Churches adopted an Outline for the study of "The Ecumenical Movement and Church Law"; it was not pursued: see Reuver, *Faith and Law*, 5.

Beal, J. P., J. A. Coriden, and T. J. Green, eds. *New Commentary on the Code of Canon Law*, 8 vols. New York: Paulist Press, 2000.

Church Law and Polity in Lutheran Churches: Reports of the International Consultations in Järvenpää and Baastad. Geneva: Lutheran World Federation, 1979.

Corecco, E. *The Theology of Canon Law.* Pittsburgh, PA: Duquesne University Press, 1992.

Cummings, D., ed. *The Rudder (Pedalion) of the Orthodox Church or All Sacred and Divine Canons.* Chicago: Orthodox Christian Education Society, 1957.

Doe, Norman. "Towards a Critique of the Role of Theology in English Ecclesiastical and Canon Law." *Ecclesiastical Law Journal* 2 (1990–92): 328.

The Legal Framework of the Church of England: A Critical Study in a Comparative Context. Oxford: Clarendon Press, 1996.

Canon Law in the Anglican Communion: A Worldwide Perspective. Oxford: Clarendon Press, 1998.

"Canon Law and Communion." *Ecclesiastical Law Journal* 6 (2002): 241.

"The Common Law of the Anglican Communion." *Ecclesiastical Law Journal* 7 (2003): 4.

An Anglican Covenant: Theological and Legal Considerations for a Global Debate. London: SCM-Canterbury Press, forthcoming June 2008.

Doe, Norman, and R. Sandberg. "The 'State of the Union', a Canonical Perspective: Principles of Canon law in the Anglican Communion." *Sewanee Theological Review* 49: 2 (2006): 234.

Erickson, J. H. *The Challenge of Our Past: Studies in Orthodox Canon Law and Church History.* Crestwood, NY: St. Vladimir's Seminary Press, 1991.

González del Valle, J. M., and A. Hollerbach, eds. *L'enseignement du droit ecclésiastique de l'état dans les universités européennes.* Leuven: Peeters, 2005.

Kuhn, Karl Christoph. "Church Order Instead of Church Law." *Concilium* 5 (1996): 29.

Hill, M. *Ecclesiastical Law*, 2nd edn Oxford: Oxford University Press, 2001.

Lambeth Commission on Communion. *The Windsor Report.* London: Anglican Communion Office, 2004.

Motiuk, D. "The Code of Canons of the Eastern Churches: Some Ten Years Later." *Studia Canonica* 36 (2002): 189.

Nedungatt, G., ed. *A Guide to the Eastern Code: A Commentary on the Code of Canons of the Eastern Churches.* Rome: Pontificio Istituto Orientale, 2002.

Örsy, L., *Theology and Canon Law: New Horizons for Legislation and Interpretation.* Collegeville, MN: Liturgical Press, 1992.

Patsavos, L., "The Canonical Tradition of the Orthodox Church," in *A Companion to the Greek Orthodox Church*, ed. F. K. Litsas. New York: Greek Orthodox Archdiocese of North and South America, 1984.

Pospishil, V. J., *Eastern Catholic Church Law.* New York: Saint Marion, 1996.

Puza, R. and N. Doe, eds. *Religion and Law in Dialogue: Covenantal and Non-Covenantal Cooperation between State and Religion in Europe.* Leuven: Peeters, 2006.

Reuver, M. *Faith and Law: Juridical Perspectives for the Ecumenical Movement.* Geneva: World Council of Churches, 2000.

Steinmuller, W. "Divine Law and Its Dynamics in Protestant Theology of Law." *Concilium* 8 (1969): 13.

Urresti, T. "Canon Law and Theology: Two Different Sciences." *Concilium* 8 (1967): 10.

Ware, T. *The Orthodox Church.* London: Penguin Books, 1963, reprinted 1991.

Weatherhead, J. L. *The Constitution and Laws of the Church of Scotland.* Edinburgh: Board of Practice and Procedure, 1997.

16 "United States Supreme Court Building," Washington, DC.

CHAPTER FIFTEEN

Religious organizations and the state: the laws of ecclesiastical polity and the civil courts

William W. Bassett

Readers in the English tradition will immediately recognize in this title the elegant and irenic work of the great Oxford divine, Richard Hooker, published in 1593.[1] Hooker's *Laws of Ecclesiastical Polity* is the classic exposition of the *via media*, the hallmark of world-wide Anglicanism and by now a literary icon of Christian religious studies. "Polity" in the title means governance, the administration of the church and its decision-making agencies. It carries the distinction between leaders and members, their respective duties and competencies within the church, and how the church internally manages its personnel, resources, and mission. It is a signature term, carrying to a large extent the self-identity, day-to-day life, and distinctive culture of the church, as a unique kind of social organization.[2]

When we discuss the interrelationship between religious organizations and the state, we necessarily draw upon the law of the state as it prohibits or permits, limits or expands the authority of government over the order and discipline, the polity, of the churches and their agencies. In this chapter, I shall focus on the law of the United States, especially as it has been interpreted by the United States Supreme Court and been applied to Christian churches, among other religious organizations. The Supreme Court has used its own idiosyncratic and not always consistent analysis of ecclesiastical polity and administration in a significant number of cases involving churches and other religious organizations. As we shall see, after two forays into construing the meaning of canon law with a later change of mind, the Court set polity as a norm of decision in cases of schisms within churches, re-thought its own conceptualization of the administration of religious schools, judged the pastoral need of a church to expand its facilities as not compelling, and construed a church's right to religious discrimination to depend on job descriptions and roles within churches.

---

[1] Richard Hooker, *The Laws of Ecclesiastical Polity* (1593), vol. 1 of 2, in *The Complete Works of Richard Hooker*, ed. Georges Edelen and William S. Hill (Cambridge, MA: Harvard University Press, 1977–1980).   [2] See further the chapter by Norman Doe herein.

Meanwhile, lower courts have superimposed their own ideas of church administration on religious trusts, employee benefit policies, collective bargaining agreements, and ascending liability models in tort litigation. These are civil, not criminal cases, involving allegations of private, not public, injury. And, of course, in each of the more than 14,000 instances in which the word "religion" or "religious" appears in federal and state statutes, the government impliedly authorizes the civil court to determine just how religious is "religious" to meet the statutory requirements.[3] Without doubt, no strict separation of church and state is involved in this jurisprudence, notwithstanding the jurisdictional coating of "neutral principles of law" adjudication. It is a question of accommodation.

My fundamental postulate in this chapter is that matters of church polity and discipline are an exercise of religious freedom under the First Amendment to the United States Constitution. The free exercise of religion entails not only the right to believe, but also the right to worship in common, to preach, teach, assemble, organize, and administer shared resources without governmental interference. State monitoring of the internal governance of the church and its agencies threatens entanglement with religion, ceding unwarranted competency to the civil magistrate. The First Amendment was meant to address and circumvent these grave political problems.

MISSIONS AND ROLES WITHIN THE CHURCHES: AN ISSUE OF RELIGIOUS BELIEF

Richard Hooker explained the episcopal structure, sacramental ceremonies, and rituals of worship and devotion of the established church in sixteenth-century England by appeal to Scripture, ancient tradition, and a reasoned disquisition upon the uses of law. It was these authorities, he explained, that the church used to construct its primary agencies of ministry and support, the dioceses, church courts, parishes, vicarages, vestries and their incumbents, and their charitable and educational agencies. The sixteenth-century Protestant Reformation, Hooker made clear, was about reform of the church as well as reform of doctrine. Both were intertwined matters of intense confrontation and debate on the Continent and in England. Both were settled historically in practical terms, though fundamentally invoking

---

[3] A LEXIS search through all existing statutes, federal and state (searching with: "religio!" [Codes library, AllCde file]) will retrieve over 14,000 statutes in which the term "religion" or "religious" appear. Religious exemptions, specifically, appear in over 2,000 statutes (searching with: "religio" w/20 "exempt!" or "except!").

in individuals the most profound issues of religious conscience, especially during the painful specter of civil intervention – whether monarchical intervention in northern Europe or inquisitorial intervention in the Latin world. The spillover of this European system in America was a pervasive fact of social discrimination and discontent roiling in the colonies where churches were often established and financially supported by public funds.

The American constitutional framers of the eighteenth century decided not to leave religious freedom to the competing interests of the plurality of churches of the time. They enacted the First Amendment guarantee that "Congress shall make no law respecting an establishment of religion, or prohibiting the free exercise thereof." The topic of this chapter, religious organizations and the state, unites both affirmations of the First Amendment – the jurisdictional restriction upon Congress making laws respecting religious establishment, and the guarantee against laws prohibiting free exercise of religion. Organizing and administering communities of faith are as much exercises of religion as are worship and public prayer. The free exercise of religion, furthermore, is hollow and almost meaningless without the protected rights of speech and association. Only by consent or in the most exigent social circumstances can the state parse out the elements of religious organizations for what courts may denominate "secular" as distinguished from "religious" functions, that is, acts stripped of the protected exercise afforded to faith-based motivation.

THE MANY FACETS OF CHURCH POLITY

Radical divisions have marked the polities of Christianity from the Reformation to this day. Christianity is split between top-down Catholic–Orthodox episcopal hierarchies and Calvinist–Evangelical bottom-up congregational ecclesiologies, with ancillary variations in connectional, auxiliary structures for support typified by the "gathered churches." Related to the essentials of church order, of course, and supported by faith-based inspiration, are the myriad affiliated organizations of mission and service – colleges, universities, seminaries, hospitals, healthcare centers, hospices, clinics, schools, research and publication centers, social welfare organizations, retreat and retirement facilities, as well as inter- and intra-church agencies of cooperation and development. These auxiliary religious organizations and agencies that stand alongside worship centers number in the tens of thousands around the world. They figure prominently in the practical life and ministry of all the churches and bear the distinctive charism, culture, spirit, and ethos of their sponsoring religious traditions.

In order to hold title to property and effectively administer their assets with appropriate legal security, churches use various civil forms of association, both for their own incorporation and for the separate creation of auxiliary agencies. In the United States, the requirements and effects of incorporation are matters of state, not federal, law. Few American churches or religious organizations now are unincorporated associations. Most are incorporated under state statutes as non-profit corporations, as religious corporations, or as corporations sole. Public benefit agencies, such as healthcare and shelter facilities, schools, and the like usually are separately created under federal tax exemption requirements.

Religious organizations consent by implication to regulatory compliance and state surveillance when they serve the general public without discrimination and contract with the government for delivery of social or charitable programs with government funding, licensure, accreditation, or certification. Moreover, churches use the law of the state for their contracts, acquisitions, and divestments, real estate transactions, corporate formation, and other legal transactions. How the church reaches its decisions, however, and who decides for the church are matters of internal belief. For example, the role of the bishop vis-à-vis his superiors, or the pastor vis-à-vis a parish board, or the preacher vis-à-vis the trustees of a congregation, derives from ancient tradition and practice. Who in the churches may validly execute contracts binding the entire church, then, may become a matter of state law before the court. A similar question of vital importance refers to the persons whose actions or inactions may render the entire church liable for wrongdoing, thus putting into civil jeopardy the material resources and reputations of the churches before the general public.

RELIGIOUS ORGANIZATIONS AT LAW

Churches and their related healthcare, educational, and social welfare agencies have a vital interest in the integrity of titles to real estate, the enforceability of contracts, compliance with health and safety regulations, and fair and full disclosure of information necessary for reliable, legally binding choices in their administration. No doubt, like corporations generally, religious organizations are entitled to police and fire services, as well as to the advantage of associational formalities and life – the right to "legal personality," as many legal systems call it. When religious organizations appear in court or before civic agencies, therefore, judges and public officials must know how they are operated, at least for purposes of determining their standing in court, the court's subject-matter jurisdiction, and the verification of the party's legal representation. Some level of scrutiny of church polity by the state is inevitable in such cases. Constitutional separation of religion and government was never intended to be absolute, nor can it be.

Beyond participation in neutral public benefits and sharing society's necessary burdens, however, the relationship of religious organizations to the state becomes a more problematic exercise in line-drawing. Here American courts have woven an asymmetrical net to catch the intrusion of the regulatory state upon the free exercise of religion. To illustrate, I shall discuss briefly four areas in which the courts have probed deeply the polity of religious organizations – with grave civil consequences.

The law of trusts

In *Watson v. Jones* (1872),[4] the United States Supreme Court took diversity jurisdiction over a bitter schism within a Kentucky Presbyterian church over issues of slavery and abolition. The Walnut Street Church in Louisville had voted itself out of the General Assembly of the Presbyterian Church, and sought affiliation with "The Presbyterian Church of the Confederate States." The Civil War tore apart the national Presbyterian Church, as well as many others. The dividing issue here turned on the refusal of local church members to assent to the General Assembly's resolution in support of the federal government and for the abolition of slavery as a moral evil. The schism in membership left title to the local parish properties in doubt.

The Circuit Court found the subject matter of the dispute strictly ecclesiastical in character. Since the Presbyterian Church was hierarchical in polity, it upheld the jurisdiction and decision of the General Assembly as the highest authority in the church. The United States Supreme Court affirmed, holding that a court may not violate the free exercise rights of a church to decide for itself issues of ecclesiastical polity without civil interference. The Walnut Street Church, the Supreme Court reasoned, belongs rightfully to the loyal members designated by the General Assembly, not to the dissidents. If a church is hierarchical in government, its members by implication consent to the authority of its highest decision-makers. In effect, in hierarchical churches an implied trust exists over property issues essentially turning upon theological controversies, church discipline, ecclesiastical government, or the conformity of the members of the church to its standard of morals. The rule in *Watson v. Jones*, likening churches to civil

---

[4] 80 US 679 (1872).

trustees, required deferral to ultimate church decisions in matters of title and beneficial use of property after a threshold finding of the church's hierarchical polity.[5]

Later, in the chill of the Cold War, the state of New York attempted to preempt litigation over rights to church properties belonging to the Russian Orthodox Church. The state added to its Religious Corporations Law a provision that brought all the churches subject to the Patriarch of Moscow into an administratively autonomous metropolitan district covering all of North America, called the Russian Orthodox Church of All America and Canada. The purpose of the designation was to prevent political use of the churches by the appointee of the Synod in Moscow, which was presumably under Bolshevik Party influence. In a 1952 case that sought to confirm ownership of St. Nicholas Cathedral in New York, the Supreme Court struck down the state law as a violation of the Free Exercise clause of the First Amendment. The state had impermissibly intruded upon a matter of ecclesiastical government, the freedom of a church to select its own clergy.[6] In a hierarchical church, the Court reasoned, the properly authorized trustees to protect properties are the leaders of the church, not state officials.

This line of cases was capped in 1976 by the Supreme Court's decision in *Serbian Eastern Orthodox Diocese for the United States and Canada v. Milivojevich*.[7] Here, the Supreme Court of Illinois had presumed to interpret the canon law of the Serbian Orthodox Church against the highest church authorities themselves. The Holy Assembly of Bishops of the Serbian Orthodox Church in Belgrade had defrocked Bishop Dionisije Milivojevich of the American–Canadian Diocese of that church and then proceeded to reorganize the church into three dioceses. Illinois found the proceedings procedurally and substantively defective under the canon law of the church, and therefore declared the church's decision arbitrary and invalid. The Supreme Court reversed, ruling that both the inquiries made by the Illinois Supreme Court into matters of ecclesiastical cognizance and polity as well as the Court's subsequent orders were in contravention of the church's constitutional rights.

---

[5] Denial of jurisdiction to civil courts to decide issues of doctrine or internal church governance was reaffirmed in 1969 in a case of schism within a church caused by dissent in a local congregation against ordination of women: *Presbyterian Church in the United States v. Mary Elizabeth Hull Memorial Presbyterian Church*, 393 US 440 (1969). But see the following year the Supreme Court in a *per curiam* opinion upheld the Maryland Court of Appeals which had settled a church property dispute by use of neutral principles of state laws governing title to property: *Maryland and Virginia Eldership of the Churches of God v. the Church of God at Sharpsburg*, 396 US 367 (1970).
[6] *Kedroff v. Saint Nicholas Cathedral*, 344 US 94 (1952); aff'd., *Kreshnik v. Saint Nicholas Cathedral*, 363 US 190 (1960).   [7] 426 US 696 (1976).

Finally, in *Jones v. Wolf* (1979),[8] the Supreme Court brought to an end its long meditation upon the demands of the First Amendment upon courts seeking to resolve church property disputes. Title to the property of the Vineville Presbyterian Church of Macon, Georgia, was in the trustees of the church. In 1973, a majority of its members, including the pastor, voted to disaffiliate from the Augusta–Macon Presbytery of the Presbyterian Church in the United States and to join another denomination, the Presbyterian Church in America. The minority faction brought a class action suit in state court seeking to establish its right to possession and use of the church property. The Supreme Court of Georgia affirmed the trial ruling for the majority faction, based on "neutral principles of law." The court examined the deeds to the church, the state statutes dealing with implied trusts, and the denomination's Book of Church Order to determine whether there was any basis for a trust in favor of the general church. Finding nothing that would give rise to a trust in any of these documents, the Georgia court awarded the property on the basis of its legal title, which was in the local church. Without further elaboration the court decreed that the local congregation was represented by the majority faction.

The Supreme Court found that a civil court could examine property deeds as well as the church's constitution and corporate charter in purely secular terms to avoid entanglement with religion or breach of neutrality. Neutral principles of adjudication avoid both interpretation of doctrine and analysis of polity to seek the locus of authority in churches. *Jones v. Wolf* was the last case in which the United States Supreme Court heard an appeal in an intra-church property dispute. Thereafter, administrators of religious organizations were put on notice to provide in documents of title the exact rights of ownership should religious differences cause schisms within the churches.[9]

The Supreme Court's mandate to the lower courts to adhere to neutral principles of adjudication and to avoid entanglement in religious controversies continues to pose serious dilemmas where judges wade into property transactions, employment contracts, or charitable donations made to the advancement of religion. Briefly, in the latter case, the most fundamental premise of trust law, namely, that the law will provide enforcement of the settlor's intent in making a lasting gift to a religious charity, is put

---

[8] 443 US 595 (1979).

[9] *Jones v. Wolf* is generally followed in state law. See, e.g., *Protestant Episcopal Church v. Barker*, 115 Cal. App. 3d 599 (1981), *cert. den.*, 454 US 864 (1981) ("California has rejected the hierarchical theory as a basis for resolution of church property disputes and has adopted in its place neutral principles of law.").

into jeopardy. If a trust is settled upon a purpose of advancing religion, or a specific religion, or to be administered according to religious law, without naming a specific civil corporation as trustee or beneficiary, it will be unenforceable for lack of neutral principles adjudication. Neutral principles adjudication holds evidence of the settlor's religious beliefs to be inadmissible.

Public aid to religious schools

The United States Department of Education oversees a vast budget of over 500 programs providing funding to state and local school administrations, accredited colleges and universities, and individual students throughout the United States. In 2007, for example, the Department guaranteed $62 billion in new student loans. The Department's funding of programs in which religiously affiliated educational organizations may participate are too numerous to list here. Added to this enormous pool of money are the billions of dollars provided by the separate states, not only to public education but also to separate remedial and enrichment programs more broadly available. The jurisprudence of the Supreme Court respecting First Amendment issues where religious organizations contract for funding with federal or state governments is sufficiently complex to illustrate a significant part of the relationship of law and religion in the arena of public service.

The administration of colleges and universities affiliated with the churches has been profoundly affected by the availability of government funding; that of secondary and elementary parochial schools less so, but still significantly. The cost of dependency upon the state has sometimes resulted in the loss of religious identity by the church. Programmatic funding conditions, as well as subsequent surveillance for compliance purposes, are often more stringent than the demands of licensing and accreditation.

A good example is the Supreme Court case of *Tilton v. Richardson* (1971).[10] To meet a strong nationwide demand for the expansion of college and university facilities to meet the rising numbers of students in need of higher education, Congress in 1963 passed the first major program of federal aid to supply construction subsidies to build and upgrade academic facilities in both private and public colleges and universities. As they had participated in the GI Bill earlier without question or legal challenge, religious colleges and universities expected to have a share in this more permanent

---

[10] 403 US 672 (1971).

federal program, too. Title I of the Higher Education Facilities Act of 1963 provided construction grants and guaranteed long-term low interest loans for buildings and facilities used exclusively for secular educational purposes, but not for sectarian instruction, religious worship, or divinity schools or departments. Four small Catholic colleges in Connecticut received funds under the Act. Two used the money to build libraries, one added a science center; another a language laboratory; and the last a music, drama, and theatre building. A coalition of taxpayers sued in federal court to invalidate the appropriations as a violation of the Establishment Clause of the First Amendment.

The Supreme Court, in a 5–4 decision, over a bitter dissent, affirmed the constitutionality of the federal funding program, with one important caveat. After finding Congressional intent to include in the Act all colleges and universities regardless of religious affiliation, the Court confirmed the facilities were in compliance with its conditions. There had been no religious services or worship in federally financed facilities, there were no religious symbols or plaques in or on them, and they had been used solely for non-religious purposes. Regardless of compliance, petitioners urged that the Act itself was unconstitutional to the extent public funds went, directly or indirectly, to religiously affiliated institutions. The Court disagreed, distinguishing higher education from elementary and secondary schools, for which the ban on funding was absolute.[11] Religion does not so permeate the secular education supplied by church-related colleges and universities, the Court reasoned, that their religious and secular functions are, in fact, inseparable. Academic freedom characterized the schools rather than religious indoctrination. All four institutions subscribed to the "Statement of Principles on Academic Freedom and Tenure" endorsed by the American Association of University Professors and the Association of American Colleges. None imposed religious restrictions in admissions, required attendance at religious activities, compelled obedience to doctrines and dogmas of the faith, required instruction in the sponsor's theology and doctrine, or worked to propagate a particular religion. The single section of the Act the Court found unconstitutional was a twenty-year sunset on the conditions. The Court struck out any limit under which the facilities could ever be converted to religious use. *Tilton v. Richardson* was quickly broadcast, with the Court's findings in fact and in general turning into a list of compliance factors for religious colleges and universities to use to

---

[11] *Tilton* was issued together with *Lemon v. Kurtzman,* 403 US 602 (1971) (banning state salary supplements to teachers in parochial grade and high schools).

qualify for federal grant monies. Religious symbolism disappeared from sub-
sidized buildings at religious colleges and universities. Devotional faith slipped
from center stage into catalogues of elective courses in "religious studies."[12]

While the Supreme Court, from 1948 forward, busied itself with
purging the nation's public elementary and secondary schools of every
vestige of religion, it also found time to track down for condemnation
every measurable trace of public aid it could find in parochial schools.[13]
In the process, the Court subjected the parochial school systems, administrators, teachers, and textbooks to exacting investigation. The focus of
their inquisition ran from state reimbursement of incidental educational
costs to parents, to salary supplements for teachers, to textbooks on loan,
to possibilities of sharing collateral student services, to use of instructional
materials.[14]

Some of the Court's decisions had tragic consequences. *Aguilar v. Felton*
(1985)[15] is a good case in point. The school district of New York had suc-
cessfully administered federally funded remedial education programs on
the premises of parochial schools for nineteen years before being stopped
by a taxpayers' lawsuit. Title I of the Elementary and Secondary Schools Act
of 1965 authorized the Secretary of Education to distribute financial assistance to local school districts to meet the needs of educationally deprived
children from low-income families. Federal funds paid teachers to staff programs approved by local and state educational agencies in public and
private schools. The subject matter of the courses was entirely secular. The
Court, however, held that the Establishment Clause constitutes an "insur-
mountable barrier" to the use of federal funds to send public school teachers and other professionals into religious schools to carry on instruction,
remedial or otherwise. New York's carefully written guidelines to secure
neutrality, to separate religious and state personnel, and to strip classrooms
of religious symbols were not enough to save the program. The Court based

---

[12] In *Hunt v. McNair*, 413 US 734 (1973), the Court approved South Carolina's creation of an agency
to issue state bonds, proceeds of which were to be used by subsidizing religious colleges. In *Roemer
v. Board of Public Works of Maryland*, 426 US 736 (1976), the Court sanctioned unrestricted annual
grants to private colleges, including religious ones, subject only to the condition that no funds be
used for "sectarian purposes," to be verified annually by affidavit.

[13] See *Board of Education v. Allen*, 392 US 256 (1968) (secular textbooks loans permitted); *Lemon v.
Kurtzman*, 403 US 602 (1971) (state salary supplements for parochial school teachers not permitted);
Committee for Public Education and Religious Liberty v. Nyquist, 413 US 756 (1973) (reimbursement
for expenses of state exams not permitted); *Meek v. Pittenger*, 421 US 349 (1975) (loan of textbooks
upheld; auxiliary aid struck down); *Wolman v. Walter*, 433 US 229 (1977) (lists of permissible and
non-permissible instructional aids); *Committee for Public Education and Religious Liberty v. Regan*,
444 US 646 (1980) (costs of correcting state exams non-reimbursable).

[14] Only Minnesota's across-the-board educational expenses tax deduction for parents of both public
and private schools survived; see *Mueller v. Allen*, 463 US 388 (1983).   [15] 473 US 402 (1985).

its decision on two considerations: (1) partnering the school board with parochial school administrators to provide for logistics and scheduling would require monitoring, which could lead to excessive entanglement of the state with religion; and (2) impressionable schoolchildren may mistake the presence of volunteer public employees in the schools as an endorsement of religion. The salient finding of the Court was that aid would be provided to and in a "pervasively sectarian environment." Thus, nothing could save the program from excessive and enduring entanglement as long as it was conducted on parochial school premises, even after normal school hours. *Aguilar* spawned a new bureaucracy and a multimillion-dollar industry leasing off-premises mobile classrooms to public school districts to keep Title 1 programs just outside the property line.

A decade later, in *Agostini v. Felton* (1997),[16] the Supreme Court reversed *Aguilar* and vacated the injunction against on-premises Title 1 instruction, leaving the program unchanged except for the location of classes. The Court abandoned the presumption that any aid to a parochial school necessarily aids religion, as well as the suspicion that religious schools are so pervasively sectarian that they cannot teach secular subjects with a neutral perspective.

As to the presence of publicly salaried personnel on premises of parochial schools, one of the major worries in earlier cases, the Court flinched a bit in an opinion, simply approving their presence where reasonably necessary for the well-being of disabled students. In *Zobrest v. Catalina Foothills School District* (1993), the Court upheld provision to pay a sign-language interpreter, under federal disability law, to accompany a deaf student in a Catholic high school.[17] The Court approved of the aid as part of an overall statute that "distributed benefits neutrally" to students in public, private, and religious schools and simply allowed the family to choose the school for their child. The interpreter would be in the school only as a result of parental decision, not by a direct government grant to the school.[18] She was a conduit of the religious message taught, not an advocate.

Following *Agostini* and depending upon its authority, the Court in *Mitchell v. Helms* (2000)[19] upheld a lending program to parochial schools "of educational and instructional materials, library services and materials, assessments, references, computer software and hardware for instructional

---

[16] 521 US 203 (1997).   [17] 509 US 1 (1993).

[18] In *Witters v. Washington Department of Services for the Blind*, 474 US 481 (1986), the Court upheld a state vocational rehabilitation assistance to the blind program cash grant to a blind student who was studying for the ministry in a Christian college. The Supreme Court upheld the grant as a benefit to the person, not the school directly, despite the issuing state program's argument that the grant benefited the school.   [19] 530 US 793 (2000).

use, and other curricular materials" funded by the federal government. In *Zelman v. Simmons Harris* (2002),[20] the Court further upheld a state-funded voucher program that allowed parents with children in a chronically failing public school to send their children to alternative public or private schools, including several cooperating Christian schools. The Court found that the voucher program did not have the "purpose" or "effect" of advancing or inhibiting religion, but was a neutral aid program implemented by the pure private choice of the parents. The Court disregarded the danger of "divisiveness" and "religious strife" as an independent factor of Establishment clause analysis.[21]

Employment policies of churches and religious organizations

From 1979 to 1986, the Supreme Court handed down decisions in four cases specifically involving religious organizations and religious employers. The lower courts have built upon these cases, adding rules derived from the intra-church dispute decisions, to emphasize the free exercise rights of churches to control ministerial appointments as the "lifeblood" of their missions. In these cases, the civil courts held their jurisdiction in deference. A short review of the Supreme Court's cases will preface consideration of some newer issues in employment law for religious organizations.

In *National Labor Relations Board v. The Catholic Bishop of Chicago* (1979),[22] the National Labor Relations Board had taken jurisdiction of lay faculty members in various parochial schools and certified elections preparatory to mandatory collective bargaining. Several high schools challenged the Board's jurisdiction under the First Amendment. Because of the intimate role of teachers in parochial schools in fulfilling the religious mission of the schools, as well as the possibility of impermissible entanglement in adjudication of "unfair labor practices" in administrative decisions in the schools, the Court held the Board lacked jurisdiction absent a clear expression of Congress to the contrary.

United States v. Lee (1992) involved an employer who refused to withhold and remit social security payments for employees on the basis of conscientious objection to the national social welfare program. The Court held that the national interest in the integrity of the social security system, in which

---

[20] 536 US 639 (2002).
[21] Since *Zelman* the Florida Supreme Court has denied the state constitutionality of school vouchers to pay tuition in parochial schools: see *Bush v. Holmes*, 919 So. 2d 392 (Fla. 2006).
[22] 440 US 490 (1979).

as many workers as possible are enrolled and contributing, prevails over the religious objections of the employer.[23]

In *Tony and Susan Alamo Foundation v. Secretary of Labor* (1985), a religious foundation was charged with violating the wages, hours, and reporting provisions of The Fair Labor Standards Act in operating small businesses by the use of services freely contributed by its members. Even though the Foundation sought to prove the religious mission and nature of its overall program of drug and alcohol rehabilitation, the Court refused a religious exemption, finding instead that the secular activities were a predominant part of the Foundation's work.[24]

In *Corporation of the Presiding Bishop of the Church of Jesus Christ of Latter-Day Saints v. Amos* (1987),[25] the Court upheld a federal exemption that allowed religious organizations to discriminate on the basis of religion in all their activities (secular as well as religious). In this case, a maintenance engineer in a church-related recreational center was dismissed from his employment for failure to observe his religious obligations. The Court reasoned that, without the broadened exemption allowing religious employers to engage in religious discrimination, it would be a "significant burden on a religious organization to require it, on pain of substantial liability, to predict which of its activities a secular court will consider secular."

From these Supreme Court precedents, the Fifth Circuit Court of Appeals has fashioned what is known as the "ministerial exemption" from anti-discrimination laws. In *McClure v. Salvation Army* (1972),[26] an ordained minister brought an action against the church for wrongful dismissal, as well as discriminatory employment practices based upon her gender. The Fifth Circuit held that where ministers of religion are concerned, the courts completely lack jurisdiction to object on any of the statutory discriminatory grounds.[27] Today, the federal courts and most state courts concur in upholding the "ministerial exception." The exception, indeed, has been extended beyond the category of ordained ministers to professors of theological subjects, teachers and principals in parochial schools, kosher supervisors, and choir directors. Decisions in all of these cases necessarily require courts to probe the polity of church organizations and distinguish employment roles in them as religious or secular in nature.

---

[23] 455 US 252 (1982).

[24] 471 US 290 (1985). See also *Jimmy Swaggart Ministries v. Board of Equalization of California*, 493 US 378 (1990), holding that when a religious crusader (taxpayer) chooses to engage in commercial activities (selling books and souvenirs), it should be treated as a business for tax purposes.

[25] 483 US 327 (1987).   [26] 460 F. 2d 553 (5th Cir. 1972).

[27] See also *Rayburn v. General Conference of Seventh-Day Adventists*, 772 F. 2d 1164 (4th Cir. 1985) (gender discrimination claim disallowed in ministerial termination case).

Civil liability

Churches and religious organizations may be sanctioned by the state for crimes committed, even by their representative agents, unknown or without consent of their membership. The First Amendment contains no defense against criminal indictment. This is the meaning of the belief/conduct dichotomy in the Free Exercise clause of the First Amendment announced by the Supreme Court of the United States in the famous *Reynolds v. United States* case in 1879 dealing with criminal liability for polygamy.[28]

Corporate liability not for crimes but to pay compensation for civil injuries caused by the intentional acts or negligence attributed by law to the entity itself is a complex matter of another kind. These civil cases crowd court dockets regularly. They concern what is known at law as "ascending liability." Each case turns not only on fault and/or causation, but also on the polity of the institution charged with payment. Who was at fault? What was the person's role or position in the organization? What is the standard of care, and how did the breach occur? How much of the organization's resources can be reached for compensation? What are the terms of title or the limits upon insurance coverage? To address these kinds of questions, courts, lawyers, accountants, expert witnesses, insurers, and plaintiffs must know the ecclesiastical law, as well as the charter and by-laws of the civil shell giving anonymity to the personnel administering the religious organization, be it a sanctuary of worship, a school, a hospice, a shelter, or a workplace that is before the court. Where crimes, creditors' claims, compensation for personal injury, or bankruptcy are at issue, the state combs deeply the organizational fabric of a given religious organization to answer these types of questions.

For example, under what circumstances can the act or omission of an individual render an entire church or religious school liable for satisfaction and compensation? In fact, case law distinguishes the responsible party by role, that is, whether the person is an officer, director, an employee, or a volunteer of the church. The law also determines whether the act or omission falls within a course of conduct proper or beneficial to the organization, or under its official control. Finally, case law finds legal significance in the expectations of persons and entities dealing with the church or religious institution.

To render these final decisions, the courts must indulge in comparisons and analogies. Judges and juries will see religious organizations and activities

---

[28] *Reynolds v. United States*, 98 US 145, 164 (1879): "Congress was deprived of all legislative power over mere opinion, but was left free to reach actions which were in violation of social duties or subversive of good order."

through the mirror of their secular counterparts. The more closely they resemble the secular, the more secure the courts are in adjudication of their affairs along entirely neutral, or non-religious, grounds. Two reported cases will exemplify the central role of ecclesiastical polity and governance in the resolution of civil liability cases brought against churches and religious organizations.

A classic decision is *Barr v. United Methodist Church* (1979),[29] involving a failed retirement home located in California and 1,900 claimants seeking recovery of the money they had invested in lifetime retirement contracts. The home itself was separately incorporated and administered, though it bore the name and in its literature professed to follow the mission of the United Methodist Church in caring for the bodily and spiritual needs of its guests. The disappointed claimants urged the California court to take under submission the polity and governance of the national church, which was not a separate corporation, but rather, in California law, an unincorporated association. In state law, an unincorporated business association could be held liable for the obligations of its members. The state court held the rule applicable even though the national Methodist Church had never received any of the claimants' money. Moreover, on the basis of name and literature, the court found that persons investing in the retirement contracts would expect to have those contracts guaranteed by the United Methodist Church itself. Thus determined, the court required the United Methodist Church nationwide to reimburse $21 million to the contract-holders. In spite of the best efforts of the administration of the retirement home to follow the state law of non-profit corporations to protect their corporate independence, the court used the Methodist Book of Discipline to impose its own notion of church governance on the national church. The court imagined the United Methodist Church to be like a business corporation.

A second case, *John Does 1-9 v. Compcare, Inc.* (1988),[30] comes out of the library of reported cases of liability for negligent supervision that are snaring the corporate assets of Catholic dioceses to pay the claims of abuse victims of wandering clergymen. In this case, a priest was placed on leave for therapy, the bishop in good faith doing all he could to protect possible victims as well as assist the priest under the terms of the canon law. The offending priest was incardinated in the Catholic Diocese of Lafayette, Louisiana. His bishop sent him to Spokane, Washington, paid for the expenses of therapy there, entrusting him to the licensed medical facility.

[29] 90 Cal. App. 3d 259 (1979), *cert. den.*, 444 US 973 (1979).   [30] 763 P. 2d 1237 (Wash. 1988).

After releasing the priest from therapy, the treatment center informed the bishop that the priest should not be assigned to any work with adolescent boys. On his own, the priest obtained a position as a counselor in an alcohol rehabilitation center in Spokane. Several months later he was fired from the center because of complaints of sexual abuse by former patients. In the lawsuit brought by the victims joining the Catholic Diocese of Lafayette with the facility in Spokane, the court interpreted the canon law of the Catholic Church to find that the diocese of incardination had control over the priest in all phases of his life, notwithstanding the suspension and the fact that the priest was no longer on the diocesan payroll. Knowledge of the priest's continued propensities was imputed to the Bishop of Lafayette, with corresponding negligence in supervision. In fact, the canon law provides no such control, nor is there any basis whatsoever in church law for the decision imputing knowledge of the prospect of harm to the bishop. A higher standard of care was imposed on the church than would have been conceivable if the offender had been a public school teacher from Louisiana, changing his domicile and job to Washington.

CONCLUSIONS

Churches and other religious organizations are privileged at state law, not because of the charity they do, the public welfare they provide, the art and education they inspire and underwrite, all of which otherwise would be a charge upon the government, but because of what religion is and was understood to be by the framers of the United States Constitution. Religion can be thought of as the service of God; in this sense, it is a transcendent claim upon personal conscience superior to the government and antecedent to its creation. The Free Exercise of religion is not a right created by the state, capable of being withheld or subdivided as government property. It is the inalienable human right of persons and communities for the protection of which citizens consented to the formation of government originally.

The First Amendment protects religion in this country because it serves in and of itself a transcendent role in personal and social life. The First Amendment religion clauses in both their constitutional affirmations are not esteemed as instrumentalities of the state for the tranquility of order, or used to motivate the greatest sacrifices in hard times, or to gird the purest forms of patriotism. Religion is a supreme value in itself, not a hybrid. It is not because religion or personal spirituality are unimportant that they are separated from the authority of the Congress or the state legislatures.

Rather, the opposite is true: the Constitution, without any doubt, deems religion so supremely important that the state is radically limited in its ability to comprehend or control its expression.[31]

The First Amendment protects the religious freedom of both individuals and groups. It withholds from Congress legislative authority not only to establish religion, but also to quell denominational rivalries, or even to provide disincentives to competition and political discourse. The Establishment Clause is used to prohibit Congress from sponsoring, endorsing, funding, advancing, or promoting a church or a number of churches, or from active involvement in religious activities in general. The purity and greatness of the American experiment with religious liberty is that the Constitution puts religion above legislative authority by separating it as much as humanly possible from the fray of politics or the din of litigation. The protection of religion did not aim to create a secular society stripped of its vitality, but, on the contrary, a society strengthened by its creativity and voluntary call to conscience. Religion engenders, instills, motivates, and sustains values that the state cannot create, not by what it does, but by what it is.

This chapter has outlined some results of the great efforts jurists in the American legal system have made to balance the needs of organized religion with those of society through nearly two hundred years of intense scrutiny of the polity of the churches. The administration, functions, missions, roles, and competencies of Christian churches have never been overlooked by the courts, and, frequently, have been evaluated by analogy to civil counterparts. Out of this legal history has come a peculiar vocabulary of trust law, cast upon a screen of constitutional ambiguity that is the notion of incorporation itself and of its relationship to distinctively American notions of federalism and freedom.

RECOMMENDED READING

Ariens, Michael S. and Robert A. Destro. *Religious Liberty in a Pluralistic Society.* Durham, NC: Carolina Academic Press, 1996.

Bassett, William W. *Religious Organizations and the Law.* 2 vols. Eagan, MN: Thomson-West, 1997–2007.

Curry, Thomas J. *The First Freedoms: Church and State in America to the Passage of the First Amendment.* New York: Oxford University Press, 1986.

Farewell to Christendom: The Future of Church and State in America. Oxford: Oxford University Press, 2001.

Esbeck, Carl H. "The Establishment Clause as a Structural Restraint on Government Powers." *Iowa Law Review* 84 (1998): 1.

---

[31] See further the chapter by David Little herein.

"Dissent and Disestablishment: The Church–State Settlement In the Early American Republic." *Brigham Young University Law Review* (2004): 1385.

Hamburger, Philip. *Separation of Church and State*. Cambridge, MA: Harvard University Press, 2002.

Laycock, Douglas. "Formal, Substantive, and Disaggregated Neutrality Towards Religion." *DePaul Law Review* 39 (1990): 39.

McConnell, Michael W. "The Origins and Historical Understanding of Free Exercise of Religion." *Harvard Law Review* 103 (1990): 1409.

"Establishment and Disestablishment at the Founding." *William & Mary Law Review* 44 (2003): 2105.

McConnell, Michael W., John H. Garvey, and Thomas C. Berg. *Religion and the Constitution*. 2nd edn. New York: Aspen Publishers, 2006.

Nichols, Joel A. "Religious Liberty in the Thirteenth Colony: Church–State Relations in Colonial and Early National Georgia." *New York University Law Review* 80 (2005): 1693.

Noonan, John T., Jr. *The Lustre of Our Country: The American Experience of Religious Freedom*. Berkeley: University of California Press, 1998.

Noonan, John T., Jr., and Edward McGlynn Gaffney, Jr., *Religious Freedom: History, Cases, and Other Materials on the Interaction of Religion and Government*. New York: Foundation Press, 2001.

Serritella, James A., ed. *Religious Organizations in the United States: A Study of the Identity, Liberty, and the Law*. Durham, NC: Carolina Academic Press, 2006.

Witte, John, Jr. *Religion and the American Constitutional Experiment*. 2nd edn. Boulder, CO: Westview Press, 2005.

CHAPTER SIXTEEN

Christianity and the large-scale corporation

David A. Skeel, Jr.

Ask most people what they associate with "Christianity and the corporation" and, at least in the United States, they may mention activist nuns calling for shareholder votes on sweatshop labor, nuclear weapons, or divestment from South Africa, or perhaps a newspaper story about mutual funds that invest only in "faith-friendly" corporations. Each is a contemporary manifestation of relations that run far deeper, and date back well over a thousand years. The church spawned many of the largest corporate enterprises of the Middle Ages, and tenaciously promoted the concept of a collective entity distinct from the state. When the modern large-scale corporation emerged in the nineteenth century, Christian responses were more complicated. Many worried about the effects of limited liability, and Evangelical populists insisted that railroads and other large corporations needed to be tamed by governmental regulation. But others held very different views. More recently, Christian perspectives have tended to divide between those who view large-scale corporations as an essential counterbalance to state power that should be free from governmental interference, and those who favor a much firmer regulatory grip.

This chapter traces these Christian attitudes toward and influence on the large-scale corporation. The chapter begins with the pre-history, the emergence of key attributes of the corporate form in Western Europe in the late Roman Empire and thereafter. From there, it turns to England and the United States, where the corporation achieved its modern form in the mid nineteenth century. The remainder of the chapter focuses on the United States, which saw a remarkable proliferation of large, widely held corporations as a result of the so-called Great Merger Wave at the end of the nineteenth century. We are now in the midst of another upheaval. While the corporate form itself has not changed, the advent of new financing techniques has simultaneously provided new tools for, and put more pressure on, corporate managers. It is too early to define the Christian contributions

17 "Erie Railway, Bradford Division, Bridge 27.66."

to these developments with any precision, but it is just the right time to consider some of the possibilities.

Because the chapter focuses on large-scale corporations, it treats partnerships and some of the new business entity forms that have emerged in recent decades only in passing. But it will refer to exciting recent work that explores these other developments. Because of my own religious orientation, and because the center of gravity shifts to the United States when large-scale corporations emerge, the chapter also has a somewhat Protestant feel. But Catholic thought and influence feature both in the beginning and in the end.

PRE-HISTORY OF THE MODERN CORPORATION

The standard definition of the corporation focuses on five key characteristics: (1) limited liability (meaning that the corporation's shareholders are not personally liable for its debts); (2) free transferability of ownership interests (shares can be sold by one investor to another); (3) continuity of existence (the corporation is "immortal"; it continues indefinitely, even if individual shareholders die or go bankrupt); (4) centralized management (the management role is distinct from ownership, so that the corporation can be run by professional managers who need not own stock); and (5) entity status (the corporation is a distinct entity with, among other things, the power to hold property and to sue or be sued in its own name). By contract and in its constitutional documents, a corporation may waive one or more of these attributes. Small corporations often restrict the transferability of the company's stock to ensure that it does not get into undesirable hands, for instance, and shareholders relinquish a portion of their limited liability if they agree to guarantee a key corporate obligation such as a bank loan. But in principle, corporations have each of the five characteristics.

The most recognizable and consciously sought after attribute is the first, limited liability. Limited liability is indeed hugely important; as we shall see, it occasioned sharp rhetorical clashes in nineteenth-century England, with theological artillery used by all sides. But in a series of pathbreaking recent articles, Henry Hansmann and Reinier Kraackman (joined in their most recent effort by Richard Squire) contend that the key historical development actually was legal recognition of the last of the attributes, entity status.[1] Of particular importance is the quality they call "entity shielding."

---

[1] Henry Hansmann, Reinier Kraakman, and Richard Squire, "Law and the Rise of the Firm," *Harvard Law Review* 119 (2006): 1333; Henry Hansmann and Reinier Kraakman, "The Essential Role of Organization Law," *Yale Law Journal* 110 (2000): 387.

If the entity is governed by "weak" entity shielding, as partnerships are, creditors of the entity have first claims to its assets, prior to any claims of creditors of the owners of the entity. Thus, if a partnership fails, its assets are distributed to partnership creditors before any creditors of individual partners are entitled to any share. With corporations, which enjoy "strong" entity shielding, another type of entity shielding is added: liquidation protection. Neither a shareholder nor a personal creditor of a shareholder can force the corporation to pay out the shareholder's ownership stake in the corporation. It is far more difficult than with a partnership for shareholders to liquidate their stake; consequently, the corporate entity has superior staying power.[2]

Not only does entity shielding provide essential benefits (it simplifies the monitoring that entity creditors need to do, and reduces the risk that vibrant enterprises will be dismembered if an owner dies or goes bankrupt), it also is the only attribute of a corporation that enterprising business people could not have achieved privately, even with clever use of contractual provisions. To make sure that the claims of entity creditors came first, each owner would need to persuade every one of her current and future personal creditors to agree by contract to subordinate their own claims against entity assets to creditors of the entity. To make matters worse, each owner would be tempted to cheat, since creditors might be willing to extend personal credit on more generous terms if their potential claim against the entity were *not* subordinated. The law solves this dilemma by providing entity shielding as one of the attributes that comes with the decision to form a corporation.

The key characteristics of the corporation emerged fitfully over the centuries, with bursts of innovation occurring at irregular intervals.[3] Its antecedents are often traced to ancient Rome, which developed a variety of private business forms that foreshadow the modern corporation in some respects. The *peculium*, which governed assets managed by a Roman's slave, appears to have enjoyed limited liability: creditor suits against the slave's master were limited to the value of the *peculium* itself. When a group of investors bid on state contracts, they established an entity, the *societas publicanorum*, that functioned very much like a modern limited partnership. Investors who did not participate in management enjoyed limited liability, whereas managing partners were personally liable for the debts of the

---

[2] The most elaborate form of entity shielding, "complete" entity shielding, insulates the entity from claims by anyone except the entity's creditors. Hansmann *et al.*, "Law and the Rise of the Firm," 1338 (listing non-profit corporations and trusts as familiar examples).

[3] The discussion in this paragraph draws on *ibid.*

venture. Ownership interests were freely traded, and the *societas publicanorum* appears to have been subject to strong entity shielding with respect to its limited partners.

A few centuries later, in medieval and Renaissance Italy, the resurgence of vibrant commercial enterprise was accompanied by another cluster of new business forms. The *compagnia*, the principal partnership form, evolved to provide a geographically oriented form of weak entity shielding: local *compagnia* creditors enjoyed priority, a status both reflected in and reinforced by the hub-and-spoke framework used by the Medici banking empire, with separate partnerships for each of the cities where the bank established a presence. Like the Roman *societas publicanorum*, the Italian *commenda*, which was first used for shipping ventures, resembled the modern limited partnership, with limited liability, strong entity shielding, and tradable partnership interests. Later still, in the seventeenth and eighteenth centuries, the forbears of today's giant publicly held corporations emerged. The Dutch East India Company and England's East India Company were given limited liability and strong entity shielding by their respective sovereigns; these protections, as well as the monopoly privileges the companies enjoyed, fueled a vibrant market in their shares.

Throughout this early history, the Catholic Church played a prominent role in legitimizing corporate enterprise. "[T]he church rejected the Roman view that apart from public corporations . . . only collegia recognized as corporations by the imperial authority were to have the privileges and liberties of corporations," Harold Berman has written. "In contrast, under canon law any group of persons which had the requisite structure and purpose – for example an almshouse or a hospital or a body of students, as well as a bishopric or, indeed, the Church Universal – constituted a corporation, without special permission of a higher authority."[4] The participants in Christian enterprises, which included many of the largest businesses of the medieval and early modern period, entered into contracts and defended against debt collection actions as a collective, rather than as individuals. Only much later did they begin to own property collectively, however; Christian enterprises hewed to the Germanic practice of holding assets in the names of each of the members.[5] One scholar has recently attributed the popularity and acceptance of corporate enterprise to the absence of strong states after the decline of the Roman Empire. "The consequent power vacuum provided incentives

---

[4] Harold J. Berman, *Law and Revolution: The Formation of the Western Legal Tradition* (Cambridge, MA: Harvard University Press, 1983), 216, 219. See further the chapters by Berman, R. H. Helmholz, and Brian Pullan herein. [5] Berman, *Law and Revolution*, 219.

as well as opportunities to institute private legal systems as a means of enhancing organizational efficiency," he argues, with particular reference to the development of canon law. "The resulting process of incorporation fed on itself as new corporations increased experience and familiarity with decentralized governance."[6] The church-related corporations that thrived in this environment differed from modern for-profit corporations in crucial respects due to their non-profit status. Other than salaries, they were not permitted to make distributions to their members; nor did they have tradable ownership interests. This meant that many of the characteristic dilemmas of modern corporations, such as the need to police distributions and to protect minority shareholders from oppression by the majority, did not arise in the same way in even the largest Christian enterprises. But the church was squarely in the middle of the early evolution of the corporation, not just acceding to the idea of collective, non-public enterprise but serving as its most important exemplar.

NINETEENTH-CENTURY IDEOLOGY AND THE MODERN CORPORATION

While there were important predecessors, such as the Dutch East India Company and the East India Company in the seventeenth and eighteenth centuries, the modern corporation truly came into its own in England and the United States in the nineteenth century. Two further regulatory developments set the stage. The first was a radical loosening of the constraints on forming a corporation. In 1720, England had enacted the Bubble Act to curb the formation of joint-stock companies, the predecessors of the modern corporation. The Bubble Act "was widely understood to have been enacted for the benefit of the South Sea Company," historian Stuart Banner has noted, "as a means of driving a large swath of alternative investment vehicles from the market, thus channeling more capital into South Sea shares."[7] But when a bubble of speculative investment burst shortly after its enactment, the Bubble Act served as a general indictment of joint-stock companies. Under the Act, the only way to obtain all the benefits of the corporate form was to petition the crown for a formal charter. It was quite difficult to obtain a charter, which meant that the number of new corporate charters was quite small.

---

[6] Timur Kuran, "The Absence of the Corporation in Islamic Law: Origins and Persistence," *American Journal of Comparative Law* 53 (2005): 785, 793.

[7] Stuart Banner, *Anglo-American Securities Regulation: Cultural and Political Roots, 1690–1860* (Cambridge: Cambridge University Press, 1998), 76.

The same stance toward corporations also made its way across the Atlantic to America. From the beginning, the states were the ones who dispensed corporate charters (this tradition explains why so much of US corporate law continues to be regulated by the states today); and state lawmakers initially were quite stingy with this privilege. Most states granted only a handful each year, and most went either to non-profit entities like churches or schools, or to very specific projects. If a state needed a bridge or canal, it would grant a charter to a bridge- or canal-building company. In practice, these corporations were more like branches of state government – like little administrative agencies – than like the corporations of today.

During the course of the nineteenth century, however, the genteel pattern of carefully regulated corporate charters began to break down as opportunities to make money in mining, manufacturing, and other areas proliferated. In England, entrepreneurs had long evaded the strictures of the Bubble Act by creating unincorporated joint-stock companies, which relied on a combination of partnership and trust law to achieve many of the benefits of incorporation. In 1844, parliament abandoned its century-long resistance to corporations and enacted legislation permitting nearly anyone to form one. In the United States, Louisiana led the way, abolishing the system of special incorporation in 1845. A number of states adopted dual systems with both special and general incorporation thereafter, but by the last two decades of the nineteenth century, specialized incorporation had been abandoned everywhere. In 1800, there were 335 corporate charters in the USA. By 1890, the number was nearly 500,000.[8]

The second key development was limited liability. Here, the watershed came in 1855, when parliament amended the 1844 Act to authorize limited liability at the discretion of the entrepreneurs who established a corporation. The fact that limited liability came eleven years after the original legislation is not accidental. Although limited liability was not a new idea, providing it as a standard feature of general incorporation proved quite controversial. Christian leaders featured prominently in the debate, which unfolded against the background of the larger debate about free market economics in nineteenth-century England.

In the first half of the nineteenth century, mainstream Evangelical leaders vigorously supported the free trade policies known as laissez-faire economics. "Barriers to Free Trade," they argued, as recounted by a British

[8] Cited in Margaret M. Blair, "Locking in Capital: What Corporate Law Achieved for Business Organizers in the Nineteenth Century," *UCLA Law Review* 51 (2003): 387, 389 n.3.

historian, "like monopolies, protective duties, and preferences, not only offended the unprivileged, but were elements of friction obscuring God's clockwork providence."[9] Free trade was thus equated with the recognition of God's providence in all of life. Thomas Chalmers, the leading spokesman for the Evangelical perspective, also extolled the chastening effects of free markets. He argued that fear of disaster would encourage businessmen to practice moral restraint in their business ventures, and that the failures of those who did not would chasten them, perhaps spurring an attitude of repentance for their excesses.

In the debate over limited liability in the 1850s, both sides tried to characterize their views as a manifestation of free market economics. Opponents insisted that limited liability interfered with the market by limiting an entrepreneur's exposure to the risks he undertook; enthusiasts countered that entrepreneurs should be permitted to set up whatever structure they wished, so long as they provided full disclosure to potential investors. Most mainstream Evangelicals took the former view. "In the scheme laid down by Providence for the government of the world," as one limited liability critic put this view, "there is no shifting or narrowing of responsibilities, every man being personally answerable to the utmost extent for all his actions."[10] Groups such as the Christian Socialists, who defended limited liability and argued that it might enable people of modest means to invest in corporate enterprise, were a distinct minority among Christians. But the range of people who would benefit from limited liability (such as existing, well-off investors) or who favored it on social grounds was wide and deep by the 1850s. Within a few years, the argument that business people should be exposed to the full rigors of the market would lose much of its resonance in English politics, even among Evangelicals.

In the United States, Christian groups seemed to show much less concern about the advent of limited liability than their English peers. It was not limited liability so much as its fruits that stirred Christian leaders and groups into action.

REGULATING AMERICA'S NEW LARGE-SCALE CORPORATIONS

The large-scale corporation, as we now know it, was born in the late nineteenth century, most pervasively in the United States and particularly

---

[9] Boyd Hilton, *The Age of Atonement: The Influence of Evangelicalism on Social and Economic Thought, 1795–1865* (Oxford: Clarendon Press, 1988), 69.   [10] J. R. McCulloch, quoted in *ibid.*, 260.

in the railroad industry. As the railroads expanded, revolutionizing transportation and at the same time benefiting from the markets created by this revolution, they adopted increasingly hierarchical business structures, with a class of middle managers between the railroad's workers and its executive officers. So long as shareholders enjoyed limited liability and thus were not responsible for its obligations if it failed, it was not necessary that they actively manage or oversee the business. This made it much easier to separate ownership from management and to develop a specialized class of managers, and it radically expanded the pool of potential investors.

The same railroads that emerged as America's first large-scale corporations also provided the first great corporate scandals.[11] Railroad owners could make enormous profits by taking control of important segments of track and charging as much as the market would bear. The swashbucklers who played this game, men like Jay Gould, Daniel Drew, and Jim Fisk, have long been known as the robber barons. (The Erie Railway, the subject of the most infamous of the railroad battles in the early 1870s, became known as the "Scarlet Woman of Wall Street" because of the rampant bribery and other misbehavior used in the fight for control by both groups of combatants, one led by Cornelius Vanderbilt and the other by Daniel Drew and Jay Gould). In 1873, the travails of America's second transcontinental railroad, the Northern Pacific, toppled Philadelphia banker Jay Cooke and his bank, triggering a nationwide economic depression. Cooke's failure spurred a populist backlash that ultimately led to the enactment of the Interstate Commerce Act of 1887, which established federal regulation of railroads; and the Sherman Antitrust Act of 1890 to prohibit monopolization of industry.

By 1890, the railroads were not the only large-scale corporations. To circumvent state corporate laws that prevented one corporation from owning the stock of another, John D. Rockefeller and others created "trusts" to consolidate control of a variety of industries, from oil to sugar and tobacco. Although the Sherman Act was designed to thwart monopolization of industry, it was narrowly construed by the Supreme Court in 1895. In part as a result, the decade that followed, which became known as the Great Merger Wave, saw even greater consolidation. Although some of the new behemoths were controlled by a Rockefeller or Havemeyer, many were midwifed by J. P. Morgan and other investment banks. These

---

[11] The scandals and the regulation they prompted are described in more detail in David Skeel, *Icarus in the Boardroom: The Fundamental Flaws in Corporate America and Where They Came From* (New York: Oxford University Press, 2005).

companies were held not by a single controlling individual group, but by thousands of shareholders, each of whom may have held a relatively small stake.

The emergence of large-scale corporations raised two related, but conceptually distinct, kinds of concerns. First, there was the risk that the managers and directors of a corporation would take actions that benefited themselves rather than shareholders. In several of the railroad scandals, the managers started construction companies, which built track under contracts that plumped the managers' bank accounts at the expense of the railroad and its shareholders. The second concern was that a corporation would act in a way that benefited both itself and its stakeholders, but harmed outsiders. Here, as already noted, the overriding concern was monopoly – the danger that corporations would snuff out competition in their industry and charge exorbitant prices to consumers.

While it is difficult to trace precisely the Christian influence on American corporations in the nineteenth century, due to the limits of existing historical scholarship and because Christianity was often a pervasive but unstated background assumption in American life, it is probably fair to say that the same factors that produced American denominationalism and Christian support for free markets assured a general sympathy for the corporate form. But this enthusiasm receded when it came to the corporate trusts, which struck many as inconsistent with market competition and some as a form of private socialism.

By nearly any yardstick, the nation's most visible and influential Evangelical Christian in the late nineteenth and early twentieth centuries was William Jennings Bryan, the charismatic orator whose "Cross of Gold" speech had propelled him to the Democratic presidential nomination for the first of three times in 1896. From the outset of his political career, Bryan's Populist attacks on corporate power were a signature theme, along with his insistence on loosening links between the dollar and gold. Excoriating the effects of the Great Merger Wave in the 1900 campaign and arguing for more competition, Bryan concluded: "There can be no good monopoly in private hands until the Almighty sends us angels to preside over the monopoly."[12] Bryan briefly went so far as to argue for government ownership of the railroads, but backed off when it became clear that advocating federal control would cost him any hope of support in the South.

---

[12] Quoted in Michael Kazin, *A Godly Hero: The Life of William Jennings Bryan* (New York: Alfred A. Knopf, 2006), 96.

Although a large majority of Christians and of Americans seemed to have worried about the power of large corporations, Christian opinion was not monolithic even on this point. J. P. Morgan, the architect of many of the leading trusts, was himself a committed Christian. Morgan believed that unbridled corporate competition was destructive, and that trusts run by himself and others with genuine character could produce goods and provide services much more efficiently than fragmented industries with numerous competing corporations.

A third major figure was Walter Rauschenbusch, one of the leaders of the Social Gospel movement, which advocated greater Christian involvement in social change. Although Rauschenbusch, like his Social Gospel peers, was more theologically liberal than Bryan, the two admired one another and shared similar views of corporate regulation. Drawing on Jesus' parables on stewardship, Rauschenbusch called for federal oversight of trusts, especially "natural monopolies" like railroads and utilities. These corporations, he wrote:

are stewards and have acted as if they were the owners. The present movement for rate-regulation, for instance, is simply an effort to assert the rights of the owner over the steward, and the aggrieved astonishment with which this movement has been met by the class that owns the railways is interesting proof that the usual historical process was very far advanced.[13]

By the turn of the century, immigration had vastly increased the number of Catholics among American Christians. Some of the campaigns with which leaders like Bryan and Rauschenbusch were associated, such as the Temperance movement, were at least in part anti-Catholic and anti-immigrant. But their concern about corporate influence echoed emerging Catholic views in important respects. Pope Leo XIII's 1891 encyclical letter *Rerum novarum* inaugurated a tradition of Catholic social thought that has generally defended the interests of labor and called for restraints on the power of corporations.[14]

As reflected in the major Protestant Christian periodicals of the time, the weight of Christian opinion seems to have favored at least some governmental regulation of corporations. *Outlook*, a leading Social Gospel magazine,

---

[13] Walter Rauschenbusch, *Christianity and the Social Crisis* (New York: The Macmillan Company, 1916) (first printed 1907), 385. Rauschenbusch's life and teachings are recounted in Christopher H. Evans, *The Kingdom is Always But Coming: A Life of Walter Rauschenbusch* (Grand Rapids, MI: Wm. B. Eerdmans Publishing, 2004).

[14] Pope Leo XIII, *Rerum novarum* (May 15, 1891), in Michael Walsh and Brian Davies, *Proclaiming Justice & Peace: Papal Documents from Rerum Novarum Through Centesimus Annus* (Mystic, CT: Twenty-Third Publications, 1991), 15.

opined that "corporations deriving their existence from the hands of the people must submit to regulation by the people," a view repeated by other articles of the time.[15]

In keeping with the overwhelming emphasis on the second of the dangers posed by the emergence of large-scale corporations, monopoly, much of the regulatory response in the early twentieth century focused on counteracting the market power of the largest corporations. The single most successful initiative was Theodore Roosevelt's "trust busting" campaign, whose landmark achievement was a 1904 Supreme Court decision that broke up the Northern Securities Corporation, a trust that combined the two transcontinental railroads. The Roosevelt administration also saw the enactment of the Railway Rate Regulation Law in 1906, and the 1907 Tillman Act, which prohibited corporations from making contributions directly to political candidates. Roosevelt even threw his weight behind proposed legislation that would have federalized the incorporation of the nation's corporations. The failure of this last initiative, federal incorporation, ultimately contributed to a sharp distinction in American law between internal corporate governance issues (the conflicts of interest between managers and shareholders that are regulated primarily by the states) and "external" concerns such as antitrust, employment law, and environmental law (much of which are now regulated by federal law).

The legislative and judicial efforts described in the last paragraph have historically been attributed to the Progressive movement, which achieved its greatest prominence during the early twentieth century. After the Democrats finally regained the White House in 1913, the Progressive movement achieved several additional regulatory victories with the enactment of the Clayton Antitrust Act in 1914, which restricted directors from serving on the boards of directors of their competitors, and the creation of the Federal Trade Commission to police the trusts. While Progressivism was not conspicuously Christian in orientation, there were close links to the Social Gospel movement. Some historians have suggested that the Social Gospel movement laid the groundwork for Progressivism through its support for labor and social change, and Social Gospelers were both participants in and cheerleaders for the Progressives' efforts to enact corporate regulation.

By the second decade of the twentieth century, then, large-scale corporations were generally accepted, but a variety of measures had been put in

---

[15] Editors, "The Supreme Court on Railway Regulation," *Outlook*, March 3, 1906, at 493. For a description of the increasing Christian concern about the corporate trusts, see Henry F. May, *Protestant Churches and Industrial America* (New York: Octagon Press, 1963), 130–33. My thanks to Zheng Zhou for the stellar research on which the discussion in this paragraph relies.

place to protect competition within the marketplace. These measures reduced the risk of monopoly (at least by industrial corporations; J. P. Morgan and a small group of other investment banks continued to monopolize American corporate finance.) Although less identifiably Christian than Prohibition or even Women's Suffrage, the Progressive reforms seem to have been influenced by the Social Gospel (as well as the Evangelical constituency represented by William Jennings Bryan) and to have reflected the general views of most American Christians.

THE FEDERAL COUNCIL OF CHURCHES AND THE NEW DEAL

The New Deal brought sweeping federal regulation of American corporate and financial life, establishing what still are the basic parameters of American corporate regulation. Perhaps most dramatically, Congress completely restructured the banking industry. The Glass–Steagall Act drove a wedge between commercial and investment banking by prohibiting banks from providing both loans (the standard fare of a commercial bank) and underwriting (investment banks' bread and butter). The goal, quite candidly stated by the New Dealers, was to destroy the monopoly J. P. Morgan and its peers had on American corporate finance and to limit their influence over large-scale American corporations. To enhance oversight of and confidence in the securities markets, Congress enacted new securities regulations in 1933 and 1934. The securities acts require extensive disclosure by large-scale corporations; and they created the Securities and Exchange Commission to police the markets on investors' behalf.

In several of the speeches laying the groundwork for corporate and financial reform, Franklin D. Roosevelt employed distinctively religious rhetoric. One of the most important economic speeches of Roosevelt's 1932 campaign condemned Chicago utilities magnate Samuel Insull, whose dramatic collapse had stunned and infuriated the nation, and vowed to take arms against "the Ishmael or Insull, whose hand is against every man's."[16] While this call to protect the little guy against the predations of a corporate titan echoed Bryan's earlier Democratic presidential campaigns, the religious landscape in American politics had dramatically shifted by the outset of the New Deal. Starting in roughly 1925, the year of the Scopes trial (about teaching evolution in public schools) and Bryan's death, Evangelicals had

---

[16] The speech and Roosevelt's New Deal initiatives are recounted in Skeel, *Icarus in the Boardroom*, 75–106.

increasingly absented themselves from American political life. One can find occasional articles in Evangelical magazines condemning the corporate scandals that followed the 1929 stock market crash, but Evangelicals did not play any visible role in the Roosevelt administration or the New Deal generally.

Christian involvement in Roosevelt's New Deal coalition seems to have come not from Evangelicals, but from mainline Protestants (the principal heirs of the Social Gospel), and from Catholics. The Federal Council of Churches, which was founded in 1908 and had become the leading interdenominational voice of mainline Protestantism, was actively involved in New Deal labor and work legislation and seems to have supported the banking and securities reforms, though not as visibly. At the outset of the New Deal, *The Christian Century*, the most widely read journal of progressive Christianity, ran a series of articles on economic issues, most applauding the New Deal initiatives and some calling for even more radical regulation (in one case, for government control of banks).[17]

Catholic Americans were the other major Christian New Deal constituency. By the early twentieth century, Catholicism claimed more adherents than any of the Protestant denominations – and most supported Roosevelt and his reformers. Perhaps the most visible representative of progressive Catholic support was Father John Ryan, who had popularized the term "living wage" (several decades earlier) and mounted a spirited defense of New Deal legislation that included skirmishes on the radio and in print with demagogic priest Father Coughlin.[18]

Christian views on the New Deal business and financial legislation were no more monolithic than the views of Americans generally. Nor were Christians the most visible advocates of the reforms. But leading figures in mainline Protestantism and among progressive Catholics defended the New Deal program, and the reforms can be traced, at least indirectly, to the political vision that Bryan and the Social Gospel promoted decades earlier.

THE NEW CORPORATE AND FINANCIAL MARKETPLACE

In the past twenty-five years, the governance of large-scale corporations has been transformed yet again, though more through the marketplace

---

[17] "Nothing less than a permanent banking bill," the editors wrote, "that goes far, far beyond [existing proposals] in the direction of government control, protection of depositors, and protection of investors, will ever restore public confidence. "An Approaching Crisis at Washington," *Christian Century* (April 5, 1933): 446.

[18] See Francis L. Broderick, *The Right Reverend New Dealer: John A. Ryan* (New York: The Macmillan Company, 1963), 211–43.

than by regulation. Corporate takeovers have been a standard feature of the corporate landscape for several decades, and shareholder-centered governance is increasingly the norm not just in the United States and England, but in much of the world. Seemingly endless innovation in financial instruments and the rise of equity and hedge funds has provided new sources of financing and new ways to manage risk, as well as intense pressure to perform. The American corporate scandals subjected these developments to scrutiny, but did not significantly alter any of the underlying trends.

Protestant views on these issues fall into two major camps. The mainline Protestant denominations, at least at the leadership level, have favored extensive governmental oversight of corporations, as they did during the New Deal. Although the Evangelical left in America differs with mainline Protestants on other issues, they generally share a desire to rein in large corporations. Both enthusiastically supported the corporate responsibility reforms that the Congress enacted after the Enron and WorldCom scandals. The Evangelical right (which includes a substantial majority of Evangelicals by most accounts) has been much less supportive of intervention. Since their re-emergence in American political life starting in the 1970s, most of these Evangelicals have favored free markets and limited government involvement.

Catholic perspectives fall into a similar pattern. Although Catholic theologian Michael Novak is best known for his fervent, theological defense of free market economics, he has also defended the corporation and called for limited governmental intrusion, arguing that this best accords with the tradition of Catholic social thought.[19] Others argue that a more hands-on regulatory approach is most consistent with the concerns of Catholic social thought.

One difficulty in making sense of current Christian perspectives on corporate regulation is that corporate regulation has been a secondary concern for many Christians, particularly Protestants. The Evangelical right has invested less energy on economic issues than on social ones, and the principal economic emphasis has been free markets and a general distaste for regulation rather than corporate and securities law. Mainline Protestants and the Evangelical left have been most concerned with the pervasive biblical concern for the poor and for other social issues such as race relations. Corporations have figured more prominently in Catholic discourse, due in important part to the papal letters of Pope John Paul II on economic issues, but here too they have not loomed as large (particularly in the United States) as other issues.

[19] See, e.g., Michael Novak, *Toward a Theology of the Corporation* (Washington, DC: American Enterprise Institute Press, 1990).

Christian perspectives on corporations also can be very difficult to distinguish from secular perspectives. Perhaps this was inevitable. Once the corporate form and the legitimacy of limited liability were accepted, and so long as government ownership of corporations is largely ruled out, the range of internal corporate governance issues around which one might develop a theology of the corporation was relatively limited. The hiving off of antitrust, employment law, and other issues "external" to the corporation from corporate law in the United States, and treating them as separate bodies of law, has reinforced this narrowness.

Yet the opportunities for developing a distinctively Christian critique of contemporary corporate law, and for shaping the coming generation in this time of great transition, are extraordinary. One approach is to construct a theology of the corporation and of corporate responsibility. Drawing on Catholic social thought, a small group of Catholic legal scholars has taken tentative first steps toward such a theology.[20] Protestant scholars have been slower to develop a careful theological analysis of the corporation, but the seeds of such an analysis are scattered through modern Protestant theology, in the work of Rauschenbusch, Abraham Kuyper, Reinhold Niebuhr, and others.

Other scholars may come at these questions from a slightly different perspective: how much can, or should, the secular law do to regulate corporate life? In recent work, William Stuntz and I have argued that, while God's law is pervasive, human law should be far more modest in its aspirations.[21] Because regulators and law enforcers are sinful, just as ordinary citizens are, we should be wary of laws that are too broad to be systematically enforced; sweeping discretion invites discriminatory enforcement. Law works best if its ambitions are modest, leaving wider scope for ordinary morality. In corporate law, this modest rule of law principle suggests that it is a mistake to try to legislate the do's and don't's of proper manager and director behavior – especially through criminal sanctions. A narrower objective might be to focus principally on removing obvious structural perversities in the market and regulatory framework. Structural flaws were a major factor in the corporate scandals of the early 2000s. The oversight of auditors and securities analysts, for instance, was undermined by structural conflicts of

---

[20] These scholars have offered sharply diverging perspectives on the appropriate scope of governmental intervention. The principal advocate for deference to corporate managers has been Steve Bainbridge. Susan Stabile has interpreted the Catholic social teaching emphasis on the common good as calling for more regulatory intervention. See analysis and sources in Mark A. Sargent, "Competing Visions in Catholic Social Thought," *Journal of Catholic Social Thought* 1 (2004): 561.

[21] David A. Skeel, Jr. and William J. Stuntz, "Christianity and the (Modest) Rule of Law," *University of Pennsylvania Journal of Constitutional Law* 8 (2006): 809.

interest that discouraged each from giving candid, honest assessments of the companies they investigated in the 1990s. The tendency to overuse stock option-based compensation, which can tempt corporate executives to pump up the company's stock price through any means possible, was exacerbated by a tax rule that rewarded companies for paying executives with options rather than cash. Some of these structural problems have been fixed; others (such as the compensation rule) have not.

Christianity also offers insights that are more cultural than legal in form. One of the most sobering lessons of the recent corporate scandals in the United States was the extent to which sin can pervade every facet of institutional life. Perhaps the most vivid illustration was Enron, whose employees were herded into a room and pretended to conduct a vibrant trading market when a group of analysts made the trip to Houston to visit the firm. The psychological literature suggests that our tendency to conform to those around us, even if what they do is clearly wrong, and to obey authority, helps to explain the poisonous internal culture at companies like Enron. But the literature also shows that if even one person takes a stand, the likelihood of misbehavior sharply declines. Christian Scripture offers rich insight into the benefits of maintaining a moral compass, not least in the emotionally honest prayers of the psalms. "I have laid up thy word in my heart," one Psalmist sings, "that I might not sin against thee" (Psalm 119:11). Jesus' servant and steward parables provide similarly useful instruction on fiduciary relationships, and might contribute to a board's deliberations about its fiduciary responsibilities.[22] As each of these illustrations suggests, it took more than law alone to create large-scale corporations, and it will take much more than law to sustain and improve them.

RECOMMENDED READING

Banner, Stuart. *Anglo-American Securities Regulation: Cultural and Political Roots, 1690–1860*. Cambridge: Cambridge University Press, 1998.

Berman, Harold J. *Law and Revolution: The Formation of the Western Legal Tradition*. Cambridge, MA: Harvard University Press, 1983.

Blair, Margaret M. "Locking in Capital: What Corporate Law Achieved for Business Organizers in the Nineteenth Century." *UCLA Law Review* 51 (2003): 387.

Broderick, Francis L. *The Right Reverend New Dealer: John A. Ryan*. New York: The Macmillan Company, 1963.

Editors. "The Supreme Court on Railway Regulation." *Outlook*, March 3, 1906.

---

[22] See, e.g., Lyman P. Q. Johnson, "Faith and Faithfulness in Corporate Theory," *Catholic University Law Review* 56 (2006): 1.

Evans, Christopher H. *The Kingdom is Always But Coming: A Life of Walter Rauschenbusch.* Grand Rapids, MI: Wm. B. Eerdmans Publishing, 2004.

Hansmann, Henry, and Reinier Kraakman. "The Essential Role of Organization Law." *Yale Law Journal* 110 (2000): 387.

Hansmann, Henry, Reinier Kraakman, and Richard Squire. "Law and the Rise of the Firm." *Harvard Law Review* 119 (2006): 1333.

Hilton, Boyd. *The Age of Atonement: The Influence of Evangelicalism on Social and Economic Thought, 1795–1865.* Oxford: Clarendon Press, 1988.

Johnson, Lyman P. Q. "Faith and Faithfulness in Corporate Theory." *Catholic University Law Review* 56 (2006).

Kazin, Michael. *A Godly Hero: The Life of William Jennings Bryan.* New York: Alfred A. Knopf, 2006.

Kuran, Timur. "The Absence of the Corporation in Islamic Law: Origins and Persistence." *American Journal of Comparative Law* 53 (2005): 785, 793.

Leo XIII. *Rerum novarum* (May 15, 1891), in Michael Walsh and Brian Davies, *Proclaiming Justice & Peace: Papal Documents from Rerum Novarum Through Centesimus Annus.* Mystic, CT: Twenty-Third Publications, 1991.

May, Henry F. *Protestant Churches and Industrial America.* New York: Octagon Press, 1963.

Novak, Michael. *Toward a Theology of the Corporation.* Washington, DC: American Enterprise Institute Press, 1990.

Rauschenbusch, Walter. *Christianity and the Social Crisis.* New York: The Macmillan Company, 1916 (first printed 1907).

Sargent, Mark A. "Competing Visions in Catholic Social Thought." *Journal of Catholic Social Thought* 1 (2004): 561.

Skeel, David. *Icarus in the Boardroom: The Fundamental Flaws in Corporate America and Where They Came From.* New York: Oxford University Press, 2005.

Skeel, David A. Jr. and William J. Stuntz. "Christianity and the (Modest) Rule of Law." *Pennsylvania Journal of Constitutional Law* 8 (2006): 809.

Index to biblical texts

OLD TESTAMENT

Genesis
1:27	169
1:28	206, 215
1:31	205
2:15	4, 206
2:23	174
2:24	169, 171
3:19	197
6:11	37
9:1–17	37
18:19	145

Exodus
12	36
20	36
20:13	36
21:1–3	144
21:6–8	144
23:7	144

Leviticus
19:18	63
24:10–14	114
25	214
25:23	214
26	145

Numbers
5:11–18	156
35:33–34	216
35:34	206

Deuteronomy
5	36
6:2	158
6:11	205
6:17–21	211
7:3–4	43
10:14	215

10:18–19	185
15:1–3	44
15:7–11	185
17:11	43
17:14–20	37
18:15	38
19:14	211
19:17	158
20:10	36
21:23	58, 59, 62
24:1–4	65
29:15–27	145

1 Samuel
8:4–22	37
17:45–50	156

2 Samuel
4:11	145

1 Kings
2:32	145
8:31	160
8:32	144, 145
8:39	228

2 Kings
22	2
22:8–23:3	38

1 Chronicles
29:11	206, 215

2 Chronicles
6:22	160
6:23	144
34:14–33	38

Nehemiah
8:1	38

Psalms
7:8	144
7:11	145
37:5ff.	145
72:1ff.	144
73:18	45
132:9	145

Proverbs
24:24	145

Isaiah
2:3–4	37

Jeremiah
12:1	145
33:25	36

Ezekiel
33:11	233

Malachi
2:11	38

APOCRYPHA

Ecclesiasticus (Sirach)
3:30–31	185
4:1–10	185
17:26	158

NEW TESTAMENT

Matthew
1:23	63
2:17	63
4:8–10	113
5–7	57, 66
5:20	57, 65
5:33–37	114, 160
5:38–39	114
5:39–40	109
5:43–48	241
6:24	207
7:2	147
10	57
13:43	155
16	57
16:18–19	66
16:19	11
16:24	211
18	57, 66

18:23–35	230
19:3	169
19:3–9	65
19:4–6	170
19:10–12	65
19:19	170
19:21	206
20:1–16	170, 210
20:16	170
22:21	7, 112
22:37–39	63
25	189
25:23	xiv
25:31–46	185
25:34–40	243
25:36	231
25:40	4, 211
27:11–16	146
28:18	59

Mark
6:1–6	57
8:38	64
10:2–11	65
10:11–12	65
10:21	211
10:25	207
12:13–17	57, 66
12:17	267
12:29–31	63
15:2–15	146
15:15–25	57
15:27	58

Luke
6:20	211
6:30	211
8:5–15	186
9:3	206
10:7	64
10:25–27	63
10:25–37	221
11:45	72
12–14	66
12:33	211
14:26	223
16:18	65
16:19–31	185
17:7–10	210
22:38	12, 66
23:3–25	146
23:5	58
23:19	57

John
7:24	147
8:23	113
13:34	241
15:13	241
15:18–19	21
17:14–16	21
18:28–19:16	146

Acts
2:45	211
4:1–22	59
4:32–35	214
4:34–35	211
4:35	207
5:17–40	59
5:29	267
6:12–8:1	59
9:1–2	59
13:46–47	59
13:50	59
15:20	114
15:28–29	114
16:20–21	60
18:6	59
21:27–31	59
25:1–12	61
25:11	60
28:16	60
28:25–28	59
28:30–31	60

Romans
1:16	59
2:14–15	91, 266
3:19–20	266
3:23	213
5	62
9:1–11:36	59
10:4	63
10:9	62
10:10	157
12:2	21
13:1	7
13:1–2	60, 113
13:1–7	60, 111, 146
13:3	267
13:3–6	113
13:5	267
13:8–10	63

1 Corinthians
1:30	145
2:16	63
3:17	64

4:2	216
4:5	146
4:7	216
5	157
5:12–13	155
6:12	93
7:7	172
7:10	64
9:1	62
9:14	64
10:29	266
12:3	62
13:12	206
14:1–33	64
14:38	64
15:45	62

2 Corinthians
3:6	62
5:17	62
9:13	158
11:23–29	59
13:1	158

Galatians
3:10	72
3:13	58, 59
5:14	63
6:2	63
6:11–12	59
6:15	62

Ephesians
5:21–33	171
5:25	169, 171
5:28	171
5:31	171
5:32	171, 173

Philippians
1:12	61
2:5	63
2:11	62
3:20	67

Colossians
3	62

1 Thessalonians
2:14–26	59

2 Thessalonians
3:10	197

1 Timothy

2:1	156
2:1–2	60
2:4	156
3:16	158
5:17	64

2 Timothy

4:16	61

Titus

3:1	146

James

2:7–13	63
5:12	160

1 Peter

2:13–14	146
2:13–17	7, 60, 113, 156

1 John

2:15–17	21
3:14	241
4:8	240
4:16	240

Revelation

17:1–18	60
17:14	58

General index

Note: Christian churches and church bodies not otherwise indexed will be found under 'Church law (modern)'

Abelard, *Sic et Non* 75
absolute monarchy 99–100
Ackerman, Bruce A. 217
agape see love, Christian
Agobard of Lyons, Archbishop 156
Alexander, Frank S. 32, 123
Alexander III, Pope 76
Alfred of England, King 9
almoners 200
almsgiving 186–87, 190, 191, 196, 197, 198
Althusius, Johannes 24
Amato, Paul 182
Ambrose of Milan 8
Ambrosiaster 157
An-Na'im, Abdullahi A. 248
Anabaptism 20–23
Anglicanism 19–20 *see also under* church law
    (modern)
Ansegis 157
Apostolic Church Order 67
Apostolic Constitutions 67
Aquinas, Thomas 13, 110, 155, 182, 189,
    202
    and conscience 267
    and marriage 173–75
    and natural law 94–96, 99
    and resistance 117–18
    and secrecy of confession 159
Ariens, Michael S. 309
Aristotle 6, 89, 173, 174, 182
Asher, Jacob ben 47
assisted reproductive technology (ART) 165, 166,
    168
Assmann, Jan 161
atheists 262–63, 265
Augustine 91, 110, 155–56, 182
    and capital punishment 232–33
    City of God 8–9

and marriage 172–73
and resistance 115–16

Baldus de Ubaldis 13
Ball, Milner S. 31, 217
Bammel, E. 69
Banner, Stuart 327
baptism, adult 21–22
Barmann, Johannes 141
Barth, Karl 30
Bartholomaios, Metropolitan 289
Bassett, William W. 309
Bayle, Pierre 259
Beal, J.P. 290
Beccaria, Cesare Marchese, *On Crimes and
    Punishments* 154
begging 196, 198, 199
Bellomo, Manlio 86
Benediction against Heretics 59
Bentham, Jeremy 126
Berg, Thomas C. 310
Berger, Raoul 141
Berlin, Isaiah 102
Berman, Harold J. 31, 86, 141, 217, 327
Bernard of Parma *Glossa ordinaria* 78
Bernardino of Siena 185, 202
Beveridge Report (UK, 1942) 202
Beza, Theodore 24
Bill of Rights (England, 1689) 20
birth control 167
bishops, and judges 147, 148
Black, Christopher F. 202
Blair, Margaret M. 327
Bodin, Jean 17
Bonhoeffer, Dietrich 30, 245
Boniface VIII, Pope, *Liber sextus* 78
Book of Discipline, US Methodist 84
Booth, Alan 182

Boyle, Kevin 269
Brennan, Patrick McKinley 234
Brinig, Margaret 178–82
Broderick, Francis L. 327
Browning, Don 182
Broyde, Michael 52
Brugger, E. Christian 234, 248
Brundage, James A. 31, 86, 161
Bryan, William Jennings 320
Burchard of Worms 74
Burns, J.H. 122
Burtt, Donald X. 234
Butler, Joseph 225, 226, 234

Calvin, John 16, 117, 176, 177, 267–8
Calvinism 23–26, 118, 119
canon law 3, 10, 11–12, 16, 17, 71–86, 176, 177–78
    and church councils 72–73, 77
    codification 13, 91, 126–27, 273–64, 275,
        277, 279, 281–82
    collections
        Clementines 78–79
        Code of Canon Law (1983) 273
        Codex iuris canonici (1917) 86
        Collectio Hispana 73
        Corpus iuris canonici 13, 78–79, 85
        Didache 7, 67, 72
        Extravagantes 79
        Gratian's Decretum 13, 74–76, 80, 91–92
        Libri duo de synodalibus causis 73
    and contract law 127–31, 133
    and De differentiis legum et canonum 79
    and excommunication 71
    glosses 76
    ius antiquum 72–74
    ius novum 74–79
    and just price 83
    and marriage 76, 77, 80, 82, 85
    medieval 79–83
    modern Catholic 85–86
    non-Catholic codes 273–74, 275, 277, 279,
        281–82
    and Ordines iudiciarii 79
    and poor relief 83
    and procedure 80, 150–53
    and Protestantism 16, 83–84
    rights and liberties 14–15
    and Roman civil law 79–80
    and sacraments 80
    and tithes 82
    and US church–state relations 298, 307–08
    and usury 80, 83
capital punishment 231–33, 246–47
Carbasse, Jean-Marie 161
Carbone, June 167

Carlson, John D. 234
Carmella, Angela C. 31, 217
Carter, Warren 182
Cassidy, R.J. 69
celibacy 176
Chalmers, Thomas 318
chantries 197, 198
charity 186–91
    and Charitable Uses Act (England, 1601)
        188
    early modern Catholic 198–99
    early modern Protestant 196–98
    and religious fraternities 193–95, 197
    and taxation 189, 190–91, 195, 196, 201
    and welfare state 201–02
Charity Organization Society 200
Charlemagne, Emperor 9
Charles I of England, King 19, 20
Charter of Fundamental Rights (2000) 246
Christian Century, The 324
Christian law 63–67
    and doctrine of the church 67–68
    and Jesus 56–58, 63, 64–66
    and primacy of individual conscience 68
    and St. Paul 59–60, 62–63, 66
Christian right (USA) 30
Christianity 3
    and Jewish law 61–63
    and law in modern age 26–30
    persecution of 60–61
Chrysipus 90
church
    doctrine of, and Christian law 67–68
    freedom of 14
    legal role in society 23–24
    privileges
        actio spolii 148
        privilegium fori 82, 148
    as social institution 25
    visible and invisible 18
church law (modern)
    and church government 279
    and church–state relations 287–88
    churches
        Anglican Communion 274, 276, 278,
            279, 281, 283, 284, 285
        Baptist Churches 277
        Church of England 287–88
        Church of Ireland 288
        Church of Scotland 288
        Church in Wales 288
        Eastern Catholic Churches 273, 275, 284
        Lutheran Churches 276, 279, 281–82,
            283–84, 285
        Methodist Churches 276, 279

Old Catholic Churches 274, 278, 281,
283, 286
Orthodox Churches 273, 275, 277–78,
283, 284, 285, 287
Presbyterian Church in America 276,
282, 284, 285, 286, 287
Presbyterian Churches 276, 284, 288
Quakers 276–77
Reformed Churches 276
Roman Catholic Church 273, 275, 277,
283, 284, 285–86, 287
and civil law 286–88
and codes of canon law 273–74, 275, 277,
279, 281–82
and constitutions 274, 276, 278, 279
and customs 274, 276
and divine law 283–84
and doctrine 280
effect and enforcement 284–86
and instruments of church order 276–77,
278
international 272–75, 277–78, 284–85
Baptist World Alliance 274, 278
Baptist World Congress 278
Leuenberg Agreement 284
Lutheran World Federation 274, 278,
281, 284, 286
World Alliance of Reformed Churches
274, 278, 284, 286
World Council of Churches 275, 278
World Methodist Council 274
local 275–77, 278–79, 285
and ministry 279–80
purposes 280–84
sources and forms 271–77
and theology 282
and worship and rites 280
church–state relations
and criminal liability 306
Religious Corporations Law, New York
state 298
and Roman law 8
separation of powers 21
two kingdoms theory 18
and US Constitution, First Amendment
294, 295, 298, 301, 306, 308–09
US Supreme Court decisions 308–09
and canon law 298, 307–08
cases: *Agostini v. Felton* (1997) 303;
Aguilar v. Felton (1985) 302–03; *Barr v.
United Methodist Church* (1979) 307;
*Church of Jesus Christ of Latter-Day
Saints v. Amos* (1987) 305; *John Does
1–9 v. Compcare, Inc.* (1988) 307–08;
Jones v. Wolf (1979) 299; *McClure v.*

Salvation Army (1972) 305; *Mitchell v.
Helms* (2000) 303; *National Labor
Relations Board v. The Catholic Bishop
of Chicago* (1979) 304; *Reynolds v.
United States* (1879) 306; *Serbian
Eastern Orthodox Diocese v.
Milivojevich* (1976) 298; *Tilton v.
Richardson* (1971) 300–01; *Tony and
Susan Alamo Foundation v. Secretary
of Labor* (1985) 305; *United States v.
Lee* (1992) 304–05; *Watson v. Jones*
(1872) 297; *Zelman v. Simmons Harris*
(2002) 304; *Zobrest v. Catalina
Foothills School District* (1993) 303
and church polity 295–96, 298
and civil liability 306–08
and employment policies 304–05
and property 297–98
and public aid to religious schools 293,
300–04
and religious discrimination 293
and trusts 297–300, 309
Cicero 6, 89–90, 91, 93, 145–46
civil disobedience 107–08, 109–12, 121–22
Clement V, Pope
Clementines 78–79
Constitutio Saepe 152
Pastoralis cura 152
Cochran, Rober F., Jr. 31, 217
Code of Canons of the Eastern Churches (1990)
273
cohabitation *see* marriage
Cohn, Haim H. 52
Cole, Elizabeth 269
common law 80, 84, 170
Commonwealth, English 20
confession 157–59
as *amende honorable* 151
annual 158
secrecy of 159
conscience 3, 266–68
freedom/sovereignty of 22, 68, 260–62
conscientious objection 105–06
and Christian principles 109–12
and submission to political authorities
112–15
Constantine, Emperor 7, 147
Constitutio Criminalis Carolina (1532) 153
contract law 125–41
American 125–26
and assumpsit 134–35
autonomy theory 126, 132, 140
bargain theory 136, 138, 140
and calculability 140
and canon law 127–31, 133

contract law (*cont.*)
  and consideration 134–35, 136
  English
    and commercial law 140
    and common law 134–37
    and courts system 133, 134
    Paradine v. Jane (1647) 136–37
    and Puritan Revolution 135–39
    Slade's Case (1602) 134
  and equity 131–32, 137, 139
  European 126–27
  Germanic 129, 130
  and human state 138
  moral theory 137
  promise theory 130–31, 136, 139
  and Puritan theology 138–39
  Roman 129–30
  and sovereignty of God 138
  and theology of covenant 138–39
  and unconscionability 131–32
  will theory 126, 132
Convention on the Rights of the Child (1989) 138, 178
Cooke, Jay 319
Corbin, Arthur 125
Cordero, Franco 161
Corecco, E. 290
Coriden, J.A. 290
corporations 4, 311–28
  characteristics of 313–14
  Christian perspectives 325–27
  church-related 316
  in England (eighteenth to nineteenth centuries) 316–17
  and entity shielding 313–14
  and free market economics 318
  and general incorporation 317
  and limited liability 313, 317–18
  and medieval and Renaissance Italy 315
  Religious Corporations Law, New York state 298
  restraints eased 316–17
  and Roman Catholic Church 315–16
  and Roman law 314–15
  and special incorporation 317
  US regulation 317, 318–27
    Clayton Antitrust Act (1914) 322
    and Enron 325, 327
    and Evangelicals 323–24, 325
    and Federal Council of Churches 324
    Glass–Seagall Act 323
    and Great Merger Wave 311, 319, 320
    Interstate Commerce Act (1887) 319
    and mainline Protestantism 325, 326
    and monopoly 319, 320, 322

    and New Deal 323–24
    and Progressivism 322–23
    railroads 319
    Railway Rate Regulation Law (1906) 322
    and Roman Catholic Church 321, 324, 325
    Sherman Antitrust Act (1890) 319
    and Social Gospel Movement 321–22, 323
    Tillman Act (1907) 322
    and WorldCom 325
Council of Chalcedon 72
Council of Nicaea 72
Council of Sardica 73
Council of Trent 17, 76, 85, 156, 187
Council of Vienne 187
courts
  church 13, 80–84, 151
  secular 81, 82
  see also church–state relations: US Supreme Court decisions
Cranmer, Thomas 16
Critchlow, Donald T. 202
Crowe, M.B. 103
Cummings, D. 290
Cunningham, Andrew 202
Curry, Thomas J. 309

D'Entreves, A.P. 103
Daly, Martin 182
Danchin, Peter G. 269
Danielou, J. 69
Dauge, David 31
Dawson, John P. 141
Deane, Herbert A. 122
Declaration of the Rights of Man and Citizen (France, 1789) 260
Declaration on the Elimination of Intolerance and Discrimination (1981) 249
Declaration on the Rights of Persons Belonging to National or Ethnic, Religious and Linguistic Minorities (1993) 254
decretals 76–78
  commentaries on 78, 79, 85–86
  Gregorian *Decretals* 78, 79, 83
  Quinque compilationes antiquae 77–78
democracy 24, 25–26
Denning, Lord 234
Destro, Robert A. 309
Didache 7, 67, 72
Didascalia Apostolorum 67
Dilcher, Gerhard 32
discrimination, religious 249, 253, 293
divine right of kings 98
divorce *see* marriage

Doe, Norman 86, 290
Dorff, Elliot N. 52
Dorwart, Reinhold 202
Draft Declaration of the Rights of Indigenous
    Peoples (1994) 254
Drew, Daniel 319
Drexel, Jerome 189
Duff, R.A. 234
Duns Scotus, John 96
Durantis, William, *Speculum iudiciale* 79
Durham, W. Cole, Jr. 269, 270
Dworkin, Ronald 102

Edict of Milan 61
Ehler, Sidney Z. and John B. Morrall 31
Ellickson, Robert C. 217
Elon, Menachem 52
Elshtain, Eric P. 234
Emancipation Acts (England 1829, 1833) 20
Enlightenment 5, 26–27
Erickson, J.H. 290
Esbeck, Carl H. 309
ethics, perfectionst v. conseqentialist 109
European Convention for the Protection of
    Human Rights and Fundamental
    Freedoms, Protocol 13 (2002) 246
Eusden, John D. 141
Evangelicals
    American 22–23, 323–24, 325
    British 318
Evans, Christopher H. 328
Evans, Malcolm D. 269
evidence
    and confession 157–59
    and credible witnesses 158–59
    and documents 160
    and exceptions to standards 155, 157
    and guilty pleas 156–57
    and improper witnesses 159
    and introduction of juries 160–61
    and notoriety 157
    and oaths 159–60
    and ordeals 155–56, 160
    and proof 154–61
    and torture 158
Eymericus, Nicholaus 79

Fagnani, Prospero, *Commentaria in libros
    Decretalium* 85–86
Falk, Ze'ev W. 52
family 25, 170–71
family law 163–82
    and assisted reproductive technology
        (ART) 165, 166, 168
    and birth control 167

and Christian jurisprudence 168–82
    and modernity 165, 167
    and *Principles of the Law of Family
        Dissolution* 167–68, 180
    Protestant 175–77
    and socio-economic change 165–66
    see also marriage
fear of tyranny v. fear of anarchy 111
Field, Lester L. 31
Filmer, Robert 17
Fineman, Martha 167–68, 181, 183
Finnis, John 102, 103
Fisk, Jim 319
forgiveness
    and criminal punishment 220–21
    and excuse 227
    and justification 227
    and love 221–25
    and mercy 227–28
    and motive for legal punishment 229, 231,
        233
    and reconciliation 228–29
Freehof, S.B. 52
Fried, Charles 141
Friedman, Lawrence 167, 183
friendly societies 197
Fuller, Lon 31, 102

Gaffney, Edward McGlynn, Jr. 310
Gaita, Raimond 230, 234, 244, 248
Gaius 6
Gallagher, Clarence 86
Gandhi, M. K. 121
Gandinus, Albertus 152
Garvey, John J. 310
Garvey, Stephen P. 234
Gausted, Edwin S. 269
Gelasius, Pope 8
Geremek, Bronislaw 202
Gershom of Mainz 48
Gerson, Jean 97
Giddens, Anthony 165–66, 183
Gierke, Otto von 103
Gillissen, John 161
Gilmore, Grant 125, 126, 141
Glendon, Mary Ann 248
Gonzales del Valle 290
Gooch, G.P. 123
Goodman, Christopher 24
Gorringe, Timothy 234
Gort, Jerald D. 248
Gould, Jay 319
governments
    basis 120
    role 110, 190, 201–02

governments (*cont.*)
    and taxation for social welfare 189, 190–91,
        195, 196, 201
    trust in 100–01, 110–11
Gratian 157
    Decretum 13, 74–76, 80, 91–92
Green, T.J. 290
Greenawalt, Kent 123
Gregory VII, Pope 9–10
Gregory IX, Pope 77–78
Gregory the Great, Pope 8, 155
Grell, Ole Peter 202
Grotius, Hugo 27, 98–99
Gui, Bernardo, *Practica officii inquisitioni*
    152
Guild of Help 200

Hamburger, Philip 310
Hampton, Jean 234
Hansmann, Henry 328
Hanukkah 43–44
Häring, Bernard 69, 231–32, 234
Helmholz, R. H. 31, 86, 161
Henry VIII of England, King 19
heresy 152, 155, 158
Hill, Christopher 141
Hill, M. 290
Hillel the Elder 44
Hilton, Boyd 328
Hincmar of Reims, Archbishop 150
Hippolytus, *The Apostolic Tradition* 67
Hispanus, Vincentius 155
Hobbes, Thomas 99–100, 154
Hollenback, David 248
Hollerback, J.M. 290
Holmes, Oliver Wendell, Jr. 126
Hooker, Richard 20, 293, 294
Horton, John 269
hospitals 198
Hostiensis (Henricus de Susa) 13, 79
House, H. Wayne 234
Huber, Wolfgang 31
Hugh of St. Victor 13
Huguccio 92, 192–93
Huguenots 119
human nature, state of 110
human rights
    and abolition of capital punishment
        246–47
    Christian basis 239–44, 244–47
    UN Convention on the Rights of the Child
        (1989) 138, 178
    and doctrine of *simul justus et peccator*
        24–25
    European Convention for the Protection of

    Human Rights and Fundamental
        Freedoms, Protocol No. 13 (2002) 246
    and human inviolability 238–39, 244
    and inherent human dignity 238–39, 244
    law of 237–38, 246–47
    morality of 237–44
    and religious liberty 251–58
    and Ten Commandments 24
    Universal Declaration of Human Rights
        (1948) 102, 178, 237–38, 249
    and unwarranted suffering 245–46
    see also natural rights
Hume, David 26, 101

Index of Prohibited Books 85
Innocent III, Pope 151
Innocent IV, Pope 152
    commentary on *Liber Extra* 155
Innocent VIII, Pope, *Summis desiderantes
        affectibus* 152
Inquisition 152
Institoris, Heinrich 152
Insull, Samuel 323
International Bill of Rights 237, 238
International Covenant on Civil and Political
        Rights (1966) 237, 249, 251, 258
    Second Optional Protocol (1989) 246
International Covenant on Economic, Social,
        and Cultural Rights (1966) 237
Irenaeus 91
Isidore of Seville 92
Islam 33, 35, 48–49
Isserles, Moses 48
ius commune (common law of Europe) 80, 84
Ivo of Chartres 74

James I of England, King 19
Jannsen, Henry 248
Jefferson, Thomas 26, 259, 260–61, 262
Jesus
    and divorce 64–65
    and Greco-Roman view of the family
        170–71
    and law 56–58, 63, 64–66
    as Messiah 61–62
    resurrection of 58
    trial and death of 57, 58, 146
Jewish law 55–56
    biblical 35–39, 40
    and covenant 35, 37–38
    and monarchy 37
    and prophecy 37–38
    and synagogue 39
    and Temple and priesthood 37, 39, 40
    and Christianity 61–63

codification 46–48
    Jacob ben Asher, *Arbaah Turim* 47
    Joseph Karo: *Bet Yosef* 47; *Shulhan Arukh* 48, 49
    Maimonides, *Mishneh Torah* 47
modern Judaism 49–52
    and *halakhah* 50, 51
    and Hebrew Jurisprudence 51
    and Reform Judaism 50–51
    and Zionism 51–52
post-Talmudic 45–49
    and codification 46–48
    and local ordinances 48
    and rabbinic responsa 46, 49
rabbinic 39–45
    and *Babylonian Talmud* 42, 45–46, 56
    and decrees 43
    and enactments 43
    and *halakhic midrash* 41
    and *halakhot* 40
    and House of Interpretation 40
    and *Mishnah* 41–42, 45, 56
    and *Palestinian Talmud* 42, 46
    and Pharisees/Rabbis 40
    and *prosbul* 44
    and Tosefta 42, 46
and religion 35
and *Talmud of the Land of Israel* 56
see also Torah
Jews
    and Christianity 33, 48–49
    and Islam 33, 48–49
    and justice 143–45
John XXII, Pope 7, 97
John XXIII, Pope 102
John Paul II, Pope 246, 325
John of Paris 13
John of Salisbury 13
Johnson, L.T. 69
Johnson, Lyman P.Q. 328
Jones, Gareth 202
Judah the Prince (Rabbi Judah) 41, 42, 56
judges
    and bishops 147, 148
    independence of 154
    lay 161
judgment
    and arbitrary punishment 152
    and bishops 147, 148
    and the Last Judgment 149
    and the pope 149–50
just price 83, 131
just war 107, 120–21
justice 143–46, 148, 220
Jutte, Robert, 202

Kant, Immanuel 27, 220, 222, 228, 234
Karo, Joseph 47–48
Katz, Jacob 52
Kazin, Michael 328
Kemp, Eric Waldron 86
Kery, Lotte 86
Kierkegaard, Søren 222–23, 234
King, Martin Luther, Jr. 30, 102, 122
Kingdon, Robert M. 183
Klassen, Walter A. 31, 123
Knox, John 118
Kohen, Ari 248
Korkman, P. 103
Kraakman, Reinier 328
Kugel, J.L. 69
Kuhn, Karl Christoph 290
Kung, Hans 248
Kuran, Timur 328
Kuttner, Stephan, 86
Kuyper, Abraham 30

Lactantius, *De mortibus persecutorum* 146–47
Lancelloti, Paulo, *Institutiones iuris canonici* 86
Langdell, Christopher Columbus 126
Lateran Council, Fourth 77, 151, 156
law
    of Christ, 63, *see also* love commandment
    and religion 1, 3–4, 28–29
    sources and forms 14
    see also canon law, common law, Jewish law, natural law
Laybourn, Keith 202
Laycock, Douglas 310
LeCocque, Andres 183
legal philosophies, secular 27–28
legal tradition, Western 4–5, 5–30
Leo XIII, Pope 29, 328
    Rerum novarum (1891) 178, 321
Leopoldo, Pietro 195
Lerner, Natan 269
Levita, Benedictus 157
limited liability 313, 317–18, 326
Lindholm, Tore 269
Litewski, Wieslaw 161
Little, David 269
Locke, John 100–1, 111, 119–20, 259, 261–63
Lombard, Peter 173, 174
Lord Hardwicke's Marriage Act (England, 1753) 76
love
    and forgiveness 221–25
    and indifference 230, 233
    and justice 220

love, Christian
    and capital punishment 231–33
    and criminal punishment 224–25
    and love commandment 4, 63, 221–25
Luther, Martin 16, 18, 83, 110, 116–17, 118, 174,
    176, 202
Lutheranism 18–19, 118–19

Machiavelli, Niccolò 17
Madison, James 259, 261, 262
    Memorial and Remonstrance (1785) 261
magistrates, role of 18–19
Magna Carta (1215) 15
Maimonides 47
Makinen, V. 103
Malik, Charles 178
Mallus Maleficarum (1487) 152
Maritain, Jacques 29, 103, 178
Marquardt, Elizabeth, 183
marriage 3–4, 17, 166–82
    and canon law 76, 77, 80, 82, 85
    Christian views 168–75
    classical Greek views 172–74
    and cohabitation 166, 167–68, 180–81
    and common law 170
    as contract 169, 179
    as covenant 168, 169, 172, 179–80
    and covenant marriage 181
    and decree *Tametsi* (1563) 85
    and divorce 64–65, 169–70, 177, 181
    as firm or franchise 180
    as institution 173, 175
    and kin altruism 173, 174–75, 176
    and Margaret Brinig 178–82
    as mystery 171, 174
    and new institutional economics
        179–80
    and Roman law 80, 173–74
    as sacrament 168, 171, 173, 175
    as status 169, 172
Martin, J. Paul 270
Marty, Martin E. 31
Mausen, Yves 162
May, Henry F. 328
McClain, Linda 168, 183
McConnell, Michael W. 31, 217, 310
McLanahan, Sara 183
Meier, J.P. 69
Melanchthon, Philipp 23, 154, 176
    Mendus, Susan 269
mercy 189–90, 227–28
Merrill, Thomas W. 217
minority rights 21, 254
    and ban on Muslim dress in French state
        schools 255–56

    and Native Americans 263, 265
    and US Native American Church
        employees 256–57
miracles 155, 156
Mollat, Michel 203
Moltmann, Jurgen 248
Montaigne, Michel de 153
Moptiuk, D. 290
moral law, universal 264–65
More, Thomas 153
Morgan, J. P. 319, 321, 323
Morrall, John B. 31
Moxes, Halvor 183
Muratori, Ludovico Antonio 203
Muratori of Modena 188
Murphy, Jeffrie 234
Murray, John Courtney 29

natural law 3, 27, 29–30, 89–103, 117–18, 185
    and absolute monarchy 99–100
    and Aquinas 94–96, 99
    and canon law 91–97
    civil and theological uses 23
    and divine right of kings 98
    educational use 23
    as inherent human attribute 93–94
    medieval to modern 97–101
    modern period 101–03
    and natural rights 94, 102
    as permissive law 93, 95, 98
    and procedure 154
    and Roman law 6
    and St. Paul 91, 93
    and trustworthy government 100–01
natural rights, 29, 94, 102, 268–69, *see also*
        human rights
Nedungart, G. 290
neo-Thomism 29
Nero, Emperor 60
Newman, L.E. 52
Nichols, Joel A. 310
Nicolas, Pope 157
Niebuhr, Reinhold 30, 120, 123, 234
Nietzsche, Friedrich 228, 231
Noll, Mark A. 31
Noonan, John T., Jr. 141, 162, 310
notoriety, doctrine of 157
Novak, David 52
Novak, Michael 325, 328

O'Connor, Flannery 234
O'Donovan, Joan Lockwood 31
O'Donovan, Oliver 31
Odo of Dover 92–93
1 Clement 67

Orsy, L. 290
Owens, Eric C. 234

pacifism 106, 114
Panormitanus (Nicholas de Tudeschis) 79
Parker, Charles H. 202
Parsons, Theophilus 127
Patsovos, L. 290
Paul, St.
    and Christian law 59–60, 62–63, 66,
        67–68
    and Torah 62
Pedalion (1800–) 273
Pelikan, J. 69
Pennington, Kenneth 86
Perry, Michael 32, 248
Peters, Victor 217
Peterson, Merrill D. 270
Pharisees 40, 55–56
Philo of Alexandri 55
Pius XI, Pope 178
Plato 6, 172–73
Pliny the Younger 60
political authorities, submission to 14, 112–17,
    146–47
political realm, importance of 109–10
Polycarp, Letter of 67
polygamy 48
poor laws 195–96, 197
poor relief 83, 194–95, 200
Pospishil, V.J. 290
prison, sexual abuse in 225, 230
procedure 143–54
    and canon law 80, 150–53
    early Christian view 146–57
    exceptions for heresy or treason 152
    and Jewish law 143–45
    and justice 143–46
    minimum standards 152–53
    and natural law 154
    processus extraordinarius 152
    Protestant 153–54
    and Roman law 145–46, 147, 148, 156
    and torture 154
proof *see* evidence
property 4, 16, 205–17
    and concurrent ownership 212–13, 214
    as control 208, 216
    and "covenants, conditions, and
        restrictions" 214
    and environmental laws 215, 216
    and fee simple absolute ownership 212
    as identity 208, 216
    intellectual 210
    legal and theological concepts 207

as mine (private) 205–06, 208, 209–10
as ours (shared) 209, 212–14, 217
as power 208, 216
renunciation of 207
and "the problem of the commons"
    213
and theology
    creation 205–06
    dominion as stewardship 209, 214–16,
        217
    the fall 206, 210, 213, 217
    the Jubilee 214
    redemption 206, 210, 213
    and trusts 216
    US law 209–10
    and adverse possession 210
    and first/subsequent possessor 210
    and usufruct 216
    as yours 208, 209, 211–12
Protestantism 5
    15–26, 30, *see also* Anabaptism,
        Anglicanism, Calvinism, Lutheranism
    and absolute monarchy 17
    and canon law 16, 83–84
    and charity 196–98
    and church power and property 16
    and education 17–18
    and family law 175–76
    and marriage 17
    and procedure 153–54
Pufendorf, Samuel 101
Pullan, Brian, 203
punishment 4
    arbitrary 152
    capital 231–33, 246–47
    criminal 220–21, 224–25
    extraordinary 158, 160
    motives for 229, 231, 233
purgation 160
Puza, R. 290

Quakers 114, 276–77
Qumran sectarians 55

Radin, Margaret Jane 217
Rauschenbusch, Walter 22, 321, 328
Rav Ashi 45
Ravina 45
Rawls, John 121, 123, 219
Raymond of Peñaforte 77
reason v. Scripture or tradition 109
Rebuffus, Petrus, *Praxis beneficiorum* 86
reconciliation 228–29
Regino of Prüm, Abbot 73
religious fraternities 193–95, 197

religious liberty 4, 22, 68, 249–69
  and attitude to atheists 262–63, 265
  and the Enlightenment 258–60
  and fascism 251–52
  and freedom from discrimination and
    intolerance 253
  and freedom from religion 265
  and freedom from religious hatred and
    hostility 254, 258
  and freedom of thought, conscience and
    religion 252–53
  and hate speech laws 257–58
  and human rights 251–58
  and minority protection 254
  and natural rights 268–69
  as "soul liberty" 264
  and Statute for Religious Freedom
    (Virginia, 1786) 260
  and US Constitution
    First Amendment 256–57, 261
    Second Amendment 261
  and US Religious Freedom Restoration Act
    (1993) 257
religious standards, application of 112
resistance 107–08, 115–21
  and Calvinists 118, 119
  Christian justification 106–07, 115,
    120
  and general Christian principles
    109–12
  and Huguenots 119
  and Lutherans 118, 119
Reuver, M. 291
Reynolds, Noel B. 270
Rhode Island colony 263
Ricoeur, Paul 183
rights v. duties 111
Rockefeller, John D. 319
Roman Catholic Church
  Congregations 85
  medieval jurisdiction
    governance of sacraments 10–11
    keys of the kingdom 11
    two swords theory 12
  see also canon law, church law (modern),
    corporations
Roman Empire
  Christian attitude to 7, 57, 60–61
  Christian conversion of 5–9
Roman law 5–6, 55, 61, 128
  and civil law 6, 79–80
  Codex Theodosianus 7
  and contracts 129–30
  and corporations 314–15
  Corpus Iuris Civilis 7–8, 53, 80

  and imperial cult 6–7
  and justice 145–46
  and law of nations 6
  Lex Duodecim Tabularum 53
  and marriage 80, 173–74
  and natural law 6
  and procedure 145–46, 147, 148, 156
  and rights, freedoms and capacities 6
  and subordination of church to state
    8
Rome, fall of 9
Roosevelt, Franklin D. 323
Rose, Carol M. 217
Rota Romana 81
Rouner, Leroy 248
Rousseau, Jean Jacques 26, 259, 260
Ruston, Roger 248
Ryan, John A. 324

sacraments 10–11, 80
Salter, Frank R. 203
Salvioli, Giuseppe 162
Sanchez, Thomas 17
  De sancto matrimonii sacramento 86
Sandberg, R. 290
Sandefur, Gary 183
Sanders, E.P. 69
Sanhedrin 43, 45
Sargent, Mark A. 328
Schulz, Fritz 141
Scripture, role in ethics 109
  see also under church law (modern)
Segal, A.F. 69
Selden, John 137–8
Sen, Amartya 244–5, 248
Seneca 6
Serritella, James A. 310
Shaffer, Thomas 221, 225, 227, 229, 231, 235
Sheen, Juliet 269
Sherwin-White, A.N. 69
Sigler, Mary 230, 235
Silberg, Moshe 52
Simons, Menno 16
Simpson, A.W.B. 141
sin 25, 26
Skeel, David 328
Slack, Paul A. 203
Smallwood, E.M. 69
Smith, Adam 27
Smith, Henry E. 217
Social Gospel Movement 22, 321–22, 323
Spinoza, Baruch 36
Sprenger, Jacob 152
Stackhouse, Max L. 248
Stahnke, Tad, 270

state
    as social institution 25
    see also church–state relations
Statute 2000 (Old Catholic Bishops United in
    the Union of Utrecht) 274
Steinmuller, W. 291
Stoljar, S.J. 141
Story, William 127
Strauss, Leo 102, 103
Suarez, Francisco 17, 98, 99, 118–19
subsidiarity 178
Swann, Abram de 203

Tahzib-Lie, Bahia G. 269
Taylor, Charles 247, 248
Taylor, Paul 270
Tellenbach, Gerd 32
Temple, William 219–20
Ten Commandments 18, 24, 91
Teutonicus, Johannes 188
    glossa ordinaria 76
the poor, deserving and undeserving 187,
    191–93
Tierney, Brian 32, 103, 132–33, 142, 203, 270
Tinder, Glenn 248
tolerance, religious and cultural 265
Toleration Act (England, 1689) 20
Tomas y Valiente, Francisco 162
Torah 55, 61
    and Jesus 57, 63
    Oral 39–40, 41
    and St. Paul 62
    Written 36–37, 39, 40, 41
torture 154, 158
Traer, Robert 248
Tribe, Laurence 217
trusts 216, 297–300, 309, 319, 322
Truth and Reconciliation Commission (South
    Africa) 229
Tuck, Richard 103
Tutu, Desmond 102

Ufficio di Pieta dei Poveri (Milan, 1405) 187
Ullman, Walter 87
Ulpian 6, 90
*United Church of Christ, Constitution and Bylaws
    of the* 84

United States Conference of Catholic Bishops
    247
Universal Declaration of Human Rights (1948)
    102, 178, 237–38, 249
Urresti, T. 291
US Constitution
    First Amendment
        and church–state relations 294, 295, 298,
        301, 306, 308–09
        and religious liberty 256–57, 261
    Second Amendment, and religious liberty
        261
usury 80, 83, 132

Vallauri, Luigi 32
van Caenegem, Raoul 161
Vanderbilt, Cornelius 319
Vatican Council, Second 29
Vaughan, Robert 270
Vázquez, Fernando 17
Vining, Joseph 234
Vitoria, Francisco 97–98
Vitoria, Thomas 17
Vives, Juan Luis 153
von Gierke, Otto 27
von Savigny, Friedrich Karl 27
Vroom, Hendrick M. 248

Waldron, Jeremy 123
Walzer, Michael 123, 142
Ware, T. 291
Weatherhead, J.L. 291
Webb, Beatrice 201
Weber, Max 183
welfare state 201–02
William of Mandagoto 79
William of Ockham 13, 96–97
Williams, Roger 263–66
Williston, Samuel 125
Wilson, Margo 182
Witte, John, Jr. 32, 87, 123, 142, 183, 234, 270,
    310
Wolff, Christian 93

Yoder, John Howard 234

Zamagni, Vera 203

Printed in Poland
by Amazon Fulfillment
Poland Sp. z o.o., Wrocław